While writing his critically successful novel *Upon a Wheel on Fire*, set against the origins of World War Two, **Paul Grieve** became interested in similar events in the eastern Mediterranean, particularly the collapse of the Ottoman Empire, and the origins of the State of Israel. In order to understand the resulting conflicts through to the present, Grieve decided to study Islam. After two years at the Mosquée de Paris, he spent a further three years in the Middle East studying Islamic history, jurisprudence, politics and Arabic, with experts at Cairo University and the American University in Cairo. The result is this book and a second novel. Grieve now lives in London.

D1358852

A BRIEF GUIDE TO ISLAM

History, Faith and Politics:
the Complete Introduction

Paul Grieve

ROBINSON
London

Constable & Robinson Ltd
3 The Lanchesters
162 Fulham Palace Road
London W6 9ER
www.constablerobinson.com

This edition published by Robinson,
an imprint of Constable & Robinson Ltd, 2006

A copy of the British Library Cataloguing in
Publication data is available from the British Library

ISBN 13: 978-1-84529-274-4
ISBN 10: 1-84529-274-x

Printed and bound in the EU

3 5 7 9 10 8 6 4 2

For my friends and mentors:

Abd al-Rahmān Salem
Muhammad Serag

CONTENTS

A Stroll Through the City of God

The walled Old City of Jerusalem is beautiful, dramatic and bitter. Transfigured by a stark white light and surrounded by what were once unforgiving rocky hillsides, good for nothing more than biblical sheep and goats. Or for property development: because today the Old City is also bitterly and dramatically buried, taking on the role of religious theme park to the banal, even ugly conurbation with which the State of Israel has enveloped the historical centre. Dull high-rises, marbled pseudo-palace hotels, shopping malls and vast archipelagos of belligerent housing settlements accessed by thickly fenced bypass roads are now the Jewish 'built facts' that overshadow the Ottoman walls. So whether the real estate was conquered, stolen or bought has lost all practical relevance. The 120 square kilometres of development that has become 'Greater Jerusalem' since the Arab–Israeli wars of 1948 and 1967 is now the apparently irrefutable physical statement that the 1 square kilometre within the stone walls belongs irreversibly to an exultant Israel, the eternal 'City of David', right up to the heavens.

Within the Old City, however, these recent encroachments are surprisingly shut out. A distinctly petrified atmosphere fills the narrow pedestrian streets, with the Mamluk and Ottoman centuries still clearly discernible behind the pervasive veneer of religious tourism.

But look deeper still and the terrible rivalries in the name of God that have created this city are soon exposed. After only an hour or two on foot the informed observer cannot remain a mere spectator. Such is the power of Jerusalem, that by the end of the walk the pressing presence of history has inspired either faith or revulsion.

Begin at the Dung Gate on the south side. Pass through Israeli security and an electronic search, show your passport and see in the heavily armed policeman's bored expression that it is not you he is looking for. Out on the polished stone plaza that leads to the Western Wall, walk the ground where a Palestinian community once lived, stretching back to the beginnings of recorded time, then bulldozed flat in a few days in 1967 to create this large open space, glistening so impressively in the sunshine. The former residents are invisible now, living only God knows where in a cinder block refugee camp.

Facing Herod's huge foundation stones, now know as the Western Wall, observe Jews at prayer, divided like Muslims between male and female, each in their own enclosure. Many carry automatic rifles over their shoulders as they follow the detailed rites their God has prescribed for the salvation of His chosen. Some, you will observe, wear on their heads the knitted kippa of the Gush, showing their radical commitment not just to a Greater Jerusalem, but to a racially pure Greater Israel.

Through more security and past more weapons, climb a long ramp towards the Haram, and the golden dome of the Muslim sanctuary. Stand here, up on Herod's platform and admire the view across the Kidron valley. The entire facing hillside is solid with the tombs of the Jewish faithful who have had their bodies brought to Jerusalem for burial from all over the world. For here is where the Jewish rising will take place when the Messiah of the Torah comes, and those well placed at the front can expect a headstart on eternity. Now look around you and imagine thousands of other bodies filling the space between the two structures of the Haram. See the bodies of Jews and Muslims, piled five or ten high by the victorious Crusaders on the stone flags under your feet. Blood and gore in the name of Jesus Christ so deep as to come up to the chest.

Or imagine you are standing on the same spot one thousand years earlier again, and all around you is the Roman army, up on this same platform, putting an end to four years of Jewish insurrection ignited by the purely religious questions of the sanctity of the holy of holies in Herod's temple, and the ceremony of sacrifice.

> While the Temple blazed, the victors plundered everything that fell in their way, and slaughtered wholesale all who were caught. No pity was shown for age, no reverence for rank; children and greybeards, laity and priests alike were massacred.
>
> (Josephus, *War*, VI, 5)

Then take the Haram tour, allow your Muslim guide to show you the very place where al-Burāq, the winged ass, was tied up on the night of the *Isrā*, while God's chosen Prophet ascended to heaven on his *Miʿrāj*. Run your fingers over the very iron ring. And once inside the Umayyad marvel that is the Dome of the Rock, see the very imprints of Muhammad's feet, magically etched into the rock from which he was assumed heavenwards to be given God's instructions for the salvation of the world.

Before leaving the Haram, look down on the Jews praying at the wall of their ruined temple below, and know that among those knitted skull-caps down there are many who even at this moment are asking their God to level everything around them, so that the Third Temple can be built and the end of the world can begin. Run your hand over the bullet holes in the walls from the last violent attempt by the Gush to lay their foundation stone in the Haram courtyard. In the Haram museum inspect the bloodstained clothes of the seventeen Muslims (but no Jews) who were killed on that day.

The Haram and the Western Wall

Then back in the crush of the covered streets of the Arab quarter, examine other faces, look into other eyes. Feel the fear and the hatred that is everywhere. Know that the centuries of Muslim tolerance, even though decreed by the Prophet himself, are over, and that a terrible revenge would be taken on those same Jewish supplicants back at Herod's wall if only these Palestinians all around you had the means.

And if this crowded scene were up in the new Jewish city, on Ben Yehuda Street, or in Zion Square, the person standing next to you might at this very moment be preparing to blow you straight to a Qur'ānic paradise of cool streams and attentive virgins. And here there are more of the flak jackets and loaded automatics of the Israeli Defence Forces, itchily alert behind their dark glasses, nervously covering every street corner.

Now move on to the Via Dolorosa and watch a group of Filipino nuns struggling up the stone steps of the passage on their knees, crossing themselves and mumbling their prayers at each Station of the Cross. Here, they believe, their Redeemer carried a wooden beam towards his coming hours of unspeakable suffering, of blood, nails and mockery. But an agony, they believe, that will be the salvation of all who have their particular brand of faith. Walk on to where the nuns are headed, the Church of the Holy Sepulchre. A dense crowd fills the building and out into the square in front. They are lined up this tightly to kiss the floor over the tomb of the Son of God, then the place where the True Cross once stood. But even the guidebooks know that they are all of them mistaken. Via Dolorosa has taken many different routes over the centuries and the present Via is merely the most convenient route for the capture of tourist dollars by the trinket-sellers, while the sacred tomb itself (not to mention the tomb's alleged former occupant) is nothing more than myth and tradition. And the men who run this church in the name of that same pacifist Redeemer are themselves so bitterly divided between Romans, Greeks, Armenians, Syrians and Copts, that they need a Muslim to lock and unlock the front door for them every morning and evening. For centuries they have not even been able to agree on which one of them should hold the key.

And further up, at the Jaffa Gate, you recognize the place where, in 1918, General Allenby, fresh from his victory over the Ottoman Empire, dismounted from his horse to enter Jerusalem on foot as his mark of respect. The Europeans were in charge once again. But although they were to be better behaved than in 1099, Britain's subsequent thirty-year Christian rule was to bring to the City of Peace a century of hate.

And here in this holy Jerusalem you really thought that you would find calm, even some personal benediction from above. But instead, in this other, this earthly Jerusalem, you are overwhelmed by a devilish frustration. So strong, as you stand by the Damascus Gate at the north end of the city, looking back over the route you have just walked, that rage is overtaking you. Because what you have just seen, you come to realize, is not the faith that you were looking for, the faith that should redeem souls, move mountains, bring peace to the world. But, rather, all you have found is a compassionless group amnesia that obliterates facts and consumes reason, that manufactures deadly illusions, perverts texts, and make curses out of the most sacred prayers. So that now a great sorrow is rising up within you, mixed with the anger. Then something like an interior fulmination deep within, and a sudden vision of how events could and should have been. And in that same instant you also find you have a prophecy for the future. Yes, now you know for certain that you alone have the answer, you are St John the Baptist come again, or the new Imam, you are the awaited Messiah himself . . .

The popular definition of your condition is 'the Jerusalem Syndrome'. Like hundreds of visitors before you, you have succumbed, and your cell awaits.

I

IN THE BEGINNING

I Muslims, Christians and Jews: Similarities

Islam is a significant presence in one hundred or more countries all around the world, and the majority religion in over forty. There are almost a billion believers, a figure comparable to Buddhism and second only to Christianity. By the year 2020, if present trends continue, half the world will be Muslim. With such size and reach, Islam is inevitably divided by politics, culture, language, history and dogma, but nevertheless unshakably united in the central Muslim credo: 'There is no god but God and Muhammad is His Messenger.'

A simple way of making a start on this vast subject is to understand that much of Islam consists of concepts familiar to a Westerner, but seen in an unfamiliar light. To illustrate, here are ten points of similarity between Islam and Judeo-Christianity.

1. *Islām* is an Arabic word meaning submission or commitment to *al-Ilāh*, the God, or *Allāh*. Islam is the humble recognition of the relationship between man and his divine Creator and resonates with the familiar words from Judaism and Christianity: 'Almighty God, Creator of heaven and earth'. But Islam goes beyond acknowledgement and devotion. The true believer surrenders himself or herself to the will of Allah, and in this way defines his or her identity as a member of the community of the faithful, or the *'ummah*. In modern times the word Islam has come to mean the faith of the way of *al-Islām*, and those who observe the faith are *muslim*, or Muslims.

2. In Muslim belief, Muhammad was Allah's chosen Messenger, or Prophet, for the delivery of Allah's Message which was revealed to Muhammad little by little over a period of twenty-two years. The revelations were recited by Muhammad as they were received and memorized by his followers. After Muhammad's death the revelations were assembled into a holy book called the Qur'ān, the equivalent of the word 'Bible', but taken from the Arabic word *kur'ān*,

meaning 'recitation'. The Qur'ān contains many references to stories found in the Jewish Torah as well as the Christian New Testament. Many of the characters familiar to readers of the Judeo-Christian texts appear in the Muslim scripture, beginning with Adam.

3. Muhammad did not set out to found a new religion; rather he saw himself as following on from the biblical patriarchs familiar to both Christian and Jew, from Adam to Noah, to Abraham and Moses, and including the teaching of Jesus Christ. Islamic tradition recognizes prophets from any language and culture from around the globe who submitted themselves to the will of God. But each of these earlier revelations is considered by Islam not to have been final. For Muslims, God only revealed His final message with the words of the Qur'ān, making Muhammad the last messenger in the prophetic cycle by which God's Word is believed to have been transmitted to man over the millennia. Ironically, Muhammad saw the unfolding revelation of the Qur'ān as sent to unite and complete all that had gone before, joining Arabs, Jews and Christians together. He expected to be accepted as a prophet by both Jews and Christians, at least to his own people. Islam only developed into a separate religion when this concept of Muhammad as the final Prophet, and the Qur'ān as the Final Word, was rejected by the Christians and Jews of his time.

4. The message of the Qur'ān was delivered to Muhammad by the angel Jibril or Gabriel who spoke in Arabic transmitting the words of Allah, who never appeared to Muhammad directly. Many of the verses of the Qur'ān begin with Gabriel's injunction to Muhammad to speak with the word اقْرَأ: *Say* or *Recite*, followed by the revealed verses. This contrasts with the revelations of the preceding Judeo-Christian prophets which were delivered by the indirect means of human interpretation drawing on an internal inspiration, implicitly claiming to be divine, but only occasionally purporting to speak with the direct words of God. Even the words of Jesus Christ in the New Testament are reported speech, however much emotion, wisdom and intangible truth the narrative may contain. And the record of Christ's life comes to us from writers in a subsequent generation as well as through a number of intermediate languages, giving rise to the possibility of faulty transmission. The Qur'ān, in

contrast, is believed by Muslims to be the unerring and direct word of God from start to finish.

5. Unlike the general Jewish view of the Torah and the Christian view of the New Testament, therefore, the Qur'ān is regarded by Muslims as the literal word of God, revealed in Arabic. For this reason translations should reproduce the original text above or alongside the non-Arabic words. Such works may only be titled 'The Meaning of the Holy Qur'ān' and cannot be represented as the Qur'ān itself. No other language is considered to be capable of providing a true rendition. That the Arabic words of the Qur'ān are believed to have come literally and directly from God the Creator is at the core of Islam, and the key to understanding many aspects of the faith.

6. Through His words Allah shows that He wishes nothing more than the reform of the world and the happiness of mankind, a theme that is closely matched in the teachings of Jesus Christ: 'Thy Kingdom come. Thy will be done in earth as it is in heaven.' Similarly, Allah in the Qur'ān, like the God of the New Testament, is All-Forgiving and All-Merciful and these qualities in God form the true basis of Islam, so often perverted by so-called Muslims and so readily distorted by non-Muslims.

7. The Qur'ān, like both the Torah and the New Testament, is literature of poise and beauty, and the work is unmatched in all Arabic letters. An imperfect comparison would be to imagine Shakespeare under divine command writing the Bible directly in English, creating the most sublime and defining language of our culture, as well as setting out the basis of our religion. Yet Muhammad was a Bedouin trader with no formal education who was certainly illiterate when his ministry began.

8. The Qur'ān contains extensive references to and veneration of Jesus Christ together with his mother Mary. But although the story of the Virgin birth is repeated in the Muslim text, Jesus is treated as a prophet not as a divine. 'And they take as their Lord, Christ, the son of Mary; Yet they were commanded to worship but One God' (*Al-Tawbah* (The Repentance) Surah 9, verse 31). In the Qur'ān, Jesus speaks and specifically denies that he is anything but human and he reproaches his disciples for treating him as God. Similarly,

although Jews originated the concept of a messiah, Judaism obviously does not accept Jesus Christ as the one.

9. Abraham, or Ibrahim, is acknowledged by the Qur'ān as the father of Islam, just as he is regarded as the original source of Judaism and therefore of Christianity. 'He was true in faith and bowed his will to that of God (which is Islam) and he was not an idolater' (*Āl Imran* (The Family of Imran) Surah 3, verse 67). But in contrast to the Torah, in the parallel Muslim tradition, Abraham was ordered by God to kill his eldest son, Ishmael, whose mother Hājar was a Canaanite or Palestinian, not the youngest, Isaac, whose mother Sarah was a Hebrew or a Jew. However, these details are not given in the Qur'ān, and the story may have been modified in a later century to suit the purposes of Arab rulers. But in any event, the importance of the story is to show Abraham's unquestioning obedience to God, rather than to score a political point. The substitution by God of the ram as sacrifice in place of Ishmael (or Isaac) is the basis of the Muslim Eid al-Adha, or Feast of the Sacrifice.

10. Geography is a further characteristic shared by all three religions. Muhammad reputedly said: 'There is not a prophet but that he has dwelt in the desert': the dry open spaces of what are now Saudi Arabia, Jordan, Israel and Egypt were the training grounds of the patriarchs, where God 'teaches by taking away'. Whether the colossi of our religious histories are mythical, factual or irrelevant, all three religions agree that they lived in the same general area, under the same conditions. This common thread stretches from Muhammad, alone in his desert cave awaiting his revelations, back to Jesus Christ, fasting and resisting temptation in the wilderness, and back further through St John the Baptist, to Job and Moses, and our most ancient traditions of deserts and deprivation.

At the moment of creation all are together – Muslim, Jew and Christian – making up the vast majority of the population of the globe.

> Praise be to Allah, Who created the Heavens and the Earth
> And made the darkness and the Light.
>> The Qur'ān, *Al-An'ām* (The Cattle) Surah 6, verse 1

To Him is due
The primal origin
Of the heavens and the earth.
When He decreeth a matter
He saith to it: 'Be,'
And it is.

                    The Qur'ān, *Al-Baqarah* (The Heifer) Surah 2, verse 117

In the beginning God created the heavens and the earth. The
earth was a vast waste, darkness covered the deep and the
spirit of God hovered over the surface of the water. God said
'Let there be Light', and there was light; and God saw the
light was good and he separated light from darkness.

                    The Pentateuch, Book of Genesis, verse 1

In the beginning the Word already was. The Word was in
God's presence, and what God was, the Word was. He was
God at the beginning, and through him all things came to
be; without him no created thing came into being. In him
was life, and that life was the light of mankind. The light
shines in the darkness and the darkness has never mastered it.

                    The New Testament, Gospel According to John, verse 1

These words express a universal human sentiment: our awareness of
an original force beyond ourselves that is the spring of faith.
Whether this consciousness is focused through the dogma of a
formal religion, left unresolved as a personal enigma, or approached
as a product of imperfectly understood natural laws, this is our condition as human beings: tentative and mortal, here exposed in a few
short sentences at the bedrock of all three mighty religions; a
moment when all can agree, at least on the fundamental question,
before the detritus of history and the sands of time obscure our
sameness. Here is the moment of unity before the varying details of
each faith develop into bitter differences of culture and politics, generation after generation, century after century.

And the divisions come quickly. Genesis goes on to say, in verse
27, that God created man 'in his own image', an insuperable heresy
to Islam in which God is described essentially in the negative: unseeable and unknowable; having no partner; not similar to His creation.

John claims in verse 16 that God the Father can only be known through Jesus Christ, the Son. But the Christian Trinity of Father, Son and Holy Ghost as both One and Three is a belief entirely repudiated by Jews and is complete anathema to Muslims for whom God can only be One.

In the face of these direct contradictions and the thousands more that follow, can anyone really be sure that the religion into which he or she was born is right and all the others wrong? Or conversely, does our Western cynicism and declining observance, which merely obscures the issue rather than providing an explanation, permit us to denigrate the intricacies in which others do find faith? Does certainty and salvation in whatever guise, religious or secular, really belong only to one group?

After thousands of years of crimes perpetrated in the name of rival gods by religions claiming to be based on love and forgiveness, the answers to these questions must surely be self-evident. The premise of this book, therefore, is that no absolute truth is to be found in any faith. Rather, it is the very divergence of human belief that really unites us, in our common inability to explain the cosmic mystery of existence. By attempting to understand Islam, the transcultural explorer begins to see how one man's approach to such an explanation has grown into the huge edifice of practice, history and politics, that is today one of the most misunderstood pieces of a fractured world.

II Muslims, Christians and Jews: Differences

The story, or metaphor, of the Creation is just one of a number of beliefs shared by Judaism, Christianity and Islam, in principle if not in detail. But the most important common ground between the three is monotheism, the recognition of a single God whose revelation replaced all that had gone before: the multiple gods of the Greeks and the Romans, the sacred rocks and idols of the pre-Islamic Arabs, or the many false gods with which the Jews were tempted from time to time during the events described in the Old Testament. The Christian God has three persons in one God; for Jews, God has a special relationship with the Children of Israel; for

Muslims, God speaks definitively only through the Arabic Qur'ān. But all three images are nevertheless linked by their monotheistic essence.

All three faiths purport to set out God's plan for the world, involving commandments for life and specific methods of worship, even though man, by his human nature, will inevitably fail to meet these divine standards. And while penalties are prescribed for transgressions, forgiveness and mercy are qualities ascribed to the Almighty by all three faiths.

But it is differences between us, not the similarities, that attract attention. Here are a few short statements of differentiation as an overview.

Judaism was established amid the repeated disasters and enslavements that befell the Children of Israel in the days of the Patriarchs, mitigated by a few minor victories and the short-lived rule of the House of David. Later, after the Babylonian captivity and the Roman destruction of Jerusalem, the religion developed in an atmosphere of homelessness and defensiveness, sustaining Jews who were spread around the world in the diaspora. Judaism was solidified further during the Christian era by the massacres of Jews in Britain during the Crusades, by the Spanish Inquisition, the Russian pogroms and finally by the Nazi Holocaust which led to the establishment of the State of Israel and to the nominal end of the diaspora condition.

Christianity travelled up through the veins and arteries of Rome, from the peripheries to the heart. Then Christianity prospered as Europe prospered, intertwined with the artistic and political developments of the last two thousand years. And starting in the sixteenth century, European exploration and colonialization carried Christianity to every continent of the world.

Islam grew as the simple belief of the illiterate desert dweller. The message is easy to grasp, offering a universal brotherhood of equality beyond race, beyond political hierarchy or ethnic origin. The dramatic appeal of Islam to the poor and the powerless is readily understandable.

Judaism speaks to one people, to the Jews. The history of Judaism is the history of the Jewish people and the practice of Judaism was developed over the three thousand years of their history, not delivered by any single prophet or saviour. While Judaism seldom proselytizes and there are very few converts, the Jewish concept of God the Creator, the all-powerful and the all-seeing, is the seed from which Christianity and Islam have grown to encircle the globe.

The **Christian** God of the New Testament is personal, pacifist and universally loving, although this central message is now diffused across an incoherent spectrum of conflicting denominations. Unlike Judaism and Islam, most Christian Churches carry extensive centralized hierarchies that claim control over dogma and many have become institutions of substantial wealth and temporal power.

Sunni **Islam**, the faith of the vast majority of Muslims, exists without any church structure. Muslims are held together by the simple concept of the One God, by God's Word as revealed directly to man in the Qur'ān, and by the uniform practice of the Five Pillars.

Judaism is characterized by God's injunctions to the Jews to obey His commandments as set out in the Torah, by which man may, in time, rectify his original disobedience in the Garden of Eden. Devout adherence to these laws will hasten the coming of the messiah and the establishment of God's kingdom on earth, an event in which Jews believe they will have a special role, which is the essence of the concept of the Election of Israel. But behind this emphasis on practice, there is no 'Jewish Creed', making for a remarkable freedom of religious thought and a wide diversity of opinion within Judaism on such topics as heaven and hell, the nature of evil and the core problem of free will.

The essence of **Christianity** is that man who was born in sin can only be redeemed by Christ through His own death and resurrection. Thus through faith, man may similarly overcome death to live an eternal life in the presence of God. But beyond this central theme of the life and death of Jesus Christ as the Son of God, Christian beliefs and practices differ widely. A personal spirituality has come to dominate modern Christianity while belief in the physical resurrection of the body, in a concrete heaven and a burning hell has generally declined together with church attendance. Christianity is open to all, but some form of initiation is required, usually baptism, symbolic or actual, together with instruction.

Islam, like Judaism, emphasizes practice through ritual, although the Five Pillars of Islam are much simpler than the multiple laws of the Torah and the resulting Jewish rites. But unlike Judaism, the Qur'ān lays out a vivid and detailed system of belief in addition to the external forms of observance. The Last Day is anticipated in a physical sense, and heaven and hell are very real.

> For the wrongdoer We
> Have prepared the Fire
> Whose smoke and flames
> Like the walls and roof
> Of a tent, will hem
> Them in: if they implore
> Relief they will be granted
> Water like melted brass
> That will scald their faces.
> How dreadful the drink.
> How uncomfortable a couch
> To recline upon.
>
> *Al-Kahf* (The Cave) Surah 18, verse 29

The culmination of the haj, or pilgrimage, is the rite of the Standing, when the pilgrim asks God for forgiveness of his or her sins, and this day is interpreted by many as a literal pre-enactment of the events of the Day of Judgement. Conversion to Islam is the simplest of all, requiring only the profession of the *Shahādah* from the heart. 'I attest that there is no god but God and that Muhammad is the Messenger of God.' Learning the faith begins then, at conversion not necessarily before, and it is a Muslim's duty to improve his or her knowledge of the faith, and therefore of the Qur'ān, continuously over a lifetime.

III   The Torah, the Bible and the Qur'ān

The Hebrew Bible consists of the Torah or the 'Five Books of Moses' (Genesis, Exodus, Leviticus, Numbers and Deuteronomy) followed by the Prophets and the Writings. The Torah is the story of the Creation, and of man's original sin of disobedience against God, followed by the core mythology of Judaism: the enslavement of the Jews in Egypt and their subsequent escape, followed by years of wandering the Sinai desert, ended by the bloody invasion of Canaan as the Promised Land. But for Jews these are also books of love, enabling man to say 'yes' to God by following the 248 positive and 365 negative commandments set out in the text, so moving towards the dream of a new paradise on earth, a state which may eventually replace the original paradise lost.

The Christian Bible opens with the Hebrew Bible as the Old Testament (although some of the later Christian components of the Old Testament are not part of the original Jewish twenty-two sacred works), followed by the New Testament which consists principally of the four Gospels (Matthew, Mark, Luke and John). Each Gospel relates the life of Christ from a slightly different point of view and each contains varying details and emphases. The Gospels are followed by the writings of the early church leaders who first put Christianity into practice, of whom St Paul is the dominant spirit.

The Qur'ān is entirely different, having no narrative thread in the same sense as the Torah or the New Testament. There are frequent references to the prophets who have gone before, and the reader is presumed to be already familiar with the names. But rather than a story, the Qur'ān is an exhortation addressed to man by God, urging a better world through a social and religious order that follows His will. These rules of conduct and of belief that will lead man to everlasting life are to be found diffused throughout the book.

The Qur'ān is approximately 120,000 words long, about the same length as the four Christian Gospels together. To a western reader, the Qur'ān may seem obscure and repetitive, even contradictory. Study and frequent reading are required to come to the message that underlies the text. Faced with an apparent inconsistency or a statement that appears to run against science or scholarship, the devout Muslim may seek further interpretation, textual reconciliation, or the words may have been abrogated, but ultimately he or she has only two choices: either he or she has faith that the words are divine and acknowledges that it is the reader who has yet to understand, or he or she ceases to be a Muslim. This bare and inescapable certainty in the Word of God lies at the heart of Islam and at the core of many misunderstandings between Muslims and non-Muslims.

Because Muhammad's life is so clearly recorded making him the only prophet to live in the full light of history, modern scholarship has made little impression on the facts of his career as accepted by Muslims. Whether or not the reader believes in the divine authorship of the Qur'ān, the text has indisputably come down to us from the seventh century CE, from the mouth of Muhammad and substantially unchanged.

In contrast, the status of both the Torah and the New Testament have gradually deteriorated from 'God-sent' to myth. Only Jewish (and Christian) literalists still assert that the five books of the Torah were written by Moses and most modern scholarship places the authorship between the years 800 and 150 BCE, reaching full canonical form only in the first or second century CE, and after much adding and subtracting. This is nowhere near the beginnings of recorded history, which in Mesopotamia and Egypt push back 2,000 years before even the oldest parts of the Torah. Further, the biblical stories are not all original, but many compare with and draw upon the ancient traditions of Babylon and Egypt as well as Phoenicia, Canaan and Persia. Nor are there any archaeological or other records to support such events as the construction of the first or the second temple of Zion in Jerusalem, the Flood, or the Egyptian captivity and release. And few Christians or Jews still believe in such events as the seven-day Creation, which has foundered on the new truth of evolution.

But the Torah succeeds brilliantly as great literature, giving form and order to the myths of the Hebrews, while at the same time constructing a façade of justification for the Jewish claim to be the Elected of God. Written for the most part during the days of low morale following the collapse of the House of David and through the captivity of Judah in Babylon, the Torah can be viewed as a masterpiece of uplifting propaganda. The books also work as a political tract that conjures the moral title-deeds to Palestine, territory which as Canaan, was in fact won and lost by the Jews on numerous occasions through nothing more mysterious than force of arms: from the legendary Hebrew invasion after the Exodus to the creation of the modern State of Israel in 1948.

The New Testament was written between half a generation and a full generation after the death of Christ and comes to us in a language (Greek) different from that spoken by the participants in the events described (Hebrew or Aramaic). The evangelists had no direct personal knowledge of the content of their writing and many assertions in the Gospels do not match historical fact, starting with the date of the Nativity. While the Gospels may be 'inspired', no claim is now made for anything but human authorship. Furthermore, the books were merely four of a number of contradictory versions of the life and sayings of Christ that circulated in the early Christian Church. Only during the first three centuries CE was the present canon agreed upon, after which all texts other than Matthew, Mark, Luke and John were banned by the church and have since fallen into obscurity, or were destroyed at the time.

IV   The Nature of Islam

At the heart of Islam is the wish to enlighten mankind to an awareness of God.

> Light upon Light
> God guides to His light whom He will.
> *Al-Nur* (The Light) Surah 24, verse 35

However, the text of the Qur'ān and the beliefs of Islam are so overlaid with misinterpretation and reinterpretation from both inside and outside that this light is often obscured. The universal message of Christianity would be similarly diminished to the point of darkness if the faith were to be defined only by reference to the sectarian murders in Northern Ireland, the history of the Spanish Inquisition, or the sad stories of lust and greed in modern television evangelism. So the following summary of the nature of Islam may seem surprising, even dubious to a Western reader, but behind all the inflammatory headlines and the misunderstandings, for a devout Muslim, these are the true characteristics of his or her faith.

● **Discipline**. Laws are to be found throughout the text of the Qur'ān, which, as a divine revelation, are therefore considered to be the laws of God. These formal statements of law in the Qur'ān are

supplemented by the Sunna, the sayings and reported actions of
Muhammad during his lifetime, which set out the detailed regulations that complement the more general injunctions of the Qur'ān.
The discipline expected of a Muslim starts with his or her personal
life: regular prayers; respect for the body by following rules of diet;
cleanliness in all things; politeness in public conduct. Then laws for
the family, which lie at the heart of Islam, followed by rules for society as a whole, with an emphasis on the maintenance of public
order. The entire structure of Qur'ānic law is accepted by Muslims
as God's will and is known collectively as the Shariah, literally 'the
Road'. This body of laws has an absolute 'God-given' character,
therefore, although softened by the possibility of forgiveness for
human frailty and the promise of paradise for repentant sinners.

> Say: 'If you love Allah,
> Follow me: Allah will love you
> And forgive you your sins.
> For Allah is Oft-Forgiving
> Most Merciful.'
>
> *Al-'Imrān* (The Family of 'Imrān) Surah 3, verse 35

But unlike Christianity, Islam recognizes no intermediary
between man and God. Obedience to the will of Allah, as expressed
in the Shariah is confronted directly by the believer. There is no
equivalent to the Christian prayer formula, 'through Jesus Christ,
Our Lord. Amen'.

> And your Lord says:
> 'Call on Me; I
> Will answer your prayer.
> But those who are
> Too arrogant to serve Me
> Will surely find themselves
> In Hell – in humiliation!'
>
> *Al-Ghāfir* (The Forgiver) Surah 40, verse 60

● **Moderation**. A practising Muslim believes in *wasat*, meaning
the way between two extremes.

And be moderate
In thy pace, and lower
Thy voice; for the harshest
Of sound without doubt
Is the braying of the ass.

Luqmān (Luqmān the Wise) Surah 31, verse 19

Moderation takes the form of consensus in arriving at decisions, in preferring the middle ground, in understanding a few things well rather than many things superficially, in personal modesty and in good relations with those whose life the devout Muslim touches. This is the horizontal axis of the Muslim faith, the creation of good relations between man and man. The vertical axis, the relationship between man and the will of God, is of primary importance, but the faith consists of maintaining both axes in equilibrium.

● **Community**. While each believer enjoys his or her own direct relationship with God, Islam is also a commonwealth of the *'ummah*, meaning the Muslims as a distinct society. Ideally, this Muslim community forms a self-helping, self-regulating and self-leveling society standing openly and solidly for the faith. The combination of parity with solidarity is expressed through all aspects of the practice of Islam and is emphasized frequently in the Qur'ān. The simple universality of the Muslim community is shown most convincingly in the saying of daily prayers within fixed times, with the entire brotherhood and sisterhood of believers facing toward Mecca from all around the world, following the same prescribed formula. The annual haj is another expression of the egalitarianism of Islam, drawing millions together from the majority of the nations, races, cultures and languages of the world to follow the orders of God and His Prophet on an entirely equal basis.

● **Tolerance**. Throughout the history of Islam, racial prejudice has been entirely absent and religious tolerance has been shown towards Christians and Jews, both considered to be People of the Book.

Say, O Muslims: We believe in Allah
And that which is revealed unto us and that
Which was revealed unto Abraham,

And Ishmael and Isaac and Jacob
And the tribes and that which Moses
And Jesus received and that which
The Prophets received from their Lord.
We make no distinction between any of them
And unto Him we have surrendered.

Al-Baqarah (The Heifer) Surah 2, verse 36

There have been famous periods of conflict between Islam and other faiths: during Muhammad's confrontation with the Jewish communities in Medina for example, during the Christian Crusades, in the Balkans, in Spain when Asian Muslims fought against Catholic Europeans. And in modern times the effective partition of Palestine and the creation of the State of Israel has led to over eighty years of political tension and violence between Muslims and Jews. But generally, over the centuries of Muslim rule in the southern and eastern Mediterranean, Christian and Jewish communities, although usually subject to a special poll tax, have lived peacefully under Islamic governments, carrying on their lives unmolested and frequently holding public office. Pogroms, ghettos, inquisitions and concentration camps are European inventions and have no equivalents in Islam. The Qur'ān expresses frustration at the continued divisions between Christians, Jews and Muslims following the revelation of Muhammad's message, but offers an optimistic view of potential unity:

Say: 'We believe
In the Revelation which has
Come down to us and in that
Which came down to you;
Our God and your God
Is One: and it is to Him
That we bow in Islam.'

Al 'Ankabut (The Spider) Surah 29, verse 46

Muhammad himself decreed tolerance towards both Christians and Jews living in the Muslim-controlled Commonwealth of Medina, as well as ordering protection for their places of worship, provided that they did not attempt to undermine the state. This historical sufferance goes against the popular Western view, yet the record of Islam compares very favourably with the frequent Christian persecutions of Muslims and Jews through the ages, reaching right down to the twentieth century.

V   The Divide: Islam Misunderstood

Islam has an entirely different image among many non-Muslims. Muslims are frequently labelled as narrow-minded, extremist or violence-prone, while the West, seen from a Muslim country, is decadent and immoral, an evil menace.

Possibly the West is pre-conditioned to see Islam as hostile. Such a view is certainly embedded in Western culture, with the heroic legends of the Crusades, the language of Shakespeare in *Othello*, of Dante and of Voltaire, or in words derived from the Old Testament such as 'Philistine', 'Chosen People' and 'Promised Land'. Such words have set Ishmaelite against Israelite from the start of biblical history and the same words have set Arab against Jew in the Middle East for the past century, right up to and including today.

Muslims are similarly programmed, usually seeing the godless West only through the excesses of our scandal-loving media. Or we appear as armed aggressors, from the colonial era through to the West's apparently unconditional support for Israel, for example, in the bombing of Libyan and Afghan civilians, the starving of Iraqi children followed by the bombing and invasion of their country, and the ruination of Chechnya, acts perpetrated against Muslims for the purposes of easy domestic political advantage, while avoiding the core issues of justice and true democracy. Even an elementary examination of some of the areas of conflict between Muslims and the West through Muslim eyes, produces a quite contrary view.

Most acts of political violence within Muslim states, especially attacks on tourists, are broadly intended to destabilize 'pro-Western' corrupted regimes and to bring about government based on Islamic *shurā* (meaning 'consensus', and to be discussed later) and the Shariah. Such acts, starting with those of September 11th, 2001, have then developed into attacks on foreign targets, but with the same objective: to force the departure of foreign occupiers so that

Islamic government can begin. However despicable in themselves, these incidents are the expression of a deep tension springing from a legitimate historical injustice. Most Muslim countries were liberated from European colonial rule only within the last fifty years. Liberation to what, though? The nation-state that the West advocates as the liberal solution for the problems of the world, a non-religious administration subject (in theory) to democratic control, is a system that took hundreds of years and untold millions of deaths to develop in Europe and America. The idea that such a structure could be imposed successfully on former colonies of a different culture over a single generation has proved to be wildly optimistic.

Further, the secular nation-state based on the Western model is a concept that runs directly contrary to Muslim traditions, which stretch back to the original community of the 'ummah, established, as we shall see, by the Prophet in Medina in the seventh century. Here was the ideal Muslim society with no national boundaries and a merged church and state, ruled by the laws of God. In contrast, most of the recent attempts to create secular nation-states in countries with Muslim majorities have produced corrupt ruling elites without a popular mandate, that are only nominally Muslim and whose flawed leaders are frequently supported by the West in the name of 'national security' and 'global stability'. There are many examples both past and present, from the Shah of Iran to General Suharto of Indonesia, to the rigged elections of Hosni Mubarak's Egypt, to Saddam Hussein himself, whose power was built up by the West when it suited us, during the Iran–Iraq war of 1981–88. The result is that in most Muslim countries, neither democracy nor *shurā* and Shariah have been achieved, neither the Western utopia nor the Muslim version, but only new forms of dictatorship and repression. Lurking instability and an intensification of violence in the name of religion has been the inevitable result.

Islam is a system of rules for all aspects of life, based on faith, forming an all-embracing 'social project', whereas Western liberalism specifically seeks to avoid the regulation of personal behaviour unless the rights and freedoms of others are affected. Islam can therefore appear to be 'intolerant' in imposing restrictions that Westerners would find unconscionable in their own lives. But in this view the Western observer overlooks the core Muslim belief that the rules of

Islam originate with the direct word of God in the Qur'ān. For a believer, therefore, the rule of the Shariah is to be welcomed not resented. And by extension, Western liberalism transgresses God's commandments in every possible way and is therefore 'decadent' and 'culpable'.

This divide between Western 'decadence' and Islamic 'repression' also coincides generally with the division between the rich world and the poor. Western democracy, political freedom, transparency and a secular state appear to lead to wealthy societies with high levels of personal consumption. In the Muslim view, however, the West pays a price for these advances in the form of intangibles: declining 'family values', increasing rates of divorce and births out of wedlock, drug and alcohol abuse, drunk driving, high crime statistics and loss of community. These are the very defects that the Western right-wing perennially promises to repair, and values which are still very much alive and well in most Islamic countries.

With the charges of 'intolerance' against Muslims and 'degeneracy' against the West go the popular but misinformed images. Muslim women wearing the *burqa*, compared with the Western use of the female form as a sales expedient; the apparent cruelty of the Islamic penal code compared with the elevated levels of crime and suffering in Western countries, to name but two. This is a divide that can never be bridged, only understood. The West may think that the spread of affluence and material comforts is the long-term solution to the wrongs of the world, but in reality the 'God-sent' light of Islam will give way to secular materialism only with the greatest of difficulty, if ever. Each encroachment by the US-dominated world produces the counter-reaction of a greater commitment among Muslims to their code.

The Salman Rushdie affair encapsulated the divide perfectly. Citizens in the West have struggled for centuries, and at great cost, for the right to freedom of speech, which is now inalienable. The West, and the UK in particular, was therefore infuriated by an attempt at censorship through a fatwa, a legal ruling that included a death sentence, issued by a foreign cleric to punish the authorship of a book published in London by a British citizen. While the fatwa is, of course, indefensible, Rushdie's novel, *The Satanic Verses*, mocks the very essence of Islam (as well as the personalities of both

Muhammad and the Ayatollah Khomeini), ridiculing exactly the process by which God through Gabriel revealed the verses of the Qur'ān to Muhammad. For many believers who consider the Qur'ān to be a revelation from God, not just mere words or an option of faith, this was a crime worse than murder. Further, in a society where sexual reticence is the accepted standard, portraying Muhammad's wives as prostitutes in a brothel ensured that Muslims would be outraged. *The Satanic Verses* is not an easy or a rewarding read and the book would probably have dropped quickly out of sight, together with the author, had the fatwa not been invoked. Instead, Rushdie is now world-famous and commands huge advance payments for his work and appearances. Ironically, the painfully constructed position of Muslims in Britain as law-abiding and industrious citizens has been deeply damaged by the actions of a few extremists in calling for Rushdie's death, creating (together with September 11th 2001 and July 7th 2005) the opportunity for the conflict to develop in the British press into the open denigration of Islam as a whole.

For the Pakistanis of Bradford, however, the Rushdie incident was a clear example of Britain's reluctance to allow Muslims to defend their own identity within society and the issue soon escalated on the Muslim side to include complaints about the funding of Muslim schools, political representation and unemployment. (According to British government figures, 60 per cent of the Pakistani and Bangladeshi community in the UK live below the official poverty line, compared with 16 per cent of whites as a whole.)

Muslims also argue that freedom of speech in Britain is not in fact absolute, being already limited by laws against pornography, racism, personal libel and national security. Meanwhile the government has periodically attempted to criminalize hatred against a group defined by religious beliefs, or 'religious hatred'. For Muslims, therefore, adding an offence against religious sensibilities such as blasphemy to the list of curtailed freedoms would be an extension of the existing list of exceptions, rather than a fresh departure. However the intention of British law is to protect the person not the faith, while 'blasphemy' involves the protection of a belief, and an official judgement about that belief, which is well beyond the level of intervention in private lives that the British electorate would accept.

In many cases Westerners attribute such divergences to the inflexible canon of Islam, when in fact the reasons for our differences are often the political and economic objectives of the West itself. The Ayatollah Khomeini, former leader of the Islamic Republic of Iran, called the United States the 'Great Shaytān' because America had for so long supported the regime of the Shah, a deeply corrupt ruler with precious little earned or inherited legitimacy. The Shah consistently suppressed the popular religious life of Iran, calling the process 'modernization'. But to Khomeini and the vast majority of Iranians, the Shah and his Western backers were working against God's law, thus allying themselves with the devil. But all the while, the real reason for Western support of the Shah was nothing to do with his social ideas, but because he maintained part of the front line against the USSR in the Cold War years, and cooperated with British and American oil interests. Then, in order to foster popular support for the policy of maintaining the Shah in power against the will of his own people, the West 'manufactured consent', by characterizing internal opposition to the Shah as 'fundamentalist', 'revolutionary' and 'Islamic', when to Western governments the real issues were, in fact, purely strategic and economic. This process of demonizing Islam has been repeated again and again by the West: in Algeria, the Sudan, Iraq and Afghanistan, to name but a few. A comparison closer to home is Ireland, where the words 'Catholic' or 'Protestant' usually precede all other descriptions of the antagonists, whereas, in fact, the root cause from which the dispute arises is not religion but relates to an historical injustice over the confiscation of land and the imposition of outside rule and migration, perpetrated by force of arms by one people on another.

A further example of the misunderstandings between Islam and the West is the refusal of many teachers in France to conduct classes attended by Muslim girls wearing headscarves (which are now prohibited by law). The official reason scarves are considered a threat in French schools is because church and state are strictly separated in the Vth Republic, religion having no place therefore in a state-run institution. But Muslims reply that miniskirts and exposed midriffs, or necklaces with crosses or stars worn to school are equally symbolic, although these infractions are rarely prohibited. However, many teachers assert that the real reason for their opposition to the scarf is because it is 'imposed' on young Muslim girls by male-ordered traditions. The possibility that the wearer of the scarf may herself wish to follow the injunctions of the Qur'ān as to personal modesty appears not to be taken into account. The headscarf reached the pitch of a national scandal in France, once again symbolizing the status of Muslims in Europe as eternal immigrants.

So is the West more advanced? Isn't an affirmative answer to this question proved by the numbers of immigrants from Muslim countries living in the West and the almost total absence of the reverse? Or by Western rates of per capita income which are up to fifty times higher than those in the poorest Islamic states? The answer is indisputably yes, the West obviously *is* ahead, at least in a material sense. But the question that follows is why, in a country like Egypt with a 5,000-year history, self-sufficiency in oil and food, a friendly cohesive population and a key geographical position, is the average per capita income one twentieth of that of France? Why, when Egypt and South Korea had much the same standard of living in 1950, is South Korea's income per capita now over six times as high? The answer that comes readily to a Western mind is: because of the backwardness of Islam. But in the opinion of this observer the exact opposite is the case. Egypt is poor while South Korea is prospering and France is rich because Islam is *not* followed in Egypt. Muhammad 'Abduh, the great Egyptian *mujtahid,* or Islamic thinker and innovator from the late-nineteenth century, made the following observation after his first trip to Europe: 'In France I saw Islam without Muslims, but in Egypt I see Muslims without Islam.' Islam decrees hard work, honesty and fairness; Islam prohibits political repression and corruption: all the conditions that are generally to be found in the West. But in Egypt, for one example, and there are many others, corruption and waste at the top are a way of life, sapping the energies of the people, limiting growth, diverting the assets of the country into the pockets of the few, and converting the country into a nation of cheats from top to bottom. The poor grow poorer, saying their prayers five times a day and hoping for justice in the world to come, while the rich plunderers grow richer, openly supported by us, the West. This is not the fault of Islam and the injunctions of the Qur'ān are clear:

And do not eat up
Your own property among yourselves
For vanities, nor use it
As bait for rulers
With intent that ye may
Eat up wrongfully and knowingly
Other people's property.

Al-Baqarah (The Heifer) Surah 2, verse 188

2
THE COMING OF THE PROPHET

I Early History

The history of Islam begins with Muhammad and the Qur'ān. The low level of importance given by Muslims to the events before Muhammad is illustrated by the Arabic term for the preceding century: *Jāhiliyyah*, the Time of Ignorance.

Islam has no ordered pre-history to tell, no 'Muslim Old Testament' in the Judeo-Christian sense, no pre-Revelation story to cover the period between the Creation and the birth of Muhammad. This is another example of the absolute primacy in Islam of the text of the Qur'ān and the life of the Prophet. Muhammad's message did not flow from a religious continuum like the scriptures of the Hebrews, or from a tradition of messianic expectation. Rather, Muhammad physically overthrew the pre-existing pagan order in Arabia.

Jesus Christ was a Jew from the House of David, from an 'Elected People' already 'Chosen of God', and from a culture with a tradition and a history of prophecy purportedly stretching back to the beginnings of time. This neat fit of faith and history has dominated Western religious tradition for two thousand years, forming until recent agnostic times the backbone of our collective psyche. Christianity built a vast structure of belief on these foundations, tying together an entire cycle of stories, from Adam's fall, representing the sins of mankind, to the potential redemption of the world by the crucifixion of Christ.

Muslim early history is much sparser and more confused. No writings have come down to us from the *Jāhiliyyah* or the early years of Islam that are even remotely comparable to the works of the early Hebrews. The nearest equivalent to a 'Muslim Torah' is *The Exegesis of Tabari*, written by Muhammad ibn Jarir al-Tabari in the tenth century CE, almost three hundred years after the death of Muhammad. This massive work, recently translated into English for the first time, funded by UNESCO and the National Endowment for the Humanities of the United States, runs to twenty-two volumes. There is, however, no central narrative running through the material; rather the work consists of sayings, myths (known as *Isrā'iliyyat*) and multiple layers of opinion relating to every surah in the Qur'ān, the sources for which are often obscure and unsubstantiated.

Before the revelation of the Qur'ān Arabic existed as a grammatical but almost exclusively oral language. No original documents remain from the period, however, only anthologies and recollections assembled by later generations. Poems composed to be recited in public were greatly valued by early Arab society. Poetry was the noblest expression of language, and language is the supreme Arab art, known under Islam as *sihr halāl*, the 'permitted magic', even though the early poets were probably illiterate, like Muhammad himself. In the *Jāhiliyyah*, epic verse sustained the *diwān*, or collective memory and honour of each tribe from generation to generation. The highest form of this early poetry was the *qasida*, or ode, which was both rhyming and metred, running to as many as sixty couplets or more. The content of a *qasida* followed a well-understood form, bearing an underlying message that spoke of the transience of life. First the poet would evoke a faraway place, a deserted encampment or a lost or distant love.

> *But what think you now of the Lady Nawar, so far away,*
> *And every bond with her broken, new cord alike with old?*
> *A Murrite she, who dwells now in Faid and for neighbours takes*
> *The Hejazi folk: how can you still aspire then to come to her?*

Then a dangerous journey would be described in which the narrator regains his equanimity in the face of the inevitability of death, through feats of strength or endurance.

> *Then I pricked her on, to run like an ostrich and fleeter still*
> *Until, when she was warm and her bones light and pliant,*
> *Her saddle slipping about and her neck streaming with sweat,*
> *And the foam of her perspiration drenching her leather girth;*
> *She tosses her head and strains at the rein but rushes on,*
> *As a desert dove flutters with the flight swiftly to water.*

Finally, with the listeners' attention assured, the poet launches into his panegyric: lines in praise of a benefactor, in praise of nature and the desert, or the poet's tribe.

> *When alarmed to battle, there they are with their helmets on*
> *And their coats of mail, the rings of them gleaming like stars.*
> *Unsullied is their honour and their deeds are not ineffectual,*
> *For their prudent minds incline not after capricious lust.*
>
> Excerpts from *The Centenarian* by Labid

To conclude that the Qur'ān was an extension of this poetic tradition is tempting. But even though the Qur'ān uses the high Arabic language of poetry, transcending tribal variations, this would be an error. For Muslims the word of God defies all human categorization.

Belief in a single paramount god preceded Islam. God was *Il* to the Babylonians and to the Canaanites, later to the Israelites he was *El*, and to the primitive Bedouins he was *al-Ilāh*. This was the god of a linear creation in which man is born and dies through divine will, rather than participating in a recurring cycle of reincarnation. But there were also hundreds of other lesser gods in pagan Arabia, forming a richly diverse Arab religious culture. Many of these gods were represented by stones or clay idols, though all were mere intermediaries between man and *al-Ilāh*. The monotheism of the first Hebrew Commandment, 'Thou shalt have no other gods before me', took many centuries for the Jews to refine. In Islam, in contrast, the move from polytheism to the One God that almost overwhelms the Qur'ān, took place only from the commencement of the message, and matured over a period of merely twenty-two years. Jewish and Christian tradition may have assisted in the formulation of Allah, the One God of Islam, but the concept itself was not issued to the Arabs by any outside religion. *Al-Ilāh* of the *Jāhiliyyah* was understood to be the ultimate source of power and above all other gods and may also have been associated with certain dietary laws and the rite of male circumcision, practices that were extended and codified by Islam.

The Ka'bah (literally 'cube') is the rectangular chamber made of hewn stone (measuring 13m × 10m × 7m high) that is now surrounded by the vast courtyard of the Great Mosque in Mecca. The Ka'bah is the physical centre of the Muslim world, and the city of Mecca constitutes Islam's holiest *haram* or sanctuary, and was long recognized in pre-Muslim Arabia as a place of pilgrimage and sacrifice set apart from conflict. The building is evidence of a strong Arab religious tradition, although in the era immediately before

Muhammad the Arabs were ardently polytheist. The present-day structure of the Ka'bah was already in existence long before the birth of Muhammad, although periodically repaired and altered, and there appears to be no historical explanation of the origin of the structure in the Arab record to match against the Muslim legend. In this legend, Abraham, in order to give thanks to God for His mercy in sparing Ishmael from sacrifice, rebuilt the present Ka'bah on foundations first laid by Adam, the original superstructure having been washed away in the Flood.

Ibrahim, or Abraham, existed in Arabic mythology long before his appearance in the Qur'ān, although the tradition may have derived from Arab contact with Jewish legends. To the early Arabs, Abraham was the patriarch of the race and the builder of the Ka'bah in Mecca. By the time al-Tabari was writing in the tenth century CE, the story of Abraham had been spruced up to create the present orthodoxy by which Abraham (who was conveniently neither a Jew nor a Christian) is regarded as the father of both the Arabs and the Jews, the former through Abraham's oldest son Ishmael by his Canaanite wife Hājar, the latter through the younger son Isaac by Abraham's Hebrew wife Sarah. In the Muslim version of the story, which may only have come into existence as Islam sought to create traditions separate from Judaism, the aborted sacrifice took place on the Mount of Mercy outside Mecca, not on the Temple Mount in Jerusalem as in the Jewish tradition. And, as we have seen, Ishmael the proto-Arab was the intended victim, not Isaac the proto-Jew.

A number of early Arab prophets are referred to in the Qur'ān who do not appear in the Old Testament, with names such as Hud, Salih, Dhu-'l-Kifl, Luqmān, Idris and Shu'ayb. The reader is expected to be familiar with these personalities and no coherent explanation is given of the lives or teachings of these men, whose detailed history is now lost. Muhammad's purpose in citing preceding prophets was to reinforce the moral themes of the Qur'ān, rather than to tell a series of stories. Further, in order to present Islam as the perfection of all that had gone before, God's previous messengers are represented as delivering the same essential message as Muhammad and sharing some of his experiences. The Qur'ān then reinterprets the old teachings in the new light of God's final word: that on the Last Day the righteous will be rewarded and the wicked punished.

II   Islam and the Torah

Islam has a forthright response to the 'missing' story that would link
the dawn of time to the birth of the Prophet. Since the Creation, in
the Muslim view, God in his wisdom has revealed to man, through
a succession of prophets from all cultures and races, that part of the
divine message which He deemed to be suitable for each age. Thus,
all who preceded Muhammad and believed in the One God were
'inspired', and even considered by Islam to be 'Muslim', in that they
submitted to the will of God. But from Adam to Jesus, none of the
earlier prophets possessed the definitive text because the moment of
ultimate revelation had not yet arrived. Not until God's revelation
to Muhammad did man receive the complete message. The Qur'ān
is regarded therefore as definitive or 'final', meaning that the message is sufficient to carry us through to the Last Day with nothing
else needed for our salvation. This belief allows Islam to co-opt, yet
at the same time to reduce in importance, all that went before,
making the absence of a 'Muslim Old Testament' irrelevant.

As a further response, Islam asserts that the God-sent messages
delivered by earlier prophets were perverted at the time, or misunderstood later, or diminished through imperfect transmission over
subsequent generations.

> They change the words
> From their right places
> And forget a good part
> Of the Message that was
> Sent them, nor wilt thou
> Cease to find them –
> Barring a few – ever
> Bent on new deceits.
>
> *Al-Mā'idah* (The Repast) Surah 5, verse 13

What we read in the Torah and the New Testament, therefore, in
Muslim belief, is a corrupted version of a pure truth that is now lost.
This human interference is then brought into further useful service
by Islam to account for the discrepancies between the Qur'ānic versions of the patriarchal stories, and those found in the religious writings of the other two older faiths. For Muslims the most crucial of

these wilful distortions relate to the teachings of the main Hebrew prophets. Moses, for example, appearing as Musa in the Qur'ān, is also a prophet of Islam even though Jewish. But through the lens of Islam, Musa's divinely inspired message of the One God was purposely revised by the Jews into a narrow cult based on Hebrew tribalism, turning the 'true word' to the support of such ethnocentric concepts as the Chosen People, the Promised Land and the Election of Israel. Thus, any discrepancies between the Qur'ān and the Torah or the New Testament that may be smugly pointed out by non-Muslims as evidence of Muhammad's lack of qualifications, are viewed by Islam as deviations on the part of the critic's faith, not deficiencies in Islam.

The idea that Moses's message was wilfully corrupted by his followers also accounts for the inclusion of the story of the Exodus in the Qur'ān, followed by the Hebrews' search for the Promised Land, when Canaan, or Palestine, the territory the Jews finally invaded with such savagery, was at the time occupied by Canaanite Arabs, who the Jews then attempted to cleanse from the land. This would seem to be an awkward reference in an Arab work, especially one regarded as the Word of God. But once again, in the Muslim view, human greed and ambition perverted the purity of God's original message into the justification by the Jews for wholesale murder and destruction.

This inclusion by Islam of all that preceded the Qur'ān in other faiths has produced the persistent criticism over the centuries that Muhammad plagiarized the Torah, and to a lesser extent the Gospels. Such complaints began in the Jewish community in Medina during the Prophet's lifetime, and developed into ridicule of Muhammad and the Qur'ān. The strands of a Muslim prehistory can nevertheless be drawn together to produce a mythical story that is similar to but different from the Judeo-Christian version, possibly pointing to a common legendary source from outside either religious framework.

In the alternate Muslim version of the familiar Bible stories, Adam and Eve are expelled from Paradise by Allah for yielding to the temptation of *Shaytān*, disobeying God and eating of the forbidden fruit. They fall down to earth a long way apart, finding each other again on the bare rocky plane of Arafāt, a few miles from the site of the future city of Mecca. After one hundred years of remedial toil for his sin, Adam is granted forgiveness by Allah, and builds a House of Rest, which is the Ka'bah in Mecca, a location that is directly under the throne in the celestial firmament. From there Adam and Eve's progeny populate the earth.

Later, the Flood washes the House of Rest away, but, the foundations of the structure are subsequently uncovered by Abraham, an immigrant from Chaldees on the banks of the Euphrates and the common father of both Jews and Arabs. Abraham rebuilds the structure which, subject to some damage and renovation over the millennia, is essentially the Ka'bah of today. Muslim legend goes on to have Abraham, after the construction had been completed, undertake the first pilgrimage to the Ka'bah, which is the original precedent for the present-day haj.

After the establishment of monotheism by Abraham, the Arabs fall back into polytheism and idolatry until the advent of Muhammad, who cleanses the Ka'bah of the stone and clay images of the Arab heathen gods, and both the monotheism and the pilgrimage of Abraham are reintroduced. The haj in final form, as prescribed by Muhammad, enacts in advance the Day of Judgement, which some Muslims believe will take place physically on the same plain of Arafāt where according to legend, Adam and Eve met at the beginning of the world. This informal belief seeks to tie the origins of the sins of the world to the cleansing 'pre-death' experience of the haj, in a way that is similar to the Christian ritual celebrating Christ's redemption, through his death, of Adam's original sin.

III   The Judeo-Christian Prophets and the Qur'ān

> With all that We relate to thee
> Of the stories of the messengers
> We make firm thy heart: in them cometh
> To you the truth.
>
> *Hud* (The Prophet Hud) Surah 11, verse 120

The Qur'ān refers to twenty-eight previous messengers and prophets and these references take up a quarter of the work. As we have seen,

Islam recognizes all prophets previous to Muhammad, although at a lower level of importance.

> We did aforetime send
> Messengers before thee: of them
> There are some whose story
> We have related to thee
> And some whose story we have not related
> To thee.
>
> *Ghāfir* (Forgiver) Surah 40, verse 78

Adam is the first prophet of Islam and the story of the Fall coincides with the Judeo-Christian version at the outset. But in the Qur'ān, Adam regrets his sins, is forgiven by God and becomes His Vice-Regent on earth. In Muslim belief, therefore, man's original sin has already been expunged and no equivalent of the Christian Redeemer is necessary. Man is assured of happiness in this life and paradise in the next if he follows the path prescribed in the Qur'ān.

Noah struggles to deliver the message of the One God to his contemporaries, whose failure to listen leads to their destruction by flooding. He is preserved by God in the ark and conveyed safely to dry land, and expresses his gratitude to the Almighty. (There is no mention, however, as in the Torah, of the patriarch's weakness for wine.)

Abraham occupies a special place as Muhammad's spiritual predecessor and the father of all Arabs. He, like Muhammad would be in his time, is jeered at and his life is endangered for his attempts to replace the worship of idols with the message of monotheism.

The story of Joseph, the twelfth son of Jacob, is told, exceptionally, in continuous narrative.

The birth of Moses and his encounters with Pharaoh take up the most number of lines dedicated to the preceding prophets. The story illustrates a number of core Qur'ānic principles: that oppression cannot last forever, that no temporal ruler, no matter how powerful, can withstand the will of God, that he whom God blesses is bound to succeed in the end.

Job is portrayed as the epitome of suffering and patience in the name of Allah.

Jesus appears in the Qur'ān as the Messenger Isā whose mission is to restate and enlarge upon previous revelations, and to prepare the world for the final word yet to come. The story of the virgin birth is repeated, but Mary has no Joseph, giving birth on her own under a palm tree, while in the care of angels. Mary is then accused by her family of being unchaste, but the baby speaks from the cradle, exonerating her and announcing his divine message. Jesus is given special powers with which to convince the population of the truth of his teaching. He cures leprosy, he makes birds out of clay and breathes life into them. Jesus is not crucified; rather Judas Iscariot (although not specifically named other than as the betrayer) is transformed to look like Jesus and dies in his place, and Jesus is later taken up into heaven. The Christian Trinity is specifically denied and Jesus addresses Christians from the Qur'ān, asking them to stop associating him with the One God. The theme of God being above having a son, is returned to frequently throughout the text.

Words attributed to Jesus in the New Testament, in John 16: 12–13, are considered by Muslims to be a justification of the Qur'ānic version of Jesus' life and proof that Jesus' mission was to foretell the ministry of Muhammad.

> I have yet many things to say unto you, but ye cannot bear them now.
> Howbeit when he, the Spirit of truth is come, he will guide you into all truth: for he will not speak of himself; but whatsoever he shall hear, that shall he speak: and he will shew you things to come.

The words 'whatsoever he shall hear, that shall he speak', are further interpreted by Muslim scholars as referring explicitly to the method by which the Qur'ān was received.

To the contemporary reader these crossovers between Jewish, Christian and traditional Arab stories may appear strained when considered against the intervening centuries of hostility between Christians, Muslims and Jews. And in modern times the implied endorsement by Islam, through the life of Abraham, of the murderous myth of the Promised Land on which the State of Israel is based, and from which Palestinians have suffered for so long, is particularly difficult to understand. But in the Muslim view the original Word of God was manipulated by the Jews to justify their territorial ambitions, while the Qur'ān remains forthrightly ecumenical.

> Say ye: 'We believe in Allah, and
> The revelation given to us, and
> To Abraham, Ismā'il, Isaac, Jacob
> And the descendants (children
> Of Jacob) and that given to
> Moses and Jesus and that given
> To all Prophets from their Lord:
> We make no difference
> Between one and another of them
> And we bow to Allah in Islam.'
>
> *Al-Baqarah* (The Heifer) Surah 2, verse 140

The Messenger Isā

The relationship between Islam and Jesus Christ, described by Professor Tarif Khalidi in his remarkable transcultural book, *The Muslim Jesus*, as 'a love affair', began with the appearance of Jesus as the Messenger Isā in the Qur'ān. Later, the story of Jesus became a living moral force in Islam, identified with the 'Spirit' and the 'Word', as well as a focus of popular piety and Sufist devotion.

But the relationship of Isā to Islam is much more significant than mere interfaith sentimentality. Jesus in the Qur'ān, by specifically rejecting, as we have seen, the very concept of the Trinity (thus his own deity, and so the core of Christianity) plays a central role in the mission of the Qur'ānic text, which is to demolish polytheism. There is no Crucifixion, therefore, in the Muslim story of Isā, no Salvation or Son of God, but Jesus remains nevertheless, very much the New Testament man of peace:

> 'So peace is on me
> The day I was born
> The day that I die
> And the Day that I

Shall be raised up
To life again.'

Maryam (Mary) Surah 19, verse 33

Jesus is also a prominent character in Muslim eschatology (the belief in judgement after death leading to an eternity of heaven or hell). The Qur'ān promises that Jesus will reappear as a Sign of the Hour of Judgement, and will prepare the way for the universal acceptance of Islam. Further, the Shi'a tradition within Islam, to be discussed in detail in Chapter 6, has drawn heavily on the tradition of Jesus. In imitation of Christ, the Shi'a Imams are believed to have been born with perfect knowledge, and the last in line was taken into divine 'occultation', rather than suffering the finality of death. Only one Qur'ānic story of Jesus, however, matches the New Testament verbatim: the parable comparing the passage of the rich man into heaven with a camel passing through the eye of a needle (although appearing in a different context).

Over the centuries, following the revelation of the Qur'ān, hundreds of fresh sayings and stories ascribed to Jesus appeared in Islamic literature. This growth in both the quantity and quality of Muslim writing on Jesus well exceeds the treatment given by Islam to any other prophet, except Muhammad himself. The source of much of this material is judged by scholars to be the result of Islam's close contact with Christianity during the first three centuries AH (principally in Syria, Iraq and Egypt), reinforced by the conversion of many Christians to Islam who would have brought their traditions of the life of Christ with them. Then, over the years, the material was edited and polished by Muslim writers to become a body of purely Islamic literature of a high order. By this route, among others, the canon of the Muslim Jesus draws on gnostic sources historically wider and culturally deeper than the four 'official' gospels of Matthew, Mark, Luke and John, on which the present Christian tradition rests.

For a Christian (or post-Christian), familiar with the life of Christ through the front door of Christian tradition, a fascinating side view on to the character of Jesus emerges from the Muslim sources. This Jesus fears the Day of Judgement, participates in debates about free will, the problem of the sinful ruler, or the role of scholars in society. He is fiercely ascetic, a sorrowing traveller for whom the world is a ruin. But he is also a miracle worker, a healer and a social commentator.

Satan passed by while Jesus was reclining with his head on a stone. 'So then Jesus, you have been satisfied with a stone in the world!' Jesus removed the stone from beneath his head, threw it at Satan and said, 'Take this stone, and the world with it! I have no need of either.' (Abu Bakr ibn Abi al-Dunya)

The day that Jesus was raised to heaven, he left behind nothing but a woollen garment, a slingshot and two sandals. (Hannad ibn al-Sariyy)

Jesus said, 'Blessed is he who sees with his heart, but his heart is not in what he sees.' (Abdallah ibn Qutayba)

Jesus was asked, 'Spirit of God, who is the most seditious of men?' He replied, 'The scholar who is in error. If a scholar errs, a host of people will fall into error because of him.' (Abdallah ibn al-Mubarak)

Jesus used to say, 'Charity does not mean doing good to him who does good to you, for this is to return good for good. Charity means that you should do good to him who does you harm.' (Ahmad ibn Hanbal)

(All translations by Professor Tarif Khalidi)

A further point of connection between Islam and the life of Jesus is the Muslim belief that Jesus foretold, or prepared the way for Muhammad, and that because of the significance of the relationship, no prophets were sent by God between the two. The verse in the Gospel of John, interpreted by Muslims as Jesus's announcement of the coming of Muhammad, has already been given above. The Qur'ān makes a matching claim, which is the basis for what Islam regards as a special affinity between Muhammad and Jesus Christ:

And remember, Jesus
The son of Mary, said:
'O children of Israel!
I am the messenger of Allah

> Sent to you confirming
> The law which came
> Before me, and giving
> Glad Tidings of a Messenger
> To come after me
> Whose name shall be Ahmad.'
> > *Al-Saff* (The Battle Array) Surah 61, verse 6

A popular Muslim assertion is that the early Christian Church suppressed, for the sake of doctrinal and political unity, all versions of the life of Christ except the four Trinitarian gospels remaining today. The Gospel of St Barnabas, for example, allegedly written by a close disciple of Christ, but repudiated by the Christian Church as a forgery from a much later date, contains a specific prediction of the coming of a last Prophet, named in the text as Muhammad.

The Muslim Jesus also has strong relevance to the twenty-first century. As Professor Khalidi writes: 'Amid the current tensions, it is salutary to remind ourselves of an age and tradition when Christianity and Islam were more open to each other, more aware and reliant on each other's witness.'

IV   The Life of Muhammad

The landscape

At the beginning of the seventh century CE, when Muhammad began his ministry, the forbidding steppes of Arabia were an uncharted territory. This was a landscape unchanged since the days of the mythical Abraham, known only to the Bedouin and hardly touched by the surrounding civilizations. To the north, the rich and settled lands of the eastern Mediterranean were part of the Roman Empire, by then ruled from Constantinople and called the Byzantine Empire, after Byzantium, the original name for the city. The fertile plains of Mesopotamia to the east, watered by the rivers Euphrates and Tigris, were ruled by the Sassanians, forefathers of the modern Persians. To the south, the kingdoms of Yemen and Ethiopia controlled either side of the Red Sea and, like the Byzantines and Sassanians, were often at war with each other.

Nomadic Bedu society was brutal and fatalistic, summed up by the description in the Qur'ān of *Jāhiliyyah* philosophy.

> And they say: 'What is
> There but our life
> In this world?
> We shall die and we live
> And nothing but Time
> Can destroy us.'
>
> *Al-Jathiyah* (The Kneeling Down) Surah 45, verse 24

Each tribe raiding the other to plunder their mean resources was the way of desert life, only saved from severe bloodshed and complete anarchy by the development of rigid rules of engagement. Manliness, honour, the protection of the weak and generous hospitality are the famous attributes of nomadic Arabs which originate with these primitive times. But the dark side included obsessional hatreds and the vendetta as a chronic state of mind, destroying any possibility of social advancement. This was an age with no state and no controls, so that the ancient law of the unregulated, *lex talionis*, was the only behavioural restraint: an eye for an eye, a tooth for tooth. These words appear in both the Qur'ān and the Torah.

Christian monks were known to retreat into the desert, and Jewish communities originally expelled from Palestine by the Romans in the first century CE lived in the oases of western Arabia. But the main point of contact between Arabia and the outside world was through trade, and the centre of Arab trade was Mecca, Muhammad's birthplace. The town was controlled by the great merchants of the Quraysh tribe, avaricious and corrupt by Muhammad's time, certainly not keen to hear of any judgement day or the possibility of eternal damnation as the penalty for sin.

The story of Muhammad's life resonates with elements in the lives of both the Old Testament prophets and the New Testament story of Jesus Christ. But Muhammad was not only a religious leader, he was also a politician who organized a community and protected his faithful through warfare. He invoked the name of God for his assistance and he suffered both victory and defeat. He saw himself and his followers as fighters in the cause of Allah, a stance

towards the hostile and sceptical world that is articulated frequently
in the Qur'ān.

> Therefore listen not
> To the unbelievers, but strive
> Against them with the utmost
> Strenuousness.
>
> *Al-Furqān* (The Criterion) Surah 25, verse 52

But unlike the Hebrew warrior-prophets, Muhammad only defended,
or he responded to threats to his community. He never initiated hostilities or led his people in the name of God to live in an ethnically
cleansed land.

Muhammad was also a great conciliator and law-giver, establishing unprecedented unity between tribes who had been mortal enemies through centuries of *Jāhiliyyah*. Muhammad sought a peaceful
solution wherever possible and displayed almost faultless magna-
nimity in victory. He was persecuted himself and on a number of
occasions only narrowly escaped assassination. Many of his contemporary followers were tortured and murdered for their beliefs.

Muhammad was broad and sturdy, his black hair and beard were
thick. He enjoyed a robust constitution which he attributed to time
spent in the desert in his early years. In his childhood, in the foster
care of the tribe of the Bani Sa'd, he accompanied his milk-brother
tending animals, then later in his teens he tended sheep and goats on
his own for his uncle Abu-Tālib and for other Meccans. His eyes were
black with a touch of brown, his mouth was full and he usually wore
a smile. His manner was quick and economical, he always walked fast
and purposefully. But Muhammad was also given to sadness and to
long periods of silent thought, although when active he was always
occupied with some project, he was never idle and always determined.
In dealing with his followers he was tactful above all, with great
human feeling for the suffering of others. Accounts of his life relate
how he loved children and animals, yet he was courageous and resolute when tackling the spiritual and political affairs of the Muslims.

Muhammad as mortal
Muhammad never claimed to be anything but mortal.

I tell you not that
With me are the Treasures
Of Allah, nor do I know
What is hidden.
Nor claim I to be
An angel. Nor yet
Do I say, of those whom your eyes do despise
That Allah will not grant them
All that is good:
Allah knoweth best
What is in their souls.

Hud (The Prophet Hud) Surah 11, verse 31

Inevitably, however, with the development of profound veneration for both Muhammad's person and his legacy, elaborations on the facts of the Prophet's life have become widespread among Muslims, especially the Muslims of Pakistan. The Sunna, the reported sayings and doings of the Prophet, have been instrumental in ordering the life of Muslims, as we shall see, but in more primitive societies stories about Muhammad have magnified the man to majestic or supernatural levels, so distorting the essential message of Islam. Yet even for those who avoid the extremes of devotion to Muhammad's person, a central mystery remains: as a man he was illiterate (described by the Qur'ān as 'unlettered'), certainly until close to the end of his life, yet over a period of twenty-three years he accumulated a work of profound religious significance, in an Arabic of transcendental beauty, unmatched before or since.

Unlike all previous prophets, the core events of Muhammad's life are historical fact not myth. In addition to the record of the Qur'ān, Muhammad's words and anecdotes of his life have been preserved as recorded by over 800 of his followers, and the outline facts of Muhammad's biography appear in the records of contemporary civilizations well beyond Arabia.

Childhood

Muhammad was born in 570 CE, or shortly after. The year was known in Arabia as the Year of the Elephant, when the Ethiopian viceroy and ruler of the Yemen marched north to threaten Mecca with his army, which included an elephant.

Muhammad had almost no family from a very early age. His father died before he was born, his mother when he was six and his grandfather and guardian two years later. At age nine, Muhammad passed into the care of his uncle, Abu Tālib, head of the minor and relatively impoverished Meccan clan of Hāshim, a division of the town's dominant Quraysh tribe.

There are a number of well-known legends about Muhammad's childhood: his recognition as a future holy man and the Seal (or Last) of the Prophets by a Christian hermit in Syria; his foster mother swelling with milk and her animals prospering from the time she began as his wet nurse; the appearance of angels in the desert carrying snow with which to wash Muhammad's heart while he was with his milk-brother following the flock; his mother visited by an angel during her pregnancy, accompanied by a strong white light and the instructions to name her child Muhammad, meaning 'The Praised'. Substantiated facts about these years, however, are few.

Muhammad as trader

Similarly, only the barest outline is known of the period from Muhammad's childhood to the time of the first revelations of the Qur'ān. As a poor boy without an active sponsor, even though he came from a recognized clan, Muhammad's options were limited. In the city of Mecca, surrounded by forbidding hills of untillable barren granite, there was no route to prosperity other than through trade. But Muhammad did not have sufficient capital to become a trader in his own right and as the manager of the affairs of others he felt that his talent for administration was not being sufficiently used. His solution was to marry Khadijah, probably in 595 CE, when Muhammad was twenty-five years old and Khadijah was ten or more years older. Khadijah was both divorced and widowed, with two daughters and a son. She was an independent woman of property, however, and the partnership with Muhammad prospered for the next fifteen years. Nothing is known of Muhammad's travels or his dealings, except that his honesty was highly regarded. Khadijah bore Muhammad two boys who died young and four girls who survived, and clearly Muhammad regarded his marriage as more than just a useful arrangement. Khadijah was the first person to accept that Muhammad's revelations came from God and during her lifetime Muhammad took no other wives. Khadijah died in 619 CE when Muhammad was forty-nine, approximately eight years after the revelation of the Qur'ān began.

Muhammad as preacher

Muhammad's career as the Apostle of God falls into two distinct periods: his years as a preacher in Mecca and his final years as leader of the Muslims, based in Medina. Separating the two is the hijrah, the Prophet's migration from Mecca to Medina to avoid assassination, and the event with which the Islamic era formally began.

For all his prosperity with Khadijah, Muhammad was dissatisfied with his life in Mecca and appalled by the all-consuming thirst for wealth among the city's traders. From time to time he took to solitary contemplation in a cave a few miles from the city and there his visitations began. Muhammad described his visions as being of a 'Glorious Being' or a 'Strong and Mighty One', who he later identified as the angel Gabriel, rather than God Himself. These first supernatural events, starting in 610 CE approximately, in which the angel instructed Muhammad to recite the words revealed to him, were the spring for all that came after. Later on in his ministry, when Muhammad suffered doubts, reversals and persecutions, his memory of the initial visitations in the cave of Hira sustained his belief in his divine mission.

> O thou wrapped up
> In a mantle!
> Arise and deliver thy warning!
> And thy Lord
> Do thou glorify.
> *Al-Muddaththir* (The One Wrapped Up) Surah 74, verses 1–3

Although the Qur'ān took more than two decades to complete, none of the transmissions was as dramatic as the first, and many were made without the agency of an apparition. The Qur'ān refers to God speaking from 'behind a veil', which is taken to mean that, as the process continued, Muhammad found the words in his heart, not from an external source. Muhammad's revelations were often accompanied by physical pain or by the sound of a bell ringing in his head, and observers reported beads of sweat on Muhammad's brow during his periods of concentration, even on the coldest days. Near the end of his life, Muhammad described the first revelations to his wife, 'Ā'isha: 'in the beginning the revelation for the Messenger of God was true vision, coming like the break of dawn'.

In the beginning there were intervals between revelations, periods during which Muhammad would often be assailed by doubts as well as by concerns for his sanity. But once the revelations resumed, Muhammad regained his conviction that he was a divinely ordained prophet.

His first converts to the One God and the new morality that would become Islam, were his wife Khadijah, 'Ali his cousin, his freed slave and adopted son Zayd, and Abu Bakr, a friend and moderately successful merchant, whose later services to the Muslim community were considerable. This group had expanded to about 200 believers, including their families, by the time Muhammad left Mecca, made up of a cross-section of society that included young men from merchant families, liberated slaves and a few women converts. By no means, therefore, could early Islam be regarded as a movement of disaffected 'down-and-outs', or jealous 'have-nots'.

When Muhammad emerged from an initial period of uncertainty following the first revelations, at the age of forty-three in 613 CE, he began to preach his message publicly. Mecca was in a state of moral decay. The pursuit of greater and greater trading wealth, and the power that wealth brings, had obliterated the traditional Arab concepts of honour and morality followed by the primitive desert-dwelling tribes. The Qur'ān directly addressed this deteriorating condition, urging that an upright life in the present and the attainment of Paradise in the life to come should replace the existing humanistic malaise. Muhammad preached of God's goodness and absolute power, of the calamity that would befall unbelievers on the Last Day, of man's duty to worship God in obedience and gratitude and of man's duty of generosity to his fellows, even as God is generous to man.

To the men of Mecca in the top strata of wealth, Muhammad's message was as much a political and economic threat as an exhortation to spiritual improvement.

> Nay nay! But ye
> Honour not the orphans!
> Nor do ye encourage
> One another
> To feed the poor!
> And ye devour inheritance
> All with greed
> And ye love wealth
> With inordinate love.
>
> *Al Fajr* (The Dawn) Surah 25, verses 17–20

In criticizing the behaviour of the ruling merchant class, Muhammad was attacking a way of life. If the old tribal morals of the desert were to be reintroduced, the wealthy would have to spend time, energy and money on helping the poor and the weak. Then there was the question of the haram, or traditional sanctuary of Mecca: if the pagan gods were to be abandoned in favour of the One God, would the city and the surrounding pagan shrines retain their same lucrative attraction as places of pilgrimage and trade? Finally, the religious power of Muhammad's message, with particular attraction for the poor, had the potential of making him into a rival political power should he so choose. The tension created by these underlying issues intensified as the doctrines of the Qur'ān emerged, blurring the border between religion and politics in a way that would become an indelible characteristic of Islam.

The principal religious question raised by Muhammad's preaching was monotheism as opposed to polytheism, with the Meccans arguing that Muhammad was deviating from the practices of their polytheist forefathers. This is an argument that resonates strongly in conservative Arab sensibility, illustrated by the word *ikhtilaq*, of which Muhammad was accused, which can mean 'heresy' to a conservative or 'innovation' to a liberal. In response Muhammad pressed preceding prophets into service, replying that his message came from a long tradition and he was not, therefore, preaching *ikhtilaq*, either innovation or heresy.

Muhammad's opponents also ridiculed the proposition that a long rotted body could be physically brought back to life for a Day of Resurrection of the flesh. To this the Qur'ān makes frequent response:

> Does man think
> That he will be left
> Uncontrolled and without purpose?
> Was he not a drop
> Of sperm emitted
> In lowly form?
> Then did he become
> A clinging clot,
> Then did Allah make
> And fashion him
> In due proportion
> And of him He made
> Two sexes, male
> And female.
> Has not He the same
> Power to give life
> To the dead?

Al-Qiyāmah (The Resurrection) Surah 75, verses 36–40

Attempts were made to categorize Muhammad as merely another soothsayer or sorcerer inspired by jinn, or traditional desert devils, accusations which explain Muslims' strong resentment of any attempt to describe the Qur'ān as self-inspired poetry. Muhammad was also attacked as insincere and his claimed prophethood was ridiculed as unsupported by any miracles. His real motivation was alleged to be the wealth and power which had been denied him during his previous career as a merchant. Muhammad did indeed achieve wealth and power later on, but only when thrust upon him by his position as leader of the victorious Muslims.

The famous 'satanic verses' fit into this early Meccan period. Muhammad was a strong character, a powerful preacher and a rising potential force opposed to the existing order. If, therefore, the ruling class of Mecca had been able to co-opt him and make him one of their own, the threat to the prevailing order would have been eliminated. Thus, when Muhammad declaimed the latest in his series of revelations, appearing to concede some form of compromise recognition to three of the principal pagan gods of Mecca, al-Lāt, al-Uzzā and Manāt, in the lines underscored in the excerpt quoted on the opposite page, the ruling merchants perceived that a possible accommodation was opening up. Muhammad would be recognized as a prophet and suitably rewarded, but the intercessory powers of the three pagan gods with the Muslim supreme God would be retained and the old and profitable order left undisturbed. So when, shortly after the first recitation of the verse, the two lines were denounced by Muhammad as coming from *Shaytān* and withdrawn, with further sardonic lines added (shown in italics) repudiating the Meccan goddesses, the bitterness of the Meccans against Muhammad was proportionately increased.

> Have ye seen
> Lāt and Uzzā
> And another,
> The third goddess Manāt?
> <u>These are exalted females</u>
> <u>Whose intercession is verily to be sought after</u>
> *What! For you*
> *The male sex*
> *And for Him, the female?*
> *Behold, such would be*
> *Indeed a division*
> *Most unfair.*
> *But these are nothing other than names*
> *Which ye have devised –*
> *Ye and your fathers –*
> *For which Allah has sent*
> *Down no authority whatsoever.*
>
> *Al-Najm* (The Star) Surah 53, verses 19–23

Many Muslim commentators question the 'satanic' version of the story. They maintain that the verse was delivered whole when first recited, but without the fictitious underscored lines (which do not appear in the Qur'ān), and was intended as a repudiation of the Meccan deities from the outset. In this version of the story there was no two-part revelation and no change of heart, and subsequent historians are accused of inventing the offending lines. This view is supported by earlier verses in the same Surah, suggesting that Muhammad's message is infallible. 'Nor does he say aught of his own desire. It is no less than inspiration sent down to him' (*Al-Najm* (The Star) Surah 53, verses 3–4).

But in any event, there is surely nothing to deny or to suppress in the 'satanic' version of the story, which can be compared to the temptations of Christ. For Christ, too, was offered power and wealth by the devil in the temporal world if he would only subvert the word of God.

> Again, the devil taketh him up into an exceeding high
> mountain, and sheweth him all the kingdoms of the world,
> and the glory of them;
> And saith unto him, All these things will I give thee, if thou
> wilt fall down and worship me.
>
> Matthew 4: 8–9

A solution to the growing hostility of the Meccans towards the new religion of the Muslims had long troubled Muhammad. But if he was tempted to compromise, he like Christ, withstood, and events took their course. This incident, and possibly the temptation of Christ, appears to be referred to in later revelations, in Surah 22 *Al-Hajj*, verse 52, for example: 'Never did We send a messenger or a prophet before thee, but when he longed, *Shaytān* threw suggestion into his longing.'

But, once again, the controversy over Rushdie's book was not because the two 'satanic' lines were repeated in his text, since the story of the verse is to be found in many works by devout Muslim commentators. Rather, objection was taken to the insults directed at Muhammad himself and his wives elsewhere in the work, as well as to Rushdie's mockery of the process by which the Qur'ān was revealed. And, as has been noted, Rushdie also indulged in five pages of wicked mockery of the Ayatollah Khomeini personally.

In 615 CE, five years into Muhammad's ministry, leadership of the Meccan merchants passed to a man of the same generation, Abu-Jāhl. Economic pressure was increased on all who supported Muhammad, while those who fell outside the protection of the clan system, slave converts for example, were physically suppressed. During this period a number of Muslims were sent to Ethiopia to escape persecution, most of whom returned later to join Muhammad in Medina.

At this time Muhammad was still under protection within his clan, sponsored by his uncle Abu-Tālib, and therefore untouchable by the hostile Meccans. Policing of Arab society before the introduction of Qur'ānic laws was based on the sure retribution of *lex talionis*. Only a miscreant's own tribe could punish a member and, if harmed by an outsider, the victim's entire tribe was obliged to retaliate. For as long as the Hashim clan were not prepared to limit Muhammad's activities, therefore, he was free to continue.

So when Abu-Tālib and Khadijah both died in the same year, probably in 619 CE, and the protection of his clan could no longer be relied upon, Muhammad's situation became perilous. He had no alternative but to leave Mecca himself. During this dark time Muhammad's spiritual life apparently intensified, culminating with the dream of a journey, or in Muslim tradition with Muhammad's miraculous physical transportation from Mecca to Jerusalem and back again during a single night. The only reference in the Qur'ān to this important episode is very brief.

> Glory to Allah
> Who did take his Servant
> For a journey by night
> From the Sacred Mosque
> To the Farthest Mosque
> Whose precincts we did
> Bless – in order that we
> Might show him some
> Of our Signs.
>
> *Al-Isrā* (The Night Journey) Surah 17, verse 1

But from the Hadith and the subsequent embroidering of this story, or *Isrā*, or Night Journey, which now forms one of the core legends of Islam, has flowed the long-standing political controversy over the status of the Haram at Jerusalem, comprising the Dome of the Rock and al-Aqsa (or the Farthest) mosque. These famous buildings, which give physical form to Muhammad's experiences, whether mythical or existential, together constitute the third holiest site in Islam after Mecca (the site of the Sacred Mosque containing the Ka'bah) and Medina (the site of the Mosque of the Prophet containing Muhammad's tomb). But the ground on which the two Muslim structures stand in Jerusalem is also claimed by Jews to be the Temple Mount, the central location in the Torah prophecies relating to the Election of Israel. The political dimension of this emotive question will be discussed later; here only the story of the Night Journey itself is relevant.

In the dream, or the myth, or in fact, Muhammad was awoken by Gabriel during the night of the 27th of the lunar month of Rajab in 621 CE to be transported from Mecca to Jerusalem on the back of the *burāq*, a miraculous beast in the shape of an ass but with wings. After arriving in Jerusalem, on the bare rock that is now enclosed within the Dome, and after praying with Noah, Moses, Abraham and the other patriarchs from former times, Muhammad was taken up to heaven and to the outer presence of God. Muhammad's ascension to heaven following the *Isrā*, or Night Journey, is known in Islam as the *Mi'rāj*, or Ascension. During the *Mi'rāj*, God permitted Muhammad a glimpse of Paradise and instructed him on how his followers should say their prayers. Initially God prescribed fifty prayers per day, with Moses's assistance this was negotiated down to five per day, with each devout prayer counting for ten. The *burāq* then returned Muhammad to his bed in Mecca, where his wife had failed to notice his absence.

The hijrah

The Arabic word *Hijrah*, or the frequently used Latin equivalent *hegira*, means more than 'flight' or 'emigration', rather giving a sense of the severing of relations with a previous family or clan, and attachment to another. The hijrah to Medina was Muhammad's response to his weak and vulnerable position in Mecca. The journey of about 400 kilometres, exposed to his enemies and without tribal protection so that discovery would have certainly led to his death, took place over ten or twelve days in September 622 CE and the Muslim era dates from this event. The date is of more significance in Islam than the date of Muhammad's birth, for example, or the beginning of his ministry, since the hijrah was the event that permitted the first implementation of the ideals of the faith.

Islamic Dating

Primitive man had three alternative methods with which to mark the passage of time. First, the terrestrial day: the precise period from noon to noon during which the earth completes a single revolution. Second, the lunar month, the 29½ days that the moon takes for a single orbit around the earth. Or third, the solar year, equal to the 365¼ days of the journey of the earth around the sun. But 12 lunar months (12 × 29½ days = 354 days) do not equal one solar year (365¼ days) and as civilization progressed a choice had to be made.

The Christian solution, since the introduction of Pope Gregory's calendar in 1582, is to add a leap year every four to the standard year of 365 days (so making up the missing ¼ day), then to divide the months into 28 (or 29), 30 and 31 days without reference to the moon but matching the agricultural seasons. In the *Jāhiliyyah*, the Arabs divided time into 12 lunar months, then added an extra month every two or three years to keep the lunar cycle synchronized with the seasons, a process known as 'intercalation'.

But there was no order to this system and the extra month was manipulated by the Meccan Quraysh, who had traditional control over practical implementation, to allow the holy months in which fighting was prohibited to fall to suit short-term political and trade objectives. Intercalation was ended by a Qur'ānic injunction coming near the end of Muhammad's life, which resulted in the Muslim calendar being detached from the seasons, so bringing a form of order to the previous chaos.

The consequence of the Qur'ānic method is that the Muslim year of 12 lunar months is 11 days shorter than the solar year, and slightly different again from the Gregorian or Western year. This in turn sees the festivals of Islam move backwards through the full Western year, only appearing in the same place every 32 Gregorian years. Thus the timing of the haj, for example, performed in the lunar month of Dhu'l-Hajja will rotate over the years between summer and winter, substantially altering the severity of the experience. More importantly, the rotation of the fast during the month of Ramadan will fall during all seasons and the lengthening and shortening days of fast will be equally borne over the years by Muslims in both hemispheres.

The Prophet embarked on the hijrah, the event that opens the Islamic era, during September 622 CE. But 'day one' of Anno Hegirak, or AH, was not the day of Muhammad's departure from Mecca, or the day of his arrival in Medina almost two weeks later, but the first day of the first lunar month (al-Muharram) of the pre-Islamic year during which the journey fell: 16 July 622 CE, over two months before. Then the years AH have been calculated in lunar years ever since, with the consequence that AH and CE are not only 622 years apart in history, but AH years are also 11 days (plus the small discrepancy between the solar and Gregorian calculations) at odds with Western time. To translate from AH to CE, therefore, or in the opposite direction, the following formula is required:

$$AH = CE - 622 + (AD - 622 \text{ over } 32)$$
$$CE = AH + 622 - (AH \text{ over } 33)$$

To find the equivalent of a specific day between AH and CE is much more complicated, however, as the Muslim calendar also adds a form of leap year periodically, called a *kabisa* year, to rectify the half day by which a lunar month exceeds 29 full days. The *kabisa* year and the Gregorian leap year do not coincide and the only practical solution is to consult translation tables.

At the same time that Muhammad had been looking for a solution to his troubles in Mecca, the leaders of Medina had been searching for a resolution to theirs. Medina, unlike barren Mecca, is a large and productive agricultural oasis. By the opening of the seventh century CE the oasis was divided into landholdings by clan and tribe, each in a separate settlement rather than joined together in a common city like Mecca. During the decades preceding the Hijrah, population growth and the resulting pressure on the available arable land had led to repeated civil war within the oasis and great loss of life, overwhelming the traditional nomadic *lex talionis* method of conflict resolution, by taking a life for a life or by the payment of blood money. Medina, like Mecca, had failed to develop a workable urban way of life based on the inappropriate laws developed over many generations for a completely different desert existence. To this impasse, both the Qur'ān and Muhammad's talents as arbiter of disputes and eventual leader were directly relevant. The situation in Medina was further complicated by the presence of Jewish clans within the oasis, although the Jews like the Arabs were divided into factions and could rarely agree among themselves.

Muhammad's growing reputation in Mecca as a man of high moral purpose, but repudiated by the leaders of his own people, led a majority of the quarrelling factions within Medina to offer him the position of judge of their internal divisions in return for military protection against the anticipated Meccan hostility, as well as a place to live. This was expressed in two successive pledges made between Muhammad and delegations from Medina, visiting Mecca under cover of the pre-Islamic pagan pilgrimage to the Ka'bah. In addition to the political and security arrangements, the delegation undertook to accept Muhammad's prophethood and to obey his decisions. At the same time the nascent rules and practices of the Muslims were accepted by the delegates as a creed. This commitment from Medina permitted the hijrah to begin. Muhammad's original supporters in Mecca, subsequently to be known as the Emigrants, left the city first, then later Muhammad and Abu Bakr slipped away at night with the help of a pagan Bedouin guide, narrowly avoiding an assassination attempt by the dominant Meccan clans acting in concert.

Mecca against Medina

In Medina, Muhammad built the first mosque, which doubled as his office and residence (and has been expanded over the centuries into the present huge Mosque of the Prophet), while continuing to receive revelations that added to the Qur'ān. From this time on, the matters dealt with by the received surahs become more appropriate to political and social issues than to the doctrinal arguments that supported Muhammad's preaching in Mecca.

Despite the pledges by the delegation from Medina, Muhammad's position in the oasis community was not at first that of omnipotent judge or ruler. His prestige only reached such a level after his success in bringing peace and justice to the oasis. This was followed by Muhammad's initial triumph on the battlefield, in which he was supported by the men of Medina because of his previous success as a politician.

Most Medinans were, however, receptive to Muhammad's arrival, and were granted by the Muslims the honorific title of the Helpers.

(The Emigrants and the Helpers together form the category known as the Companions of the Prophet, defined as any Muslim who spoke to Muhammad at any time during his life.) A few men of Medina, who foresaw that they would lose power to Muhammad, remained opposed to the arrangement while nominally embracing Islam. Later the Qur'ān named this faction the Hypocrites, and would regard them as worse offenders against Islam than the non-believers who had never converted.

Muhammad's position in Medina was particularly precarious during the initial months. First, the Jews rejected Muhammad's prophethood and criticized the Qur'ān as being inconsistent with the older Jewish scriptures. Response was made to the effect that the Jewish traditions were in error, not the word of God as revealed to Muhammad, and the beginnings of a serious breach opened up. This led eventually to the first Jewish rebellion against Muhammad and the ensuing expulsion of the Jewish Qaynuqā tribe from the oasis, although other significant Jewish tribes remained, protected by Muhammad's constitution.

The original principles of Islam, as enunciated in Mecca, required modification to suit the conditions in Medina, and Muhammad's abilities and strength of character did not register with all the Medinans immediately. Nevertheless, he succeeded in negotiating a comprehensive settlement to the troubles of Medina, subsequently set out in a document that has come to be known as the Constitution of Medina. Over the following fourteen centuries to the present day, from these modest beginnings, the concept of a utopian Shariah community was to develop, militantly fusing religion and politics into a single 'divinely ordered' social scheme. The tremendous nostalgic reverence given to this period by recent Muslim societies justifies a close consideration of the text of the constitution, which is reproduced in full at the end of this chapter as Appendix 1.

The expression *al-salafi al-salih*, meaning the 'pious forefathers', has come into use during the last 150 years by Muslims seeking a simpler, more certain and protected faith. So the word *salafi*, or even *salafist* now describes the literalist movement in Islam, giving an ultra-conservative reading to the text based on the outward meaning alone. This narrow view, usually focusing on bellicose language taken out of context, rejects centuries of Qur'ānic interpretation by which the basic principles of the text have been filtered into Shariah jurisprudence for use in the real world. The rise of the *salafist* attempt to return to the roots of Islam coincided in the nineteenth century CE with the advancing threat of Western colonization, and the present *salafist* trend in the twenty-first century may well be in reaction to the increasing pressure on Islam from the West. In fact the 'pious forefathers' treated the text of the Qur'ān as flexible and tolerant, and in the period of Muhammad's rule the new religion was stretched and pulled to accommodate the needs of the emerging community. This was followed by further innovation as the Muslim empire expanded.

The most important feature of the constitution is the opening paragraph, where the Muslims are said to be 'a single community distinct from all other people', although the religious toleration demonstrated in the text, as well as the fusion of religion with politics, are also of significance for the future. Islam was overcoming the old irreconcilable tribal divisions to create a new '*ummah*, or community, subject to a new form of egalitarian law and justice that predates Magna Carta (the first attempt in post-medieval Europe at a workable division of powers in the form of a written constitution) by almost 600 years.

There was also the question of how the Emigrants were to support themselves since the Helpers could not afford to feed the new arrivals for long. As part of the solution to this practical problem, Muhammad took to raiding the caravans of the Meccan merchants. But more as a form of business retaliation rather that piracy, seeking to undermine the trade routes to and from Mecca in revenge for the destruction of the livelihoods of those who had been forced to emigrate due to Meccan hostility, and who were being deprived of their fractional clan ownership in the caravans under attack. This initiative was supported by a timely divine revelation, but of only limited application to the specific conditions then facing Muhammad (contrary to the aggressive *salafist* reading of the same verse, which is often quoted in jihadi literature).

> To those against whom
> War is made, permission

> Is given to fight, because
> They are wronged – and verily
> Allah is Most Powerful
> For their aid.
> They are those who have
> Been expelled from their homes
> In defiance of right –
> For no cause except
> That they say, 'Our Lord
> Is Allah.'
>
> *Al Hajj* (The Pilgrimage) Surah 17, verses 39–40

Muhammad's first ambush was against a small Meccan camel train, achieved only after a number of failed attempts, and the attack soon led to tension between the communities of Mecca and Medina. After a further attempt by Muhammad on a much larger caravan led by the Meccan noble Abu-Sufyān, the Muslim raiding force of a little over 300 men met with a superior Meccan force of 1,000 men at the site of a well near the settlement of Badr, on the coast road north to Syria. While Muhammad prayed, his men routed the Meccans, who had many of their leaders killed and many men of substance taken prisoner, as well as great quantities of booty lost to the Muslims. The Battle of Badr (16 March 624 CE) was a great turning point for the Muslims who believed that Allah had endorsed their enterprise by sending angels to assist in the fight against such overwhelming odds.

> It was not ye who
> Threw at them; it was Allah.
>
> *Al Anfāl* (The Spoils of War) Surah 8, verse 17

After Badr, during which Abu Jāhl was killed, Abu-Sufyān, a member of the ascendant Umayyad clan of the Quraysh tribe, became leader of Mecca. His son Mu'āwiyah was to become an important figure in the history of Islam. While back in Medina, Muhammad, as the victor of Badr, was able to consolidate absolute power, and those Arabs from within the oasis who still resisted now capitulated. The critical Qaynuqā' Jews were expelled for clear breaches of the constitution and Muhammad strengthened his alliances further by various marriages.

Skirmishing occupied the two sides for the following months and a large Meccan caravan was captured by the Muslims. A year after Badr, the men of Mecca set out to take their revenge on both Muhammad and Medina with a force of 3,000 including cavalry. As the Meccan army approached the oasis they were met in the desert by a Muslim force of 700 men, led by Muhammad himself, wearing armour. The Muslims took up position on the hill of Uhud, after which the battle was to be named. The course of the engagement was very confused. Muslim tactics had the initial advantage, but, thinking that the battle was won, Muhammad's archers abandoned their covering position on the high ground, thus allowing the Meccan cavalry to attack from behind. At the end of the day more Muslims had been killed than Meccans, and Muhammad was wounded and had lost a tooth. But Abu Sufyān withdrew, having failed to achieve either the destruction of Medina or the elimination of Muhammad.

Uhud, however, was a spiritual defeat for the Muslims. How could God allow such a result to befall his faithful? Where were the angels of Badr? Muhammad's answer was to predict that the Meccans would not benefit from the outcome (which was how events turned out) and to blame the Muslims themselves for their lack of steadfastness.

> Allah did indeed fulfil
> His promise to you
> When ye with His permission
> Were about to annihilate
> Your enemy – until ye flinched
> And fell to disputing
> About the order
> And disobeyed it.
>
> *Al-Imrān* (The Family of Imrān) Surah 3, verse 152

Following Uhud, the contest between Mecca and Medina widened as Abu Sufyān sought assistance from distant nomadic tribes to assemble an even larger force with which to renew the attack on Muhammad. Plots, ambushes and assassinations followed, during which a second Jewish clan within the oasis of Medina, the an-Nādir, intrigued against Muhammad. The Jews were besieged by the Muslims and expelled, with their armour and their lands taken over by poor Emigrants.

Two years after Uhud, Abu Sufyān was back. Despite Muhammad's diplomatic efforts with the desert tribes of the Hijaz, the Meccans had been able to form a confederation to raise 10,000 men, including the exiled Jews of Medina. Muhammad could muster only 3,000, with the remaining Jewish clan within the oasis, the Qurayzah, purporting to remain neutral.

This time the Muslims did not offer pitched battle; instead they prepared Medina for siege by digging a defensive trench across the only level approach to the oasis accessible by cavalry, which was further defended by infantry with spears and bows. This previously unknown method of warfare frustrated the provisionless Meccans, and their political confederation, camped out beyond the ditch, rapidly disintegrated into squabbling factions in the face of inaction. Unseasonably cold April weather together with a wind storm hastened their departure.

During the siege, the Jewish Qurayzah clan attempted to shed their promised neutrality, offering to let the confederate tribes into the oasis at Muhammad's rear, which would have been fatal to the entire Muslim cause. Once the enemy had departed, Muhammad besieged the Jewish forts, from which the tribe asked to be allowed to depart under the same conditions as had been applied to the an-Nādir. Due to the mortal threat that the Jewish treachery had represented, this was refused, and a judge was appointed from an Arab tribe having connections to the Qurayzah to preside over a trial of the Jews. The sentence was death, justified ironically, by the application of the vengeful terms of the Book of Deuteronomy. The Jewish males were executed, with their women and children sold as slaves. The decision was supported by the entire Muslim community and was not unusual for either the times or the offence. Those smaller groups of Jews within the oasis of Medina who had remained true to the Commonwealth were permitted to stay unmolested.

The Meccan cause was now lost. Their greatest efforts had not unseated Muhammad and their trade routes were no longer secure. But rather than a war of vengeance, Muhammad launched a series of diplomatic, missionary and military deputations to the outlying tribes, leading to the establishment of a blockade against

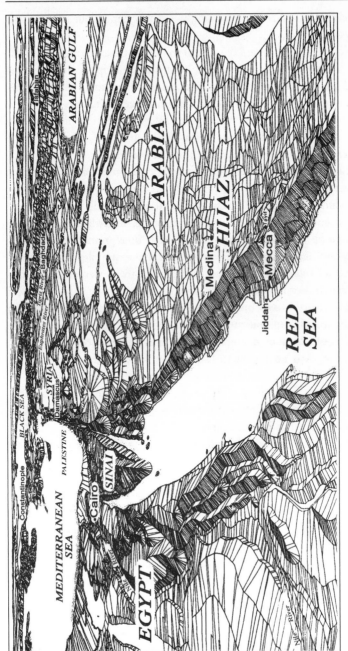

Map of the Hijaz

Mecca, whose citizens were almost entirely dependent on overland imports.

The first signs of a *pax Islamica* were emerging: traditional hostilities between the tribes replaced by spiritual discipline and peaceful economic expansion by treaty. Instead of destroying Mecca by starvation or invasion, Muhammad demonstrated his talents as a statesman. With 1,600 men, and inspired by a dream, he approached the city as an unarmed pilgrim, with the intention of performing the lesser haj or '*umrah* at the Ka'bah, in the pre-Islamic form. Religious and political objectives had replaced the desert tradition of mere military victory.

Muhammad halted at the well of al-Hudaybiyah where a treaty was negotiated with Mecca, restoring peace. The Meccans were free to resume their trade caravans, although their monopoly was now lost, and in return the Medinans could make the pilgrimage unmolested the following year, while the nomadic tribes were released from the remains of their confederation with Mecca. In practice the effect of this treaty was to bring almost all the tribes of the Hijaz over to Muhammad, thus making him invincible, while undermining the leaders of Mecca by demonstrating to the ordinary people of the city that they had no reason to fear retribution by the Muslims. Islam sought only their conversion, not their enslavement, with Mecca invited to join with Medina at the core of the new religion. For Muhammad's ambitions for a larger Arab confederacy to succeed he needed both the administrative abilities of the senior Meccans, as well as the two principal cities of western Arabia, unified voluntarily under him.

The Treaty of al-Hudaybiyah was followed by the final confrontation with the Jews exiled from Medina. These tribes had re-established themselves in the oasis of Khaybar to the north, where they were again using their wealth and abilities to undermine Islam. Apart from the security and material advantage that would flow from their defeat, an irreconcilable conflict of ideas was also present. The Jews regarded themselves as the Chosen of God, so if a true prophet could appear from among the gentiles, their divinely ordained primacy must collapse. Conversely for the Muslims, if the Jews held a monopoly on relations with God then Muhammad could not be God's Messenger and the basis of Islam must collapse.

This contention had already found form in the rejection by the Jews of Muhammad's ministry, and their subsequent military treachery. In response, the Muslims had turned their backs on the Jews, quite literally changing the direction of daily prayers in 624 CE from Jerusalem to Mecca. Five years later Khaybar was besieged, reduced to vassalage, and the power the Jewish opposition to Muhammad was broken forever.

The Treaty of al-Hudaybiyah also enabled Muhammad to establish his own confederacy well beyond the immediate area of Medina. By tradition he sent messengers as far as Egypt and Ethiopia, calling the nations to Islam. Then in the following year, Muslims took up their treaty rights to make the pilgrimage to the Ka'bah in Mecca, with the Meccans withdrawing from the city for three days to avoid tensions. The Muslim pilgrims were an impressively disciplined force and Muhammad took the opportunity of the visit to reconcile with his uncle al-'Abbās with whom he had quarrelled earlier. Al-'Abbās, patriarch of the 'Abbāsid dynasty (to be of importance later in the history of Islam), was to play a crucial part in the final denouement that now followed.

The occasion for the final submission of Mecca came with the renewal of a tribal dispute between a group within Muhammad's confederacy and a Meccan clan. The terms of the Treaty of al-Hudaybiyah were broken when the Meccans opened hostilities against Muhammad's allies, placing Muhammad by custom in the position of being able to invade the city in retribution. To forestall inevitable disaster from Muhammad's overwhelmingly superior forces, the increasingly divided Meccan leadership sent Abu-Sufyān in person to Medina to ask for leniency, an open admission of how matters then stood. Abu-Sufyān reached an agreement with Muhammad by which bloodshed was prevented, but from then on the end was inevitable.

During January 630 CE Muhammad arrived before the city with a force of 10,000 men. Abu-Sufyān came out to submit formally to the Prophet of God as had been previously agreed in Medina, and Mecca was occupied the next day, with amnesty given to those who offered no resistance. There was little bloodshed and reprisals were taken only against a few, a poet who had mocked Muhammad among them. No plundering was permitted, but most importantly, the polluted Ka'bah was cleansed of idols, reputedly 360 in number. The grand idol Hubal was toppled, the false god to which Abu-Sufyān had attributed his pyrrhic victory at Uhud, and the separate shrines of the infamous al-Lāt, al-Uzzā and Manāt were also destroyed. A new order had arrived, the tyranny of the rich had been abolished, and the poor now embraced Islam in gratitude for their deliverance.

The image of the victorious Prophet overthrowing the pagan idols with his own hand as he gave thanks to Allah remains a potent force in Islam. From his apparently hopeless situation during the hijrah, Muhammad, the hated self-styled prophet, had re-entered the main city of Arabia as the all-conquering Apostle of Allah. In modern Islamist rhetoric, America is often cast in the role of 'the Hubal of the age', which in due course will be overthrown. American materialism is thus equated with idolatry, and Arab leaders doing the bidding of the West are cast as the back-sliding Medinan Hypocrites. Similarly, Muhammad's rise from nothing, through faith alone, was used by Osama ibn Laden to explain the successful October 2000 attack on the American destroyer USS *Cole* in Aden harbour, by a motor boat. 'In this world,' he said, 'the destroyer represented the capital of the West, and the small boat represented Muhammad.'

Immediately after the victory over Mecca, known as the 'opening' due to the lack of bloodshed (although all subsequent Muslim victories were to be called 'openings', whether bloody or not) Muhammad faced his greatest military challenge. The Hawāzin tribe from north of Mecca assembled a force of 20,000 men with the intention of plundering the defeated city as the culmination of years of a separate hostile rivalry. The Muslims, in seeking to protect their new possession, were thus, within a month of their victory over the Meccans, obliged to become the champions of their former enemies. Muhammad's forces with Meccan reinforcements moved against the Hawāzin at Hunayn and inflicted a defeat, the outcome of the battle turning on Muhammad's personal valour.

After Hunayn, the Hawāzin also accepted Islam, together with the remaining Meccans, many of whom were to become ardent Muslims, rising to positions of great importance during the subsequent expansion of the Arab empire. This second Muslim victory within a month forced the pace of reconciliation between Mecca and Medina and opened the way for Muhammad to achieve absolute power.

Rather than sending delegations out to the tribes as in the early days, the tribes now came to Muhammad and by the date of his death the circle of Muslim alliances had spread through most of western and northern Arabia. At the same time levies paid by the confederated tribes to the 'treasury of God' were increasing the community's wealth. In addition, Muhammad followed the traditions of pagan Mecca and kept for his own use, and to pay the costs of his leadership obligations, one fifth of all booty from the Muslim conquests, which was to be spent in the public interest. When Muhammad set out on his last major expedition, to Tabuk, to take control of the road north to Syria, he commanded 30,000 foot-soldiers and 10,000 cavalry, compared with the mere 300 men and 2 horses available to him at Badr.

The Commonwealth of Medina

All the traditional powers of the Quraysh tribe were now in Muhammad's hands: the custody of the Holy House, control over the pilgrimage and the intercalation of the year, generating a colour of right and a due reverence from the other tribes even without the Prophet's spiritual leadership and his 'divinely guided' status. During the remaining two years of his life Muhammad wove all these elements together, pagan traditions with the new faith of Islam, civil obedience with religious submission, to create the system of combined faith and politics that was about to convulse the known world. Islam was initiating a fusion of community structure, religion and economics to create the seed of the 'social project', or 'complete way of life' that would inspire the faithful down the centuries, while the few years of Muhammad's Commonwealth, and the pattern of Muslim society in the first decades after the Prophet's death, remain acutely relevant to the political and religious aspirations of many militant Muslims in the present day.

The original Constitution of Medina was expanded by the continuing revelation of the Qur'ān as well as through Muhammad's living words and his practice (the Sunna), together establishing the broad principles that were to become the Shariah, or Islamic law. Later Muslim societies, however, were left to struggle with the development of both the theory and the details of the law, in a continuing attempt to find solutions suitable for changing times and circumstances.

From the profusion of detailed sources available from the Medinan period, the following general themes emerge from Muhammad's rule:

● In place of the ties of the tribal system, formerly the only reposi-tory of Arab loyalty, Muslims were to be brothers in the new *'ummah*. This was the key social reform that ended inter-tribal war-fare and unlocked the potential of Arabia. On this horizontal plane of brother and brother, the highest standards of behaviour were expected between Muslims, from personal politeness to absolute respect for property and life. The fierce independence of the desert-man was retained, however. There was to be no priesthood or hier-archy in this society of equals, with prayers led by the military commander or any other suitable person, as an equal. And where before there had been internal strife between Arabs, now the faithful were to apply their zeal to the protection of each other against the outside world.

● On the vertical plane, between man and God, the rules of obser-vance were established for Muslims to practise together as the *'ummah*. Daily prayers were said in a set form, and the rituals and procedures that now constitute the Five Pillars of Islam were initi-ated. Following the example of the Prophet, God was to be recog-nized at every stage of the day in both speech and action.

● The commandments of the Qur'ān, universally accepted by the last years of Muhammad's life as the direct Word of God, were to be obeyed without exception. This concept of the constitution of the Muslim community as a 'divine order' gave the state a degree of sta-bility that would have been impossible to achieve by mere human agency. The surahs revealed during this late period establish rules for a wide variety of situations. Especially protected are slaves, the poor and the weak, and orphans, matching Muhammad's condition as a child. But beyond the frequently recurring subjects of inheritance, marriage, slavery, murder, property and commercial issues, which are extensively 'legislated' in the text of the Qur'ān, in practice Muhammad treated legal issues on the merits of each individual case. This set the precedent in Islamic law by which case-specific judgements had the 'punishment fit the crime', an approach that became at least as important as adherence to an overall legal theory. Only later in the history of the Shariah were these case-by-case decisions by Muhammad analysed and codified into a form of Islamic jurisprudence known as *fiqh*.

● In addition to the new equality between Muslims and the reduction of importance of tribal loyalties, all other religious groups were to be tolerated, Jews, Christians, even pagans, provided that Muhammad's position as head of state was accepted and provided that there was no cooperation by non-Muslims with outside enemies. The power of the desertman's old xenophobia was broken, and Islam had found the basis on which entire peoples beyond the boundaries of Arabia could be ruled.

At this point an explanation should be offered of the Muslim use of the expression 'the Holy Land'. The Muslim term is equivalent to the Christian version (the land where Christ lived in Palestine), meaning the physical region where Muhammad lived in the Arabian province of the Hijaz, or at least the two cities of Mecca and Medina. But the difference between Muslim and Christian practice is, of course, that there is no restriction on non-Christians visiting Palestine (and the area is in any case inhabited by Jews and mostly Muslim Arabs), while non-Muslims are strictly excluded from Mecca and Medina, theoretically on pain of death (and in practice from the whole of Arabia, which allows very little tourism and none to the Hijaz).

During the Prophet's lifetime, however, no such restriction existed, and Muhammad received Christians at his mosque in Medina, most famously a delegation from Najran in Yemen who were accommodated on the premises, while Jews lived in Medina until they breached the terms of the Constitution. The same openness would have applied to Mecca had the circumstances arisen. In fact, the restriction of non-Muslims was initiated by the Caliph 'Umar in the first decade after Muhammad's death, to prevent infiltration by potential enemies into the Arab homeland while the Muslim armies were in distant Syria attending to their conquests. The rule excluding non-believers from the Muslim Holy Land has since been widened and hardened, despite the absence of authority in the Qur'ān or in any secure Hadith, which generally advocate a high degree of inter-faith tolerance.

The death of Muhammad

The story of Muhammad's last months is well known. He led the haj again in March 632, known as the Farewell Pilgrimage, during which the present-day form of the rite was finalized. Many of the ancient pagan rituals were retained for continuity, but with all trace of idolatry eliminated. On the last day of the pilgrimage Muhammad preached his final sermon sitting on his camel on the slopes of the Mount of Mercy in the middle of the plain of Arafāt. During his discourse the last revelation was received.

> This day have I
> Perfected your religion
> For you, completed
> My favour upon you
> And have chosen for you
> Islam as your religion.
>
> *Al Ma'idah* (The Repast) Surah 5, verse 3

On 8 June 632, after a short illness following his return to Medina from the haj, Muhammad died, his head in 'Ā'isha's lap. Although in his sixties, he had appeared to be in good health until very near the end, and his undiagnosed illness had been regarded as nothing more serious than a passing ailment. The Muslims were profoundly shaken, therefore, and many at first refused to accept the stunning news, even though at heart none of the Companions regarded Muhammad as anything more than mortal. The shock was due more to the unexpectedness of the event, to the lack of preparation, the removal of the security that Muhammad's leadership had provided, and to the prospect of an errant future that had suddenly opened up before them.

Historical assessment

Until the twentieth century, Muhammad may have been the most maligned man in history. He was 'the great enemy' to Christian Byzantium and to Zoroastrian Persia. To medieval Europe

Mohammad was a constant threat, as well as being the antichrist occupier of the Christian Holy Land. Prejudices have possibly waned in modern times, but Muhammad personally is still frequently denigrated by non-Muslims. The criticisms fall into three categories.

Firstly, Muhammad is said to have been insincere, to have consciously composed the text of the Qur'ān from his own imagination, or by plagiarism, or both, then to have passed the work off as coming from 'outside himself'. The fortuitous arrival of certain surahs to match the Prophet's political needs or personal desires of the moment is given as further evidence of falseness, as is the abrogation of earlier verses by later revelations, an issue that will be discussed in a subsequent chapter.

This criticism confuses the question of the claimed divine origins of the work with the question of whether or not Muhammad himself believed in the revelations. The response is to separate the two. Whether the Qur'ān is accepted by the individual reader to be the Word of God is a matter of personal faith. But Muhammad's vast achievements during his lifetime, his personal humility and evenhandedness, and his establishment of a powerful world religion which has produced followers of great saintliness and devotion as well as improving the lives of many, must surely resolve any doubts about his own sincerity in the Prophet's favour.

Secondly, treachery and cruelty are obvious criticisms of Muhammad's life. He attacked Meccan caravans during the pre-Islamic holy month, war was waged on the assumption that God approved of the bloodshed, the Qurayzah Jews were massacred and so on. But are these actions to be judged by the standards of seventh century Arabia, or by Western ideals at the beginning of the twenty-first century? If the former, then there is a practical reply to every accusation. The holy month at the time was pagan, for example; the Meccans initiated hostilities with their violent persecution of Muhammad and Islam; and the intention of the Jewish Qurayzah was the overthrow of Muhammad, which would have led to the eradication of the entire Muslim community by the Meccans. If judgement is on the latter contemporary basis, then the destruction and loss of life perpetrated by the West, even in the recent past, in order to promote 'freedom and democracy', which has yet to be realized in such countries as Afghanistan, Iraq, Libya and Somalia, to name but a few, makes the penalties paid in blood for the vast improvement of conditions in Arabia brought about through Muhammad's unification seem inconsequential.

Thirdly, the religious heritage of the West centres on the strong image of Jesus Christ, the ultimate man of peace who 'turned the other cheek', who rendered unto 'Caesar the things which are Caesar's', and unto God 'the things that are God's'. In the Christian view therefore, how could Muhammad claim to be both the believable Prophet of God and a warrior. But Christ avoided crossing the line between the ideals of religion and the practicalities of politics. On the high mountain He was tempted with civil power by the devil, and He refused. Yet until Church was separated from State every human attempt to implement Christianity in the political world, from the persecution of early schismatics in the name of dogmatic conformity, to centuries of doctrinal European wars, to the worldwide destruction of native cultures by Christian missionaries, has produced episodes of devastation in the name of the Christian God unrivalled by any other human motivation. The difference between Christianity and Islam is that in Islam the two parallel forces of religion and politics were recognized as fused from the start.

Finally, Muhammad's wives represent a further difficulty, when judged beside standards of Christian monogamy and the tradition of celibate priests, motivated by the desire to emulate Jesus himself. But this Christian ethic has created a link in the West between sex and sin which is entirely absent in Islam, where there is forthright acknowledgement of sexuality, within limits, as a gift from God. Husbands and wives are instructed by the Qur'ān to satisfy each other's desires, anecdotally evidenced, for example, by the multiplicity of winsome lingerie shops along the main streets of conservative Cairo. For Muslims, therefore, the Prophet's well-known sexual appetite carries no overtones of immorality in itself. Muslim commentators are unapologetic about Muhammad's strong interest in women. In this view the revelation of the Qur'ān to a man who understood human indulgence is a further dimension to the miracle.

Muhammad had either eleven or thirteen wives, depending on the definition. He may have been attracted to some of his wives more than others, but all his marriages, after his first to Khadijah,

had a political or charitable basis, as was usual in contemporary
Arabia, where divorce was common, and death for men was often
brutal and early, leaving many women vulnerable. Muslims emphasize that Muhammad made every effort to follow the injunctions of
the Qur'ān (which limited the number of wives to four only after
Muhammad had entered into his marriages) to treat all wives
equally, both materially and emotionally. Further, Muhammad's
family group lived very frugal lives: Muhammad repaired his own
clothes, meals were simple and the first mosque where they lived was
a primitive structure. Sumptuous harems were created in Arab culture by corrupt rulers only in later centuries, justified by wilfully
perverse interpretations of the sources.

Appendix I

The Constitution of Medina

In the name of God, the Merciful, the Compassionate!
This is the writing of Muhammad the Prophet, between the believers and the Muslims of the Quraysh (from Mecca) and from Yathrib (Medina) and those who follow them and who fight with them.

1. They are a single community ('*ummah*) distinct from other people.

2. The Emigrants of the Quraysh, according to their former condition, pay jointly the blood money between them, and they, as a group, ransom their captives, doing so with uprightness and justice between the believers.

3. The Banu 'Awf, according to their former condition, pay jointly the previous blood-wits, and each sub-clan ransoms its captives doing so with uprightness and justice between the believers.

4. The Banu 'l-Hàrith, according to their former condition, pay jointly . . . (as 3).

5. Banu Sà'idah . . .(as 3).

6. Banu Jusham . . .(as 3).

7. Banu 'n-Najjàr . . .(as 3).

8. Banu 'Amr b.'Awf . . .(as 3).

9. Banu 'n-Nabit . . .(as 3).

10. Banu 'l-Aws . . .(as 3).

11. The believers do not forsake a debtor among them, but give him help according to what is fair for ransom and blood-wit.

12. A believer does not take as confederate the client of a believer without the latter's consent.

13. The God-fearing believers are against whoever of them acts wrongfully, plans an act that is unjust or treacherous or hostile or corrupt among the believers; their hands are all against him, even if he is the son of one of them.

14. A believer does not kill a believer because of an unbeliever and does not help an unbeliever against a believer.

15. The security of God is one; the granting of neighbourly protection by the least of the believers is binding upon them; the believers are clients of one another to the exclusion of other people.

16. Whoever of the Jews follows us has the same help and support as the believers, so long as the believer is not wronged by the Jew and the Jew does not help others against the believer.

17. The peace of the believers is one; no believer makes peace apart from another believer, where there is fighting in the way of God, except in so far as equality and justice between them is maintained.

18. In every expedition made with us the parties take turns with one another.

19. The believers exact vengeance for one another where a man gives his blood in the way of God. The God-fearing believers are under the best and most correct guidance.

20. No idolater gives neighbourly protection for goods or person to the Quraysh, nor intervenes in a Qurashi's favour against a believer.

21. When anyone wrongfully kills a believer, the evidence being clear, then he is liable to be killed in retaliation, unless the representative of the murdered man is satisfied with a payment. The believers are against the murderer entirely; nothing is permissible to them except to oppose him.

22. It is not permissible for a believer who has agreed to what is in this document and believes in God and the Last Day, to help a wrong-doer or to give him lodging. If anyone helps the wrong-doer and gives him lodging, then upon this man is the curse of God and His wrath of the Day of Resurrection, and from him nothing will be accepted to make up for this punishment or to take its place.

23. Whenever there is anything about which you differ, it is to be referred to God and to Muhammad (peace be upon him).

24. The Jews bear expenses along with the believers so long as they continue at war.

25. The Jews of the Banu ʿAwf are an ʿ*ummah* along with the believers. To the Jews their religion and the Muslims their religion. This applies both to their clients and to themselves, with the exception of anyone who has done wrong or acted treacherously; he brings evil only on himself and on his household.

26.   For the Jews of the Banu ʿn-Najjàr, the like of what is for the Jews of the Banu ʿAwf.

27.   For the Jews of the Banu ʿl-Hàrith the like . . .

28.   For the Jews of the Banu Sàʾidah the like . . .

29.   For the Jews of the Banu Jusham the like . . .

30.   For the Jews of the Banu ʿl-Aws the like . . .

31.   For the Jews of the Banu Thaʾlabah the like of what is for the Jews of the Banu ʿAwf, with the exception of anyone who has done wrong or acted treacherously; he brings evil only on himself and his household.

32.   Jafnah, a subdivision of Thaʾlabah, are like them.

33.   For the Banu ʿsh-Shutaybah the like of what is for the Jews of Banu Awf; honourable dealing comes before treachery.

34.   The clients of the Thʾlabah are like them.

35.   The *bitanah* (or Arab entourage) of the Jews are as themselves.

36.   No one of the *ummah* may go out to war without the permission of Muhammad (peace be upon him), but the *ummah* is not restrained from taking vengeance for wounds. Whoever acts rashly, it involves only himself and his household, except where a man has been wronged. God is the truest fulfiller of this document.

37.   It is for the Jews to bear their expenses and for the Muslims to bear their expenses. Between one another there is help against whoever wars against the people of this document. Between one another is sincere friendship and honourable dealing, not treachery. A man is not guilty of treachery through the act of his confederate. There is help to be given to the person wronged.

38.   The valley of Yathrib (Medina) is sacred for the people of this document.

39.   The protected neighbour is as the man himself so long as he does no harm and does not act treacherously.

40.   No woman is given neighbourly protection without the consent of her people.

41. Whenever among the people of this document there occurs an incident or quarrel from which disaster for the '*ummah* is to be feared, it is to be referred to God and to Muhammad, the Messenger of God (God bless and preserve him). God is the most scrupulous and truest fulfiller of what is in this document.

42. No neighbourly protection is given to Meccan Quraysh and those who help them.

43. Between the people of this document is help against whoever suddenly attacks Yathrib (Medina).

44. Whenever they are summoned to conclude and accept a treaty, they conclude and accept it; when they in turn summon to the like, it is a debt to them by the believers, except whoever wars about religion; incumbent on each man is his share from the side which supports him.

45. The Jews of al-Aws, both their clients and themselves are in the same position as belongs to the people of this document for so long as they are thoroughly honourable in their dealings with the people of this document. Honourable dealing comes before treachery.

46. A person acquiring guilt acquires such guilt only against himself. God is the most upright and truest fulfiller of what is in this document. This writing does not intervene to protect a wrong-doer or traitor. He who goes out is safe, and he who sits still is safe in Medina, except whoever does wrong and acts treacherously. God is the protecting neighbour of him who acts honourably and fears God and Muhammad is the Messenger of God (God bless and preserve him).

Appendix 2

Muhammad's Wives

Khadijah was Muhammad's first wife, and the circumstances of the marriage have already been related. Only one daughter, Fatima, survived the Prophet. Fatima married 'Ali, the Prophet's cousin and fourth caliph. Reverence of Fatima played a significant role in the development of the character of Shi'ism.

Upon the death of Khadijah, Muhammad married **Sawda**, the widow of one of his companions. She was over forty at the time of the marriage. Sawda already had a son from her first marriage and she looked after Muhammad's children from his first marriage. She had no children with Muhammad.

'Ā'isha was the daughter of Abu Bakr, companion of the Prophet and the first caliph or successor to Muhammad. The betrothal was intended to unite the families of Muhammad and Abu Bakr, even though 'Ā'isha was only nine years old at the time. The marriage was consummated when the bride was fifteen. 'Ā'isha, who was pretty, intelligent and independent, became very close to the Prophet and is popularly known as his 'favourite' wife. Muhammad died in her arms and she contributed much to the development of Islam in the years that followed. She bore no children and died at the age of sixty-six.

Hafsa was the widowed daughter of 'Umar, trusted companion of Muhammad and the second caliph. Hafsa's husband was killed at the battle of Badr. The marriage was contracted in order to give protection to Hafsa as a favour to 'Umar. Hafsa had no children and was reputedly a disruptive influence on the menage, often arguing with the Prophet himself.

Zainab was also the widow of a Muslim martyr. She was devoted to caring for the poor and earned the name Ummu'l-Masākin, Mother of the Downtrodden. She died three months after the marriage at the age of thirty.

Umm Salama was another war widow. She had two children with her first Meccan husband and as an early convert to Islam was badly treated by the Meccans before being permitted to leave. Reputedly Muhammad looked after Umm Salama's children as if they were his own. She was the last of the Prophet's wives to die.

Muhammad's seventh wife was the second **Zainab**, who was married to his adopted son Zayd in a union arranged by Muhammad. Following

Zayd's divorce from Zainab, Muhammad married her, allegedly smitten by her beauty. The morality of this marriage has been criticized on the basis that Zainab was Muhammad's daughter-in-law as well as his cousin. The Prophet is further accused of promoting the divorce for his own libidinous ends. A surah was received absolving Muhammad from wrongdoing, and these lines are also cited as evidence of the falseness of the Qur'ān.

> Then when Zayd
> Had dissolved his marriage
> With her with the necessary
> Formality, We joined her
> In marriage to thee,
> In order that in future
> There may be no difficulty
> To the Believers in the matter
> Of marriage with the wives
> Of their adopted sons, when
> The latter have dissolved,
> With the necessary formality,
> Their marriages with them.
> And Allah's command must
> Be fulfilled.

Al Ahzab (The Confederates) Surah 33, verse 37

But the purpose behind Muhammad's marriage to Zainab was legislative. Verse 3 of the same surah prohibits legal adoption, which was seen as erroneous because, 'Allah has not made for any man two hearts in his one body', meaning that no son or daughter could love two mothers or fathers. The prohibition thereupon became part of the Shariah, with the result that even in modern Muslim societies there is no legal adoption procedure. Nothing prevents the charitable sheltering of a child in need, but family status cannot be changed. Marriage to the wife of an adopted son was prohibited in the *Jāhiliyyah*, so by marrying Zainab, Muhammad demonstrated that the old procedures for adoption were no longer valid. This gives an entirely different meaning to the surah quoted above.

There are also two responses to be made to the accusation that Muhammad manipulated the divorce to satisfy his own sexual whim. First, Zainab was Muhammad's cousin, whom he knew well, and he could have married her at a much earlier time had he been so inclined. Secondly, at the time of the marriage, after the Farewell Pilgrimage, Muhammad was in poor health and close to death.

Juwairiya was taken as a prisoner of war from the hostile Banu'l-Mustaliq tribe. As part of Muhammad's diplomatic initiatives as his power increased, he married Juwairiya in order to confirm a peace settlement with her tribe, of which her father was chief. She was instructed in the faith by 'Ā'isha and became a devout Muslim.

Ramlah, better known as Umm Habiba, was the daughter of the infamous Abu Sufyān. She embraced Islam early, in defiance of her father, and spent time in Ethiopia during the years of persecution. On her return, her husband having died during exile, Muhammad married her as part of his peaceful 'opening' of Mecca.

Safiyyah was a Jewish princess all of whose male relatives were killed during Muhammad's last confrontation with the Jews at the Battle of Khaybar. From slavery she rose by force of personality to marry Muhammad. Objections were raised because of her status as the daughter of a Jewish enemy, but on her conversion Muhammad treated her as a Muslim and an equal.

Muhammad's eleventh wife, **Maymunah**, represented a further alliance between Muhammad and the leading Meccan families, initiated by 'Abbās, Muhammad's uncle. Maymunah was fifty-one when she married and she devoted herself to improving the condition of slaves.

Mary was sent to Muhammad as a slave by the Christian Orthodox Archbishop of Alexandria. Because Mary was a Copt the marriage has been questioned, but a son was born, Ibrahim, who died less than a year old and for this reason the relationship is usually regarded as marriage.

Muhammad's relationship with the Jewess **Rayhāna** is similarly unclear. She was a prisoner, taken after the capitulation of the Qurayzah.

THE FUNDAMENTALS OF FAITH

I The Noble Qur'ān

For a non-Muslim with no knowledge of Arabic, the Qur'ān in translation is an exasperating, punishing read, apparently without order, narrative or conclusion. Listen to the words chanted, however, by an accomplished *muqri* at a funeral, or even by chance over the radio in a Cairo taxi, and the work is spell binding. An imperfect comparison could be made with the opaque words of the Old Testament psalms, brought off the page and into life when intoned as plainsong.

This experience of hearing rather than reading the words connects the listener to the oral tradition that lies at the heart of Qur'ānic exposition. Arabs say of Arabic that when something is said beautifully the words are almost true already. And for Muhammad's followers, the repeating of the revelations, the very sound of the words, became their life and inspiration, with cadence almost as important as content. This was the voice of God on their lips and ringing in their ears, possessed with the same personal intensity that Catholics feel with the transubstantiated body and blood of Christ on the tongue. So once the words of the Qur'ān were written down and the inevitable dissection and interpretation began, the marvel was rendered slightly less marvellous.

The magic of classical Arabic, in a modern example, was a strong element in the extraordinary power exerted over the Muslim world by the televised tapes of Osama ibn Laden speaking after the events of September 11th 2001, an effect entirely lost on a Western viewer. Despite the dead eyes and the blank expression, the man spoke an incendiary Arabic, echoing the Qur'ān in the way that the rolling epic of Churchill's wartime speeches echoed Shakespeare for the British.

Ultimately, therefore, reading the Qur'ān is a matter of faith. The New Testament, and much of the Torah, is made up of stories generally understandable in their plain narrative meaning by any reader of any faith. But for Muslims, the dense Arabic words of the

Qur'ān hide an inner significance whose discernment requires the gift of God's grace as well as a pure and faithful heart. And this deeper meaning, like God Himself, does not appear directly.

> It is not fitting
> For a man that Allah
> Should speak to him
> Except by inspiration
> Or from behind a veil.
>
> *Al-Shurā* (Consultation) Surah 42, verse 51

We have discussed the Qur'ān as Muhammad's prophetic 'miracle' and we have considered the setting in which the revelations were received. The overwhelming significance of the Qur'ān as the core of the faith has also been touched on, as well as the legislative aspect of the work as the basis of the Shariah. For Muslims individually, the Qur'ān is 'eternal', 'the Book of Wisdom', a 'Message for any that has a heart', 'the Mother of Books', and 'Guidance Sure'. Now the work will be examined in some detail.

How the Qur'ān was assembled

The text of the Qur'ān refers to a number of methods by which Muhammad delivered the work: through the famous appearance of the angel Gabriel, or by struggling during the night to receive the right expression for the inspiration, or from an exterior mystic 'suggestion'. All these experiences are summarized in Surah 2, *Al-Baqarah* (The Heifer) where Muhammad is told at verse 97 that the words of the Qur'ān have been 'brought down upon thy heart by Allah's will'.

As the words were received, the pre-existing oral poetic tradition, as well as the tenacious Arab memory, enabled the work to be memorized by Muhammad's Companions. Each Companion became a guardian of a part, with a few able to recite the entire work as the revelations unfolded over twenty-three years. Committing the whole Qur'ān to memory (and so becoming a 'reciter') has ever since been regarded as one of the ultimate acts of Muslim devotion.

Contrary to popular presumption, reading and writing were common in *Jāhiliyyah* Mecca, though far from universal. By legend,

the most admired poems were reproduced in golden letters and suspended from the side of the Ka'bah for all to admire. Some of the
Companions were fully literate and able to record excerpts of the
Qur'ān in a more permanent form than recitation, but the entire
work was not assembled as a single document during the Prophet's
lifetime.

The first collection of the elements of the Qur'ān was undertaken
by Zayd ibn-Thābit, Muhammad's principal amanuensis during his
later years, and who also served Abu Bakr during the two years of his
caliphate as the first successor to the Prophet. This departure into
writing, for which there was no direct authority to follow, away from
the dominant oral tradition practised by Muhammad himself, was
justified by the loss of a number of reciters during the apostasy wars
that followed Muhammad's death. The community feared that the
Qur'ān might be lost forever before the words could be passed on to
a new generation of reciters.

Sections were taken by Zayd from the 'hearts of men' while the
words were still fresh in their memories, others from writing on
pieces of parchment, stones, bones and boards. And during his last
years in Medina, when the more complex legislative surahs were
revealed, Muhammad employed scribes, so that at least part of the
work had been written down as the revelations occurred. In Surah
10, *Yunus* (Jonah), at verse 38 those who claim that the Qur'ān is
forged are challenged to 'Bring then a surah like unto it', from which
scholars have concluded that during his lifetime, Muhammad had
organized at least part of the work into recognizable surah divisions,
even if not in finished form. Probably the surahs were expanded
during the process of assembling the components, by adding those
memorized parts which did not appear in the incomplete written
records. This entire procedure, from the original revelations in separate episodes over many years to collection from various sources and
allowing for later insertions, goes some way, in some commentaries,
to account for the disjointed character of the work.

But the story of Zayd's collection is tradition only, no copy of the
original collection authorized by Abu Bakr has survived. There was
no definitive version of the Qur'ān in circulation until the rule of
'Uthman, the third caliph, which began twenty-three years after
Muhammad's death. He ordered an 'official' compilation as well as

the destruction of the previous partial versions prepared by various Companions (including the putative Abu Bakr version) in an attempt to end disputes about the readings of the Qur'ān that had developed among the troops carrying Islam's early expansion. The 'Uthman version, overseen by Zayd ibn-Thābit once again, was widely distributed, but took the form of a shorthand aide-memoire for those already familiar with the work and was still not a complete text in the modern sense. For the existing reciters, however, the Qur'ān continued to be the subject of a number of conflicting 'readings', although the differences related to minor matters only.

Refinement of the text continued into the tenth century, together with the Arabic language. The oldest copy of the complete Qur'ān, written on gazelle skin and held by the Egyptian National Library, dates from AD 688, fifty-eight years after the death of Muhammad.

Native Arabic speakers who are non-Muslim (Arab Christians, for example) assert that this constant refinement of the text by great scholars over two or three centuries was the means by which the magnificent language of the Qur'ān was produced, and not by the original revelation or composition. In fact, emerging modern scholarship of early Islam provides some support for this view. Then later in Muslim history, Shi'a would claim that verses favouring the right of 'Ali, Muhammad's cousin, to the succession had been omitted, although no evidence for this exists, and 'Ali himself, once he became caliph, made no changes to the 'Uthman version. There have also been questions raised by academics over the years. The authenticity of certain surahs has been questioned, those predicting Muhammad's death for example, or praising Abu Bakr, and the possibility of omissions has been examined. Modern Western scholars have 'deconstructed' the text and claim to have found inconsistencies in style.

But all such questions are quibbles. No other work in history has survived more than thirteen centuries from inception with so comparatively pure a text.

The form of the Qur'ān
The text is divided into 114 surahs or chapters, subdivided into *āyas* or verses which range from long and complicated to short and blunt.

The work is also traditionally divided into thirty portions of approximately equal length, indicated by a fraction sign in the margin. This arrangement assists in reading the Qur'ān right through over the days of a lunar month.

The first surah, named *Al-Fātiha* (The Opening) is comparable in Islam to the Lord's Prayer in Christianity. The *Fātiha* is reproduced in the original, then phonetically, and then in translation in Appendix 2 to this chapter.

The reader's confusion begins at the second surah, with the discovery that the order of Surahs 2–114 is mostly based on length, with the longest, consisting of 286 verses, at the front and the shortest, consisting of only 3 verses, at the back. But even this rule is not precisely observed and there is no other relevance in the order of the surahs – for example, by subject matter, chronology or place of revelation. Further, the surahs are for the most part named by reference to a prominent word in the text which often has little or nothing to do with the contents (Surah 2, *Al-Baqarah* (the Heifer), for example, or Surah 16, *Al-Nahl* (The Bee)). Then the composition of a surah can be disjointed internally, full of apparently unrelated issues and plagued by non-sequiturs. These difficulties can only be overcome by careful study and by constant reading and rereading.

How far the order of the surahs was set by Muhammad himself has not been determined. He certainly regarded certain surahs as forming sequences, probably linked by the appearance of the mysterious letters in the opening lines (see the box on page 84). According to Muslims, Gabriel reviewed the entire text with Muhammad during his last Ramadan, and reciters during Muhammad's lifetime must have given the surahs an order of which he approved, but there is no tradition dealing with the question. Much research has been undertaken to divide the surahs into those of Meccan origin and those of Medinan origin to determine the correct chronology. The former are generally shorter and inspirational, relevant to Muhammad's role as preacher in Mecca; the latter are more prosaic, concerned with the establishment and running of the community at Medina. But even this method of categorization is imperfect since verses within the surahs have been identified from different periods, as a result of faulty collection or through revisions and insertions made during Muhammad's lifetime.

All surahs (except one, for historical reasons) open with the invocation, known as the *tasmiyah*:

بِسْمِ اللّهِ الرَّحْمَنِ الرَّحِيمِ

Bi-smi llāhi r-rahmāni r-rāhim
In the name of God, the All-Merciful, the All-Compassionate

This formula is now in universal use in Islam for a range of purposes (usually in the shortened version: *basmala*), from the opening invocation in a letter, to the start of a personal prayer. A Hadith of the Prophet says that any significant act undertaken without the saying of the *tasmiyah* is deficient in the sight of God. But note that neither this invocation nor the titles of the surahs are considered to be part of the revealed text.

The work is presented on the page in Arabic as continuous lines of prose, broken only by the verse numbers which do not begin on a new line, and no uniform metre is detectable. The verse breaks create the pauses where the spoken word would rest naturally. Some lines do rhyme and verses often end with repeated refrains, significant to the recital of the text.

The Mysterious Letters

Twenty-nine surahs of the 114 begin with an Arabic letter standing alone, or a group of separate letters. The first two verses of Surah *Al-Baqarah* (The Heifer), for example, are written as follows:

   1. Alif Lam Mim (letters A L M)
   2. This is the Book
   In it is guidance sure, without doubt

or Surah 26, *Al-Shu'arā* (The Poets):

   1. Ta Sin Mim (letters T S M)
   2. These are the Verses of the Book
   That makes things clear.

Patterns can be detected, and certain letters are repeated more than others, while the surahs using the same letters are arranged generally in sequential blocks. But no satisfactory explanation for the significance of the letters has been found in more than thirteen centuries of study.

Many theories have, of course, been put forward. The most convincing suggestion interprets the letters as referring to the reciters from whom Zayd obtained the originals. Academics have attempted to link the letters to specific individuals with such knowledge, but again, no satisfactory scheme of explanation has emerged. Attempts have also been made to show that the letters are contractions of previously used titles, but no coherent rationale has been put forward. Tortuous but unsatisfactory arguments have been made, purporting to show that the content of the surahs beginning with certain letters share a common thread of subject matter.

Muslim scholars are more prepared to give the letters symbolic or mystical significance, as possibly reproducing the signs from a heavenly book, for example, to which Muhammad was given some form of access. Then two of the letters have been linked to a Muslim battle-cry, 'Hā mim, they shall not be aided', which has led to the interpretation that the letters are signs from God that He will come to the assistance of Muslims. In a further interpretation, the letters could be from Syriac or Hebrew and refer to the texts in those languages with which the surahs in question may be linked.

The most sympathetic construction is that the presence of the letters reminds the reader that the Qur'ān is made up of just such common elements as letters, used by all Arabic speakers, yet the linguistic skill of the Arabic text is impossible to match. The eloquent among Muhammad's detractors are challenged in the Qur'ān to produce one equivalent surah, or ten verses, or even one single verse, but none succeeds.

No explanation fits exactly, however, and the mystery continues.

The 'voice' of the Qur'ān is generally that of an unidentified party addressing Muhammad in the third person, which is consistent with Muhammad's experience of the revelations coming to him from outside himself. Muslim belief is that this is the voice of God, speaking through Muhammad to mankind, via the agency of Gabriel.

Sometimes the voice speaks in the first person:

> I have only created
> Jinns and men, that
> They may serve me.
>
> *Al-Dhariyat* (The Winds that Scatter) Surah 51, verse 56

But more often the regal third person is employed:

> We created men from sounding clay
> From mud moulded into shape.
> And the jinn race We had
> Created before, from the fire
> Of the scorching wind.
>
> *Al-Hijir* (The Rock) Surah 15, verse 26

On other occasions the voice speaks directly to Muhammad in the second person singular. This is the voice that instructs Muhammad to recite, that encourages, that rebukes and gives advice. Sometimes the voice turns from this second person singular ('O thou . . .' in biblical language) to the second person plural ('O ye . . .')

Apparent difficulties arise in the frequent passages where God speaks of Himself in the third person, or where the voice is clearly that of the angels. Often the angels speak in the first person plural as 'we', confusing their voices with that of God. Or on other occasions God is referred to in the third person singular (as 'the Lord', or equivalent) then the form will change abruptly to the first person, and again from singular to plural.

> Now I do
> Call to witness
> The Lord of all points
> In the East and the West,
> That we can certainly
> Substitute for them
> Better men than they;
> And We are not
> To be defeated
> In Our Plan.
>
> *Al-Ma'arij* (The Way of Ascent) Surah 70, verses 40–41

What is clear and consistent, however, is that Muhammad is never more than the mouthpiece. The words only pass through him and are never represented to the reader as being of his own composition. Even such a passage as Surah 11, *Hud* (The Prophet Hud) verse 120 (quoted on page 34) where the speaker is clearly Muhammad himself, the originating command from Gabriel on behalf of God, 'Recite' ensures that the reader understands clearly that Muhammad's position is that of the mere messenger for words provided for him. Thus all the voices which may appear to belong to a speaker other than God are in fact dramatic devices only. The entire text is still believed by Muslims to be the direct word of God, whatever the apparent form.

The content of the Qur'ān

No discussion of the Qur'ān can be complete without an attempt at a minimum statement of the substance of the work. Richard Bell's authoritative *Introduction to the Qur'ān*, sums up the content under five headings, which are here summarized:

1. The One God, without peers or partners occupies most of the work. He is Omnipotent, as demonstrated by His power to create. His existence is evidenced by His Signs visible in the natural world: the sun, the moon, night and day, etc. Man is utterly subordinate, unable to do or will anything unless God allows, to which the only correct response by man is complete surrender to His will.

2. Other spiritual beings are described, jinns living in a parallel world, similarly created by God, and who, like man, may be benign or malevolent, either Muslim or unbeliever. Similarly, angels are recognized as further created creatures, consisting of pure goodness and the direct servants of God. *Shaytān*, the fallen jinn, is permitted to tempt man, seductively whispering his evil suggestions, and making wrong fair-seeming.

3. Muhammad's prophethood is stated and elaborated as bringing the message of the One God to man. Man will be punished like those before him if the Word of God is not heeded.

4. Muhammad is also the 'warner' of the Last Day. Omnipotent God will restore man to life on that day to be judged and then either

rewarded with everlasting bliss or condemned to everlasting torment. Hell and Paradise are frequently described in compelling detail.

5. God prescribes laws by which the faithful are to live: the Five Pillars, the commandments of Surah 17, prohibitions against certain foods, against the drinking of alcohol and against usury, followed by the detailed social provisions that have become the Shariah. But for those who try and inevitably fail, God is Most Gracious and Most Merciful.

To Bell's summary, this observer presumes to add two further issues:

6. The history of salvation occupies a substantial portion of the text. God has sent many messengers before Muhammad to guide mankind and the lives of a few are recounted in some detail. But God's messengers have been ignored, or their warnings perverted to some human end. Muhammad's ministry and the message of the Qur'ān, as the Last of the Last, now represents God's final word, which man ignores at his peril.

7. The brotherhood of man is emphasized in numerous contexts. Muslims are specifically said to be brothers, beyond all other affiliations (especially tribal or ethnic), united by their belief. Non-believers are nevertheless to be tolerated, with Christians and Jews recognized as People of the Book, or believers sharing with Muslims a common source of faith, and their prophets are accepted as men of God. Those who profess faith with their lips, but not with their hearts (The Medinan Hypocrites, for example) are threatened with particularly harsh punishment on the Last Day.

The message of the Qur'ān was hardly original, Jews and Christians had followed monotheism for centuries. But to Muhammad's listeners the message was largely new, and above all, Arab, while the medium, the language, was captivating, adorned with proverbs, recited with an almost musical elegance, and capturing all the power of ancient desert lore.

The Meccan and Medinan periods

As we have seen, the revelation of the Qur'ān covered both phases of Muhammad's ministry: from the first revelation through to the hijrah, the twelve-year Meccan period; then from the hijrah through to Muhammad's death, the ten years he spent in Medina. In Mecca, Muhammad saw his task as calling his listeners to Islam, to righteous conduct, to comprehension of the Oneness of God and away from polytheism, and to an apprehension of the coming judgement. In Medina, the Prophet's initial ministry to mankind as a whole gave way to his concern for the establishment of the Muslim community. The surahs from the two periods generally reflect these different purposes.

Thus the Meccan surahs are mostly short and exhortational, dealing with the fundamental questions of God's existence and the authenticity of Muhammad's message, addressed to all who will listen:

> O Mankind. It is
> Ye that have need
> Of Allah: but Allah is
> The One Free of all wants,
> Worthy of all praise.
>
> *Fatir* (The Originator of Creation) Surah 35, verse 15

Medinan surahs are longer, usually dealing with laws and social issues, addressed to those who are already members of the community and who have accepted Muhammad as a prophet of God:

> O ye who believe.
> If ye fear Allah,
> He will grant you a Criterion
> To judge between right and wrong,
> Remove from you all evil
> That may afflict you
> And forgive you:
> For Allah is the Lord
> Of grace unbounded.
>
> *Al-Anfal* (The Spoils of War) Surah 8, verse 29

Interpretation of the Qur'ān

The process of determining what the Qur'ān means, by attempting to expose the themes that underlie the text, is as old and as complex as the work itself. And since the Qur'ān is also the source of the 'legislation' of Islam, interpretation quickly merges with jurisprudence and the Shariah.

The Qur'ān is first to be explained by the Qur'ān itself. Difficult passages should be read in conjunction with clear passages and earlier episodes should be matched with later ones on the same subject to produce a comprehensive whole. In Surah 2, *Al-Baqarah* (The Heifer) at verse 37, for example, Adam learns unspecified words of inspiration from his Lord. In Surah 7, *Al-A'rāf* (The Heights), the reader learns at verse 23 what those words were:

> They said, 'O Lord
> We have wronged our own souls.
> If Thou forgive us not
> And bestow not upon us
> Thy Mercy, we shall
> Certainly be lost.'

An intimate knowledge of the Qur'ān will allow the reader to link such passages, creating a more coherent whole than is apparent on first reading.

Secondly, the Qur'ān is explained by the Prophet. There are numerous examples of such explanations in the Sunna, but these traditions are not all reliable, an issue to be discussed below.

Lastly the interpretations of experts may be considered. Clearly the most significant interpretations are those of the Companions of the Prophet, provided that authenticity can be established, followed by the acknowledged masters from Muslim history, down to the present. This process can, of course, degenerate into mere unsupported opinion so that the status of the commentator is always of great importance.

In some cases, Muslims acknowledge, God abrogated a few of the earlier verses. Where a preceding injunction was of a temporary nature, His commands changed with the changing circumstances of the Muslims. This is accepted doctrine and does not dilute in the

Muslim view, the integrity of the work. Apparently abrogated verses are retained in the Qur'ān as the word of God, and God moreover is free of all restraints.

Translations of the Qur'ān

The Qur'ān rendered in a language other than Arabic cannot achieve the depth of the original, and loses many important characteristics. Further, translation cuts the reader off from the oral tradition that originated with the revelation to Muhammad himself: the sounds that can move the hardest desertmen to tears of ecstasy. Rendering the work in another language is a tremendous challenge, therefore, and the translator himself must first come to a precise conclusion about the meaning of the Arabic words, which in turn requires considerable knowledge of the wide dimensions of the language. Three translations into English of the 'meaning of the Qur'ān' from the twentieth century are widely recognized, and from each one, verse 22 of Surah 34, *Saba* (Sheba), is quoted for comparison and to demonstrate the difficulties, each is laid out in the form favoured by the translator.

Muhammad Marmaduke Pickthall (1875–1936) This work is especially valued by Muslims because Pickthall was a convert to Islam as well as a Qur'ānic expert and a native English speaker. His volume is subtitled 'An explanatory translation', and his foreword warns bluntly that 'the Qur'ān cannot be translated'.

> Say, O Muhammad: Call upon those whom ye set up besides
> Allah. They possess not an atom's weight either in the
> heavens or on earth, nor have they any share in either, nor
> hath He an auxiliary among them.

'Abdullah Yusuf 'Ali (d. 1953) This version by a truly bilingual Indian scholar and devout Muslim is the translation followed throughout this book. The revised 'Ali edition comes complete with 6,310 footnotes, the author's verse commentary, a full index and the Arabic text laid out alongside the translation. The tone is biblical, but fluent and convincing.

> Say: 'Call upon the other gods
> Whom ye fancy, besides Allah;
> They have no power –
> Not the weight of an atom
> In the heavens or on the earth;
> No sort of share have
> They therein, nor is any of them
> A helper to Allah.'

Arthur J. Arberry (1905–69) A profound and inspiring teacher at the universities of London and Cambridge during the first half of the twentieth century and the author of over sixty works on Persian and Arabic topics. This version by a non-Muslim is more free-spirited, but more readable.

> Say: Call on those you have asserted
> apart from God: they possess not so much
> as the weight of an ant in the heavens
> nor in the earth; they have no partnership
> in either of them, nor has He in them
> any supporter.

The translation by the well-known Orientalist Richard Bell, however, is suspect to Muslims. His version alters radically the order of the surahs and asserts boldly in the commentary that Muhammad, not God, was the author of the work.

Qurʾān Reciters

An inadequate comparison was made in an earlier chapter between the language of the Qurʾān and that of a hypothetical 'Shakespeare under divine command'. This goes some way towards describing for a non-Arabic speaker the richness of the text, and the aphorisms, allegories and riddles that are woven into the lines. This simile could be taken further, by comparing the cultural position of the Qurʾān in Muslim life to the combination, for an English speaker, of Shakespeare's *King Lear*, Handel's *Messiah* and The Gospel According to St Matthew, all rolled into one. But even then, the significance of the work would still not have been adequately captured because almost all Muslims know large parts of the work by heart to a degree that has never been matched for any Western work in any age. And until recently the study and memorization of the Qur'ān made up a substantial part of the syllabus of a Muslim's education.

Only a brave man, therefore, stands up in public to recite. To satisfy his inevitably knowledgeable listeners his memory must be perfect, down to the last nuance of the reading that is to be followed, his diction must be exact and between the lines his rendering must deliver meaning in a way that meets the highest expectations for the Word of God. The tones that result from this art, wafting plaintively and timelessly from tape players in shops and ateliers out into the street, is one of the defining characteristics of a Muslim city.

Here is the living connection back to the Companions and to the Prophet himself, returned from an all-night vigil in his cave to deliver himself of a fresh revelation before those sceptical existentialists in the dusty streets of Mecca. Here also is where standard Western cynicism about the way in which the Qur'ān was collected after Muhammad's death meets the dimension of faith. There must have been considerable discrepancies between reciters, the criticism goes, so that the assembled text must be a form of compromise, rather than accurately capturing the Prophet's original words. But even today, almost fourteen centuries later, if a visitor to the humblest rural mosque were to make a mistake in his recital, just a single word in a single passage, there would be present four or five local amateur reciters, or partial memorizers, able to correct the error immediately. With such intensity of application and devotion, mistakes among the original reciters would have been impossible.

The Qur'ān is the six times the length of *Henry V*, and takes about fifty hours to deliver, or longer if a slow speed is chosen. The words can be spoken as *tajwid*, or intoned as *tilawa*, giving a quasi-melodic artistic embellishment to the text. Both forms follow strict rules that have been developed in response to the command of the text itself: 'And recite the Qur'ān in slow, measured rhythmic tones' (*Al-Muzzammil* (The Enfolded One) Surah 73, verse 4). Detailed recital conventions cover the articulation of consonants, the vocalization of syllables and the duration and emphasis of individual sounds. These may vary from master to master, linked to long-standing oral traditions reaching far back into Muslim history.

Future reciters start as boys, first mastering the words themselves. Only half a lifetime later is a reciter able to deliver a distinct and telling resonance. Recital competitions take place all over the Muslim world and are especially popular in Malaysia, where a famous contest is held each Ramadan. The Egyptian government runs an annual competition, funded by Saudi Arabia, offering substantial prizes in a poor country.

Strict rules cover personal readings, and begin with cleanliness. 'None shall touch but those who are clean' (*Al-Wāqi'ah* (The Inevitable) Surah 56, verse 79). Women, for example, are not to handle the book or to recite during menstruation. Next, learning, reading and reciting out loud must be approached with the correct intention: for the sake of Allah's pleasure only and not for any other reason; free of all other preoccupations; in humility and respect while sitting on the ground, preferably facing Mecca. No believer's day should pass without some reading, even if only a few verses.

The physical text itself is also to be respected. The Qur'ān must always be stored on a high shelf, never allowed to touch the floor, and nothing must be placed on top of the cover.

II   The Hadith and the Sunna of the Prophet

If the Qur'ān is the Word of God, then Muhammad was His chosen instrument for the delivery of His Message, and Muhammad's divinely appointed status is frequently confirmed in the text. Muhammad is the 'Lamp spreading light', for example, the 'Seal of the Prophets', and a 'universal Messenger to men'. Believers are enjoined by the Qur'ān 'to obey Allah and obey the Messenger'.

Muhammad is regarded by Muslims as the 'perfect man', so inevitably the Prophet's life has become a source of example and emulation covering all aspects of the believer's life, from religious doctrine to personal politeness and cleanliness, from breaking wind to yawning:

> Abu Sa'id al-Khudri relates that the Holy Prophet said:
> When one of you yawns he should close his mouth with his hand, else Shayt'ān would enter.
>
> (Muslim, *Riyād as-Salihìn* 141/889)

The behaviour enjoined on a believer through the Prophet's example is long and detailed, covering amongst many other things, how to dress, how to eat, preferred crockery to be used, how to pass water, how to lie in bed, prohibitions against spitting, or wearing silk, and so on. The list can be made to look petty and invasive, and more sinisterly, questionable Hadiths can be resurrected from earlier ages and different circumstances, or even invented, to support all manner of unreasonable behaviour.

Nevertheless, if the life of Abraham, or the life of Jesus Christ especially, as the postulated Son of God, had been contemporaneously observed in detail and recorded, no doubt traditions based on those lives would have developed in a similar way. How did a man in communication with God, or who is considered to be God Himself in the case of Jesus Christ, deal with the trials of the mundane world? What did such a man eat or wear, what was his attitude towards women (all prophets and gods being male) or towards his opponents? And most importantly, what light did the conduct of the man's life shed on the message itself?

The Qur'an does not stand alone, therefore. The Word of God may be supreme, but His Message in the Qur'an is generalized. Form is given to the outlines laid down in the Qur'an by the Sunna of the Prophet, by which is meant the precepts and examples that Muhammad set during his lifetime. The traditional examples of the Sunna explaining the Qur'an are those covering prayer and fasting. Both are required of a believer by the Qur'an, but no detail is given in the text itself as to how these devotions are to be accomplished. Muslims rely on the instructions and actions of the Prophet which enlarge on the general requirements in order to create the practical rules and procedures to be followed.

Sunna literally means 'path' or 'beaten track', and the practice of recording tradition originates with pre-Islamic tribes who sought to preserve their history and continuity by following the tribal customs of those who had gone before. The Sunna, therefore, is essentially a conservative institution, favouring established practice over innovation.

The source of the Sunna is the Hadith, but these words are almost interchangeable and require careful explanation. The Sunna refers to the practice of Islam, following the injunctions, actions, examples and tacit disapproval of certain practices, expressed by the Prophet during his lifetime. As we have seen, the issues covered range from the vital specifics of the practice of the Five Pillars, down to very questionable minutiae of behaviour. The Hadith is the vehicle that carries the Sunna, and consists of the written records, from the secure to the dubious, from which the Sunna has been extracted.

In the first years following the death of Muhammad the recording of his sayings and his practices was considered to be a detraction from the primacy of the Qur'ān. Muhammad himself opposed the development of any form of divinity based on his person. 'Take from me only the Qur'ān', he is supposed to have said, in the famous anti-Hadith Hadith. But by the third and fourth centuries of the Islamic era, the collection of reports that make up the Hadith had become a vast and rising tide.

The task of codifying the Hadith was begun in the eighth century CE, two hundred years after the death of Muhammad, principally by Muhammad ibn Ismā'il al-Bukhari (810–70) and Muslim ibn al-Hajjaj (d. 875). These scholars attempted to categorize the hundreds of thousands of individual Hadiths in circulation into a secure few thousand for which the chain of guarantors was discernible, reaching back to one or more Companions of the Prophet. The following is an example of a secure Hadith:

> Malik informed us that ibn Shihab reported from Abu Bakr, born 'Ubaydallah, from 'Abdallah, born 'Umar, that the Apostle of Allah (may the blessings and peace of Allāh be upon him) said: Whenever any of you eats, let him do so with the right hand, and drink as well with the right hand, for the devil eats and drinks with his left hand.

As in the example above, a secure Hadith must begin with an identifiable chain of reputable transmission back to a known Companion or Companions (here Abu Bakr and 'Umar, the first and second caliphs). This is often written in a form of shorthand, naming only the reporter in cases when he is well known and reliable. More examples of secure Hadiths are given in Appendix 1 to this chapter.

Modern analysts are sceptical of the origin of almost all Hadiths, but this has done little to alter the practice of Islam. Informal Hadiths are still a popular repository for every local proverb and saying across the Muslim world, as well as for heroic anecdotes credited to Muhammad, in numbers that would have required many lifetimes to fulfil. Here the search for purity struggles against popular piety and the need to humanize the unfathomable, in a way that resonates with the 'personal' Jesus and is thus contrary to pure Islam. Purity must even struggle against abuse by unscrupulous salesmen, for example, who will offer 'lemons like the Prophet liked to eat'.

The highest form of Hadith is *Hadith Qudsi*, or Holy Hadith, in which the Prophet relates in his own words what God has said or done. This is not to be confused with the direct Word of God in the Qur'ān, which remains the ultimate authority. The following is an example of *Hadith Qudsi*:

> Abu Huraira reported that Allah's Messenger (may peace be upon him) said: 'Allah (Mighty and Exalted is He) said: If my servant likes to meet me, I like to meet him, and if he dislikes to meet me, I dislike to meet him.'

The Sunna is also the point of schism between *ahl al-sunna*, the People of the Sunna, or Sunni Muslims, and the Shiʿa ʿAlì, or Shiʿite Muslims. Since, in the Shiʿa view, as we shall see, the Companions of the Prophet erred in electing Abu Bakr and his successors to the caliphate over ʿAli, the Prophet's cousin and son-in-law, then the records of the Prophet's saying from those same Companions cannot be trusted either. The Shiʿa hold to their own form of Hadith, therefore, derived from ʿAli and his separate line of successors.

But the importance of the Hadith goes beyond mere written record. The fabric of both Sunni and Shiʿa society, each in their different way, has been created by the emulation of the reputed way of life of the Prophet. In this way the Hadith has been more influential than the Qur'ān itself. From prayers to business, from birth to death, the perceived conduct of the Prophet, his approval and his disapproval, has been the basis of Muslim tradition for almost 1,400 years.

III   The Five Pillars of Islam

Islam as a practised faith consists of two fundamentals: *imān*, the outward expression of belief and *ihsān*, doing right. Both are necessary for a Muslim to fulfil the will of God and so to achieve God-consciousness.

But what is meant by 'doing right' is not set out in any all-embracing Muslim code, with the result that the moral concepts of Islam cannot be definitively listed in a way that matches the official catechisms of Christian churches. There have been attempts by individual thinkers to encompass the moral basis of Islam, but there is no Muslim equivalent of the central decision-making hierarchy that is to be found in most Christian sects, responsible for the generation of a detailed dogma in written form. Many of the beliefs of Islam are quoted in this book, taken from the Qur'ān and the Sunna. Obedience, kindness, justice, tolerance, modesty and consideration for others are frequently mentioned. But ultimately, the 'rightly guided' life is a matter of conscience between the believer and his God, Who is All-Seeing and All-Hearing, who is 'closer to man than his jugular vein' (*Qāf*, Surah 50, verse 16).

Conversely, through the Qur'ān and the Sunna, the external acts required of a Muslim are defined down to the smallest detail. Thus, based on these authorities, the outward manifestations of the faith (without which a Muslim ceases to be a member of the '*ummah*) take on a 'divinely ordered' importance without parallel in other religions. There are some general comparisons to be found in Christianity and Judaism, where certain rituals are regarded as initiated by God directly. Christian Communion or Mass is an obvious example, based on the specific precedent set by Christ himself at the Last Supper, although the import of the words Jesus reportedly spoke has been a source of conflict since the Reformation and the form of the ritual has changed dramatically over two millennia. In Judaism there are the commands of Deuteronomy 5: 'Now therefore hearken, O Israel . . .', the teaching of the young, the 'binding of the arm' with the words of God 'which shall also be frontlets between thine eyes', and there are many others. But generally Christian and Jewish practice consist of intricate rituals built up by the faithful over the centuries, rather than being based on a claim that both content and detail follow specific divine command.

The ceremonial duties of Islam also serve as outward emblems of personal and communal identity, opening into a form of worldwide solidarity through universal and uniform practice. These observances set Muslims visibly apart from other religions, but at the same time the acts emphasize the equality of all believers before God, regardless of race, status, birth or wealth. This levelling aspect of Islam is the faith's dominant external characteristic and possibly one reason why so many of the world's poor and disadvantaged are such ardent adherents. To them will come the ultimate rewards, regardless of the present unjust ordering of things in this transitory life.

Muhammad said that Islam is 'constructed on the Five', which have since come to be known as the Five Pillars of Islam.

Shahādah: The Open Testimony

The First Pillar is the believer's confession of faith, reduced to a few words that every member of the faithful from every continent and background can understand, from the illiterate nomadic herdsman in the deserts of northern Kenya to the sophisticated trilingual businessman of Paris or Riyadh.

أشهد أن لا الله إلا الله وأشهد أن محمداً رسول الله

Ashhadu allā ilāha illa' Llāh, wa anna Muhammadan rasul' l-Lāh.

> I bear witness that there is no god but God and that
> Muhammad is the messenger of God.

This is the essence of Islam, known as *tawhid*, the central act of affirming Allah to be the One, absolute, transcendent Creator, Lord and Master of all there is. No words in the entire world are more often uttered than these. These are the words that are first heard by a new-born and the last to be spoken by the dying. The saying of these words from the heart is alone sufficient to make the speaker a Muslim. The words form part of daily prayers, which means that the formula is repeated a minimum of twenty times each day by a devout practitioner. The words are also at the heart of the call to prayer of the muezzin, and are the words on the lips of the mujahid, the fighter in the cause of God, who thus becomes *shaheed*, or witness and martyr if subsequently killed in battle.

The specific words of the *Shahādah* come from the Sunna and were established by Muhammad in the form that is used today. The words in various similar forms also appear repeatedly throughout the Qur'ān underlining the essential creed that 'there is no deity but He'.

Muhammad used the word *rasul* in the *Shahādah* to describe his mission, which translates as 'messenger', even though he is commonly referred to in European languages as 'Prophet', which is technically incorrect but widely accepted. Muhammad carried a message from God to man: his function was not to prophesy the future, except in the limited sense of warning of the punishments that await sinners who ignore the message. The word 'messenger' also encompasses the idea of the place Muhammad claimed in the long line of 'messengers' that had gone before him, from Noah to Jesus Christ.

Salāt: Ritual daily prayer

The Second Pillar is the central act of righteousness in Islam, the very essence of the life of a Muslim. In popular belief, a believer's record of prayer will be the first question asked of him or her on the Day of Judgement.

Here a significant difference with Christianity emerges. Many Christians believe that through prayer they can enter into a 'conversation with God from the heart', or 'come into the presence of God', concurrent with almost any other daily activity. In contrast, a Muslim prays only by way of performing certain prescribed physical acts and spoken words. Observing a ritual serves to concentrate both body and mind exclusively on God, devoting solely to Him, without outside distraction, the few minutes required to complete the procedure. For this reason, for therefore, the form of prayer cannot be random or haphazard, and for a Muslim's prayer to be 'accepted' the believer must accomplish a strictly disciplined routine. Ultimately only the righteousness of the believer reaches God, but the execution of the drill is the necessary means to that end.

Prayers are said five times each day, facing the direction of the Ka'bah in Mecca, so bringing the city into the very centre of day-to-day Muslim life in a geographical as well as a spiritual sense. The times for prayer vary with the seasons and the progressively earlier or later appearance of the sun. The specific times are calculated in advance and a prayer schedule is displayed in the entry of most mosques, covering the following month or two, set out like an almanac or a tide chart. The basis for calculating the due times for prayers is as follows:

subh	When the sky is light but before sunrise. The test for *subh* given in the Sunna is the moment when distinction can be made between a white and a black thread.
zuhr	After midday, with the sun at the highest point in the sky.
'asr	Between three and half past three in the afternoon.
maghreb	In the evening, just after sunset.
'ishā'	About one hour after sunset.

Apart from noon prayers on Fridays, the time that a believer chooses to say his or her prayers is a matter of personal discretion. A prayer is punctual if said at any time after the appointed time but before the next prayer is due. Only the *subh* prayer has to be said between dawn and sunrise. In practice, however, in large cities and in many other modern circumstances, especially in the West, Islam is coming to accept that men and women may be unable to stop for prayers or to find a suitable place, and that the missing cycles may then be caught up at home with the *'ishā'* prayers. But the *subh* prayer should still be said separately before the day's activities begin, and before sunrise.

The prayers of a traditionally devout Muslim start with the muezzin calling *azān*, for the faithful to congregate. The call is always made at the due time, so that all the mosques in one area generally call *azān* simultaneously. The muezzin is a volunteer who should be a God-fearing man educated in Islam, but usually not the imam of the mosque. He may receive a stipend if his functions prevent him from obtaining other employment. At the level of popular belief, the muezzin who calls for God's pleasure only, not for his own gain, is declared to be 'free of hell-fire'.

The call of the muezzin from the balcony of the minaret of the mosque was once a plaintive incantation of great inspiration and beauty, but in recent times tradition has been compromised by electronics. The artistry of the modern caller rarely survives the harsh distortions, clicks and feedback that inevitably accompany the amplified variety of the call, made into a microphone from ground level and broadcast from speakers on the roof of the mosque or hung on the minaret itself. While amplification may carry further and thus embrace more of the faithful, once all the mosques in a city use the same broadcast technique, whatever advantage there may have been is lost.

Beyond the call to congregation, the *azān* has a function similar to the ringing of church bells in a Christian town to mark the passage of time (but not to announce a wedding or a funeral). In Islamic culture, even if the individual listener has no plans to attend, the voice of the muezzin assures him that he lives in a 'land of God's Peace' from which, through the saying of prayers, 'the Devil is on the run'. The call is also a reminder of the summons which the listener will hear on the Day of Resurrection.

The *azān* of the muezzin is only the audible half of a set of invocations and responses that take place between the caller and the faithful. The words, which must be in Arabic, are as follows:

MUEZZIN	*Allāhu akbar, Allāhu akbar.* God is the Greatest. God is the Greatest. (This frequently used formula is known as the *Takbir.*)
LISTENER	*Allāhu Akbar, Allāhu Akbar.*
MUEZZIN	*Ashhadu allā ilāha illa'Llāh, ashhadu allā illāh illa'Llāh* I bear witness that there is no god but God, I bear witness that there is no god but God.
LISTENER	*Ashhadu allā ilāha illa'Llāh, ashhadu allā illāh illa'Llāh.*

MUEZZIN	*Ashhadu anna Muhammadan rasul 'l-Lāh, ashhadu anna Muhammadan rasuu 'l-Lāh.* I bear witness that Muhammad is the messenger of God, I bear witness that Muhammad is the messenger of God.
LISTENER	*Ashhadu anna Muhammadan rasul 'l-Lāh, ashhadu anna. Muhammadan rasulu 'l-Lāh.*
MUEZZIN	*Hayy 'ala'ssalāh, hayy 'ala'ssalāh.* Come to prayer. Come to prayer. *Hayy 'ala' 'l-falāh, hayy 'ala' 'l-falāh.* Come to fulfilment. Come to fulfilment. (For the *subh* prayer, the words, 'Prayer is better than sleep', are added.) *Allāhu Akbar, Allāhu Akbar.*
LISTENER	*Allāhu Akbar, Allāhu Akbar.* (Here the call is acknowledged with the listener's *niyyah* or intention to pray.)
MUEZZIN	*Lā ilāha illa' llāh.* There is no god but God.
LISTENER	*Lā ilāha illa' llāh.*

Ablutions, or ritual washing, which can either be performed before leaving home or at the mosque, are mandatory preconditions to an acceptable prayer. The steps of ablution are accompanied by a further statement of intention through a similar formula of words. Washing is a prerequisite to prayer under all circumstances, even in the desert where clean sand may be substituted if the use of water would create hardship. There are eight steps to ablution, extending to the hands, mouth, nose, face, arms, ears and feet, with damp hands passed over head. Every mosque is equipped with a minimum of washing facilities, even in the poorest parts of the most decrepit Muslim cities. After sexual intercourse and after menstruation the entire body must be washed before prayers can be said. Women cannot say prayers during menstruation.

Prayer consists of thirteen separate movements, together with the repetition of the words that accompany each stage. The procedure was developed by Muhammad during his ministry and he usually led the prayers of the faithful in congregation himself. The words are preferably learned in the Arabic original, but certainly for new converts, the vernacular is acceptable for an initial period of time.

At the core of the prayer sequence is the physical act of islam, with seven points of the body resting on the floor: forehead, palms, knees and toes. There is no adequate word in English to describe the position, so this observer has taken *prosterner* from French and adapted to English to create the word 'prosternate'. This will serve to remind readers of the intricacies of the act, which differs entirely from 'prostration', the English word usually used, which means merely to lie flat on the ground.

1. At the start of each *rakʾa,* or cycle of prayer procedure, the believer stands with hands lifted to the height of the face and says the *Takbir.*

2. With hands crossed flat over the abdomen the *Fātiha* is recited, followed in some prayers but not others by other verses from the Qurʾān as may be appropriate for a personal circumstance.

3. Step one is then repeated as a prelude to the inclining of the body. The *Takbir* is repeated.

4. In the inclined position, the following formula is repeated three times: *Subhana rabbiaʾ l-ʿadhim* (Glory and praise be to the All-Powerful).

5. In preparation for the prosternation of the entire body, step one is repeated once again, accompanied by the following words: *Sami'a-l-lāhu li man hamidah* (God will listen to those who praise Him).

6. In the second stage of preparation for prosternation, the hands are left free, accompanied by the following words: *Rabbana wa laka-l-hamd* (All praise flows to God).

7. The third stage of preparation for prosternation, and immediately before kneeling, is to repeat the *Takbir* again.

8. Now the believer kneels then prosternates in *islam* (submission) before God. The floor is usually covered by a carpet or other material, consistent with the pre-prayer ablutions. During prosternation the following words are repeated three times: *Subhana rabbia 'l-a'la* (Praise and Glory be to God on High).

9. Returning to the kneeling position the believer repeats the *Takbir*, followed by *Subhana rabbia 'l-'adhim* (I ask for forgiveness O, God) three times.

10. The prosternation of step eight is then repeated a further three times together with the same words.

11. Returning to the standing position and the hands once again level with the face, the *Takbir* is repeated once again. At this point a second *rak'a* begins where required and varying with the prayer to be performed, which consists of the repetition of steps two to ten.

12. After the second prosternation of the last *rak'a*, instead of standing, the believer remains kneeling and repeats the words of the *Tashahhud* (a prayer formula from the Hadith).

13. The final step of the entire sequence is to take the sitting position, turning the head to the right with the words, *As-salamu 'alaykum wa rahmatu-l-lāh* (May the peace and forgiveness of God be upon you). Then to the left with the same invocation.

The number of *rakʿāt* (plural of *rakʿa*) to be performed varies with the time of day. The words to be repeated are spoken in an alternating audible and inaudible voice, which also follows a strict pattern.

At the end of each prayer sequence, the believer who has followed all the requirements precisely reaches a blessed moment, a possibly transformed state and may make *duʿāʾ*, or a supplication to God of a personal nature, accompanied by further prayer formulas. Traditionally, Muslims believe that God will always answer, so that whatever may befall the believer thereafter will be better than the worse fate that awaited had the intercession not been made. And here again the difference between Islam and Christianity is clear. Where a Christian's prayers are essentially personal from the outset, the consideration of oneself in Islam can only begin after the outward formula has been followed and an 'acceptable' prayer has been accomplished.

During times of communal calamity, an extra *rakʿa* may be said in supplication or *qunut*, asking for God's mercy, against flood, droughts or war, for example. 'May God destroy America', is a popular request.

The objective of the call of the muezzin is to gather men together at the mosque to pray together in congregation. Women do not usually attend the mosque, and prayers are in any event segregated to avoid distraction. Tradition emphasizes that women should pray at home, but there is no impediment to praying at the mosque, and this was the practice during the life of the Prophet.

Definite rules apply to the formation of congregations, covering such questions as who leads, or the length of the wait between the end of the call of the muezzin and the beginning of the prayers. But the underlying purpose of the congregation is to reinforce the sense of the Muslim community of the faithful as a cohesive self-aiding society.

Congregations are very orderly and the faithful entering the mosque in response to the *azān* quickly remove their shoes and arrange themselves into neat straight rows facing the *qibla*, or prayer niche, in the direction of Mecca. Men join shoulder to shoulder and foot to foot, hands are held to the side and eyes fixed on the place on the floor that the forehead will touch. According to a Hadith there are extra benefits to be gained from standing in the front row, to which 'Allah and his angels send down blessings'.

The atmosphere in a mosque during prayer is calm and pious and a conscious effort is made before the start to clear the mind of all thoughts other than the love of God. A leader is always chosen for prayers, a man of strong character and respected religious knowledge, usually but not necessarily the imam of the mosque. He stands at the front, his back to the ranks and his timing of the movements is to be followed precisely. If any member of the congregation makes a mistake in his prayers or is unsure, more experienced members have a duty to correct or instruct.

Salāt expresses some of the most important elements of the faith. Discipline imposed from the outside was entirely alien to the desertman and his pride in his independence was a vital part of his character. The straight rows of prayer and the act of islam, the most abject position of submission imaginable, are a powerful demonstration, therefore, of his obedience to the will of God. Similarly the brotherhood of Muslims as equals, no longer divided by tribe or race, is expressed in the solidity of the ranks and the unison performance.

This communal dimension to the efficacy of prayer in Islam is another deep distinction from Christianity, where the effort of the individual is of primary importance. Muslims are obligated to attend the mosque at least once a week and other prayers may be said alone, but all prayer is always more acceptable to God in community.

The *zuhr* prayers on Fridays at noon carry a particular importance, and in practice a Muslim who may miss congregation on other days will make a special effort to attend on Friday. This is the only prayer of the week that strictly speaking is required to be in community: a minimum number is needed to meet the definition of a congregation, the figure varying from five to forty depending on the interpretation followed. The Qur'ān established Friday as the Muslim holy day, which distinguishes Islam from Judaism (Saturday) and Christianity (Sunday). But the day is not exactly comparable with the biblical 'day of rest', since the faithful are enjoined by the Qur'ān when prayers are over to 'disperse through the land and seek the Bounty of Allah' (*Al-Jumu'ah* (Friday) Surah 62 verse 10), in effect, to return to business.

Prayers on Fridays are heavily attended and on this occasion the *rak'āt* are preceded by a sermon or *khutba* lasting for about thirty minutes. This is a stern, almost liturgical address by the imam of the mosque, usually based on a verse of the Qur'ān, but which may extend to issues of concern to the particular congregation. In the Friday *khutba*, religion and politics often mix or conflict, for example when an imam instructs the faithful how to vote, or gives an opinion on whether to accept or reject the current temporal power. Frequently, one mosque will promote a more political agenda than the majority, leading to political activism based on that institution fuelled by radical religious interpretation. In many Muslim countries, however, the difficult border between religion and politics is carefully controlled by the government.

With the Friday *khutba*, the distortions of the daily amplified *azān* are brought to an apocalypse as each imam bellows his sermon through the amplification system used for the call to prayer, trying to have his voice heard over the exhortations of the next mosque which may be less than a hundred metres away. In Islamic Cairo, for example, between noon and half past the hour on a Friday, the city almost comes to a complete halt while hundreds of mosques overflow with rows of the faithful out into the street. The air becomes one reverberating shimmer of competing declamations as over 400 mosques launch into their *khutbas* simultaneously.

Apart from the personal spiritual experience, the defining characteristic of prayer in congregation is equality: from the prosternation of rich and poor side by side, right down to the last words, '*May the peace and forgiveness of God be upon you*', a greeting that recognizes no rank and no hierarchy. Muslim prayers are a levelling experience, shoulder to shoulder without class or category. With the personal liberty and dignity of the desertman as the sociological bedrock of his belief, each Muslim confronts his God, not through another divinity, not through any priest or magisterium, but in a direct and individual way that goes beyond even the purity of Calvinism.

Since man cannot act other than through God's will, the name of God is often on a Muslim's lips as a form of continuing prayer. Some of the more common Arabic expressions giving effect to this all-pervading belief are given as Appendix 3 to this chapter. Another form of frequent prayer outside the set procedure of the *rak' a* is the saying of the *tasbih*, or Muslim rosary, that will often be seen in a Muslim's hands. The chaplet usually consists of thirty-three beads, which are passed around through the fingers three times in succession during mediation. The longer version of the chaplet consisting of ninety-nine beads is less common. Simultaneously with the fingering of the beads, one of two prayer formulas is repeated. Either the Ninety-Nine Beautiful Names of God can be said (given in full at the end of this chapter as Appendix 4), or the following formulas thirty-three times each:

> *Subhān' allāh.* (Glory be to God.)
> *Al-Hamdu lillāh.* (Praise be to God.)
> *Allāhu akbar.* (God is the Greatest.)

The three joints of the fingers of one hand, counted by the thumb, are often used in place of a chaplet where the *tasbih* is said after formal prayers.

Zakāt: Poor-tax

The Third Pillar is prescribed alms or a poor-tax, by which the believer gives back to Allah a portion of the bounty He has conferred. The practice started during Muhammad's Meccan period as voluntary charity, but after the hijrah the position of the Emigrants in Medinan society was so precarious that what was previously an act of piety became a form of tithe. Then, as other tribes joined the faith, *zakāt* was expected as a fundamental obligation. Once Islam moved toward codified rules and the giving of alms was recognized as one of the Five Pillars, the payment of the poor-tax became a stepping-stone to righteousness and the character of the act changed.

Zakāt is primarily an act of purification through the self-mortification of parting with something that the believer wishes to keep for himself. But in a wider sense the act also purifies the remaining wealth of the donor, while at the same time the guilt associated with possessions in societies of great diversity of circumstances is relieved. Behind that again lies the concept that *zakāt* makes the poor less envious of the rich, for the richer the rich become, the greater the alms that are due. The poor are also relieved of the humiliation of taking charity by the belief that the rich in fact give to Allah Himself, who then hands over the donation to the poor. To give is better than to receive, therefore, the upper hand is better than the lower, and in this way the receiver performs a valuable service to the giver. Then again, what is poverty? Merely the absence of wealth, which can be made up by righteousness in the present, and for which the believer will be rewarded in the next eternal world.

The rules for who can receive *zakāt* and the amount of the levy were developed while Islam was still a desert religion. Although the needy were always the principal beneficiaries, *zakāt* was also used to benefit slaves attempting to purchase their freedom, or to provide a fund for hostile tribes that needed to be bought off. The tithe was based on agrarian and nomadic revenues and was usually paid in kind. Today *zakāt* is often collected through the mosque for community work if not donated privately and amounts to approximately 2.5 per cent, and up to 10 per cent, of the donor's after-tax income, depending on the type of donation. Close friends or acquaintances in difficulty are eligible as are many formal Islamic charities. Some members of the donor's family are also eligible (uncles, aunts, cousins and nephews) but others are not (fathers, mothers, children and grandfathers).

Zakāt can be criticized in modern terms as regressive, since an equal percentage applies to the rich and the less rich alike. Or the levy can be seen as the means by which the rich can purchase *laisser-faire* at the expense of the rest of society. But *zakāt* has always been payable in addition to all other state taxes, which are usually progressive, and the obligation is spiritual, not fiscal. In some Muslim countries such as Saudi Arabia and Malaysia, *zakāt* is now administered by the government.

Zakāt also collides with the modern Western world in the attempts by the United States and allied governments to close down the funding of Islamist organizations potentially involved in hostilities against Israel or the West. Many organizations such as the Palestinian Hamas and Lebanese Hizbullah, as well as engaging in armed resistance, operate substantial social projects, among the poor of Gaza and Beirut, and raise significant sums for these purposes through *zakāt* donations. Attempts at regulation of the 'divinely ordained' obligation of one of the Five Pillars, or the freezing of assets derived from *zakāt*, by or on behalf of a non-Muslim power, will require care in order to avoid creating a great deal of resentment with little achieved.

Sawm: The Fast

The annual fast takes place during the lunar month of Ramadan, the holiest month in the Islamic calendar. During Ramadan, Muslims say, the gates of hell are closed and the gates of heaven are open. This is the month during which Muhammad received his first revelation and the occasion is celebrated during the fast as *Lailat al-Qadr*, or the Night of Power, on the twenty-sixth of the month, the most solemn festival of Islam.

The objective of the fast is to diminish the believer's love for the world and reduce his or her dependence on material things. This underlying message of withdrawal from the world of the flesh in preparation for death is also echoed in various stages of the Pilgrimage. In fact, Ramadan is a favourite time of year for most Muslims when the twenty-nine days of the month become a nightly round of celebrations and family visits, starting with *iftar*, the traditional evening meal that breaks the fast, followed before dawn with *sohour*, the meal that precedes the resumption of the fast at daybreak. In modern Muslim cities the hours of effective work decrease during the month as many people are up for most of the night, and the consumption of groceries and restaurant meals actually increases. And, just like the annual protests against the secularization of Christ's birthday, Muslim clerics can be heard railing in the background during Ramadan against the commercialization of self-denial.

Charitable donations are also given at the end of Ramadan, in addition to the obligation of *zakāt*, when every Muslim who can has a duty to help the poor. Many wealthy individuals set up dining tables in the street every night of the month, to feed those with no other means. Fasting further serves to remind the well-fed of the suffering of the needy, and to create a place for them in more affluent hearts.

The rules of the fast are simple. The duration is from dawn to dusk, which is from after the *subh* prayer to the moment the muezzin calls the *maghreb* prayer. In some larger Muslim communities other means are used to signal the start and end of the fast, the

Ramadan Cannon in Cairo, for example, or street criers. During the prescribed period of daylight, nothing may pass the lips: no food, no water, no cigarette smoke, nothing whatsoever. Sexual intercourse is also prohibited during daylight hours, but a married couple holding hands is acceptable in most Muslim societies, even in public. There are exemptions from fasting during sickness or pregnancy and women do not fast during menstruation, although the missed days must be made up before the following Ramadan.

But beyond the physical deprivation, the emphasis is on spiritual enrichment. A devout Muslim will say that he or she fasts 'not with the stomach, but with the heart'.

Fasting in Islam began in 2 AH, then developed further with the adoption by Muhammad of the Jewish fast of *'Āshurā* or Day of Atonement. Then, after the break with Judaism, when Muhammad failed to win recognition as a universal prophet, the month of Ramadan was substituted:

> O ye who believe,
> Fasting is prescribed for you
> As it was prescribed
> To those before you
> That ye may learn
> Self-restraint.

Al-Baqarah (The Heifer) Surah 2, verse 183

The words, 'To those before you', probably refer to the Eastern Christians who fasted for thirty-six days each year during Lent. There was no tradition of fasting in the Arab *Jāhiliyyah*.

Ramadan starts with the new moon at the end of the previous calendar month of Sha'bān. Although modern techniques could be used to predict the precise time for the start of the month, the traditional method is preferred: if the new moon is seen on the 29th day of Sha'bān, then Ramadan starts the next day, if not, then Sha'bān will last thirty days and Ramadan will start the day after. This can lead to different readings in different countries, resulting in Ramadan starting and ending a day earlier in cloudless Saudi Arabia, for example, than in soggy Britain.

Haj: The Pilgrimage

The pilgrimage to Mecca is the Fifth Pillar, a once-in-a-lifetime obligation for every able-bodied Muslim, both men and women, with the means to make the journey. In the haj, all the elements of Islam come together during eight days or longer of intense observance and prayer.

To summarize the importance of Mecca, the city is taken by some Muslims to be the mythical site where Adam and Eve found each other after their expulsion from the Garden of Eden. According to this legend, Adam built the first Ka'bah in the barren hills of the Hijaz on the instructions of God, as a house of worship and rest after a century of redemptive labour for his sin of pride. The structure was later swept away in the Flood. More importantly, Mecca is where Abraham offered his son as sacrifice following God's instructions. To thank God for His mercy after the angel Gabriel's intervention with the ram, Abraham built, or rebuilt, the Ka'bah, inserting a meteorite into the north-west corner of the building which is now venerated as the Black Stone. All the elements of the present-day ritual were determined by Abraham during that first pilgrimage and were performed in the presence of Gabriel. And here the legend of Abraham gives way to the words of the Qur'ān, which for a Muslim is fact:

> And remember Abraham
> And 'Ismā'il raised
> The foundations of the House
> With this prayer: 'O Lord!
> Accept this service from us:
> For Thou art the All-Hearing.
> The All Knowing.
> O Lord! Make of us
> Muslims, bowing to Thy Will.
> And of our progeny a people
> Muslim, bowing to Thy will:
> And show us our places of due rites
> And turn unto us in Mercy
> For Thou are the Oft-Returning.
> Most Merciful.'

Al-Baqarah (The Heifer) Surah 2, verses 127–8

Then two or three thousand legendary years later Mecca was the birthplace of the Prophet who cleansed the Ka'bah of idolatry upon the opening of the city when the monotheism of Abraham was reinstated. The pilgrimage represents not only a return to man's physical and religious origins, therefore, but also a recapitulation of the spiritual journey of man on earth. Just as the holy journey of the pilgrim on the haj leads to the presence of the Sacred, facing the Ka'bah, so man's life leads to death and to a corresponding encounter with the Divine. Thus for Muslims, the simple oblong stone structure, hung with a black silk covering, embroidered with verses from the Qur'ān and changed annually, has become the primordial Temple, the House of God.

In Mecca and then Medina the religion of the One was perfected by the revelation of the Qur'ān. The two cities are therefore the symbol of the entire prophetic cycle from Adam to Abraham to Muhammad.

While making their pilgrimage to Mecca, Muslims also visit the sacred places of Islam, first and foremost the Ka'bah itself, the spiritual centre to which they have turned in prayer every day of their lives. Then the cave of Hira, outside Mecca, where Muhammad first received his Message, the battle sites of Badr and Uhud where Muhammad defended his faithful from their enemies, his place of birth, also in Mecca, and in Medina the first mosque, built with the Prophet's own hands (still standing but vastly overlaid and increased in size over the centuries) and containing the Prophet's tomb. Muslims report that the two cities are permeated with a mystic *baraka*, an atmosphere of grace, similar to the feelings of a Christian visiting Assisi or Lourdes for example, or the Western Wall of the Temple for a Jew. For this reason the cities are known as Mecca the Most Honoured and Medina the Radiant.

Just as prayer is the outward manifestation of the believer's faith, so the pilgrimage to the centre and origin is an outward exertion in the path of God, or jihad, a concept that will be considered in a subsequent chapter. The haj renders physical and visible the invisible line that joins every corner of the world to the Ka'bah, which in another popular legend lies directly on the vertical axis under the Throne of God.

In addition to recapitulating both the spiritual life of man as a whole and of the believer in particular, the pilgrimage also improves the believer's life by preparing him or her for death. He or she stands before the Creator metaphorically naked in simple garments and accepts his or her mortal condition. For this reason the simple clothes worn during the haj are often washed in water from the holy well of Zamzam and retained for use as a burial shroud.

Each year almost two million Muslims make the pilgrimage, from every corner, race, culture and language of the world, from the mountains of Java to the deserts of Mauritania. And here the simple pilgrimage vestments and the dense throng of bodies serve to eradicate differences between the faithful, emphasizing brotherhood and sisterhood in Islam across all boundaries. In the pilgrim camps ideas and experiences from around the world are shared.

By the *tawāf*, the circumambulation of the Ka'bah, man follows the direct orders of God and his Prophets, Abraham and Muhammad, physically expressing submission to His will. The heart is emptied of evil, just as the Prophet emptied the Ka'bah of idols and the believer attempts to be sufficiently worthy to receive the Divine Presence.

> Such is the Pilgrimage:
> Whoever honours the sacred
> Rites of Allah, for him
> It is good in the sight
> Of the Lord.
>
> *Al-Hajj* (The Pilgrimage) Surah 22, verse 30

The pilgrimage is also an organizational task of immense proportions, starting at Jiddah airport, which welcomes over a million pilgrims in a matter of days as the rituals begin, while a further million or more arrive overland or by sea. In addition to immigration formalities, the organizers provide the pilgrims with ablutions, clothes and food. Then, for the next eight days, the organizers supply camps, transport, toilets, security, medical facilities, water, cooling, shade and communications. The haj takes place during the lunar month of Dhu'l-Hajja, which rotates with the Muslim calendar. When the pilgrimage falls during August, the organizers take on responsibility for the very survival of weaker pilgrims.

Since the discovery of oil in Saudi Arabia, billions have been spent on both pilgrimage facilities and on the massive rebuilding and extension of the mosques of Mecca and Medina (for which the principal contractor was the Binladen Group), using the very best materials from around the world. Unfortunately this same affluence has led to the vulgar commercialization of the two cities, with high-rises, shopping centres and neon signs crowding against the holy sites, and land values well in excess of London or New York.

The holy cities are never without pilgrims. The lesser pilgrimage of *al-ʿumrah* is performed year round, ensuring, as the Prophet ordered, that the Great Mosque at Mecca is never empty. In modern times, with the tremendous growth of Islam, there is a constant throng around the Ka'bah day and night, without interruption.

The haj consists of six stages:

1. Before his or her arrival at the boundaries of *al-haram*, the holy precinct of Mecca, the pilgrim performs a complete ritual ablution to wash away the impurities of the world. Then worldly clothes and jewellery are removed, replaced by two pieces of seamless white cloth worn around the waist and over the shoulders, with plain leather sandals. Women keep their own clothes provided they are simple and cover the body except for hands and face. From now on the pilgrim is in a consecrated state known as *ihrām* and must put away all evil thoughts, free from the cares of the world and from sexual passion. The simplicity and colour of the garments signify a death to the outside world and nakedness before God.

2. Upon entering Mecca the pilgrim makes *tawāf* or seven circum-ambulations of the Ka'bah and attempts to kiss the Black Stone, from which he or she may be separated by a dense fast-moving crowd. The circulation is counter-clockwise to symbolize the unwinding of the fall of man as well as the accumulated sins of the individual. The pilgrim may pray during the walk, or cry out, *lab-bayka allāhumma labbayk*, 'at Thy service, O Lord, at Thy service'.

3. The *saʿy* is the rapid walk following a set route (now within the Great Mosque itself and air-conditioned) to celebrate the desperate search by Hājar (Abraham's Canaanite wife, abandoned on the orders of Allah) for water for her son Ishmael up and down the bare

mountains of the Hijaz. The spring of Zamzam, which traditionally sprang from under the boy's heels as he beat the ground in frustration, lies beneath the mosque and water from the source is often taken home by pilgrims as a blessing for their families.

4. On the ninth day of the month, the pilgrims assemble together for the Standing, in a vast congregation on the plain of Arafāt where the deepest prayers of the pilgrimage are said and the climax of the ritual is reached. This event, lasting from noon until dusk, takes place on the ground where, in popular myth, all mankind will stand before God on the Day of Judgement or *Mahshar*. On this Last Day, the believer will face God's judgement without worldly rank or belongings, his or her only possession being the record of his or her actions as a mortal. The experience of the Standing is the believer's preparation for the day when he or she will meet the Creator in a physical sense. The site of the Standing is also important as the place where the Prophet's farewell sermon was delivered, inviting all men to peace and brotherhood. An account of Muhammad's last address is to be found as Appendix 5 to this chapter.

5. At Mina, where the Prophet uttered his last words in public during his final pilgrimage, the pilgrim throws pebbles against stone pillars representing *Shaytān*. This is an external remembrance of Abraham's escape from the devil and a representation of the believer's lifelong inner battle against sin, an unforgettable experience for a believer and a powerful weapon in the future trials of life.

6. Finally, there is the sacrifice of an animal, repeating the sacrifice of the ram by Abraham – but this is now satisfied by a donation for food for the poor. This rite coincides with Eid al-Adha throughout the Islamic world, the Feast of the Sacrifice, associated through the haj with the Day of Resurrection and with the incarnate state of the pilgrim at the end of his or her observances, as the purified servant of God.

Muslims draw great strength from the pilgrimage. Setting eyes on the Ka'bah is next only to facing God Himself, while leaving for Mecca and saying goodbye to friends and family is a foretaste of death. Standing on the plain of Arafāt is a physical reminder of the

Relief plan of the Haj route

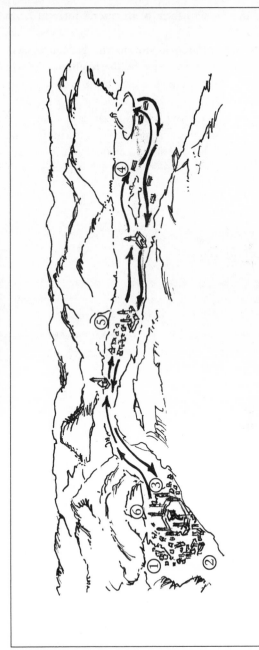

1 Ablutions completed before entering Mecca
2 *Tawāf*
3 *Sa'y*
4 The Standing on the plain of Arafāt, facing the Mount of Mercy
5 Mina, the stoning of the pillar
6 Donation in lieu of Sacrifice

Last Day, and is the physical form of the moral force of Islam for good in the world.

The haj ends with a farewell visit to the Ka'bah to seal the remembrance of the Centre, preceded by the ceremonial shaving of heads and paring of nails, with the proceeds buried at Mina. The pilgrim should now be addressed as *haj*, or *hajah* for women, and if the haj has been performed solely to please God rather than for personal vanity, his or her sins have been forgiven. On returning home the pilgrim is visited by friends and relations anxious to experience even indirectly, something of the *baraka* (or special atmosphere) of the holy cities.

The Perils of the Pilgrimage

The Al-Saud family, rulers of Saudi Arabia, founded their kingdom on assassination and bloody desert conquest, all in the name of God. But today Saudi Arabia is super-affluent and superficially peaceful, although in the awkward position of being both a vital ally of the United States as well as the leading influence in the Muslim world. The Saudi kings are the Guardians of the Two Holy Shrines as well as major patrons of many Islamic causes worldwide. For this reason the Saudis come under constant attack from elements within Islam, especially from Shi'a, who famously combine religious fervour with political action, and the haj is where the mixture becomes combustible. 'Revive the great divine political tradition of haj,' the Ayatollah Khomeini declared. 'Inform the pilgrims of their great duties to confront the aggressors and international plunderers,' referring to the United States and to Saudi Arabia as the American client state.

Demonstrations during the haj in recent years have frequently turned violent. Control of the holy city of Mecca by the al-Saud family was first challenged in 1979 by a group of radical Saudis from the clandestine religious-political opposition, one of whom claimed to be the Mahdi or 'Expected One'. The group of neo-Ikhwan, or 'brothers', took possession of the Grand Mosque and denounced al-Saud rule through the speakers on the minarets of the mosque, ironically echoing the politico-religious zeal on which al-Saud rule had been founded. After two weeks of fighting, with a substantial number of Saudi servicemen killed or wounded, the attackers were contained in the cellars of the mosque and the demonstration was finally subdued. Of those captured, sixty-three were publicly beheaded, some in each of the principal cities of the kingdom. Reputedly the (non-Muslim) French CRS police force was called in when Saudi forces were unable to capture the last of the militants. The lower levels of the mosque where the they were hiding were flooded and the water was then electrified. 'They floated out like kippers,' a witness reported.

In 1981 and 1982 pilgrims again disturbed the haj, beginning with the unfurling of banners from the walls of the mosque reading 'DEATH TO THE USA' and 'DEATH TO ISRAEL'. In 1987 and 1988 over 400 pilgrims were killed during Saudi suppression of demonstrations and 16 of the leaders, mostly Iranian, were also publicly beheaded.

Accidents also claim lives during the pilgrimage. In 1990 more than 1,400 were crushed to death by the collapse of a bridge and 270 were killed by a falling overhead walkway in 1994. In 1997, 300 pilgrims were killed and 1,500 injured when fire swept through the tent cities at Mina. Outrage followed the Saudi attempt to explain these events as 'God's unavoidable will'. The double-decked structure where the stoning of *Shaytān* takes place is especially dangerous, with the huge crowd often in a perturbed state after the emotional hours of the Standing. In 2001, for example, 35 pilgrims were crushed to death in a stampede before control could be re-established.

IV   The Commandments of Islam

The Commandments in the Qur'ān are not clearly numbered or as famously emphasized as the Ten Commandments in the Torah, and subsequently in Christianity. Twelve commandments do appear, however, in Surah 17 *Al-Isrā* (The Night Journey) at verses 22–38, quoted or excerpted below on the left, and make an interesting comparison with the well-known ten of Judaism, given on the right.

A further list of commandments appears in Surah 6, *Al-An'ām* (The Cattle) starting at verse 151. Here ten only are given, with 3, 4, 6, 9, 11 and 12 missing from the commandments of Surah 17, and four substituted: to observe justice, to fulfil the Covenant of

God, to follow no other paths, and to come not near to pollutions, outward or inward. In practice, however, the two lists overlap and the longer is the more specific and interesting, although the commandment to avoid pollutions in Surah 6 at verse 151 has been interpreted to give the Qur'ān modern relevance.

The Qur'ān

1. Thy Lord hath decreed that ye worship none but him.

2. Be kind to parents. If one or both attain old age in your dwelling, show them no sign of impatience, nor rebuke them, but speak to them kind words. Treat them with humility and tenderness and say: 'Lord be merciful to them. They nursed me when I was an infant'.

3. Render to the kindred their due rights, as also to those in want, and to the wayfarer.

4. Make not thy hand tied like a niggard's to thy neck, but squander not your wealth in the manner of the spendthrift.

5. Kill not your children for fear of want.

The Torah

1. Thou shalt have no other gods before me.

2. Thou shalt not make unto thee any graven images or any likeness of anything that is in heaven above or that is in the earth beneath.

5. Honour thy father and thy mother, that thy days may be long upon the land which the Lord thy God giveth thee.

No equivalent.

No equivalent.

No equivalent.

The Qur'ān contd.

6. Nor come nigh to unlawful sex, for it is a shameful deed, and an evil opening of the road.

7. Nor take life, which Allah had made sacred – except for just cause.

8. Do not interfere with the property of orphans, except with the best of motives, until they reach maturity.

9. Fulfil every engagement, for every engagement will be enquired into on the Day of Reckoning.

10. Give full measure when ye measure, and weigh with even scales.

11. Pursue not that of which thou hast no knowledge.

12. Nor walk the earth with insolence, for thou canst not cleave the earth, nor reach the mountains in height.

No equivalent.

Equivalent Day of Assembly on Friday prescribed in Surah 62, *Al-Jumu'ah* (Friday) at verse 9.

Covered generally by commandments 8, 9 and 10.

No equivalent.

No equivalent.

The Torah contd.

7. Thou shalt not commit adultery.

6. Thou shalt not kill.

8. Thou shalt not steal.

No equivalent.

No equivalent.

3. Thou shalt not take the name of the Lord thy God in vain.

4. Remember the Sabbath to keep the day holy.

8. Thou shalt not steal.

9. Thou shalt not bear false witness against your neighbour.

10. Thou shalt not covet thy neighbour's house.

The first and most obvious conclusion to be drawn from the comparison is that where an equivalent injunction is missing from either the Judeo-Christian list or the Muslim list, this does not mean that Islam permits the bearing of false witness, for example, or that Judaism and Christianity condone pride, or the killing of children. These matters are dealt with elsewhere in general form in the scriptures and traditions of the respective faiths. There are, for example, several verses in the Qur'ān condemning false witness, and theft is subject to the well-known fixed punishment of amputation.

Less self-evident is what lies behind both the differences and the similarities.

The first Qur'ānic commandment confirms Islam's place as the third of the world's three monotheistic religions, claiming heritage, as we have seen, from Abraham, Moses and Adam, although in the Muslim view Islam finalizes and perfects what went before. The self-helping nature of Muslim society is confirmed by the second commandment, and this is then extended by the third commandment to the *'ummah* of all Muslims, and, ideally, to all of mankind beyond. Commandment four refers to the frequent Arab practice of families ruining themselves to provide sumptuous weddings or funerals regardless of the financial consequences in the future. Commandment five ends the *Jāhiliyyah* practice of female infanticide, a daughter being of no value in a society that was perpetually at war. The extremely conservative sexual code in Muslim society begins with commandment six, with no distinction made between fornication and adultery. Commandment seven, not to take life without just cause is the practical version of the Judeo-Christian sixth commandment, not to kill, whose absolute nature is, of course, constantly breached by so-called Christian societies that go to war or inflict capital punishment. In commandments eight, nine and ten can clearly be seen Muhammad's origins as an orphan and a trader. Commandments eleven and twelve combine a warning against pride, man's original sin, and an injunction against futility, the waste of the believer's God-given talents.

At the Heart of Faith

In 2001 Pope John Paul II set foot in a mosque, the Umayyad Great Mosque in Damascus, where St John the Baptist is buried (his head, his body, or both, depending on which legend is followed). This was the first such event in the history of Christianity and could be interpreted as conferring 'holy' status on the building, since according to the Vatican, the Pope only visits 'sacred places'. But will the chasm of dogma ever close between a devout monotheistic Christian and a devout monotheistic Muslim? What are the specific beliefs that separate the two?

● The first difficulty must be the central Muslim belief that the Qur'ān is the Word of God. The work may be accepted as 'true' in a historical sense, or 'inspired', or studying the Qur'ān may open the Western reader to a greater understanding of Muslims. But embracing the belief that God actively intervened in the life of mankind through the agency of Gabriel to reveal the specific text of the Qur'ān to Muhammad, in the Hijaz, in Arabic, probably represents a high barrier.

● Many Christians believe in saints on a sentimental level, but would have difficulty in accepting the Muslim dogma of angels and jinns as God-created creatures with parallel but unseen physical lives, based on the frequent references to this other world in the Qur'ān. Similarly with belief in a living *Shaytān*, or a three-dimensional Heaven, a perpetually burning Hell, or a crowded Last Day. The Judeo-Christian equivalents have become widely accepted as metaphors for those questions which humans cannot answer, and the texts are no longer taken to be the literal truth.

● The Will of Allah may be the most difficult of all. The Qur'ān says in Surah 81, *Al-Takwir* (The Folding Up) at verse 29:6 'but ye shall not will except as Allah wills – the Cherisher of the Worlds', and in Surah 87 *Al-A'lā* (The Most High) at verse 2:6 'God hath created and balanced all things, and hath fixed their destinies and guided them'. The Sunna goes so far as to say that certain people were created 'for Hell' and others 'for Paradise'. Belief in a specific formula for predestination is not, however, a core requirement for faith since Islam has no satisfactory answer to the contradiction between an omnipotent God who controls all destiny, and man's responsibility for his own actions. Both points of view are postulated together in the text without resolution. But can any of the monotheistic religions provide an answer? This impasse has contributed to the decline of Christianity in the West and to the rise of economics, materialism and humanitarianism in place of faith as the potential (but as yet unrealized) remedies for the problems of the world. Muslims take the opposite view, saying that they rely on Allah, Most Gracious, Most Merciful, not on the uncertain works of mere men, and that God is not subject to human logic. However, the Hadith, 'first tie up your camel, then trust in God', seems to show that the Prophet himself was perplexed by the problem of predestination.

● The image of a new-born baby already stained by sin is a harsh Christian doctrine. But without original sin the concept of man's redemption by the death of Christ would not have been necessary, and the meaning of the Christian narrative would disappear. The Muslim, with the authority of the Qur'ān ringing in his ears, prosternates himself before the unknowable Ultimate Truth, relying on the lofty concept of God's justice for his forgiveness and salvation. The Christian confides in a personal Redeemer with a human face, who knows and loves him or her as an individual, but yet as a sinner. Thus both Muslim and Christian are offered access to salvation, only the routes differ: the Muslim through a holy book alleged to be the Word of God, the Christian through a legend of Crucifixion and Resurrection.

● Creationism is still part of Muslim belief, although not in the sense of an obligatory dogma. But according to the polls the same affliction also applies to a majority of Americans. In Europe, however, evolution is generally accepted as a scientific fact, similar to the earth's orbit around the sun, or the existence of the force of gravity, even though few individuals possess the knowledge to prove these postulations for themselves. Nor do these scientific facts necessarily preclude belief in God. What happened 'before the beginning' is equally as unanswerable today as at any time in history. Darwin himself, at the end of his life, hovered between agnosticism and atheism, considering the existence of God to be beyond anyone's understanding. Islam may even go so far as to accept that nature has evolved from a primordial slime on a cooling planet to produce the present environment, but in the words of the Qur'ān, God created Adam 'from sounding clay, from mud moulded into shape' (Al Hijr (The Rock) Surah 15, verse 33). Man, therefore, is different from all other living things, and man's creation was i'jāz, by a process 'known only to God'. The scientific information available about the origins of Homo sapiens is considered by Muslims to be too slight (despite the recent completion of the human genome sequence, clearly linking man to the animal world) to reduce the words of the Qur'ān to metaphor. Or, in agreement with Cardinal Schönborn of the Vatican Congregation for Catholic Education (and a close adviser to Pope Benedict XVI), Muslims argue that evolution is too blind an instrument to have forged by way of an entirely random natural selection process such a complexity as human consciousness. Higher forces, or an 'Intelligent Designer', must be at work beyond what can be demonstrated by bare science (even though many American states are under pressure to teach ID as an 'alternate science'). Possibly this doubt about evolution may decrease among Muslims with time and with the acceptance of scientific fact. The basis certainly exists in the Qur'ān for such an advance.

> Do not the Unbelievers see
> That the heavens and the earth
> Were joined together as one
> Unit of Creation, before
> We clove them asunder?
> We made from water
> Every living thing. Will they
> Not then believe?
>   Al-Anbiyā (The Prophets) Surah 21, verse 30

So are these really the differences that launched a thousand conflicts? Or should we look inwards for the reasons for the hundreds of years of confrontation between Christianity and Islam: to our own imperialist history, to colonialism and to failed politics, the subject of the next chapters?

Appendix I

Examples of Secure Hadiths from al-Bukhari and Muslim

We are informed by Abd-us-Salam b. Mutahhar, who had it from 'Umar b. 'Aly, through M'an b. Muhammad al-Ghifari, through Sa'id b. Abu Sa'id al-Maqburi, through Abu Hurairah, from the Prophet (Allah bless him and give him peace), who said:

Truly Islam is a religion whose burden is light, for no one can be too rigorous in the practice of it, without being overcome by it. Therefore be ye upright and moderate, and hope for your reward. Call to your aid the early morning and the evening prayers, also the prayers in the night. (Al-Bukhari, chapter on al-Imān)

We are informed by Ahmad b. Muhammad al-Makki, who had it from 'Amr b. Yahya b. 'Amr al-Makki, through his grandfather, through Abu Hurairah, who said:

I once followed the Prophet (Allah bless him and give him peace) when he went out to relive his necessity. He went on without looking around. When I approached him he said: 'Fetch me some stones, for my absternation' (or some words to that effect) but do not bring me any bones or animal dung. I therefore brought him some stones in the fold of my gown and placing them beside him, then I left him. When he had finished, he made use of the stones. (Al-Bukhari, chapter on ablution)

It is narrated on the authority of Abu-Huraira that the Messenger of Allah said to his uncle at the time of his death: Make a profession that there is no god but Allah and I will bear testimony of you being a Muslim on the Day of Judgement. But Abu-Tālib refused to do so. Then Allah revealed this verse:

> Verily thou canst not guide to the right path whom thou
> lovest. And it is Allah Who guideth whom He will, and He
> knoweth best who are the guided.
>
> *Al-Qasas* (The Narrations) Surah 28, verse 56)
> (Muslim, chapter of al-Iman)

Appendix 2

Surah 1, *Al-Fātiha* (The Opening)

1.
بِسْمِ اللّهِ الرَّحْمَنِ الرَّحِيمِ

Bismi-l-Lahir-Rahmāni-r-Rahim
In the name of Allah, Most Gracious, Most Merciful.

2.
الْحَمْدُ للّهِ رَبِّ الْعَالَمِينَ

Al-hamdu li'Llahi Rabbi-l-'alamin-
Praise be to Allah, the Cherisher and Sustainer of the Worlds;

3.
الرَّحْمَنِ الرَّحِيمِ

Ar-Rahmāni-r-Rahim
Most Glorious, Most Merciful;

4.
مَالِكِ يَوْمِ الدِّينِ

MālikiYawmi-d-Din
Master of the Day of Judgement.

5.
إِيَّاكَ نَعْبُدُ وإِيَّاكَ نَسْتَعِينُ

'Lyyākā na'budu wa 'lyyaka nasta'in
Thee do we worship and Thine aid do we seek.

6.
اهدِنَــا الصِّرَاطَ الْمُسْتَقِيمَ

Ihdinā-s-Sirāta-l-Mustaquim
Show us the right way,

7.
صِرَاطَ الَّذِينَ أنعَمتَ عَلَيهِمْ غَيرِ المَغْضُوبِ عَلَيهِمْ وَلاَ الضَّالِّينَ

Sirata'lladhina an'amta 'alihim ghairi'lmaghdubi 'alaihim wala'
ddallin
The way of those on whom
Thou hast bestowed Thy Grace,
Those whose (portion)
Is not wrath,
And who go not astray

Amin
Amen

Appendix 3

Common Arabic Expressions Invoking the Name of God

A'udhu billāhi min al-Shaytān al-rajim
May God protect me against Satan, he who should be
stoned.

This expression is used to ward off anger, the urge to violence, or any
temptation that should be resisted. The image is of the devil taking
hold of the believer from within, and the believer calling on God for
assistance.

Lā hawla walā quwwata illā billāh
There is no power but that of Allah

This phrase serves as an exclamation at the arrival of the unforeseen,
and to defeat feelings of frustration. Or the words can be used to mean
'I am unable to help you', or 'everyone is powerless in the face of God's
destiny', the equivalent of 'tough luck'.

Al-hamdu lillāh
Thanks be to God

Usually used in reply to the question 'how are you?' The response indi-
cates both that the speaker is well and that this is due to God's bounty
alone. The phrase also serves as the equivalent of Christian 'grace'
before meals, or in similar circumstances of receiving.

Inshah'allāh
As God wills

The most common Arabic expression of all and connected to the irresolvable debate about predestination, free will and the will of God, dealt
with earlier in this chapter. The words usually accompany an expressed
intention, to travel, for example, to see a friend again on parting, or to
invoke God's blessing on any future undertaking. The expression finds
direct authority in the Qur'ān in Surah 18, *Al-Kahf* (The Cave), verses
23 and 24:

Nor say of anything
'I shall be sure to do
So and so tomorrow' –
Without adding, 'So please Allah'.

Bismillāh
In the name of God

This is the short version of *Bi-smi Llāhi arRrahmāni ar-Rāhim*, the *Tasmiyah*, which has been examined earlier in this chapter in the context of the form of the Qur'ān. These words, spoken before an action, give effect to a Hadith, that only an act done in the name of God has any validity. The expression has a universal application as a preamble, from saying prayers to making love (but only to one's wife or husband, of course).

Tawakkaltu ala-Allāh
In God we trust

This expression is similar to the preceding words, but applies more to a situation where a decision has been taken to proceed, on a journey, for example, or with a project, and the speaker seeks God's blessing. These expressions are heartfelt among Muslims and far from the routine blasphemies so common in the West. A Western traveller in a Muslim country (even non-Arabic speaking) would be surprised at the warm reception he or she receives in response to the use of one or more these terms, even mixed in with English.

Appendix 4

The Ninety-nine Beautiful Names of Allah

Allāh		*Al-Bāhith*	The Raiser from Death
Ar-Rahmān	The Merciful	*Ash-Shahīd*	The Witness
Ar-Rahim	The Compassionate	*Al-Haq*	The Truth
Al-Mālik	The King of Kings	*Al-Wāhil*	The Guardian
Al-Quddūs	The Holy One	*Al-Kawi*	The Almighty
As-Salam	The Peace	*Al-Mateen*	The Firm
Al-Maumin	The Faithful	*Al-Walī*	The Nearest Friend
Al-Muʾmin	The Faithful	*Al-Hamīd*	The All-Praiseworthy
Al-Adhim	The Mighty	*Al-Mūhsi*	The Accountant
Al-Jabbār	The All-Compelling	*Al-Mubdī*	The Beginner
Al-Mutakabbir	The Majestic	*Al-Muʾhid*	The Restorer
Al-Khalik	The Creator	*Al-Moʾhyī*	The Quickener
Al-Bari	The Artificer	*Al-Mumīt*	The Slayer
Al-Musawwir	The Fashioner	*Al-Haiy*	The Ever-Living
Al-Ghaffār	The Forgiver	*Al-Kaīyūm*	The Self-Subsisting
Al-Qahhār	The Dominant	*Al-Wāhid*	The All-Perceiving
Al-Wahhāb	The Bestower	*As-Samad*	The Eternal
Ar-Razzāk	The Provider	*Al-Kadar*	Providence
Al-Fattāh	The Opener	*Al-Muktadir*	The All-Powerful
Al-ʿĀlim	The All-Knowing	*Al-Mukaddim*	The Forewarner
Al-Kabiz	The Closer	*Al-Mūakhkhir*	The Fulfiller
Al-Bāsit	The Uncloser	*Al-Awwal*	The First
Al-Khafiz	The Abaser	*Al-Akhir*	The Last
Ar-Rafi	The Exalter	*Ath Thahir*	The Manifest
Al-Muhizz	The Honourer	*Al-Bātin*	The Hidden
Al-Muzīll	The Leader Astray	*Al-Wālī*	The All-Governing
As-Samīʿh	The All-Hearing	*Al-Mutāhāli*	The One Above Reproach

Al-Basīr	The All-Seeing	*Al-Barr*	The Good
Al-Hākim	The Judge of All	*Al-Tawwāb*	The Relenting
Al-Hādil	The Equitable	*Al-Muntakim*	The Avenger
Al-Latīf	The Gracious One	*Al-Ghafoor*	The Rewarder
Al-Khabīr	He who is Aware	*Al-Rawūf*	The Ever-Indulgent
Al-Hālim	The Clement	*Mālik-ul-Mulki*	King of the Kingdom
Al-'Azīz	The Strong	*Dhu'l jalāl wa Ikrām*	Lord of Splendid Power
Al-Gāfir	The Pardoner	*Al-Muksit*	The Equitable
Ash-Shākir	The Thankful	*Al-Jami'h*	The Gatherer
Al-'Alee	The Exalted	*Al-Ghanī*	The All-Sufficing
Al-Kabīr	The Very Great	*Al-Mughnī*	The Sufficer
Al-Hāfiz	The Preserver	*Al-Mu'hti*	The Provider
Al-Mukīt	The Maintainer	*Al-Māni'h*	The Withholder
Al-Hasīb	The Reckoner	*An-Nāfi'h*	The Propitious
Al-Jamīl	The Beneficent	*Az-Zarr*	The Harmful
Al-Karīm	The Bountiful	*An-Noor*	The Light
Ar-Rakīb	The Watchful	*Al-Hādi*	The Guide
Al-Mujib	The Hearer of Prayer	*Al-Azali*	Eternal in the Past
Al-Was'ih	The All-Comprehending	*Al-Baki*	Eternal in the Future
Al-Hakim al Mutlak	The Judge of Judges	*Al-Warith*	The Inheritor
Al-Wadcod	The Loving	*Ar-Rashīd*	The Unerring
Al-Majid	The All-Glorious	*As-Saboor*	The Patient

Appendix 5

Muhammad's Farewell Sermon

On the eighth day of Dhu'l-Hajja, Muhammad went to Minā and spent the day and the night in that locality. There he performed all the prayers incumbent during that period. The following day Muhammad recited his dawn prayer and, at sunrise, proceeded on his camel, al Qaswa', to the Mount of Arafāt, followed by all the pilgrims. As he ascended the mountain, he was surrounded by thousands of companions reciting the *talbiyah* and the *Takbir*. The Prophet naturally heard their recitations but made no effort either to stop them or to encourage them. He commanded some of the Companions to put up a tent for him on the east side of the mountain at a spot called Namirah. When the sun passed the zenith, he ordered his camel to be saddled, and rode on it until he reached the valley of 'Uranabh.

It was there that he, while sitting on his camel, delivered his sermon in a loud voice to his people. Rabi'ah ibn Umayyah ibn Khakaf repeated the sermon after him, sentence by sentence. He began by praising God and thanking Him, and then turning to the people he said:

'O Men, listen to my words, for I do not know whether I shall meet you again on such an occasion in the future. O Men, your lives and your property shall be inviolate until you meet your Lord. The safety of your lives and your property shall be inviolate as this holy day and holy month. Remember that you will indeed meet your Lord, and that He will indeed reckon your deeds. Thus do I warn you. Whoever of you is keeping a trust for someone else shall return that trust to its rightful owner. All interest obligation shall henceforth be waived. Your capital, however, is yours to keep. You will neither inflict nor suffer inequity. God has judged that there shall be no interest and that all the interest due to 'Abbās al Muttalib shall henceforth be waived. Every right arising out of homicide in pre-Islamic days is henceforth waived. And the first such right that I waive is that arising from the murder of Rabi'ah ibn al Hārith ibn 'Abd Muttalib. O Men, the devil has lost all hope of ever being worshipped in this land of yours. Nevertheless he is still anxious to determine the lesser of your deeds. Beware of him, therefore, for the safety of your religion. O Men, intercalation, or tampering with the calendar is evidence of great unbelief and confirms the unbelievers in their misguidance. They indulge in it one year and forbid it the next in order to make permissible that which God forbade, and to forbid that which God has made permissible. The pattern according to which the time is reckoned is always the same. With God, the months are twelve in number. Four of them are holy. Three of these are successive and one occurs singly between the months of Jumādā and Sha'bān. O Men, to you a right belongs with respect to your women, and to your women a right with respect to you. It is your right that they not fraternize with any one of whom you do not approve, as well as never to commit adultery. But if they do, then God has permitted you to isolate them within their homes and to chastise them without cruelty. But if they abide by your right, then to them belongs the right to be fed and clothed in kindness. Do treat your women well and be kind to them, for they are your partners and committed helpers. Remember that you have taken them as your wives and enjoyed their flesh only under God's trust and with His permission. Reason well, therefore, O Men, and ponder my words which I now convey to you. I am leaving you with the Book of God and the Sunna of His Prophet. If you follow them, you will never go astray. O Men, hearken well to my words. Learn that every Muslim is a brother to every Muslim and that the Muslims constitute one brotherhood. Nothing shall be legitimate to a Muslim which belongs to a fellow Muslim unless it was given freely and willingly. Do not, therefore, do injustice to your own selves. O God, have I conveyed Your message?'

As the Prophet delivered his speech, Rabi'ah repeated it sentence by sentence and asked the people every now and then whether they had understood the Prophet's words and committed them to memory. In order to make sure that the people understood and remembered, the Prophet would ask his crier to say: 'The Prophet of God asks, "Do you know which day this is?"' The audience would answer, 'Today is the day of the great pilgrimage.' The Prophet would then say, 'Tell them that God has declared inviolate your lives and your property until the day you will meet your Lord; that he has made the safety of your property and your lives as inviolate as this day.' At the end of his speech, the Prophet asked 'O God, have I conveyed Your message?' And the people answered from all corners, 'Indeed so! God be witness.'

When the Prophet finished his sermon, he dismounted and performed both the noon and the afternoon prayers. He then remounted his camel and proceeded to al-Sakharāt where he recited to the people the concluding divine revelation: 'Today I have completed for you your religion, and granted you the last of my blessings. Today I have

accepted for you Islam as the religion.' When Abu Bakr heard this
verse, he realized that with the completion of the divine message, the
Prophet's life was soon to come to a close.

(Extract from *The Life of Muhammad* by
Muhammad Husein Haykal)

4

ISLAM IN THE MODERN WORLD

I The Spread of Islam

The problem of succession

In the Commonwealth of Medina, Muhammad was prophet, law-giver, prayer leader, commander of the army and head of state. So when he died, leaving only one surviving child, his daughter Fatima, and without providing for a successor or clarifying beyond doubt the method by which a successor should be appointed, the *ummah* fell into dissention. The unity of Islam would never recover from the events that were to follow over the next two decades and no satisfactory answer would ever be found to the question of the legitimacy of subsequent Muslim rulers. This uncertainty, combining religion and politics in equal measure, as well as touching on the question of free will and the nature of God, is still present in modern Islam, as veneer democracy alternates with tyranny, occupation and corruption. For how can the utopia of the 'divinely ordained' Commonwealth ever be recreated without Muhammad's presence as the 'divinely guided' ruler? Yet if God is All-Powerful and All-Knowing, does it not follow that the less-than-perfect rulers who have in fact taken power must be expressions of His will?

Succession by male bloodline was not the automatic practice in pre-Islamic Arabia, and an heir would in any event be required to seek confirmation as a 'first among equals' after a *shurā*, or consultation, among the tribe or tribal group. But in the case of the succession to Muhammad there was no male heir to consider, and two main factions came forward to claim the caliphate: the Emigrants on the one hand, represented by Abu Bakr, those first Meccan converts and participants during Islam's darkest hours, and the Helpers or Medinans on the other hand, represented by Sa'd ibn Ubādah, who had protected and sustained the Muslims when they had nowhere else to turn. There was also support for 'Ali, Muhammad's cousin, the first Qurayshite man to accept Islam, and married to Muhammad's daughter, Fatima. (Some Muslim historians name

Abu Bakr as the first Qurayshite man to embrace Islam, in which case 'Ali, young at the time, was the first *boy* to do so.) Fatima campaigned for 'Ali's election among the Companions (the Emigrants and the Helpers combined), but she was not successful. Fatima died shortly thereafter, reputedly full of bitterness, further coloured by a dispute with Abu Bakr over her property inheritance. Later, this would be seen in retrospect as the start of the great schism between Sunni and Shi'a.

The Emigrants prevailed, electing Abu Bakr as First Caliph, or 'successor' to Muhammad's temporal, but not his spiritual authority. Abu Bakr was a pious man and father of Muhammad's wife 'Ā'isha. He ruled for two years until his death, followed by Caliph 'Umar for ten years and Caliph 'Uthman for eleven. All three were former close Companions of Muhammad as well as members of the dominant Meccan tribe of the Quraysh, and each was elected by the same *shurā* procedure. 'Ali was finally elected in 656 CE on the death of 'Uthman, but shortly after this fourth improvised solution to the problem of succession, the *shurā* consensus system disintegrated.

What is now the mainstream Sunni branch of Islam regard these first four caliphs as 'rightly guided', since, through their closeness to Muhammad, the influence of the Prophet, and therefore of God, could still be felt. But here the great divide within Islam opens up. The events that followed the election of 'Ali as the Fourth Caliph were to lead to the permanent division within Islam between Sunni and Shi'a, that still exists so vividly today. The absorbing and much misunderstood issues surrounding the origins of the schism will be considered in Chapter 6.

During the twenty-nine year rule of the first four caliphs, Islam expanded and changed in ways that would have been unimaginable on the day of Muhammad's death, when Muslim power was still contained within the Arabian peninsula. Further, the Arabs came to understand during the years of the first caliphs that they had been 'saved' from their endless barbaric rounds of tribal vendetta and counter-vendetta. They were becoming a self-aware cultural fact, with an Arabic Qur'ān to match the spiritual possessions of their more civilized Christian and Jewish neighbours and they could assure themselves that they were no longer excluded from the divine plan. By submitting to the will of Allah, their obscure Arab race from beyond the borders of the known world would change the course of history within one generation. The character of Islam developed during this period, from what could have ended as nothing more than an inconsequential social experiment in remote Medina, to become a recognizable, if still unrefined, religious and political system that was ready to address the world.

First Abu Bakr undertook the *Riddah*, or Wars of Apostasy, against the tribes of Arabia beyond the Hijaz who attempted to re-establish their autonomy after the death of the Prophet, or who had never sworn loyalty to Muhammad during his lifetime. The unity that resulted from these campaigns was to bring to a final end the ancient business of inter-tribal raiding and warfare.

Then the move north began, creating over the next decades the core of the vast Muslim Empire that was to last, in various forms, for centuries. Western historians typically explain the break-out from the Arabian peninsula after the death of Muhammad as brought on by hunger. In this view, since many desert tribes had had no livelihood other than raiding their neighbours, and since this was now prohibited, but warfare still remained a way of life, the attraction of the fertile lands on the northern and eastern boundaries of Arabia became irresistible. Primary Muslim sources, however, give a more complicated picture.

In his last years Muhammad had sent envoys to the Arab Christian tribes on the borders of Sassanid Persia and Christian Byzantium, urging them to convert to Islam. The response had been the murder of one of his envoys, leading to the dispatch of a punitive expedition to take revenge, and to the first contest between the Muslims and the imperial forces of the Eastern Roman, or Byzantine Empire. The opening battle was fought at Mu'tah in what is now Jordan, and the small Muslim army was defeated, the remnants withdrawing only with some difficulty against greatly superior numbers. To maintain his prestige and safeguard Medina from attack in this moment of perceived weakness, Muhammad mounted a second campaign north in 630 CE, which he led himself, but he only reached as far as Tabuk, well inside what is now Saudi Arabia. The expedition, in harsh summer conditions, and suffering from hasty and incomplete organization, was unsuccessful in finding the Byzantine imperial army and avenging Mu'tah. But as a result of the campaign, the border tribes, together with some fringe Jewish and Christian communities, were brought under Muslim control.

Shortly before his death, Muhammad sent a third expedition against the northern Arabs, under the leadership of 'Usāmah ibn Zayd, but the Prophet's death halted the expedition. Abu Bakr felt obliged therefore, upon his accession, to remount the campaign and was further motivated by the news that the Byzantine army was gathering for a pre-emptive invasion of Arabia.

In the event, the Muslim army was unopposed as it moved north into Syria, opening the way for the great advances that were to come. When 'Umar became caliph, on the death of Abu Bakr, the campaign continued and the Muslims came under counter-attack from Byzantium. Soon a full-scale engagement was under way, culminating during 'Uthman's caliphate with the successful Muslim penetration into the distant north-east and west of Syria and Persia.

'Umar was murdered by a Persian slave and succeeded by 'Uthman. But 'Uthman favoured his own clan of the Umayyah, the Meccan late-comers under Abu-Sufyān who had held out against Muhammad until the very end (although 'Uthman himself had been an early convert to Islam). The result was that commanders of the victorious army were passed over in favour of 'Uthman's Umayyad relatives who were appointed to positions of regional authority in the new territories. The ensuing discontent, aggravated by the tight control exercised over the troops in the rich new lands in order to prevent looting, led to 'Uthman's assassination.

The astonishing advances by the Arabs into what is now Egypt, Israel, Jordan, Syria, Iraq, Iran and central Asia (and what was Palestine) were driven by the variety of internal motivations discussed above. But these moves were only made possible by a series of external historical accidents working in the Muslims' favour.

The Persian Sassanid Empire, predominantly Zoroastrian by belief, occupied the fertile plains between the rivers Tigris and Euphrates in what is now the heartland of modern Iraq, as well as the mountainous hinterland beyond, that is now in Iran. The Sassanid Empire had been weakened by years of war with the Byzantine Christian Empire, which had ruled the eastern end of the Mediterranean from the capital of Constantinople since the first half of the fourth century CE. At the same time, Persian agriculture was in decline following repeated flooding, and erosion had destroyed large areas of productive terracing.

Similarly, the Byzantine Empire, in addition to suffering from exhaustion by plagues, earthquakes and the military campaigns of the Byzantine Emperor Heraclius against the Persians, had created internal weakness by the persecution of both Jews and schismatic Christian sects. Further, the Arab tribes on the southern borders of the Empire, often employed as mercenaries by Constantinople, as well as by the Sassanians, changed allegiance once the Muslims arrived in force, leaving the defences of both eastern and southern borders inadequately defended against the unexpected invasion from the desert.

The historical moment was dramatic. With two great battles, the first and most important being Yarmuk in 636 CE, the Arabs overturned 1,000 years of rule by the Christian West in the eastern Mediterranean, while at the same time the way was opened for Islam to become the inheritor of the Sassanid Persian Empire. The second crucial battle of the two, at Qadisiyyah in modern Iraq in 637 CE, led to the fall of the Persian capital Ctesiphon and the final opening up of Persia. Suddenly, a small town in the distant Hijaz ruled the entire fertile crescent, including Ctesiphon, Jerusalem, Alexandria and Damascus, as well as vast territories beyond, stretching in the east from Herat in Afghanistan and Sind in India to modern Libya in the west.

The Battle of Yarmuk

This battle, in August 636 CE, was one of the turning points of world history, leading to the eventual end of the Byzantine Empire and the dominance of Islam in what is now the Middle East. But despite the favourable circumstances created by the decline of both Persia and Byzantium, this great Arab victory by an inferior desert force over a professional imperial army was no accident. The Apostasy Wars fought by Abu Bakr had transformed the anarchic Arabs from a bickering tribal horde into an organized fighting machine. The campaigns against dissident tribes within Arabia, following the death of the Prophet, also produced Muslim commanders of genius, while having the further effect of turning Arabia into an armed camp. The Arabs had also mastered the use of cavalry in a way that the Byzantines never matched, and camels carrying recently invented wood-frame saddles gave the Muslims the advantage of self-sufficiency, when the Byzantines were dependent on long lines of supply. Finally, the Muslims were ferocious fighters, fearless in the face of death, armed with the belief that the sensual paradise described in the Qur'ān awaited the martyrs of Islam. The Muslims were thus able to accept a much higher level of casualties than their opponents.

The Muslim forces, initially under Abu Bakr, had first moved into Palestine and Syria divided into four independent armies, with the group under the commander Khalid ibn al-Walid crossing the wastes of the Great Nafud to open the campaign by surprising and overwhelming the city of Busra from the undefended south. In response to further minor defeats inflicted on the Byzantine armies by the Muslims under 'Umar during 635 and the first half of 636, Emperor Heraclius assembled a large army for the counter-attack with which he intended to recapture Syria for the Christian Empire. In response, the Muslims, who had already taken Damascus, chose to withdraw to a site straddling the deep gorge of the Yarmuk River in southern Syria. The Byzantines followed, taking up a strong position on a peninsular projecting into the river escarpment. After two months of stalemate, attempted subversions, espionage and counter-espionage, which sapped the energy of the Christians but not the well-supplied Arabs, the two sides aligned for battle on the high plain above the river. Heraclius was able to field 50,000 troops against 20,000 Arabs, but in the heat and dust of August the desert Muslims had a distinct advantage. The Arabs initially fell back on their flanks towards their camps, but here they were met by their womenfolk, who mocked their manhood and themselves took up the fight against the enemy with tent poles and cooking pots. On the sixth day, the Christians collapsed, after the Arabs had captured a key bridge to their rear, so blocking the arrival of reinforcements as well as escape. The defeated Christian army attempted to flee south along the river, losing many of their number over the cliffs of the gorge.

Despair engulfed the Byzantine high command, which had so recently been successful against the Sassanians. Within two years of the battle of Yarmuk all the fortified towns of Syria and Palestine had surrendered and the Muslims had become the masters of a great new empire.

At first, the character of this new Muslim Empire was entirely different from what had gone before. There was no wholesale plunder of the conquered lands by the new rulers. Instead, the Arab armies were contained in disciplined garrison towns, Fustat in Egypt, for example, or Kufah in Iraq. Religious persecution of minorities by the Greek Orthodox Church came to an immediate end and tolerance was declared following the injunctions of the Qur'ān. Muslims had no preferences between the intricate factions that had formed among both Christians and Jews, ironically respecting both as 'people of the Book', despite their military defeat. (The 'Book' is not the Christian Bible or Jewish Torah, but the mystical 'divine text' from which *all* scriptures, including the Qur'ān, flow.) The occupied non-Muslims were, however, required to pay the *jizyah*, a tax levied on income in return for protection. But the levy was generally less than the previous fiscal impositions of the departing Persians and Byzantines, and non-Muslims were exempt from paying *zakāt*. Islam was not forced upon the population, rather the early conversions were as a result of the personal and community examples set by the Muslims and the ease with which this powerful new religion could be understood. Even converts, however, were not exempted from the protection tax which was needed to fund the operation of the new empire.

The Umayyads (661–750 CE)

With the assassination of 'Uthman, the Third Caliph, Muslim progress was halted and the unity of the '*ummah* was about to be irrevocably shattered. 'Ali was proclaimed caliph following a *shurā* and began to rule, attempting to maintain the discipline of his predecessors while emphasizing pure Qur'ānic standards. But for all his piety and his indirect blood relationship with the Prophet as the father of Muhammad's grandchildren, 'Ali was opposed by the Umayyad clan, now led by Mu'āwiyah, son of Muhammad's old enemy Abu-Sufyān, and cousin of 'Uthman, who had earlier appointed Mu'āwiyah governor of Syria. Here was the classic confrontation between realpolitik and idealism: between the wealth, organizational power and ability of the Umayyad clan on the one hand, and the simple-hearted 'Ali on the other, relying on his superior claim in blood and in religion, as well as his close association with the Prophet, and his *shurā* appointment.

Civil war between factions within the *'ummah* was a shocking prospect for Muslims, however, running directly contrary to the Word of God and the teachings of the Prophet, by which Muslims were to treat each other as brothers. Thus, in the first major confrontation between the two sides, Mu'āwiyah's forces broke off the engagement as an expression of their frustration. An attempt was made to arbitrate the dispute, but the negotiations raised the unanswerable questions touched on earlier, to do with the nature of God, free will, the relationship between piety and political power, and the negotiations were thus inconclusive. Mu'āwiyah once again pressed his advance into Iraq and Arabia against 'Ali and his supporters, whereupon the opposition crumbled. Then shortly thereafter 'Ali was murdered by a dissenting group from within his own party, known as the Kharijites or 'Seceders', who had objected from the start to the 'Will of God' being subjected to human arbitration.

Mu'āwiyah, the Umayyad, became the Fifth Caliph and the *shurā*-based or 'republican' period of the caliphate was over, to be replaced by dynasties until the abolition of the caliphate by the Turkish Assembly in 1924. Similarly, Damascus now replaced Medina as the capital of the Muslim Empire, symbolic to many of the faithful of the shift away from the ideals of Islam towards the power, wealth and corruption of the outside world beyond Arabia. Over the centuries 'Ali and his son al-Husayn (who was also murdered by the Umayyads at a later date as a low-level civil war continued) would come to represent the tragically lost utopia, the vanished purity of the Commonwealth of Medina and the spurned injunctions of the God-sent Qur'ān. And just as early Islam combined politics and religion in the person of Muhammad, now political opposition within Islam took on the cloak of religious dissident, a Muslim characteristic which remains strong in modern times. The name given to the disinherited followers of 'Ali was Shi'at-Ali, or the Party of 'Ali, later to become the permanently disaffected Shi'a community, always seeking the impossible and impractical political implementation of God's law, and the return to some ill-defined lost ideal.

Although Mu'āwiyah can be judged harshly by Qur'ānic standards as opportunistic, unjust, secular, dynastic and tyrannical, and although he claimed no special relationship with the Prophet, he was

a brilliant ruler and a devout believer. Moreover, the Qur'ān could be
interpreted to justify the rule of the de facto holder of power.

> Say: 'O Allah!
> Lord of Power and Rule,
> Thou givest power
> To whom Thou pleasest.
> *Āl'Imrān* (The Family of Imrān) Surah 2, verse 26

Mu'āwiyah pacified and unified the empire after the horrors of the
civil war, although the condition was to be only temporary. Arabic
became the majority language of the new Muslim lands, overpower-
ing Greek and Persian, while Islam spread to become the predominant religion among Arabs and non-Arabs alike, replacing Persian
Zoroastrianism and to a lesser extent, Byzantine Christianity.

The years of Umayyad rule achieved the Arabization of the new
empire, and the adaptation of Byzantine and Sassanid administration to Muslim rule. The influence of the Umayyads was limited by
contests for power within the dynasty as well as by frequent external
rebellions by disaffected followers of 'Ali and his descendants. But,
nevertheless, the Umayyads developed a sound system of government that was to last for centuries, as well as the central Muslim
concept of the mosque, now to be found all around the globe.
Umayyad caliphs demonstrated a passion for architecture, elevating
the simple design of the Medina prayer-hall, that doubled as the
dwelling of the Prophet and his wives, to the splendour and dignity
of the Dome of the Rock in Jerusalem and the Great Mosque of
Damascus, both still standing today. And a subsequent branch of
the Umayyad dynasty was to bring four hundred years of peace,
prosperity and outstanding cultural achievement to Spain.

The 'Abbāsids (750–1258 CE)

Umayyad rule came to a bloody end eighty-nine years after
Mu'āwiyah's accession, and was replaced by the 'Abbāsid dynasty,
who initially promised a return to the utopian ideals of the proto-
Shi'a Party of 'Ali, while claiming legitimate descent and 'divine
right' from 'Abbās, the Prophet's uncle who had assisted with the
opening of Mecca. This was the final outcome of the civil war

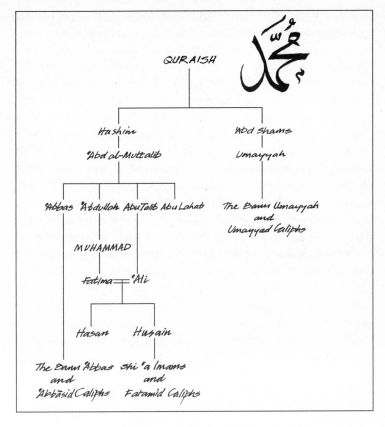

Muhammad's family tree

between 'Ali and Mu'āwiyah, and at the time it looked as if the partisans of 'Ali had won and that a new universal age of 'Alid equality, righteousness and justice would prevail. But this ideal state never came into being and eventually Shi'ism would for the most part retreat behind the borders of the old Sassanid Persian Empire, leaving the majority of the Muslim world as Sunni.

The 'Abbāsids moved the capital of the empire once again, from Damascus to Baghdad, where a large palace was built as part of the famous Round City. But although coming to power as self-proclaimed religious purists, the 'Abbāsids quickly turned to everything that the Umayyads had practised and the ascetic Prophet had abhorred: luxury, corruption and vicious tyranny. The army became a professional body of ruthless Turkish slaves and ex-slaves (later to be known as Mamluks), imported to pacify both the Persian proto-Shi'a and the Arab proto-Sunnis, and owing loyalty only to the person of the caliph. But during the first two hundred years of 'Abbāsid rule the empire enjoyed political stability and economic expansion. The 'Abbāsids became the most celebrated of the Muslim dynasties, although more Persian than Arab in character. Science and the arts were patronized and Muslims made more technical and scientific progress during this time than in all the previous years of recorded history combined. Islam grasped the inheritance of Greek learning, eventually transmitting to Renaissance Europe treasures that would have otherwise been lost during the northern Dark Ages. *Fiqh* developed, the jurisprudential definition and application of the Shariah, and, as will be seen later, the great Islamic debate about *ijtihād* (open-mindedness) began, between progressives and strict legal constructionists.

Islam in Medieval Europe

Muslim expansion into Spain was Islam's most dramatic move westward. Only seven years (710–16 CE) separated the first Arab reconnaissance of Spain from their North African base from the establishment of al-Andalus as a province of the Umayyad caliphate in Damascus. The speed of the victory reflected the ill will of the native Spanish for their Visigoth rulers, who, upon their defeat, were marched back to Syria by the victorious Arabs as captives, complete with their gold. Spanish Jews who had been continuously persecuted and subjected to forced Christian conversions by the previous regime also welcomed the Arabs. Then, from their new forward base in Spain, Muslim horsemen raided north across the Pyrenees into modern France. The Arabs captured Narbonne and Toulouse in 718 CE, but their excursions were stopped by the Frankish General Charles Martel at the battle of Poitiers (732 CE). Much has been made of this battle in the West, the implication being that had it not been for the valiant French, the Muslims would have conquered their way along the northern shore of the Mediterranean and back to Damascus, encircling the Mediterranean and establishing mosques in Paris, London and Rome as they progressed. Conversely, Muslim historians maintain that the dark ages of Europe date from the Muslim defeat: lost centuries that would have been avoided had the light of Islam been permitted to spread and shine. In reality the battle changed nothing, the impetus of Arab expansion was in any case already spent and the north was a cold and uninviting land. Nor did the defeat serve to remove the Arab presence from France, which continued in the lands north of the Pyrenees mountains for a further twenty-five years.

Certainly Islamic Spain was spared the bleak fate of the rest of Europe during the Middle Ages, stretching from the ninth to the eleventh centuries CE. The great era of Muslim rule in Spain, soon independent of the Iraqi-based caliphate that was by then controlled by the 'Abbāsids, began with the first Iberian Umayyad, 'Abd-al-Rahmān I (756–788 CE). He had escaped as a young man from the massacre of his family as the 'Abbāsids came to power in Damascus in 750 CE, when the Umayyad caliphate was overthrown. After wandering penniless across North Africa, pursued by spies and assassins, 'Abd-al-Rahmān crossed to Spain where, under his leadership, dissident Berber and Arab troops defeated the ruling 'Abbāsid governor. The Umayyads established their capital in Cordoba, which was to become the largest, richest and most civilized city in Europe during the two centuries up to the end of the first millennium. The great mosque of La Mezquita was built in the city centre, one of the most beautiful buildings in the world until punctured by a Christian church during the sixteenth century CE on the orders of Charles V, the Holy Roman Emperor (who on visiting the site came to regret his actions, even before the roof of the church was on). Islamic religious and racial tolerance formed the basis of a brilliant Arab-Iberian civilization. Science flourished, with advances made in botany, medicine, philosophy, irrigated agriculture and astronomical mathematics. Later, Spain was to contribute this fund of invaluable knowledge to the reawakening of Europe during the Renaissance. Arts of all kinds were practised: poetry, song (which has influenced Spanish flamenco and Portuguese fado to this day), ceramics, textiles and most famously of all, architecture. The Alhambra Palace in Granada was the culmination of Moorish achievement in Spain and the basis for Western Gothic architecture in subsequent centuries.

Unified Umayyad rule disappeared from Spain in 1031 to be replaced by fractured Arab-ruled kingdoms and principalities squabbling among themselves. The last of these, based in Granada, was overthrown in 1492 by the strengthening native Catholic powers from the north. Under Spanish rule, starting with King Ferdinand and Queen Isabella, Islamic tolerance came to an abrupt end. Conversions to Christianity were once again forced, books were burned, the Inquisition was established, and all non-Christian practices suppressed. Even regular washing was suspect, linked to the Muslim practice of ablutions before prayers. After a number of protest risings against Catholic persecution, the entire Muslim and Jewish populations of Spain were expelled. 'The Moors were banished: for a while Christian Spain shone on, but like the moon with a borrowed light. Then came the eclipse, and in that darkness Spain has grovelled ever since.' (Lane-Poole, *Moors in Spain*, 1934)

The decline of the Empire

From the beginning of the tenth century CE the Muslim Empire slowly disintegrated, until the caliph's writ hardly ran beyond the boundaries of Iraq. During this long decline, real power passed to a succession of militarily powerful factions within the core lands, many under temporary Shi'a influence. At the same time the distant peripheries achieved de facto independence under local sultans, or 'holders of power', giving allegiance in name only to a caliphate that no longer had any real claim to succession by bloodline from the Prophet (the Shi'a requirement for a ruler's legitimacy to be elaborated in the following chapter). The decline of the position of the caliph, from powerful and often absolute ruler to mere figurehead, led to a relaxing of the mesh between religion and politics. Islam was becoming fractured politically but more unified spiritually. Under little threat from the outside, before the later invasion of the Mongols, while temporal regimes came and went, Muslims could practise their religion unmolested in Dar al-Islam (the 'abode' of Islam, as opposed to Dar al-Harb, the 'abode' of war, or the territory beyond the borders of Dar al-Islam). Only in modern times, with Muslims once again threatened by the West, has the fervour of the Prophet's Commonwealth been reignited. Whether the threat is real or imagined, militant Islam now seeks to reclaim the simple days of Muhammad in Medina, rather than the Muslim empires that followed, however large and powerful.

The process of disintegration gathered speed with the Fatimids (909–1171), initially Shiʿa dissidents (now known as Ismaiʾilis) who claimed to be descendants of ʿAli and his wife Fatima, the daughter of the Prophet. Their rule began in North Africa and eventually included Egypt, Palestine and Syria, extending south to control the holy cities of Mecca and Medina. The new Fatamid capital of Cairo was prosperous and culturally developed, and al-Azhar university was built in 970, now the oldest seat of learning in the world and the centre of Sunni Qurʾānic scholarship. But after a short interregnum by the Ayyubids, the former Fatimid lands were conquered and ruled by the Mamluks (1250–1517), the samurai-like descendants of the former Turkish slaves employed by the ʿAbbāsids as a professional army. The Mamluks were implacable professional fighters who turned back the advance of the Mongols. And a Fatimid caliph had destroyed the Church of the Holy Sepulchre covering the traditional site of Christ's crucifixion, so providing one of the pretexts for the launch of the First Crusade. The Mamluks were the force that would finally drive the last of the Crusaders from Palestine.

Shortly before this period another Turkish tribe, the Seljuks, consolidated a large Muslim territory on the eastern flank of the crumbling empire. Their rule stretched from Central Asia to Baghdad, acknowledging the last of the ʿAbbāsids as nominal caliphs only. The Seljuk viziers were orthodox or Sunni Muslims who rolled back the influence of the Shiʿa and established Sunni religious schools deep in traditional Shiʿa territory to the east. But Seljuk rule was short-lived, dependent on nomadic forces with little interest in empire-building.

The Crusades through Arab Eyes

Muslim historians record that the Firinj took the holy city of Jerusalem for the first time on 22nd Shaʿbān 492 AH (15 July 1099 CE). Hundreds of fair-haired warriors spilled through the gates, sword in hand. Two days later, not a single Muslim or Jew was left in the city. All had been killed or taken as slaves, with their property shared among the Christians. Outside al-Aqsa mosque and through the streets, 30,000 citizens were slaughtered. Blood and gore rose to the height of the invaders' knees, sitting on their horses. With the killing over, the Firinj sang canticles and gave thanks to God at the site of the destroyed Church of the Holy Sepulchre, the traditional location of Calvary. For the next five months putrefying bodies lay unburied and the stench of death hung over the city where Christian, Jew and Muslim had lived harmoniously under *Pax Islamica* for almost 500 years. The Dome of the Rock, together with all the mosques of the city, were turned into Christian churches, and al-Aqsa mosque became a palace for the victorious knights. The city became exclusively Christian, and in contrast to the tolerance of Muslim rule, the practice of Judaism, and of Islam, was prohibited.

The Crusades accomplished nothing but death and destruction, not even proto-colonialism, and the much-admired Crusader castles were in fact built by the enslaved Muslim population at a great cost in human suffering. The Christian Church preached the Crusades, not out of religious conviction, but in response to drought and famine in Europe, and the misery and brevity of eleventh-century life. Killing and plundering beyond the borders of Europe was the solution, or at least a diversion. So wars fought at the bidding of the Church became meritorious for the souls of those who took part, while those who died in holy war would achieve paradise.

In Europe, however, the true facts of what was happening were obscured, and the Crusades (literally 'taking the Cross') were justified in ways that have affected the West's view of Islam (and vice-versa) down through the centuries. Despite the unprovoked Christian invasion and the slaughter, scholar-monks wrote of Islam as 'inherently violent and intolerant', 'only established by the sword', and conversions made 'on pain of beheading'. Muslims were 'fanatical and intolerant' and they had met the 'fate they had long deserved'.

These groundless attacks from Europe, together with the hypocritical moral and religious justification that went with them, remains vivid in the Muslim psyche, even though in the West this part of our history has become little more than an asterisk to the remote Middle Ages. But *al-Salibiyyah*, the Arabic word for the Crusades, has been readily applied to every subsequent invasion of Muslim lands by European non-believers: from the French invasion of North Africa in the nineteenth century, to General Allenby's advance through Palestine and Syria in 1917 and 1918 that led to the final fracturing of Dar al-Islam, to the force assembled in Arabia in 1991 to reverse the Iraqi invasion of Kuwait, to the American military presence in Saudi Arabia, to the latest invasion of Iraq.

The Firinj occupied Jerusalem for eighty-eight years until driven out by Salah al-Din al-Ayyubi (known in the West as Saladin) in 1187 CE. Earlier Saladin had also put an end to Shiʿa Fatimid rule in Egypt, to be replaced by the Sunni Ayyubids (1169–1252). Egypt and Syria were united under Saladin's rule and the previously suppressed religious fervour of Sunni Islam was channelled against the Crusaders. Saladin first destroyed the Firinj army at the battle of Hittin, then one after the other took most of the principal Crusader cities and castles, almost all without bloodshed. Jerusalem held out at first, threatening to destroy the Haram, but surrendered after only eight days of siege. Saladin, in emulation of Caliph ʿUmar, entered the city in peace (and coincidentally, on 27th Rajab, the day on which the mystical night journey of the Prophet from Mecca to Jerusalem, the *Isrā*, is celebrated). The Dome of the Rock and al-Aqsa mosque were restored to Islam, but there was no retribution other than the conversion of two churches to mosques, there were no massacres, and even ransom was waived for the poor. Christians and Jews were permitted to remain and worship freely, while the city resumed life under the timelessness of Muslim rule. The bloody Crusader interval was over.

This final victory of Islam over the invading Westerners has left a further impression on Muslim consciousness: as a model in the perennial search for the strong but pious leader who will bring ultimate redemption to the confused state of the Muslim world. During his first years as Egypt's 'Strong Man', the shadow of Saladin was seen behind Nasser, for example, or in recent times behind Saddam Hussein or Yassir Arafāt (for whom the 'new Crusaders' were the Jewish colonists of Israel). With each new hero the rhetoric builds up expectations among Muslims for a miraculous 'God-sent' deliverance, but events always end with predictable human failure, with corruption, with repression, and, in the Arab view, with fresh manipulation by the West.

The fragmentation of the Empire

During the thirteenth century CE, slow disintegration gave way to the complete separation of the components of the Muslim Empire, a fragmented condition that lasted for three hundred years until the rise of the Ottoman Empire.

Only the main threads of these turbulent times have made a recognizable impression on the character of modern Islam. In the first decade of the thirteenth century Mongol horsemen from Central Asia entered Muslim history by overwhelming the Seljuks. Genghis Khan was proclaimed supreme Mongol chief in 1206, claiming that he would 'rule the world'. He created a vast empire, incorporating most of Russia, China, Afghanistan and Persia. Then, under his successors, Baghdad was sacked in 1258, with Persia and Iraq occupied.

The Mongols were originally pagan, but in the middle of the fourteenth century their leaders became Muslim, and Islam was subsequently bourne eastward as far as China by Mongol agency. After the retreat of the Mongols, Islam was sustained in the near east by the Timurids (1370–1506), rulers of Persia and Iraq. The famous Timurid leader Timur Lang (or Tamerlane in English) claimed to be descended from Genghis. Both the Mongol and Timurid dynasties destroyed much and built little new, but the invasions facilitated the spread of Islam 'backwards' through vast areas of Asia.

This eastward transmission of Islam was completed by the Mughals (1526–1858), another group descended from the Mongols, who ruled Afghanistan, northern India and what is now Pakistan. Contemporaneously the Safavids (1501–1732) followed after the Timurids in the near east, giving Persia a distinct character and settled borders, able at a later date to resist incorporation into the Ottoman Empire.

The Ottoman Empire (1281–1924)

The Ottomans were Turkish Muslim tribesmen whose original territory in Anatolia was created by resisting the Mongols in the east and pushing back the remains of the Byzantine Empire in the west. From primitive tribal beginnings during the eleventh century CE, Ottoman power rose out of the defeat of the Seljuks in eastern Anatolia, and in 1453 the capture in the west of Constantinople (renamed to match the Turkish pronunciation of the word as 'Costan-pull', or Istanbul), followed by the invasion of Eastern Europe. Istanbul served as the Ottoman capital for the next 470 years, until the creation of the modern state of Turkey and the end of the Ottoman Empire in 1924.

In 1517 Sultan Selim the Grim extended Ottoman rule into Syria and Egypt by defeating the Mamluks, using the innovation of light artillery. The last of the ʿAbbāsid caliphs, by then powerless, was brought to Istanbul from Baghdad to give an appearance of legitimacy to the new empire. Subsequent Ottoman expansion further to the west took in Libya, Tunisia and Algeria, but progress was halted with the defeat of the Ottoman navy by a coalition of European powers at the naval battle of Lepanto in 1571.

Ottoman power peaked under Süleyman the Magnificent (1520–66), both territorially as well as culturally, with the sultan's vast construction projects, which included the rebuilding of the walls of Jerusalem.

Ottoman rule was passive and cruel, but strongly Muslim, covering the entire Middle East and extending as far down Arabia as the holy cities of Medina and Mecca, where the Arab tribes enjoyed considerable freedom but were still Ottoman subjects. Religion and politics were combined in the person of the Ottoman Sultan, 'the Shadow of God upon Earth', while a hierarchy of *qadi* administered his empire, whose roles included judge, prosecutor, Qurʾānic interpreter, superintendent of public works, food distributor and enforcer of military conscription.

The Ottoman Empire was seen as a constant threat by Europe and in 1683 the 'Muslim hordes' famously reached the gates of Vienna. In reality, starting with the first Ottoman defeats on the battlefield of Eastern Europe shortly thereafter, the Empire was in decline for the next two centuries.

II   Islam beyond the Empire

By the end of the fifteenth century CE, Islam was the largest ideological block in the world. On a map that did not then include the New World, Muslims worshipping the One God were to be found far beyond the limits reached by the Arab horsemen of the seventh century.

The Ottoman Turks, after capturing Constantinople had subdued Serbia and the Balkans as well as becoming the rulers of Greece and later Hungary. The old Eastern Roman or Byzantine Empire had ceased to exist. The Safavid dynasty was establishing their rule in Persia, defining the Shiʿa character of the country that has become contemporary Iran. The Mughals had created a Muslim empire in Northern India extending from the Hindu Kush to the Arabian Sea. The hinterland of Asia that today consists of the Muslim-influenced provinces of Western China and the Muslim republics of the former Soviet Union had already been converted with the 'reverse conquest' of the Mongol empire by Islam.

In East Africa, where Muhammad had sent a number of his Meccan supporters for safety during the years of persecution before the hijrah, Islam extended south along the coast from Ethiopia, through what is now Somalia, to the ports of modern Kenya, Tanzania and Mozambique. In West Africa, Muslim traders, every one a missionary for the faith, had brought Islam south across the Sahara to Mali and Ghana. Trading centres flourished at Timbuktu and Gao, mosques were built and schools for Qurʾānic study established.

The same process of trade combined with missionary zeal had brought Islam to Malaysia and the Indonesian archipelago, in the thirteenth century CE, or earlier. During his return from China in 1292 Marco Polo found entire Muslim towns on the island of Sumatra. Over the centuries almost the entire population of the Indonesian islands was converted from Hinduism, which has given a particular character to South Asian Islam, in which many Hindu practices remain, filled out with Muslim prayers. Later the Europeans established forts along the trade routes to the China and Japan and dislodged the Muslim sailors, but Islam continued to spread inland and Indonesia is today the most populous Muslim country in the world. Catholicism was able to halt this advance only in the Spanish Philippines.

But only the case-by-case facts of this expansion are notable. Although the underlying faith was undoubtedly strong, Islam was unable to exert cohesive political power commensurate with the extent of the faith, and was soon to be dominated both economically and militarily by the West. Further, the imposition of Twelvers Shiʿism, to be discussed later, as the state religion of the Safavid Empire (and thus of modern Iran) brought the two main communities of Islam into a debilitating formal conflict, similar to the Protestant–Catholic confrontation that was developing in Europe.

III   The Arrival of the West in Dar al-Islam

By the end of the seventeenth century, two hundred years after this high point of expansion had been reached, the three great Muslim empires were in decline. The Ottoman Empire was withdrawing from Hungary, Transylvania and the Ukraine, the Safavids had lost control of Afghanistan, while Persia itself was decaying and disintegrating. An attempt to impose Islam on the Hindu subjects of the Mughal Empire had led to widespread revolts and the rise of separate Indian states.

There were attempts at Muslim renewal during the eighteenth century, mostly by reforming preachers who advocated a return to the purer traditional Islam and the utopia of Medina. But religion alone was not able to reverse the inevitable, and another turning point in the history of Islam was approaching.

As the Muslim powers dissolved, Europe was growing in strength. Exploration of the boundaries of the old world by European sailors had turned into colonization around the globe. And soon the Industrial Revolution would provide the economic and technological advantage by which the European powers would come to rule almost the entire Muslim world.

Napoleon's occupation of Egypt in 1798 was the first occasion since the Crusades, 700 years before, that a European power had controlled any part of the central Muslim lands. The French withdrew in 1801, but the torpor of the Ottoman centuries had been irrevocably disturbed. Muhammad Ali took power in Egypt in 1805 and began the modernization process which led to the massacre of the last of the Mamluks. He Europeanized the country's administration and his successors built the Cairo Opera House, so symbolic of Western influence. The construction of the Suez Canal would later lead to full occupation by Britain.

Other losses of Muslim independence were to come in quick succession: France conquered Algeria (1830–47), Italy occupied Libya (1911–12), and Tunisia became a French protectorate (1881). Serbia became autonomous in 1830, Greece gained independence from Ottoman rule in 1829, Bulgaria came into existence in 1878, and Austria annexed Bosnia and Herzegovina the same year.

In India, the British had established colonial control over both Muslims and Hindus by 1848, then British power was extended over the Malay states starting in 1874. The Dutch completed the colonization of Indonesia in 1908. France had established French West Africa by 1912, and during the same period in Central Asia, Russia annexed the territories of the Muslim Kazakhs, the Turkomans and the Tajiks.

In few of these cases was the practice of Islam prohibited, the principal exception being in the Asian republics of the USSR. But the mere presence of Christian powers in Muslim lands would soon lead to the regeneration of the same mix of dissident politics and passionate religion with which the original Islamic empire had begun.

IV   The Great War and the Cairo Conference

The Ottoman Empire and the preceding Christian Byzantine Empire had been under pressure from Russia for one thousand years over the issue of control of the Bosporus, the narrow strait that gives access to the Mediterranean from the Black Sea, and from the only year-round, ice-free Russian ports. The Russians had long referred to Constantinople possessively as 'Czargrad', as if the city and the strait had already been conquered, annexed and renamed. When, therefore, war began in 1914 between Germany and Austria as the Central Powers on the one side, and the Entente of Britain, France and Russia on the other, the Ottoman Empire attempted to remain neutral. Britain had protected Turkey from Russia for many years, but if the Entente were to prevail over the Central Powers, Turkey feared the consequences of a victorious Russia. But a series of minor events was to destabilize Turkey's preference for neutrality and the Ottoman Empire joined the Central Powers, calling on all Muslims to join in a jihad against Britain, France and Russia. So began the process that would bring on the final destruction of the Ottoman Empire, followed by the occupation of the core Muslim lands by the British, and the re-demonization of Islam in the modern era.

Piracy on the Tyne

During the summer of 1914 the new revolutionary rulers of the Ottoman Empire, the Young Turks, who had overthrown the old order during the previous decade, wished to avoid the decision to join one side or the other in the coming World War. On one hand, they mistrusted Germany's Berlin-to-Baghdad military ambitions. On the other hand, the British were the traditional protectors of Turkey, and had protected the Ottoman Empire from Russian aggression at great cost through the Crimean War. But half a century on, Britain was losing patience with her cruel and ramshackle client and was considering the annexation of Egypt, nominally an Ottoman province, while Russia, now Britain's ally, once again coveted Istanbul and the Bosporus. Turkey had offered Britain a permanent alliance in 1911, but the very idea of a relationship had been summarily dismissed by the British cabinet, in high imperial style, as 'unworthy'. Germany was keen, however. Under the threatening shadow of a two-front war the Kaiser was anxious to recruit any allies available. Turkey's ruling Committee of Union and Progress accepted the German offer of alliance in principle but then dithered over the formalities, hoping for some early indication of which side might be the more likely to win. Winston Churchill, then First Lord of the Admiralty, made the Turks' minds up for them.

The revolution in Turkey that had begun in 1908 promised a secu- larized and modernized state, and was to lead to the deposing of the last caliph in the line that had started with Abu Bakr in Medina. A new navy was to be developed following the Turkish defeat in the Balkan Wars of 1912, when the Ottoman Empire had been expelled from the last Muslim territories in Europe. Two battleships were ordered from Britain, to be built by shipyards on the Tyne and armed to the standard of the most powerful new warships in the British Navy. The huge cost of the ships was met by *zakāt* subscription, with contributions made by every subject of the Empire, however poor. The *Sultan Osman* and the *Reshadieh* were completed in May 1914, but a series of excuses was made by the British to avoid delivery, even though a substantial payment had been made and 500 Turkish sailors were waiting to board their ships and sail home. In July, a week before the outbreak of the European war, Churchill seized the battleships which were renamed and turned over to the Admiralty, ready for active service. When the news reached Turkey, England immediately became the popular enemy, a sentiment which, mixed with revived religious intensity, was to end so bloodily on the beaches of Gallipoli. Sir Edward Grey, the British Foreign Minister, sent a note to the Turkish government, explaining that Britain, 'with sincere regret', required the battleships 'for her own needs during the present crisis'. The Turkish crew was interned and financial compensation was not even mentioned. Grey's telegram arrived in Constantinople on 3 August 1914. Turkey signed the German treaty on the same day.

Although the First World War went well for Turkey initially, with the defeat of a British force in Palestine, the defeat of a second British force in Iraq, and a third victory over Britain at Gallipoli, Turkey's declaration of war nevertheless precipitated the formal annexation of Egypt by Britain and the beginning of the end of empire. By 1918 the Ottoman army had been defeated in both Iraq and Palestine, with the Ottoman territories occupied as far north as the borders of Anatolia.

At first the British war aim in the Middle East had been to 'roll-up' the Ottoman Empire, starting from Egypt, with an advance around the eastern end of the Mediterranean Sea, leading to the opening of a second front against Germany and Austria in the 'soft underbelly' of the Balkans. This became especially urgent for the Allies as the Russian army collapsed in the period leading up to the Revolution of 1917, which allowed the Germans to intensify pressure on the Allied trench lines in northern France with troops no longer required to face the Russians in the east. In order to hasten the opening of the planned Balkan second front, the British enlisted the help of the Arabs against the Turks, promising the Amir of Mecca (Guardian of the Holy Places but nevertheless an Arab Ottoman official) the kingship of a united and liberated Arabia in return for the declaration of an Arab Revolt backed by a jihad to counteract the earlier jihad of the Ottoman caliph against the Allies. The correspondence between Sir Henry McMahon, on behalf of the British government, and al-Hussein ibn Ali, the Amir, promised to 'uphold the independence of the Arabs' and to 'guarantee the Holy Places'. The latter assurance included Jerusalem.

But almost concurrently with this first promise, Britain negotiated a secret treaty with France, the Sykes–Picot Agreement, by which the Ottoman territories in the Middle East would be divided between the two powers after the war had been won, and not given to the Arabs. And in a third document (the Balfour Declaration, see Appendix 1), Britain promised the Jews of the world a 'national home' in Arab Palestine with the objective of hastening American entry into the war and gaining general Jewish support for the British war effort.

After the war was over and Britain was in occupation of the Middle East from Cairo to Damascus to Baghdad, the three conflicting promises were considered by a conference convened in Cairo in 1921 by Winston Churchill, then Secretary of the Colonies. The 'solution' to the problem adopted by the conference led to almost a century of violent conflict and remains the root cause of Middle East unrest in present times.

The Arab provinces of the defeated Ottoman Empire were divided up and effectively colonized, rather than liberated. France, despite fierce local opposition, occupied Lebanon and Syria, which were split into separate countries. Britain established control over the newly imposed states of Transjordan and Iraq, while claiming Iran as a sphere of influence. At the same time, Zionism, the mass emigration of Jews from around the world into Palestine (another new British colony) to create the promised 'national home', was adopted as British policy. Thus, despite the solemn promise made during the war, the Arabs who had been Britain's only allies in the field against the Turks, found that they were to be denied both freedom and unity, and that Islam's holy city of Jerusalem was to be taken out of Muslim control.

A further long-term tragedy rooted in the outcome of the Cairo conference was the failure to implement Kurdish nationhood, which would have been possible at a time when Britain had direct or indirect control over almost all the Kurdish lands. Instead, the Kurds were arbitrarily divided by the final Cairo settlement between the emerging nation-states of Turkey, Syria and Iraq, with further tribes spread into Iran, which was also under British influence at the time. Decades of oppression, war and misery for the Kurdish people were to flow from this decision, lasting up to the present day, still with no nationhood in sight.

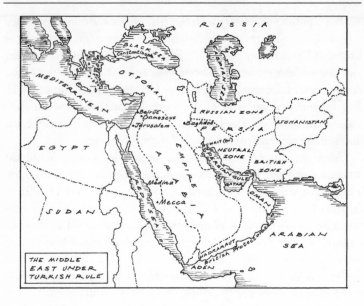

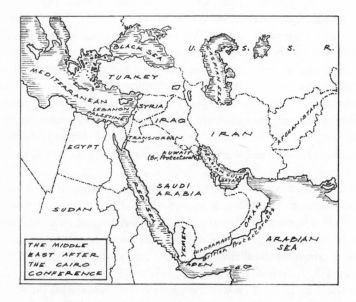

Maps of the Middle East showing results of the Cairo Conference, 1921

V   Islam in the Modern World

By the 1920s European colonization in various forms had prevailed over almost the entire Muslim world. Boundaries, where few or none had existed before, were imposed by the imperial powers, and later became the national boundaries of the states that make up the present map of Islam. Britain, France, Spain, Portugal, Holland and the former USSR all played a role.

Then, in a true historical irony, by fighting for or otherwise accepting self-rule within these new boundaries, the process by which independence was gained by the Muslim world worked to confirm the colonizers' policy of dividing Islam into separate synthetic 'states'. In addition, most emerging countries were simultaneously squeezed into the Western mould of a secular political system with no official place for religion. In this way the Europeans had, by the 1950s, effectively overturned fourteen centuries of Muslim history and tradition within one generation.

The further ironic consequence of this new 'historical geography' is that recently created and unstable nation-states with all-Muslim populations occupy a central strategic position on the face of the globe. Muslim states, moreover, control huge reserves of low-cost oil and gas in the Persian Gulf and these conventional supplies will continue long after all other non-Arab sources have been exhausted. During 2004, America already imported 56 per cent of oil and gas for domestic consumption and came into increasing competition with the Republic of China for sources of supply. (By the invasion of Iraq in 2003 the US wiped out China's entire investments in Iraqi oil production under Saddam.) The inexorable statistics of oil, mixed in with Muslims' unfulfilled spiritual and political hopes left over from the decolonization process, make it certain that Islam's effect on world events will remain significant for the foreseeable future. The only energy alternative lies in increased reliance on non-conventional oil supplies, principally the heavy oil reserves of Canada and Venezuela. (By 2030 Canadian production is projected to match current Saudi output.)

The sweeping political changes of the twentieth century were responsible for the creation of almost every one of the countries listed on p. 164.

- **Countries with an almost entirely Muslim population:**

Djibouti	Libya	Iran
Qatar	Jordan	Turkey
The Maldives	Somali Republic	Pakistan
United Arab Emirates	Tunisia	Indonesia
Bahrain	North Yemen	Comoro Islands
The Gambia	Saudi Arabia	Bangladesh
Sultanate of Oman	Iraq	Western Sahara
Kuwait	Algeria	Afghanistan
Mauritania	Morocco	Yemen
Mali		

- **Countries with an Islamic majority:**

Egypt	Niger	Turkmenistan
Senegal	Azerbaijan	Tajikistan
Syria	Guinea	
Sudan	Uzbekistan	
Chad	Albania	

- **Countries with a Muslim population of 25–50%:**

Guinea-Bissau	Gabon	Kazakhstan
Sierra Leone	Angola	Kyrgyzstan
Ivory Coast	Ethiopia	Malaysia
Nigeria	Albania	Lebanon

Before the arrival of the Europeans, almost none of these countries had existed as a separate state within their present boundaries. Most Muslim populations were passed by the hand of history directly from their previous condition as subjects of 'native' empires, first to colonial status, then to independence within an artificial nation-state, subject to a received form of Western political ideology. And these events, by their very nature, were ordered from the outside, rather than as a result of any form of internal popular choice.

Most Arabs, for example, were the subjects of the Ottoman Empire until 1918; the Muslims of India before the arrival of the British were part of various Asian empires that included many other religions; while Africans and Indonesians in pre-colonial times were generally grouped by tribe. These Arab, Indian, African and

Indonesian populations then passed from 'native' rule to European colonial rule, contained within new frontiers determined in distant European capitals with little regard for history, culture or religion. On gaining independence these colonial units became the 'nation-states' of Syria, Lebanon, Jordan, Iraq, Brunei, Sudan, Nigeria, Algeria and so on.

Only in the second half of the twentieth century did Muslim populations emerge from their previous subjections with both political independence and an Islamic majority. This has created opportunities not experienced since the days of the Prophet's Commonwealth to implement Islam as a social and political project as well as a personal religion. But the possibility of a 'return' to the imagined utopia of Medina in the seventh century CE, widely hoped for by Muslims, has come up against practical, national and international limitations.

Like most colonies, the future Muslim states struggled violently for their political independence from their colonizers, obscuring for the time being the question of what influence Islam would have on the regimes that were to follow the retreat of the imperial powers. This drive for independence resulted in widespread violence and almost all the principal Muslim states of the present day were born of armed conflict of some kind, from fierce all-out war in Algeria to the partition massacres in India and Pakistan. These events in turn threw up post-independence regimes of secular dictators, often nominally socialist, emerging victorious from anti-colonial campaigns, who held together their nation-states by force. Many such brutal arrangements were then consolidated with arms and money by either the West or the East during the Cold War. Syria, Algeria and Egypt, for example, 'went socialist', while Saudi Arabia, Pakistan and Indonesia were 'pro-Western'. And in the worldwide strategic confrontation of the 1960s, 1970s and 1980s, appalling examples of repression and mismanagement in Muslim countries were overlooked by both East and West in the name of either the 'free world' or 'anti-imperialism', with Islam once again ignored as a possible alternative form of government.

During the 1980s, the same economics that brought down the Berlin Wall also ended both American or Soviet support for many Third World dictatorships. From Yemen to Algeria, from Iran to Indonesia dictators fell or were seriously weakened. With this unwinding of the 'aligned' and 'non-aligned' divisions, the opportunity finally appeared for Islam to emerge as a system for running, or even merely influencing, society. The chance had come to sweep away the unwanted impositions, from foreign occupation to internal dictatorship, and to return to the laws that were established by the Prophet.

The concept of rule by a divine Qur'ān-based constitution, as we have seen, is what is meant by the Shariah in the widest sense. But instead of the emergence of the Shariah as the basis of a constitutional solution in the post-native empire, post-colonial, and post-Cold War Muslim world, the twentieth-century concept of the secular state has been reinforced by the West. The former bloody excesses of dictators may be retreating, but the old military men, taking advantage of the former ideological divide between communism and capitalism, have been succeeded by a new ruling elite of civilians who have replaced overt repression with state corruption, backed by formidable police powers. Once again, abuses that would be unthinkable within Western countries themselves are tolerated by the West: the absence of financial accountability, censorship of the press, ubiquitous paramilitary presence, straw parliamentary parties winning 95 per cent of the vote and full of businessmen on the make, and so on.

On the streets of Cairo or Lahore, of course, the perpetrator of all these misdeeds and injustices is not the 'West' in the general sense used here, but America specifically. America's pragmatic self-interest has frequently led to support for men like Saddam Hussein, the former Shah of Iran, or the rulers of Saudi Arabia, but then at a later date the same motivation has produced a change, ignoring the resulting injustices to the subject populations. And since American policy is consistently promoted in terms of 'democracy' and 'freedom', we can hardly be surprised that Muslims do not see the future paths of their societies as following the West into the dark side of these words: pacification by consumption, political half-truths and declining religious observance. In any event, materialist liberalism is a convenient belief for those already rich, but the creed has yet to offer any real solution to the impoverished majority of the world. Rather, the reality is that in almost all of the Islamic countries now controlled by questionable voting and corruption, a strong majority of the population would vote for the establishment of some form of Islamic state under the Shariah out of sheer frustration, if truly free elections were held.

There is, however, very little possibility that this will happen. Sitting rulers have the power of the state available to them at election time and the purist Muslim opposition is usually doctrinally split, or subject to crippling security restrictions. And, of course, the corrupt are quick to invoke the Qur'ān themselves, making a true contest between the existing hypocritical order and what are seen as God's laws almost impossible.

Thus in no Muslim country has the Shariah been given the time or the opportunity to prove whether or not the system can achieve a workable balance. Even in Iran and Saudi Arabia the historical legacy of ultra-conservatism has weighed down the possibilities of the Shariah with dogmatic rigidity and thus precipitated widespread, if suppressed, discontent.

To illustrate the general political impasse reached by much of Islam in the modern world, here are potted histories of eight Muslim states. These are countries whose problems are often sensationalized by the Western press, while the origins of their present conditions are ignored.

Algeria was united into the Umayyad dynasty and gradually converted to Islam during the eighth century CE, but stood for centuries on the edge of the events in both the Muslim and European spheres. In 1962 Algeria emerged from 132 years of French colonial rule after a bloody war of liberation. The economy of the country was destroyed and at least two million Algerians were killed. A significant number of the victims, as recently been revealed to the French public by a retired and bemedalled general, were tortured to death by French troops. And although French politicians claimed to be 'deeply shocked' and 'horrified' at the revelation, the events occurred during the time when a former President of the Republic was Minister of Justice, and the President in office at the time of writing served as an Intelligence officer in Algeria during the war. (The general, Paul Aussaresses, was tried and convicted following the publication, not for his activities in Algeria, but for writing the book, and thus 'condoning war crimes'.)

In the forty years since independence, the leadership of the victorious Algerian army, through the National Liberation Front (FLN), has ruled aggressively in the name of state socialism. During this time the secular ideals of democracy and equality that were promised by the revolutionary leaders at the end of the war have given way to stagnation and corruption, with the result that the country remains bitter and impoverished. The opposition to the present military oligarchy, the Islamic Salvation Front (FIS), has grown steadily, operating from a network of radical mosques in the principal northern cities. The party advocates the implementation of the Shariah as the political ideology of the country, combined with a form of democracy and economic reform. In 1990, in the first free elections ever to be held in Algeria, the FIS took power in a majority of the municipalities across the country. In the first round of national elections in 1991 the FIS gained 188 of 435 seats (although with only 25 per cent of the popular vote), but the army intervened to remove the civilian FLN government and impose martial law. The President of the country was deposed, the leaders of the FIS were imprisoned and all religious organizations proscribed. The French government and the Western press were jubilant, offering immediate support to the new military dictatorship in the fight against 'fundamentalism'. In a European country such a coup would have caused international outrage.

A militant group broke away from the FIS and a guerrilla war began against the Algerian military (including the bombing of targets in Paris) that cost over 100,000 lives up to the end of 2001. The deaths included the massacre of the entire population of a number of rural villages, including women and children, which were at first presumed to be the work of the ex-FIS guerrillas, the GIA (supported, of course, according to the Algerian government, by al-Qaeda). But in the last few years even the French press has speculated that these endless murders, for which no suspect has ever been arrested, much less publicly tried and convicted, may in fact have been the work of the Algerian military, attempting to discredit the GIA in the eyes of the outside world and at the same time terrorize the population at home. Further, the unrestrained campaign by the Algerian government against any dissent, with thousands of suspects executed without trial, has had the effect of driving many young Algerian men abroad to become the foot-soldiers of Islamist insurgency worldwide. Yet France, fearing above all another flood of Muslim emigration across the Mediterranean, continues to support the existing military-backed regime with arms, cash and trade.

In September 2005 the Algerian government attempted to bring an end to both the civil war and to unanswered questions about the many unsolved atrocities and over 6,000 'disappearances'. Not through any form of 'truth and reconciliation commission', but with a plebiscite praising the Algerian army for 'saving the country'. No outside observers were permitted to monitor the poll, which inevitably resulted in the granting of unconditional amnesty to the army for all previous crimes by a '97 per cent yes' vote.

Meanwhile, with bald cynicism, the government of Algeria rushed to embrace America's 'War on Terrorism'. Subsequent support from the US for the continuation of the Algerian *pouvoir* culminated in Operation Flintlock in 2005, a major training operation in the southern Sahara in partnership with the Algerian and other national armies. The considerable cost of the exercise, complete with planes, tanks, helicopters and extensive support facilities, contrasted with a tragic period of drought and starvation in Niger and Chad, for which, ironically, a charitable appeal was launched on US television. The opportunity for Algerians to settle their method of government for themselves by a free election, that would undoubtedly return a pro-Shariah majority, seems as remote as in colonial days.

Pakistan (meaning Land of the Pure) formed part of the unified Indian Raj under British rule for 300 years until the middle of the twentieth century. After the Second World War, however, Britain was no longer able to maintain her empire either financially or morally. But in the rush to unload imperial responsibility for India and to avoid the further expensive entanglement that may have resulted from the proper maintenance of public security, sectarian violence brought on by approaching independence was left to spread unchecked. This in turn led Muslims to believe that a hijrah to a separate Islamic state was their only safeguard against the Hindu majority. Then Britain's heinous incompetence in managing the ensuing partition of the country during the two years of post-imperial panic as Pakistan and India moved towards independence, resulted in the expulsion or death of millions from both communities. The new state of Pakistan, born of bloodshed, was to 'return to the original purity of Islam' in the words of Muhammad Iqbal, the intellectual founder of Muslim independence. The 1956 constitution declared Pakistan to be an 'Islamic Republic', but a state ruled by the Qur'ān turned out to be beyond the reach of imperfect politicians. The ideal of an Islamic state was compromised from the start by the very upper-class and military oligarchy that had first promoted the concept. Once the unaccountable institutions of the former Raj were in their hands, the concept of the Shariah turned from being an objective to become a threat to the existing order and only token reforms have ever been implemented, often by merely changing the titles and headings of existing legislation. Pakistan's ideal has been further compromised by the retention of virtual feudalism in the Punjab, distrust of the central government by the strongly Muslim tribes of the North West frontier, and the conduct and expense of three wars with India over the province of Kashmir, a further legacy of the Raj.

Reformist Islamist movements never took hold in Pakistan, as in Egypt, for example, the new country being too traumatized at birth (and remaining on a war footing against India ever since) or distracted by extreme poverty and the violent break-away of East Pakistan (on the other side of the Indian sub-continent) to become Bangladesh. Instead, Pakistan has developed a deeply conservative and stagnant Muslim culture, inward-looking, fearful of India and the West, and convinced that the slightest deviation from orthodoxy will sweep the country away.

Pakistan's recent history has been dominated by tension between the secular management of the state on the one hand (often by the pro-Western army), covered by a thin veneer of Islam but internally riddled with corruption, and a desire by the majority on the other for some unspecified Islamic *tawhid* or theo-democracy, based on the security of a traditional way of life. Thus the Shariah has made little progress, only trotted out when the government seeks a diversion away from any number of recurring crises. The implementation of an Islamic state is further frustrated by clashes between the minority Shi'a and majority Sunni, and between the natives of Sind and Karachi with the Muhajirs (immigrants from India from the time of partition). In addition, Pakistan's conduct of proxy wars with a religious character in both Afghanistan and Kashmir has resulted in the import into Pakistan of destabilizing armed militancy and drug-related gangsterism (not to mention, reputedly, Osama ibn Laden himself). Islamism has also been dangerously manipulated internally by successive governments and their security services as a source of political support in the wilder regions, and military support in Kashmir.

During the Cold War and the occupation of Afghanistan by the USSR, Pakistan was able to exploit geography in order to keep aid and arms flowing from the West, without any serious criticism of internal policies. In the twenty-first century Pakistan's combination of nuclear power and Muslim militancy has the capacity to frighten the West into continued support. Although this brinkmanship is often taken to the very edge, the West ultimately has no alternative. The active support given by Pakistan's military government to America's overthrow of the Afghan Taliban (former clients of Pakistan) is a further example of the same cycle. In return, Pakistan's profile in the west has been raised from isolated state to strategic ally, and the country's external debt has once again been renegotiated, without any commitment extracted to democratic reform and an end to military rule. Even the West's obsession with Pakistan's 10,000 *madrasahs* has resulted in very little change, with General Pervez Musharraf still dependent on right-wing religious support for his control over the mainstream political parties.

Kashmir, described by a Mughal emperor as a paradise on earth, attempted (under a Hindu Maharaja imposed a century earlier by the British Raj) to gain independence at the same time as India and Pakistan. When the overwhelmingly Muslim population objected, some violently, the Maharaja asked for help from the Indian Army. The first Indo-Pakistan war followed, with both sides claiming the whole of Kashmir. A Line of Control was established by a UN ceasefire in 1949, which divided the state between India and Pakistan. Both countries promptly assimilated their share, while still claiming the portion given to the other. Further fighting in 1965 resulted in a second deadlock. The Indian portion of Kashmir, renamed Jammu and Kashmir, the only Muslim majority state in the county, has been in a virtual state of uprising ever since, resulting in

direct rule by the Hindu-dominated Union government in New
Delhi. This is justified on the basis that Kashmir is essential to the
country's defence against China, and that India is a secular democracy and religion irrelevant. But at the same time India has consistently refused to hold the plebiscite mandated by United Nations
resolution as part of the 1949 ceasefire, and specifically promised to
Kashmiris at the time. Yet opponents of Indian rule are referred to
as 'terrorists', and Kashmir has long been subject to appalling
human rights abuses and corruption by the Indian Army. This, in
turn, has provoked further violence, leading to thousands of deaths
annually, as well as the inevitable collapse of tourism, once the core
of the Kashmiri economy. At the same time Pakistan claims Kashmir
as unfinished business from the catastrophic British withdrawal of
1947, and as a vital element of the state that was set up specifically
to offer a refuge to Muslims. In another version of the name,
Pakistan stands for **P**unjabis, **A**fghans, **K**ashmiris, **S**indis and the
people of Balukhi**stan**.

The Dutch colonialization of **Indonesia**, that began with spice
trading in the seventeenth century, came to an abrupt halt with the
Japanese invasion of 1942. Ironically, the Japanese, however brutal
their occupation of the Indonesian archipelago may have been,
respected Islam as an anti-European force, and in the period up to
the defeat of Japan by the Allies in 1945 the idea began to develop
among Indonesians of Indonesia as a united and independent
Islamic nation. Independence was declared from Holland the same
year with the acquiescence of the departing Japanese, but the Dutch
attempted a return after the war to 'punish the collaborators', and
complete native sovereignty was only conceded after another four
years of futile colonial brutality. The country that the new independent government inherited consists of 13,000 islands of varying
historical backgrounds that had never constituted a united political
entity before colonization. The result is that Hindu, Buddhist,
pagan and Christian societies are closely mixed with the world's
largest Muslim population, which had reached an estimated 180
million at the turn of the twentieth century. This history has given
Indonesian Islam a tolerant folkloric character, split into many
conflicting doctrinal groups. But recently outside pressure and a

worldwide Muslim self-consciousness has led to stricter Sunni observance. The development of extreme literalist elements has followed specifically the Jemmah Islamiah and the Islam Defenders Front, leading to an escalation in violent confrontation with the heretical ways of the past, almost unchecked by the central government. The Bali nightclub bombing of October 2004 was one tragic outcome.

Indonesia reversed the usual course of post-colonial history by starting with a period of political instability under President Sukarno, from 1950 to 1965, and following with a 'strong-man' dictatorship. President Suharto came to power in 1965 with his New Order, suppressing the chaotic Old Order with great ferocity during which, it is now estimated, one million civilians were killed. But rigged elections and support from the West and from the Association of South Eastern Nations (ASEAN, a Pacific version of NATO), together with considerable oil revenues, gave the regime the appearance of legitimacy and the brutal rule of the army was ignored by the rest of the world. In the name of 'development' and 'stability', rigid central authority was imposed on all regions, millions were forcibly resettled from urban to hostile rural areas, for which purpose large tracts of land were appropriated from their peasant owners.

But the stability of the New Order and the status of the country as an 'Asian Tiger' with a miracle economy proved to be a corrupt illusion and civil order collapsed during the South-east Asian economic recession which began in 1997. Most regions beyond Java have demanded devolution or outright independence from central control and many have also called for the implementation of the Shariah as the solution to Indonesia's chronic problems, once again raising the utopian ideal of the Prophet's Commonwealth. As history began to unravel with the end of Suharto's rule in 1998, communal violence spread, especially in Aceh, Kalimantan (Borneo) and the Moluccas. Despite the extremely bloody record of the Suharto government, which was heavily supported by Europe and the US for thirty years, news reporting in the West has fixed the responsibility for the current unrest on 'Muslim aggression' or 'militant Islam'. In fact the tolerant Indonesian verion of Islam is prospering under the beginnings of democracy, and regional disturbances are the product of decades of criminal mismanagement and forced internal cross-cultural immigration, resulting in violent disputes about the ownership of land.

From the time of the division of the Roman Empire into east and west in 395 CE, the territory that is modern **Turkey** was the core of the Eastern Roman or Byzantine Christian Empire. Byzantium steadily gave way to Islam, until by the 1500s the Ottoman Empire had entirely replaced the previous Christian empire in Turkey as well as in the Balkans (Greece, Macedonia, Albania, Bosnia, Bulgaria) and in the eastern Mediterranean and across North Africa. But by the end of the First World War only metropolitan Turkey remained of the old Ottoman Empire, ironically the only part to achieve full and immediate post-war independence. As a sequel to the Young Turks' revolution of 1908, a Republic was declared in 1923 under Mustafa Kemal (later known as Atatürk) to resist the punitive terms imposed by the victorious Allies.

The new national state of Turkey was defined by Atatürk as an uncompromisingly lay society with no official place for Islam, thus signifying a turn away from the Arab world and a conscious wish to be considered a part of Europe. The call to prayer was banned, Sunday rather than Friday became the official day of rest, and religious schools were closed. But almost eighty years on, the strongly centralized army-influenced state has become ossified, corrupt and violently repressive, the very afflictions that Atatürk sought to abolish with his revolution. The way in which the Turkish state deals with Islam has led to particularly bizarre results. The population is 97 per cent Muslim, yet the army men, much cosseted by the West when Turkey was on the front line of the Cold War against the USSR, impose comprehensive restrictions on all forms of Muslim observance, supposedly to protect the state against *irtica*, a nebulous fundamentalist threat that is apparently about to overtake the country at any minute. Headscarves are banned, beards and turbans are risky, mosques are strictly controlled, and heavy penalties have been imposed for the use of the word jihad in public. Protestors, from MPs to street demonstrators, have been jailed under inhuman conditions or removed from politics for life, and a hidden dirty war continues between the army and Kurds advocating cultural freedom, much less political independence. In their frustration, dissidents express the ironic opinion that membership of the European Union will guarantee civil rights, and thus permit the liberation of Islam as well as the preservation of Kurdish identity. The absence of religious and political freedom in Turkey is indeed one of the obstacles to Union membership, brought into focus once again by the arrest in 2005 of the author Orhan Pamuk for daring to suggest that the Armenian Massacre by Turkish troops in 1908 may be a historical fact. But in any event, popular European public opinion, reacting to friction with the existing Muslim minorities, is a long way from accepting an Islamic member, even under the moderate government elected in 2002. And with hundreds of reporters in Turkish prisons, a constitution edited by the military, and civil liberties viewed by even elected governments as a subversive concept, Turkey's application to join Europe remains firmly at the bottom of the list. But the historic opportunity will be lost to hinge Europe and the Middle East through Turkey as an Islamic EU member.

Afghanistan's Muslim history has been 'typical' (from native empire to European dominance, then passing through a bloody war of independence to an unstable present) but to an extreme degree not matched in any other modern Muslim nation-state, except possibly Somalia. Almost all the conquerors in the history of Islam have crossed through the country's mountain passes, including the Umayyads and the 'Abbāsids, the Mongols, the Mughals and the Persian Safavids, leaving behind them tribes of widely different ethnic origin: from the Turkic peoples of the north, connected to the nomads of Central Asia, to the Shi'a in the west (Dari speakers of Persian origin) to the Pashtuns of the south (Sunnis claiming descent from Oways, a Companion of the Prophet). Afghanistan's violent history has created a deeply cherished warrior tradition of self-reliance, combined with the Islamic ideals of equality and justice, while invasion and counter-invasion to and from Persia have produced a historic hostility between the majority Sunni tribes and the minority Shi'ites.

In the eighteenth century a recognizable Afghan state under the Pashtun Durrani dynasty finally emerged from the preceding empires, but from early in the nineteenth century on, the Durranis were besieged and manipulated by both Russia from the north and Britain from India in the south, in the era of geo-political competition known as the Great Game. The outcome was British domination of the country and the violent suppression of non-Pashtun tribes with British support. The Pashtun Durranis were deposed in 1973 and a Republic was declared by the northern tribes, who turned to the USSR for assistance, while the Pashtuns, now in opposition, were supported by Pakistan. Afghanistan thus fell into the Soviet orbit and a series of coups brought a communist government to power. This in turn led to rebellion by the devout Sunni Pashtuns and others, against the communist 'infidels', precipitating the Soviet response of invasion in 1979. The country was then at the very centre of the Cold War, with the Pashtun Mujahidin, or Fighters in the Cause of God, as the rebels called themselves, fighting directly against the Soviet army, backed in their jihad by the US, China and Saudi Arabia. During this period any inconvenience to US policy, such as mujahidin war crimes or drug-trafficking, was ignored. And a further product of US support was the creation of the 'Arab Afghans'. This cadre of 20,000 zealous warriors from mostly Arab countries, armed by America and funded by Saudi Arabia, was, however, devoted to a concept of Muslim destiny that found common cause with America against the Soviets only temporarily. Their number included twenty-six-year-old Osama ibn Laden, master propagandist, inspired quartermaster and tactician.

Al-Kifah was formed in the early 1980s to recruit new members, to be replaced by the secure inner circle of al-Qaeda in 1989 after al-Kifah had been penetrated by the secret services of Arab governments. Later, after ibn Laden's disillusionment with America following the abandonment of the victorious Afghan Muslims and the establishment of American bases in the Prophet's holy land of Arabia, the concept now known as al-Qaeda spread out into thirty or more countries, seeking the implementation of the Shariah in the Muslim world.

In the vacuum left in Afghanistan by the precipitous departure of both the Russians and the Americans, a vicious civil war was waged between the armed ethnic and tribal groups and their respective warlords, until the country had been reduced to a series of fiefdoms, with what remained of both the agricultural and the urban infrastructures utterly devastated. The former mujahidin command-ers now became the new oppressors and the flood of the dispossessed into Pakistan, that had begun in 1973, intensified. During the next twenty years a new generation came of age in the hopeless refugee camps on the Pakistan side of the border. These were the sons of dis-enchanted mujahidin foot soldiers, for whom the only available education was as a *talib*, or student of Islam, in *madrasahs* run by half-literate mullahs whose sole source was the text of the Qur'ān, misread against a backdrop of continuous war and extreme personal suffering. This group, calling themselves Taliban (plural of *talib*), began with sixteen rifles in 1994, seeing their first action with the rescue of village girls held in Kandahar in sexual slavery by a regional strong-man. But by early 1997, after a ferocious advance against the northern tribes and the rump of communism, and supported by Iran, the Taliban were in control of 90 per cent of Afghanistan, including Kabul. Their leaders immediately set about the imple-mentation of their interpretation of the Qur'ān in an attempt to turn back the clock to a mythical time when Afghanistan was peace-ful and united, based on the even more distant utopia of the Prophet's Commonwealth of Medina.

But the brutal zeal of the Taliban met with a level of inter-national criticism, relating to such single issues as women's rights or the demolition of Buddhist statues, that failed entirely to take into account the highly destructive manipulation of Afghanistan by out-side powers in the recent past (or the earlier more widespread destruction of Afghanistan's cultural heritage by the mujahidin during the time when they were important to the West). The West was delighted with the defeat of the Soviet army in Afghanistan, as the Russians had now suffered their 'own Vietnam'. In fact the vic-tory of the mujahidin contributed significantly to the fall of the Berlin Wall and the end of communism. This was only made possi-ble, however, by using the Pashtun rebels as the West's proxy fighters, supported by a flood of arms into Afghanistan through the West's client, Pakistan. And it was the Afghanis, not the West who paid the price for this terrible Cold War victory: with the destruc-tion of Herat, for example, during which over 20,000 people died and one of the oldest cities in the world was devastated, or with the ruinous mining of Kandahar and the surrounding farmlands. There were terrible tragedies both communal and individual during these years, with millions killed and injured, including many of the leadership of the Taliban, most of whom were missing a limb or an eye.

Under these circumstances the status of women and the destruction of statues were surely irrelevant to the need for peaceful reconstruction. By abandoning their valiant former proxies the US had created a new level of tragedy. Regional powers (Iran and Pakistan in particular) were free to wield power and perpetuate the fighting, international insurgency and drug-dealing had found a new sanctuary, and threatened with Islamist destabilization, the ex-USSR Central Asian republics were able to justify their harsh regimes.

With the events of September 11th 2001, Afghanistan again became the centre of world attention. The refusal of the Taliban government to give up Osama ibn Laden, presumed to be responsible for the strikes on New York and Washington, together with other members of al-Qaeda, led to an American attack on the country. Heavy bombing completed the devastation of the previous two decades, and within three months, according to Human Rights Watch, more innocent Afghan civilians had been killed than had died in the suicide attacks on New York and Washington. The enormous disparity between the power of America and the primitive resources of the Taliban resulted in the speedy collapse of the regime, which was replaced by an interim Western-friendly inter-tribal government, but with a very limited writ beyond Kabul. And the new power in the land included a disturbing number of the mujahidin elements responsible for the collapse of the country into chaos and drug-production prior to the arrival of the Taliban. Further, while the role of religion in government, the original motivation of the Taliban, may be temporarily obscured by plans for reconstruction, this core issue has not been settled by American bombs or 'regime change'.

Syria has been at the centre of Middle East history since the dawn of time, forming part of the Phoenician, Persian, Greek, Roman and Byzantine Empires, among others. Syria was the first territory to come under Muslim rule during the expansion of Islam in the seventh century and has been continuously Muslim ever since. Under the Ottoman Empire, Syria was a quasi-independent *vilayet*, or administrative district, run by Arabs but under a Turkish governor. On the defeat of the Turks in 1918, the British occupied Damascus, but passed Syria to France under the Sykes-Picot Agreement, rather than back to the Arabs as previously promised. France maintained Syria as a colony until 1946, despite unrelenting Arab opposition and great loss of life on both sides. The Syrian army ruled for the first twenty years after the defeat of the French, during which time the country suffered ten coups, the last of which, in 1970, brought Hafez al-Assad and the Ba'th Party to power. A fiercely repressive regime followed, nominally socialist and pro-Soviet, turning in the 1980s to superficial economic reforms and wholesale corruption, with the development of a patronage system based on oil revenues. The elite around the President, and particularly his own Alawite clan, grew immensely rich while the average per capita income declined steadily and military expenditure consumed 50 per cent of government revenues.

Islamist opposition was especially targeted by Syria's dozen or more secret services. An insurrection by the Muslim Brotherhood in Hama in 1982 was put down with the full force of the Syrian military, 10,000 people were killed and the town destroyed. Syria intervened in the civil war in Lebanon and occupied that country for twenty-eight years to 2005. Yet none of these obscene actions disqualified al-Assad as a suitable partner for the West in the Gulf War of 1990, and in 2001 Syria was chosen to sit on the Security Council of the United Nations.

During the 1980s Syria took virtual control of Lebanese politics initially to suppress the ambitions of the Muslim left and the Palestine Liberation Organization (PLO), but later came into direct conflict with Israel, following Israel's invasion of the South. Syria has opposed the existence of Israel since 1948, participating in all three Arab–Israeli wars, and losing in 1967 a large part of Southern Syria to Israeli invasion, and the de facto annexation of large areas of Syrian territory for Jewish settlements. Syria's participation is thus at vital to any comprehensive peace in the Middle East.

Repression in Syria of both Muslim aspirations and human rights continues under al-Assad's son Bashshār al-Assad, whose succession in 2001 created the first 'republican monarchy' in the Arab world. Syria has recently come under pressure from the United

States, but not to rectify internal injustices, or to ensure free elections. Rather, the opportunity was provided by the assassination in Beirut of Rafik al-Hariri, the former Lebanese prime minister (and outspoken opponent of Syrian influence in Lebanon) to remove Bashshār through apparently legitimate means, so ending Syria's opposition to Israeli expansion as well as Syrian support for Hizbullah. If the United Nations investigation into the huge explosion that killed al-Hariri and his bodyguard (on St Valentine's Day 2004) can be traced to Damascus, a repeat of the sanctions and no-fly zones used against Iraq may be expected. And in a possible US 'exit strategy' from Iraq, unable to prevent the break-up of that artificial state, the Iraqi 'Sunni triangle' could only be permitted inevitable association with Syria if that country's regime were first rendered 'user friendly' to American policy.

Egypt gained limited independence from Britain in 1923 as a constitutional monarchy. The new state was based on the Western-style secular nation-state, rather than on the Shariah which was clearly the preference of the majority. Instead, Islam was relegated to one clause in the new constitution, which also provided for religious appointments to be controlled by the state. An elite with European tastes took power, and political repression with a religious veneer forced the opposition to turn to the Society of Muslim Brothers, which preached rejection of the post-colonial state as a new *Jāhiliyyah*, and the building of a new state 'under God's law'. The post-colonial constitution was overthrown in 1952 by a coup led by Neguib and the Free Officers, the monarchy was abolished in 1953, and in 1954 Jamal 'Abd Nasser came to power. Nasser enjoyed great popularity in Egypt, for nationalising the banks and the Suez Canal, and for his apparent defeat of Britain and France in the Suez Crisis of 1956. His Revolutionary Command Council was initially supported by the Brotherhood, but the RCC's failure to implement the Shariah and other social reforms as promised, together with Nasser's failures against Israel, especially the disaster of the 1967 war, led to violent dissension. An unconvincing attempt on the life of Nasser, probably staged by his own police, provided the opportunity for the Brotherhood to be crushed, with many imprisoned and their leaders tortured and hanged, including Sayyid Qutb, the uncompromising intellectual theorist of the movement (whose sister was gang-raped in front of him in a Cairo jail).

Anwar Sadat came to power following Nasser's death in 1970 with a 'corrective coup', after which Soviet influence was ended and the economy was opened to the West. The immediate result was that the poor became poorer and the rich richer, while political repression continued – though cynically combined with populist Islam in an attempt to improve the regime's image. Protest continued nevertheless, culminating in the assassination of Sadat and the start of the current regime under Hosni Mubarak, a former air-force general. At the opening of the twenty-first century Egypt is America's heavily subsidized protégé to the tune of $2 billion per year, much of which is spent on infrastructure, although the programme is deeply compromised by the corruption of the state from top to bottom. And every two years, except for 2003, the year of the invasion of Iraq, American and Egyptian forces hold joint exercises in the Western Desert, codenamed Bright Star. The war games are the largest joint training exercises in the world.

But the price of even mild economic reform has been a further division between rich and poor, with public services crumbling, held together by a twenty-year state of emergency which prohibits all deviation, from homosexuality to demonstrations in support of the Palestinian intifada. Democracy is a sham, even after an attempted intervention by the judiciary, and in any event parliament operates on the same level as a European municipal council. The West appears to be influencing the separation of state and mosque in Egypt but the US clearly prefers cosmetic change to profound reform, so that political liberalization is a further sham. The main opposition party, the Muslim Brotherhood (which renounced violence a generation ago) is banned, every attempt at peaceful demonstration is outnumbered and broken up by police, detention and torture are common, while the President continues to maintain that his measures are all that stand between civil order and Islamist chaos. The government manipulates all the important issues: the budget, the media, the armed forces and patronage, while the rate of unemployment among young men is catastrophic. These are the conditions that brought on the revolution of fifty years ago.

Iraq became an independent state in 1932, following centuries of Ottoman rule ending with the Turkish defeat of 1918, and fourteen years of British rule as a League of Nations Mandate. But with independence Iraq inherited the poisonous seeds of turmoil and misery that have endured up to the present day. As part of the Ottoman Empire, what is now Iraq had been loosely administered as three distinct *vilayets* centred on Mosul, Baghdad and Basra, respectively containing majorities of three different peoples with little in common: Kurds in the north, politically dominant Arab Sunnis, and poor southern Shiʿa. As the frontline between the Ottoman Empire and Safavid Persia, the area that is the present Iraq/Iran border had been the subject of endless armed contention, leading to the capture by the Turks of the Shiʿa shrines of Najaf and Karbalā and the forcible inclusion of a substantial Shiʿa Persian population under Ottoman rule, who were then savagely persecuted by the Turks over the following centuries as enemy aliens. The border demarcation question remained unresolved, however, to be passed on to the new state via Churchill's Cairo Conference of 1921. Thus Iraq began statehood with a ready-made source of dispute with Iran, as well as unjustified national borders that packaged the three former Ottoman *vilayets* into an artificial nation-state. A form of the British 'first past the post' parliamentary system of government was imposed on the new state, wholly alien to Iraqi culture. Also imposed on Iraq was a king (Faisal, son of Husain the Amir of Mecca), who came from the far side of Arabia and whose confirmation by plebiscite was openly manipulated by the British administration. Further, during the British 'period of assistance' (1918–32) political violence became a way of life with internal opposition suppressed by the British army and the Royal Air Force with great loss of native life. Even during the interim period of direct British military rule, 1918–21, before a League of Nations Mandate was imposed, 10,000 Iraqis were killed by British occupation using air power and poisonous gas.

Independence on this synthetic basis resulted in classic instability. Coup followed coup as dominant Sunni groups competed for power and wealth, with the majority Shiʿa mostly excluded. All-out war between Baghdad and the Kurdish minority in the north-east of the country (where two thirds of Iraq's oil reserves are located) alternated with unworkable peace treaties. The British reoccupied during the Second World War in order to control oil supplies, then in 1958 the monarchy was overthrown and Faisal's grandson, Faisal II, was executed. But the new order that replaced the monarchists and their British imperialist patrons was republican only in name. General Abd al-Karim Qasim held power as a military dictator, establishing a form of fascist grip on all aspects of Iraqi life through tentacles of patronage extending into every level of society, including control of the traditional tribal sheikhs. Promises of reform (principally land redistribution and elections) were abandoned, political activity was suppressed and the army put down protests from the country's ethnic and religious groups with great ferocity. Civil war began once again between the northern Kurds and the Sunni rulers. Qasim was armed by the USSR, who also supported Iraq's renewed border claims against monarchist Iran (supported by the US), as well as Iraq's demand that oil-rich Kuwait (newly independent from, and supported by, Britain) should be 'returned' to Iraq, on the historically inaccurate basis that Kuwait had formed part of the original Ottoman *vilayet* of Basra. Five years later Qasim was overthrown and shot by a Ba'th or Renaissance Party coup in the name of 'Freedom, Unity, Socialism', supported by a group of younger army officers. Nevertheless, under a series of Ba'thist dictators, the patronage system based on oil revenues, the persecution of the Shi'a and the war against the Kurds all continued unchanged, despite the rhetoric of popular socialism.

Saddam Hussein had joined the Arab Ba'th Socialist Party (ABSP) as a young operative in 1958, taking part in a failed 1959 attempt on the life of Qasim. After a short exile which ended with the successful 1963 Ba'thist coup, Saddam moved up rapidly, developing his own patron-client system based on financial and political influence. By 1975 Saddam was effective ruler of Iraq behind the ailing President Ahmed Hassan al-Bakr, and in exclusive control of oil revenues and arms purchases, as well as the security services. The Iranian Revolution of 1979 threatened Iraq with Shi'ite unrest and Saddam took the opportunity to remove al-Bakr and to proclaim himself President. At the same time Shi'a demonstrations were suppressed by the army and over 500 senior Ba'thists from rival patronage groups were executed, many arrested during a party conference, as Saddam, smoking a large cigar, and feigning tears, looked on from the podium. He was forty-two, the son of peasants and without military experience, but poisonously charming, capriciously generous and murderously ruthless. The Ba'thist form of fascist rule was tightened up, centred on the person of Saddam, who exercised control down to the grass roots through the expansion of the ABSP organization.

Iran under Khomeini, following the overthrow of the Shah, while already providing support to Kurdish and Shiʿa dissidents within Iraq, rapidly became a revolutionary threat to the oligarchical Gulf States as well. In order to increase his international stature as a Sunni Arab leader and unite Iraq behind him, Saddam reopened the centuries-old border dispute with Iran. In September 1981, under the impression that Iran had been weakened by the Revolution, and with logistical support from both the USSR and the West, as well as financial support from the Gulf States, Iraq invaded the disputed border territory, the navigable Shatt al-Arab, or Arab River, the delta where the Tigris and Euphrates rivers flow into the Gulf. But Saddam had miscalculated: war had the effect of consolidating the Iranian Revolution and fanatical Iranian counter-attacks soon threatened both the Iraqi state and Saddam's rule. Iraq rearmed (including preparations for bacterial warfare) looking to the oil-rich Arab states for contributions following the destruction of many of Iraq's own oil facilities by Iran. Saddam also intensified nuclear development, but the principal Iraqi plant was destroyed by the Israeli air force while still under construction. An eight-year war of attrition with Iran followed, with great loss of life, especially on the Iranian side. Revolutionary Iran had now become an active military threat to the Gulf States, to the stability of the Muslim states of the USSR on Iran's northern border, and to world oil supplies. The US navy intervened to destroy half the Iranian navy, and the West, with support from Saudi Arabia, began fresh arms shipments to Iraq, as well as providing satellite intelligence. Iran, facing such overwhelming odds, reluctantly agreed to a UN ceasefire in which neither side made any territorial gains.

With the end of the conflict Saddam's domestic unpopularity could not be disguised by his claim to 'victory' and he moved to reconsolidate his position. His Republican Guard devastated those parts of the Kurdish territories, supported by Iran, which had revolted during the war. Shiʿa dissent within Iraq was also suppressed once again, and the officer corps was purged of potential rivals and their supporters. But the Iraqi economy was in ruins, more than $80 billion in debt during a period of low oil prices, as well as suffering from runaway inflation and high unemployment. When menaced by Iran, the Gulf States had appeared willing to forgive Iraq's growing war debt and assist in post-war reconstruction, but once the Iranian threat had been contained, the promises were side-stepped. Simultaneously, Kuwait began to flout OPEC-allocated oil production quotas, to Iraq's detriment, as well as reopening an old frontier dispute based on the nineteenth-century Ottoman borders.

In desperation Saddam ordered the occupation of Kuwait, which was completed in under eight hours. Saddam anticipated that his move would extract from Saudi Arabia and the smaller oil producers of the Gulf sufficient economic concessions to rebuild his patronage system, and he apparently understood (from US Ambassador April Glaspie) that his wartime ally, the United States, would remain neutral. Kuwait was formally annexed to Iraq, justified by propaganda about 'Arab unity', correcting the 'British imperialism' that had separated Kuwait from the former *vilayet* of Basra in 1921, and linking the occupation of Kuwait to Israeli occupation of Palestine. But Saddam had made an even more spectacular miscalculation than his invasion of Iran. A Western Coalition led by America, and supported by UN authority, expelled Iraq from Kuwait within four days of the launch of Operation Desert Saber in February 1991, following an intense bombardment of Iraqi infrastructure (subsequently referred to by Iraqi propaganda as the 'Mother of All Battles' and 'The Thirty-Country Aggression'). Iraq suffered 62,000 casualties, the Coalition 97.

Perceiving the regime of Saddam Hussein to be defeated, spontaneous revolts broke out in the Shiʿa south and Kurdish north, but Saddam's National Guard had been held in reserve to deal with internal security and the Western Coalition could not agree between themselves on an advance beyond the borders of Kuwait into Iraq. Further, in order to build Arab support for Desert Saber, the US had promised to limit the action to the relief of Kuwait. The result was the ferocious and unchecked suppression of the Iraqi rebels by

Saddam's military, with great loss of life. A 'no-fly' zone was imposed on northern Iraq by the Coalition, later extended to the south, in an attempt to protect the Kurdish and Shi'a communities, but no other assistance was offered to the rebels. Once the threat from Iraq against the ruling families of Kuwait, Saudi Arabia (now grown into an elite over 30,000 strong) and the United Arab Emirates had been removed, the US-led Coalition effectively chose to allow the continuation of the Iraqi regime (although Saddam Hussein himself was the target for a number of American-backed assassination attempts) over the prospect of civil war.

Internal turmoil in Iraq would, it was feared, lead to intervention by, and the strengthening of, Iran. The US also feared invasion of Iraq by Turkey to suppress Kurdish independence before the revolt could spread, while Saudi Arabia wished to prevent elections or revolution in Iraq that would lead to a Shi'a government on its border. Iraq was, therefore, to be contained by economic sanctions, imposed through the agency of the UN with the expressed aim of extracting reparations for Kuwait, paying the UN's administrative costs, and removing Saddam's ability to build weapons of mass destruction. Inspections of Iraq by a UN Special Commission (Unscom) and the International Atomic Energy Agency (IAEA) began in May 1991, searching for chemical, biological and nuclear weapons, and ballistic missiles. Over the following six years much of Iraq's capability was destroyed, but the activities of Unscom nevertheless ended in stalemate. In 1997 Unscom claimed that a residual biological warfare programme with the potential to manufacture anthrax, botulin and VX nerve gas was being concealed by Iraq. Although no direct proof was produced by Unscom, Iraq had allegedly not accounted for 17 tonnes of imported biological growth medium. But at the same time Saddam released evidence showing that the UN inspection team had been used by the American CIA and NSA for clandestine espionage beyond the UN mandate (intelligence which was then shared with Israel, Iraq's arch-enemy), and in December 1998 Iraqi cooperation with Unscom was withdrawn. President Clinton thereupon resumed the bombing of Iraq (without UN approval and using information gathered by Unscom to locate targets) to coincide with and to attempt to postpone the impeachment debate in the US House of Representatives following the Monica Lewinsky scandal.

This crass manipulation of both the inspection process and the response was to lead to a precipitous increase in Arab resentment of America throughout the Middle East.

When, therefore, following the occupation of Iraq in 2003 by the US 'coalition of the willing', the destruction of much of the country and the death of over 25,000 innocent civilians, the US and Britain were forced to admit that no weapons of mass destruction had been found, resentment turned to outright Arab hatred, from which American foreign policy may never recover. Nor have Arabs forgotten that the monstrous Saddam regime was originally created by the West during the 1980s in order to contain Iran, bringing about the conditions under which Saddam's patron and client system, the *Umana' Saddam* (Saddam's faithful) could survive and prosper by the corruption of the porous sanctions system, and the subsequent 'oil for food' programme begun in 1997. Meanwhile the people of Iraq, victims of forces beyond their control since the days of the Ottoman Empire, have been left to suffer repression, government manipulation of food and medicine supplies, shocking rates of infant mortality, near starvation, cluster bombs and fire bombs from the air, followed by occupation and virtual civil war, and the complete collapse of all government services.

This significant human tragedy has continued for over twelve years. This is hardly the background against which America can successfully preach 'democracy' to the Iraqis or to any other Arab nation.

Hiro as Hero

This observer has been consistently disappointed by the torrent of titles on Islam that have been published since September 11th 2001. The more the author, preferably with a familiar media face, has placed himself at the centre of his (or occasionally her) work, the more the book has been reviewed and presumably read. But on turning the last page, has the reader's understanding of Islam been advanced? Does the reader, for example, now appreciate even one or two differences between Sunni and Shi'a? Does the reader now recognize the significance of the Prophet's Commonwealth or the importance of Jerusalem?

In this vast new publishing enterprise that attempts to explain or to exploit Islam, one author shines, for clarity and readability, for detail and insight. Dilip Hiro, who never appears in his books, is recommended to all who seek detailed answers to the common rhetorical questions, such as 'What do they want?' or 'How did this happen?' To illustrate, Hiro's sixth work on the Middle East, *Secrets and Lies*, specifically on the origins of the occupation of Iraq, contains a detailed rebuttal of the pivotal speech made by US Secretary of State Colin Powell to the Security Council of the United Nations on 5 February 2003, justifying the coming invasion of Iraq. The following is a brief summary.

Powell: Iraq offers sanctuary to members of al-Qaeda, who run a poison factory in Khurmal, and teach chemical weapons techniques.

Fact: Khurmal, in Iraqi Kurdistan, which is allied to the US, was subsequently visited by journalists and US inspectors. Only a derelict warehouse was found, with no trace of chemicals. No link between Iraq and al-Qaeda was ever discovered, until, ironically, the start of the resistance to the US occupation of Sunni Iraq.

Powell: Rocket launchers with warheads containing biological agents have been disbursed to sites throughout western Iraq.

Fact: No such weapons have ever been found by occupying forces, anywhere in Iraq.

Powell: In order to avoid discovery by UN inspectors, Iraq uses at least seven mobile laboratories to produce chemical and biological agents, consisting of seventeen trucks.

Fact: Two suspicious vehicles were found, but on examination contained no relevant equipment or any traces of pathogens. The units turned out to be equipment sold to Iraq by Britain in 1987 and used for the manufacture of hydrogen to fill artillery balloons.

Powell: The Iraqi military is consistently hiding munitions immediately before the arrival of inspectors, and using 'chemical decontamination trucks' to hide toxic traces.

Fact: The pictures of such a location shown by Powell (Taji, north of Baghdad) were taken weeks apart, not hours, and the movement of arms was a routine matter known to the inspectors. The 'decontamination' vehicle turned out to be a fire engine.

Powell: Iraq is preparing ballistic missiles to deliver chemical, biological and 'if we let him, nuclear warheads'.

Fact: The UN inspectors had visited the same site (Al-Rafah, west of Baghdad) five times, and no prohibited weapons were discovered then or later. (And after the invasion the documents allegedly proving that Iraq had attempted to buy potential nuclear materials from Niger were shown to be forgeries.)

Powell: Iraqi scientists are threatened with death for discussing weapons programmes with the UN inspectors.

Fact: Not one such scientist has been produced in public before or during the occupation.

Powell: Iraq can convert fighter jets to spraying anthrax, and possesses drones capable of spreading chemical weapons over a large area.

Fact: One model drone (not equipped for spraying) had already been destroyed by the UN inspectors, and ground forces during the occupation never found the jets or the agents to have been used in the alleged spraying

Powell: The US is relying, in part, on Tony Blair's 'meticulously researched' dossier about Iraqi weapons capabilities.

Fact: Ninety per cent of the famous dossier was created from sources available on the internet prior to 2000, even using the original spelling and punctuation. The texts were then 'sexed-up' by Downing Street staff to indicate that Iraq was supporting terror groups against the West, and by implication al-Qaeda.

In response, the American public watching the speech on television embraced the prospect of war by over 60 per cent. The European diplomats present at the UN, with their own intelligence sources and some with personal knowledge of Iraq, maintained a diplomatic silence, while their peoples took to the streets in protest, although with no result. In the Muslim world there was total disbelief, soon to be confirmed into a bottomless spring of anger and hatred.

Morocco, or the **Maghreb** in Arabic, was at the far end of first the Roman Empire, then the Muslim Empire. The country once covered most of north-west Africa west of Tunisia, which was formerly the most distant Roman province of Ifriqiya. Conquered by the Arabs at the end of the seventh century CE, the pagan Berber population of Morocco quickly converted to Islam. But with the end of the Umayyad dynasty, followed by the contraction of the power of the 'Abbāsids centred on distant Baghdad, Morocco fell out of the mainstream of history. For hundreds of years local dynasties came and went, administering a loose and autocratic version of Islamic law, culminating in the rule of the present Alawite dynasty (not to be confused with the Alawite sect of Syria).

At the beginning of the twentieth century France and Spain partitioned Morocco between them, imposing the borders that would create the modern states of Algeria and Morocco, as well as the bitterly disputed Polisario territory that was Spanish Sahara. Although the Alawite sultans were retained in nominal power by the French administrators, agitation and rioting in support of self-rule led to the withdrawal of the French in 1956. The Alawite sultan Muhammad V succeeded in shifting his position to ally himself with the anti-French movement. On independence he became king, quickly reassuming the feudal power of former centuries. When the earlier anti-French sentiment turned into protests against the tyrannical rule of the monarchy in the 1960s, King Hassan (son of King Muhammad V and father of the present King Muhammad VI) suspended the sham and ineffective representative institutions and openly took absolute power. Dissidents disappeared into remote desert forts and bodies were dumped in the Atlantic from helicopters. In another well-documented episode in French post-colonial history, the Moroccan opposition leader Ben Barka was kidnapped outside a Paris brasserie and tortured to death in a suburban villa, watched over by the French secret service.

But King Hassan was protected from international scrutiny by virtue of his service to American policy by the provision of naval bases, by his cooperation against anti-Western Muslim leaders with the Israeli secret service (who arranged the kidnapping in Paris) and his general obedience to the West, and to French interests in particular. Hassan also accumulated enough personal wealth at the expense of his own people to be able to pay off the national debt three times over, when over 30 per cent of the country's annual budget is taken up with interest payments, so that basic services such as health and education are left to suffer. The illiteracy rate is 70 per cent, clean water available to no more than 60 per cent, and 90 per cent of Moroccans are not served by electricity. Yet this man, who personally took part in the murder and torture of his political opponents, was invited in 1998 (the year before he died) to stand alongside

President Chirac of France to take the salute at the annual Bastille Day military parade in Paris.

The utopian mission of Islam to create a single community of believers bound together by the Shariah under God seems to have no future. Muslims can look back fondly from the new *Jāhiliyyah* of modern times to the mythical era of the Prophet or to the time of the 'rightly guided caliphs' (in the Sunni version), but history appears to have doomed Islam to be ruled by a dysfunctional version of the Western ideal of the nation-state.

Opponents of existing regimes mix religion with politics to demand in the name of Islam an end to Western impositions, the elimination of tyranny and corruption and the advent of the Shariah and social justice. But even if power were ever to be transferred democratically to an opposition group, once in power the same alternatives would face the new leaders as faced the old: either a return to the bankruptcy of socialism under an Islamic guise, or following the path set by the International Monetary Fund toward neo-liberalism and the mirage of Western-style prosperity. In this harsh existential world the anguished desire of Muslims to return to the purity of God's commandments can amount to little more than minor Shariah-based changes to personal and family law, to the re-clothing of women, and laws against blasphemy, all inevitably accompanied by hollow expressions of piety.

11th September 2001

Commentators have predicted that the pictures of the World Trade Center towers crashing to the ground in Manhattan will join the other key images that define popular post-Second World War American history, such as Jackie Kennedy covered in blood at Johnson's impromptu swearing-in, the assassination of Martin Luther King, or Neil Armstrong stepping onto the moon. But those events did not change the world, while the attacks on New York and Washington have resulted in a global realignment, compared by US Defence Secretary Donald Rumsfeld with the new alliances created at the end of the Second World War. So in this post-9/11 world, has the desperate idealistic act of a few Muslim radicals improved or worsened the condition of Islam?

The significance of September 11th in the opinion of this observer, was that the after-effects of US foreign policy suddenly became an internal disaster for 'homeland' America. The shattering consequences of decisions made in Washington were no longer felt only on the Shatt-al-Arab, in Mogadishu or Gaza, but in America as well. At first the results appeared to benefit ordinary Muslims. President Bush appeared in a mosque to urge tolerance, then almost endorsed the concept of a viable independent Palestinian state. Subsequently, however, the optimism has faded. The War on Terror has developed into America's undisguised assumption of the role of global enforcer. The US government, according to John Pike of Global-Security, discovered in Afghanistan the instant formula for changing uncooperative governments. 'You add airpower, microwave for three minutes, and hey, you've got a new regime'. Previous actions against the 'rogue states' (the bombing of Serbia, for example, or the liberation of Kuwait) although American led, were nominally undertaken by international coalitions and sanctioned by the UN or NATO. Afghanistan, in contrast, was bombed by America alone, and in Iraq America bears the weight of the occupation virtually single-handed.

A single US carrier task force consists of 14 ships, 70 aircraft, 14,000 men, 2 submarines, as well as marine landing forces and helicopters. There are 12 such American flotillas. B-1 bombers can fly non-stop around the world, B-52s are available overhead anywhere within hours, from a worldwide network of bases far exceeding the reach of the British Empire at full stretch. For a non-democratic regime, therefore, obedience has become more urgent than repentance, and the rewards for unconditional loyalty soon follow.

There are some ironic examples in the new order. An early volunteer for America's War on Terror was Muhammad VI, feudal king of Morocco, who was rewarded by the withdrawal of UN support for the Polisario, the organization representing the indigenous people of Western Sahara, the former Spanish colony on Morocco's southern boundary, illegally occupied by Muhammad's father in 1975. But in a changed world, the Polisario have become the 'terrorists', and after ten years and half a billion dollars expended on a referendum that has never taken place, the UN has approved a plan recreating Western Sahara as

'the southern provinces of Morocco'. French and American oil companies with Moroccan licences have immediately begun prospecting. This
shift in favour of Morocco was expedited by an American warming
towards the government of Algeria, the former protectors of the
Polisario, because Algerian President Bouteflika also hastened to join
the WoT, his cooperation recognized by two personal invitations to the
White House in quick succession.

Similarly, criticism of the harsh treatment of dissidents by military
courts under emergency laws in both Syria and Egypt is no longer heard,
now that America has begun the same process in the infamous military
prisons of Iraq, Afghanistan and Cuba. And Jordan, already the recipient
of substantial American largesse, has been able to amend the country's
penal code without any international criticism, giving dramatic new 'temporary' powers to the government to deal with dissenters and control
the press. Pakistan, as we have seen earlier in this chapter, 'changed sides'
to join the WoT and was quickly rewarded. While the Philippines and
Indonesia (with the massacres in East Timor by the Indonesian army
almost forgotten) have come under stronger American influence
through the means of providing arms and assistance against Muslim political groups and secessionists. Even Libya has applied to join the WoT,
seeking the return from asylum in the West of the regime's political
opponents, who are, of course, according to the Libyan justice ministry,
'terrorists' with 'links to al-Qaeda'. Return would be to a certain and
gruesome death.

Most importantly, however, Israel succeeded in equating Yassir Arafat,
the Palestinian Authority, and the movements in opposition to Israeli
occupation, with al-Qaeda. Palestinians under Israeli military rule have
become 'terrorists' once again. 'It is a fact that we killed fourteen
Palestinians today', said Israel Defence Minister Ben Elezir, following an
incident shortly after September 11th, 'with the world remaining
absolutely silent'.

Osama ibn Laden (the presumed mastermind of September 11th)
would surely have been displeased with such rotten fruit from his enterprise. Even the Muslim regimes he may have supported directly, in the
Yemen and the Sudan, cooperate with America out of fear of retribution,
and the Taliban are gone. The human tragedy of Iraq continues well into
a second decade. The increase in the US defence budget alone for each
year since 2002 has matched the total of all aid from the West to the

poor nations of the world in the previous year. While the Saudi Arabian monarchy, further weakened by the events of that fateful day, in which at least fifteen Saudis took part, has become more dependent than ever on American weapons supply and logistical protection.

In addition to the thousands of innocent Muslim civilians killed since September 11th 2001, there are the secondary consequences that have rebounded on Muslims more than any other group: international travel restrictions, economic decline, rising poverty and dangerous levels of unemployment, the decimation of the tourist industry in the Middle East, and the increased isolation of many Muslim communities in Europe and America. These are the very conditions in which idealistic desperation thrives.

VI   Muslim Communities in the West

The negative generalizations that have been made about Islam in the international press cannot fail to have an effect on domestic politics in the West. Millions of Muslims live in Europe and the US, generally 'counter-colonists', refugees from post-colonial conditions already described. Or, as in the case of Germany, they were permitted to enter for the economic advantage of an industrial country short of unskilled labour on what was anticipated to be a temporary basis. Now, however, the typical emigrant group has become a permanent presence for which no satisfactory long-term solution has been found.

The common characteristic shared by Muslim minorities in the West is the unresolved conflict between the desire of Muslims to become full participating citizens of their new countries while at the same time preserving their Islamic culture and religion, a legacy to be handed down through the following generations. To this the host countries tacitly object, being broadly prepared to accept emigrants from non-white races as full citizens, but not from foreign cultures that are not prepared to blend.

In France there are ministers with Italian and Polish names, men and women who have reached the highest levels of power within three generations of the original (and at the time, unwelcome) emigration. But when a Frenchman is confronted with the prospect that one day a Boubakeur or a Bencheikh may become the Minister of the Interior following the same process, the usual reaction is outrage. But since the presence of significant Muslim communities in France, in excess of 10 per cent of the population, is now irreversible, are entire sections of the population to be regarded as immigrants for ever?

Of all the countries in Europe with a Muslim minority, **France** presents the greatest paradox. Despite the violence that accompanied the colonization and subsequent liberation of north Africa, France has left a substantial legacy to the Maghreb in the form of culture. Large segments of Tunisia, Algeria and Morocco are Francophone and Francophile, regarding France as the home of liberty and social justice, literature, human dignity, croissants and café crème. But for the six million Arab residents of France, Europe's largest Muslim community, reality has been very different. Frenchmen have resented Arab immigration since the early 1960s, even though French attempts to make North Africa part of metropolitan France precipitated the war and the resulting emigration in the first place. Arabs have been moved into sterile tower blocks in the suburbs of Marseille, Paris and other main cities, unemployment has remained twice the national average among Arab and North African youths, and the largest right-wing party in Europe (although now split), the National Front, was formed with the principal aim of forcing the return of all Arabs to their country of origin. The worst of the overtly racist anti-Arab sentiments, almost hysterical during the bombings in Paris in 1995, have receded. After the riots of 2005, Islam has become the target of a lower-key but broadly popular hostility in the media, often with a fine pseudo-intellectual gloss about culture, but all with a similar message: Arab = Muslim = trouble. Added to this is the continuing aid by France, for reasons already discussed, to the despotic regimes which many Arabs emigrated to escape. There is widespread speculation in the Arab community that the 1995 bombings in Paris were originated by the Algerian secret services themselves, with the knowledge of the French authorities, to ensure continuing French support for the existing Algerian regime and their war against 'terrorist organizations' and renewed emigration.

The symbolic issue of headscarves in schools, and the response that Church and State are separate in the Vth Republic, intended to accelerate integration, in fact confirms the long-term position of Muslims in France as aliens, leading to more radicalism and violence among second and third generations not less. The French state has concordats with both Jews and Protestants, both with lower membership than Islam, but has only recently agreed to negotiate a similar status for Muslims through the newly formed French Council of the Muslim Faith. Further, France has yet to elect a single Muslim to the National Assembly and in the centralized French system applications to build mosques have been blocked, imams in prisons are rare, no state support is offered for Muslim schools, police powers are heavily employed against Muslim minorities and state aid is inconsistently applied to cultural activities. The absence of the negotiating channel that would be provided by a concordat has led to an uncertain relationship between Islamic family laws and those of the French state. Polygamous marriages, for example, which were unilaterally outlawed retroactively in 1992, well after most polygamous Muslim immigrants had already established residency. All this cannot help but lead to more unrest among French Muslims, stemming from a deep insecurity about their position in society.

The Muslim minority in **Germany**, predominantly Turkish and Kurdish, is the hardest case in Europe. Turkey's ill-fated decision in 1914 to join Germany and the Central Powers against Britain, France and Russia has resulted in an almost post-colonial relationship between Turkey and Germany, expressed in practical terms by the direct rail link from Istanbul to Berlin. So when the German economy began to boom in the mid-1950s, Turkey was the obvious source to fill the demand for unskilled labour. These factors produced, over the next forty-five years, a *Gastarbeiter* force of Muslim emigrants that is now 3.2 million strong. The word, 'guest-labourer', speaks volumes, revealing the uncompromisingly economic and essentially temporary basis on which Germany presumed the migration would take place. Chancellor Köhl himself said many times that Germany is 'not an emigration country', despite what was in fact taking place. Now, at the start of the twenty-first century, the Turkish presence which was originally economic and temporary has become permanent and cultural, and German's Muslim minority, well into a second and third generation of confident Euro-Turks, has no intention of leaving. Recognition of this reality has been slow and reluctant. 'Ethno-pluralism' is the buzz-word used in the German media, which is double-speak for retaining the status quo and avoiding any decisions about permanent status.

However, qualification for citizenship in Germany is still based on the concept of the *Volk* bloodline, derived from the Imperial Naturalization Act of 1913, making Germany, together with Israel, ironically, the only Western countries where citizenship is based on race. This makes any attempt at full integration by Muslims not born in Germany very difficult, especially since an applicant is obliged to renounce his or her citizenship of origin when he or she is able to qualify even as a 'conditional' citizen, after eight years' residency. Few Turks are willing to do this, with the result that 9 per cent of the population are not citizens. If citizenship is to be awarded as an exception to a rule based on race, then the status could one day be taken away again for the same reasons, as happened to the Jews in Germany in the 1930s. Thus Muslims in Germany have become a marked-out and marginalized community, right in the heart of the new Europe, and still a long way from integration. Turks especially are then further menaced into protective groupings by the rabble-rousing language of hate from the Republikaner Party, the German People's Union in the east, or the Freedom Party in Austria. Violent actions by neo-Nazis and skinheads have resulted in the arson deaths of many Turkish men, women and children, with racist attacks on individuals across the country running into hundreds per year. Even the main German political parties have attracted little Turkish support. The Christian Democratic Union is seen as anti-Muslim because of the name of the party, in addition to explicit CDU opposition to Turkish membership of the EU, while the SPD precondition, an apology by Turkey for the Armenian Massacre more than ninety years ago, has the same result.

The Muslim community in **Britain** is composed of two distinct elements, broadly represented by London and Birmingham.

Freedom of speech has been a frequent casualty of Muslim history, with the result that the opponents of despotic regimes in Muslim countries (those who are not in domestic jails) are invariably emigrants or refugees abroad. This has had the effect of making

London an intellectual hub for the Middle East. The advantages offered by the city are many: the transportation hub of Heathrow Airport; a tradition of Arab scholarship; historical and colonial connections and, most importantly, a liberal political climate that condones all expression short of violence and arms dealing. Here are to be found opposition groups of every stripe: radical nationalists, pan-Arabists, Islamists, liberals, Ba'thists, monarchists and every shade of Arab, Iranian, Kurdish and Turkish dissident. While these communities may add to the multi-cultural mosaic of the city and bring substantial amounts of investment to Britain, individual residency is intended for the most part to be temporary. Since September 11th 2001, however, and then again after July 7th 2005, 'Londonistan' has become less attractive, with dozens of 'visitors' held on suspicion of supporting terrorism. Changes in the law allow non-national jihadis to be held indefinitely without trial as security Category 'A' prisoners, when even in Egypt charges must be brought within forty-five days. And in the months after the London bombings, the British government proposed yet more powerful measures against suspects, challenging centuries of freedoms and European human rights standards. But polls in Britain showed that few believed the attack was merely the work of individuals who could have been restrained by such laws, or had nothing to do with domestic Muslim alienation, and British involvement in US foreign policy.

Birmingham, on the other hand, is competing with Bradford and Leicester to becoming Britain's first 'majority-minority' city. Starting forty years ago with the emigration to the city of 100,000 Pakistanis from Kashmir, displaced by the Azad dam, the city has become home to an Asian and predominantly Muslim community of a million or more in what has been an overall success story. One third of the city businesses are now owned by Asians and there is a huge emphasis within the community on the education of the next generation and on making Birmingham a permanent home. At the same time this has been accomplished with very little surrender of religious values, so that on the changing face of Birmingham the dome and minaret of a newly built mosque now take a central place. But the penalty for Birmingham's success is 'ghettoization' by which Islam is contained within a few Midland cities, some fractiously on the edge of poverty and racial confrontation, while leaving the country as a whole unchanged. This merely practical solution to the problem, which produced the four suicide bombers of July 7th 2005, cannot be accurately described as integration.

Islam in the **United States** is a quite different case from the situations considered above. There is no universal Catholic culture to be offended, there is no bloodline requirement to US citizenship, the space limitations of Britain are absent, yet Muslims in America are still a precarious and distinct minority. There may be as many as six million Muslims in America, making Islam the second largest religious minority after Judaism, outnumbering Presbyterians, or the Mormons, Quakers, Unitarians, Seventh-day Adventists, Mennonites, Jehovah's Witnesses and Christian Scientists all combined. Approximately 44 per cent of American Muslims are native-born Americans, the majority of whom are black and are still on the edges of the mainstream of Islam. The remaining 56 per cent represent Muslims from all over the world, mostly from South Asia, with only 12 per cent from Arab countries. Muslims and their mosques are spread across the country, not grouped in communities like Britain. Nevertheless Islam in the United States faces stronger challenges than in Europe. Internally, the conservative family-based Muslim culture is under constant pressure from the surrounding society where, despite the appearance of piety on Sundays, almost anything goes, from gay pride to teenage sex to widespread drug use and the unrelenting pursuit of wealth: the values of Mammon have been raised in America to the level of a secular religion. This hedonism may be resisted by the first generation of Muslim emigrants, but the next and the next, in such a large and alien territory, are increasingly tempted to lapse. Further, Islam in America is the subject of even greater misunderstanding and prejudice than in any European country. The publicity that used to be given to the Nation of Islam, for example (see Chapter 6), has created the impression that the overtly racist and theologically absurd views of Louis Farrakhan are those of all black Muslims, when the Nation of Islam membership is in fact no more than 50,000. While for Muslims who are brown, there is a separate line of prejudgement: all Muslims are potential terrorists. The repercussions of the events of September 11th 2001 and the demonization of Osama ibn Laden to a worldwide degree never before seen, together with the accompanying media hysteria, have created an atmosphere of hate from which Muslims will escape only slowly, if ever.

The long-term success of Muslim immigrant societies in Europe will depend on a combination of adaptation by the one and acceptance by the other, for which sufficient commitment (so avoiding permanent abrasion) may or may not be found. But on the troublesome threshold of Europe, Muslims are natives, not racial intruders. In **Bosnia**, **Kosovo** and **Albania**, Islam is as European as Christianity and as long established as Protestantism in Northern Europe. The message of Jesus Christ began among the Jewish Semites of Palestine and only later became European by progressing up the arteries of imperial Rome towards the heart. Similarly, as we have seen, Muhammad's message and the religion of the desert Arab was disseminated through the means of temporal power, culminating with the Ottoman Empire. And just as the provinces of Rome accepted Christianity in the fourth century CE, significant parts of the European territories forming part of the Ottoman Empire voluntarily embraced Islam, principally Bosnia, Kosovo and Albania. There are substantial elements among European Muslims with Turkish or 'foreign' roots, but native Albanians, for example, who are 80 per cent Muslim, are as indigenous to their region of Europe as Orthodox Serbs or Catholic Croats are to theirs. Nationalist politicians who seek to enforce a 'greater Serbia' or a 'pure Croatian state' might wish that this were not the case and that Muslims could be told to 'go home to Turkey', but the facts of history are against them. Language has been pressed into the sinister service of this bigotry, so that in most Balkan vernaculars the word for 'Muslim' has become the equivalent of 'Turkish'.

But the vexed history of the Balkans tells a different story. When the region rose against the Turks with the support of Austria at the end of the nineteenth century, Bosnian and Albanian Muslims fought against the retreating Ottoman Empire side by side with Serbs and Croats. When, fifty years later, the Balkans threw off Austrian rule, Muslims were similarly involved and formed an integral part of the new multi-ethnic state that governed between the world wars (the Kingdom of Yugoslavia), and after 1945 (the communist Republic of Yugoslavia), both of which included Bosnia and Kosovo.

Albania ran a parallel course, achieving independence after the Balkan wars against Turkey, first under King Zog and later, following the expulsion of the Germans, as a maniacal and xenophobic communist regime under Enver Hoxha, with followers of Islam harshly persecuted. After the collapse of communism in Europe, Serb and Croat nationalistic enmity (exacerbated by recent history in which Croats had generally been supported by Nazi Germany and Serbs had been brought to power by the victorious Soviets) came into the open with Muslims falling victim to the ambitions of both sides. Serbs, then later Croats, attempted to 'cleanse' Bosnia-Herzegovina and to ghettoize Muslims, and later again Serb forces attempted to expel the Muslim population from Kosovo into Albania. Despite the intervention of the West, hundreds of thousands of lives were lost, millions displaced, entire communities destroyed and cities ruined. In attempting to find a workable solution to the ethnic and religious patchwork left by centuries of history and an end to the destruction, many mistakes were made by the European alliance, with the Muslim communities as the principal victims. The five days in July 1995, when Serb forces were able to massacre 8,000 Bosnian Muslim men under nominal UN protection in Srebrenica, finally galvanized Europe into the necessary scale of operation to stop Serb aggression, although the event had been widely forgotten by the tenth anniversary. Nor is the result of European and American military intervention fully satisfactory, producing a fractured and unworkable Bosnia, and a de facto Muslim Kosovo in what will always be claimed by Serbs as the inalienable heartland of their history. But the spectacle of a massive intervention by the West against the Christian Serbs on behalf of a Muslim minority (even if European) is an encouraging counter-weight to the many other situations in the world where the injustices to Islam are not recognized, and certainly not acted upon.

The **Caucasus**, the neck of land between the Black Sea and the Caspian Sea, came under Ottoman control for less than 100 years (1514–1603 CE). But as imperial Russia pushed the boundaries of the Ottoman Empire steadily south and eventually back to the borders of Anatolia, much of the reconquered territory remained strongly Muslim. Tsarist Russia made a number of attempts to eradicate Islam in the southern provinces, a cause that was taken up by the Soviet government from the 1920s on, with extreme brutality. 'In thirty years,' the Secretary of the Communist Party declared in 1928, 'Islam in Russia will only be a bad memory from long ago.' Merely owning a Qur'ān, or saying prayers, earned a Muslim a long term in a Soviet jail. Nevertheless, when the Communist government collapsed in the 1990s, sixty million Muslims remained, spread across all of southern Russia as well as the Caucasus, forming the majority in the six republics that declared independence in the south as the Soviet empire crumbled (Kazakhstan, Kyrgyzstan, Tajikistan, Uzbekistan, Turkmenistan and Azerbaijan).

The new Russian state succeeded in retaining control of a number of Muslim provinces adjacent to the new republics, motivated by nothing more logical or strategic than hurt imperial pride. Of these, Chechnya in the central Caucasus has proven the most obstinate, declaring in 1990, in response to a long history of harsh occupation, unilateral independence from Moscow as the Republic of Ichkeria. A President was elected, promising the implementation of the Shariah and by 1995 the Chechens had expelled the Russian army, but at a cost of 80,000 mostly civilian lives and the destruction of the capital Grozny. The Soviet army attacked again in October 1999 after 300 civilians were killed by bomb attacks in four Moscow apartment blocks. The deaths were blamed on the 'Muslim fanatics' of Chechnya (although nothing has been proven and Ichkeria has denied responsibility) while the timing of the Russian 'strong-man' response ensured the election of Vladimir Putin as Russian President. By the third year of the renewed war, however, the Russian army was in trouble again, sustaining heavy casualties and unable to win, but politically unable to withdraw. The destruction continued, with Grozny becoming a new Dresden and over 200,000 Chechens made homeless. Despite resolute attempts by Russian security services to exclude all reporters and foreign visitors (including kidnappings and beatings), the activities of the Russian army began to attract attention in the West. Detailed reports from both Russian and Western journalists told of mass torture, rape, wholesale theft of civilian possessions, and the imprisonment in pits and summary executions of suspected Muslim fighters. Senior staff officers finally admitted that the frustrated Russian army had turned to brutal revenge against civilians and was guilty of war crimes. In the Council of Europe, the expulsion of Russia was considered in an attempt to force a political solution to the Chechen war by recognizing the human rights and cultural aspirations of Muslim Chechens. But in return for Russia's support for the international campaign against terrorism following the events of September 11th 2001, the tone immediately softened. Chechens became 'Islamist fundamentalists', European leaders called for 'a more differentiated evaluation in world opinion', and took the issue off their agenda. 'We face a common foe,' President Putin declared recently to the German Parliament, and suddenly no European politician chose to disagree. The long tradition of Russian persecution of Islam (now over 15 per cent of the population) had become invisible once again.

Appendix

The Balfour Declaration

London 2nd November 1917

Dear Lord Rothschild,
I have much pleasure in conveying to you, on behalf of His Majesty's
Government, the following declaration of sympathy with the Jewish
Zionist aspirations, which have been submitted to and approved by the
Cabinet: 'His Majesty's Government view with favour the establishment
in Palestine of a national home for the Jewish people, and will use their
best endeavours to facilitate the achievement of this object, it being
clearly understood that nothing shall be done which may prejudice the
civil and religious rights of the existing non-Jewish communities in
Palestine, or the rights and political status enjoyed by Jews in any other
country.'
I should be grateful if you would bring this declaration to the knowledge of the Zionist Federation.

A. J. Balfour
Secretary of State
His Majesty's Britannic Government
London

5

THE PRACTICE OF ISLAM

I Faith without Priests, Feasts without Sacraments

The desertman's profound sense of equality and self-reliance on which Sunni Islam is based prevented the development of any Sunni version of a church hierarchy. There is no mystical ritual in mainstream Islam, there are no human intermediaries or divine interceders between man and God. There are no sacraments to be administered by the ordained few to the supplicant many. If God (in the Muslim version) forgave Adam for his transgression at the time, then man cannot be inherently evil, or born in 'original sin'. So, like Adam, all men can be forgiven their sins directly by God without the need for intervention by any third party, whether a Redeemer on a cross, a virgin with child, or a priestly delegate operating through the medium of a confession box.

> That Allah may forgive thee
> Thy faults of the past
> And those to follow;
> Fulfil His favour to thee
> And guide thee
> On the Straight Way.
>
> *Al-Fath* (The Victory) Surah 48, verse 2

This unadorned relationship cancels the need for baptism, confirmation, confession, extreme unction and the central Christian act of communion, as well the functions of a ministering priesthood. For many Christians, Christ bequeathed the foundation of a future church in the person of St Peter, and He ordained the method of access to the divine with the ritual of holy communion. Only through the Church, therefore, as the successor to St Peter, can salvation (and thus everlasting life) be obtained. But in the Qur'ān, Christ is merely the Messenger Isā and the sacred text itself, in

Muslim belief, is God's legacy to man, unreservedly accessible to all in the Arabic vernacular. For a Muslim, therefore, the central act of devotion is not to be found in following any supervised rite or sacrament, but by reading and contemplating God's direct word to man, set out in a book which he can open, read and interpret for himself.

Conversion to Islam, as a practical example of this straightforwardness, follows a simple formula. After repeating the words of the *Shahadah* from the heart (*I confess that there is no god but God, and that Muhammad is the messenger of God*) the speaker has become a Muslim, responsible for gathering his belief for himself directly from the original sources of the Qur'an and Sunna, although this process may, of course, be assisted by the writings or teachings of experts.

Mosques and imams

Rather than suffering configuration by a theocracy from above, Sunni Islam is organized down at the community level only, on an informal self-help basis centred on the *masjid*, or mosque, meaning place of prosternation. The Prophet ordered that a mosque should be built in every location where Muslims live, and upon his arrival in Medina Muhammad provided the example to be followed by constructing the first mosque in Islam with his own hands.

The existing inventory of mosques was for the most part built by rulers or by successful businessmen, although the names of the benefactors are rarely to be found displayed on the building. More recently, community action or central governments have been the moving forces. Once complete the premises 'belong inalienably to God' and fall outside the scope of any land title or trading system. Only the pure intention to create a mosque for the good of the community is required on the part of those carrying out the project, and in theory no sanctification or commissioning by a higher authority is necessary for the mosque to become operational.

Behind many mosques stands, or once stood, a *waqf*, or religious benevolent endowment association, supported by the local residents, to which property could be donated or bequeathed, so creating a reliable income stream with which to sustain operations. In many cases the *waqf* itself was responsible for building the mosque from donations, or where the building was pre-existing the organization may fund at least the maintenance of the fabric and the provision of light and water. In most contemporary Muslim countries, however, a version of a Ministry of Religious Affairs has taken control of the traditional *waqfs*, and often pocketed their assets. This accounts for the poor condition of most religious buildings, and under such regimes donors cannot now stipulate the specific use to which their funds are to be put.

Similarly a man who perceives himself as having a religious calling typically follows up his basic education with a period of study at a Qu'rānic school and upon graduation seeks out a position directly in a community without any formal ordination. The man may have been the student of a well-known teacher, who may then allow the student to teach in his turn in his own mosque in the teacher's name. This affords the student the opportunity to work towards becoming well-known himself, attracting students who would in turn continue with the teachings of the original teacher, and so on. In this way various schools of Islamic thought have developed, and modern teachers can often claim a connection back through generations of teachers to the original revered experts.

Upon his appointment by the community, the newly trained teacher can call himself mullah, sheikh or imam, depending on local usage. At one level all three words mean 'minister' in the Protestant sense and are interchangeable, 'mullah' being the Persian version of the Arabic 'sheikh'. But the word 'sheikh' also means a secular 'holder of power' in the wider political sense, and imam, or 'spiritual guide', is also used in Shi'a Islam to describe the true caliph or successor to the Prophet.

The principal responsibility of the mullah, imam or sheikh of a mosque is to deliver the *khutba* during Friday prayers. He may also give courses on the Qur'ān in the mosque or teach local children. The imam would be available to attend family functions, but only if invited, and his presence is not essential. His duties often include leading the prayers in the mosque five times per day and most importantly at noon on Fridays, but any male member of the community who is acceptable to the other worshippers may also lead prayers. Alternatively, the imam of a mosque may simply be a devout Muslim with a separate full-time occupation, a man who is sufficiently knowledgeable and is prepared to devote the necessary time to the community.

This effective and egalitarian system has, however, also been corrupted by big government. Tight control is exercised over the operation of mosques in order to suppress political dissent. And whereas ideally the members of a community should decide on an imam for themselves and the imam should preach according to his own learning and beliefs, in practice in most Muslim countries no imam can be appointed to an established mosque without government approval, and the content of Friday *khutbahs* are censored, so that only the brave speak out. The political power that can be achieved over the faithful through the political control of the mosque is clearly demonstrated in the case of Afghanistan. Xenophobic Taliban propaganda disseminated from pulpits across the country was able to keep the population in line for a number of years, despite the complete devastation of the country, physically, culturally and economically.

Sunni practice as outlined above, does not apply to the 10 per cent of Islam that is Shiʿa. As we have seen, Sunni Muslims accepted the de facto caliphate of Muʾāwiyah after the murder of ʿAli, the last of the 'rightly guided' caliphs, and thus achieved a limited form of practical separation between secular and religious authority. From the Umayyad caliphate on, secular power passed from dynasty to dynasty but religious authority began to fragment across the length and breadth of the Sunni Muslim territories. This in turn drove the organization of Islam down to the self-directing community level that prevails today.

The followers of ʿAli, on the other hand, opposed Umayyad power based on the belief that both spiritual and temporal power were transmitted by God together, and exclusively through the family of the Prophet. From this belief a Shiʿa hierarchy has developed, combining both political and religious power, and behind which is seen God's guiding hand. In this way the two quite different religious atmospheres of Sunni and Shiʿa have evolved, to be explored further in the following chapter.

Neither Sunni nor Shiʿa recognize the equivalent of monks or nuns, and Islam has no monasteries or nunneries. All Muslim men and women are urged to marry unless subject to a physical defect.

The Christian idea of virtuous celibacy permitting the individual to pay full attention to spiritual ends is entirely alien to Islam.

Family rites

In matters relating to the family the same self-help culture prevails in Sunni Islam, since there is no 'church' to intervene, to dispense approval or sacraments. The passage from birth to death in the presence of God concerns the individual alone, without any mediation required. Muslim social ceremonies, rather than being formally religious in character, are intended to strengthen the concept of belonging to the continuing community of Islam in which religion is ever-present. This contrasts with twilight Christianity or liberal Judaism where religion is absent from everyday life, the connection being made only when the rites of birth, marriage and death are performed.

Marriage is a great feast and celebration throughout the Muslim world, emphasizing the importance of the family as the cornerstone of the community. A marriage feast brings together groups beyond the immediate families involved in a way not duplicated in any other Islamic festival. But Muslim marriage is forthrightly contractual and not overtly religious. The relationship between bride and groom is based on a nuptial agreement that establishes the terms of the marriage within the limits of the law. In all marriages the wife's property is strictly separated from that of the husband, and the agreement may provide for the woman to enjoy the same right to divorce as the man, as well as prohibiting further wives. The contract may be formalized either at the mosque or equally validly at home, but a semi-official *maʾdhun*, or marriage contract specialist, is required for registration. The importance among Muslims of the extended family, in contrast to the Western 'nuclear family' concept, means that the choice of partner is a matter that has implications beyond the lives of the individuals, since the two families will then be closely associated. Although modern conditions have reduced the prevalence of arranged marriages, the consent of the respective families to a union is still very important in most Muslim societies. Divorce is regarded as a great tragedy (and 'most hated by God', according to a Hadith) so that when difficulties arise, the Qurʾān urges that every effort be made to achieve reconciliation. Three acts of divorce must be completed at separate times before the separation is absolute.

The birth of a child is another joyful event, a male especially. Celebrations include a feast and the distribution of food to the poor. By tradition, the words of the *azān*, the prayer that the Muslim will repeat all his life, are whispered into his or her ear at birth. The child is named by the parents without any ceremony comparable to Christian baptism. For males, one of the names of the Prophet is usually chosen as a first given name (Muhammad, Mahmud, Ahmed, Mustafa), and one of the Beautiful Names of Allah as the basis for a second. Girls often receive the name of one of the women in Muhammad's family (Khadijah, Fatima, ʿĀʾishah, Zaynab, etc.).

In early Muslim society male circumcision was performed as a rite of passage. (Female circumcision has never been an accepted Muslim practice, an issue which will be discussed later in this chapter.) In modern times the procedure is undertaken in hospital as part of the birth, or by the midwife if the birth is at home. Circumcision is required for reasons of cleanliness only and has no religious significance, although supported by a Hadith. (In a contemporary twist to the ancient practice, statistics on the spread of HIV in Africa, although incomplete, appear to show that male circumcision at least slows the spread of the virus.)

Traditional Muslim education was almost exclusively religious, learned at the feet of a master in the courtyard of the mosque. The syllabus would consist of memorizing excerpts of the Qurʾān, elementary interpretation, logic, grammar, literature and rhetoric. The ability to recite extensively from the Qurʾān by memory, or even recite the entire work, would mark the passage from childhood to adulthood. Most Muslim schools are now westernized (with some notable exceptions) and increasingly influenced by technology, with religious matters dealt with in special part-time schools or *madrasahs*. In modern times Qurʾān recital as a mark of graduation has been replaced by the granting of an academic certificate or degree, followed by the start of a working life. There is no equivalent of the bar mitzvah or Confirmation in Islam.

Death is not of itself regarded as a punishment in Islam, as in Christianity. Death simply brings to an end a stage in the process extending from birth to God's final judgement on the Last Day.

Muslim rites of death are, therefore, principally intended to improve the deceased's chance of gaining credit on Judgement Day, and once again, no sheikh or mullah is required. The body is washed then wrapped in a simple white shroud, and may be dressed in the plain white clothes of the pilgrimage if the deceased had performed the haj. There is no casket and the expense of the burial is to be kept to a bare minimum. During preparation the body is traditionally instructed on what to say when questioned by the angels, Nakir and Monkar, who are responsible for preparing the life record that will be the believer's sole possession on the Day of the Resurrection. In the grave the body is laid on the side, facing Mecca, as a further indication that the deceased was a Muslim. Traditional Muslim practice discourages tombstones: ideally the burial place should merely blend back unmarked into the desert sands. Although modern urban practice is to erect monuments, even in the most affluent Muslim cities funerary decoration falls far short of the intricacies and opulence of a Christian cemetery. Before burial, prayers are said at the graveside, and usually the body is first taken into the mosque at prayer time. A feast may be held in honour of the deceased and alms given to the poor. Mourning is inconsistent with belief in the will of God and the final resurrection, although grief is inevitable on a human level. Verses from the Qur'ān are read at such times, emphasizing patience, strength and fortitude. Cremation is forbidden out of respect for the body.

Feasts

The great feasts of Islam follow the same pattern as family rites. The saying of prayers is a vital part of every celebration, and congregational prayers are usual led by a sheikh or mullah, often followed by a *khutba*. The organization of the more important annual feasts overlays religion with a strong social aspect, reflecting the Muslim community way.

Eid al-Adha, the Feast of the Sacrifice, the principal feast of Islam, takes place on the tenth day of the Muslim lunar month of Dhu'l-Hajja, and falls at the same time as the end of the annual Pilgrimage, when Abraham's sacrifice of the ram in place of his son Ibrahim is re-enacted. This concurrence reminds Muslims everywhere of the essential message of the haj: the renewal of faith, and the importance, while experiencing 'pre-death', of how life is lived. The feast is celebrated literally with a banquet held in each family (and preceded in the more traditional areas by the sacrifice of an animal), in which the poor, as at every Muslim festival, are invited to share.

The second most popular Muslim feast is Eid al-Fitr, literally the Feast of Fast-Breaking, on the first day of Shawwāl. This event falls on the day after the end of the Fast of Ramadan, which, as we have seen in a preceding chapter, can also be a form of month-long feast. Traditionally, new clothes are worn on this day following the example of the Prophet. Before the start of Ramadan religious buildings should be cleaned, but with the heavy hand of governments controlling the *waqfs* this is rarely done. Decorative lights are hung, or Ramadan lanterns (now mostly made in China).

Mawlid al-Nabiyy, the Prophet's Birthday on the twelfth day of the month of Rabi' al-Awwal, began to be celebrated in the tenth century CE by the Fatamids in Egypt to demonstrate their close blood relationship with the Prophet. The feast also grew in importance in response to the growing Christian rite of Christ's birthday. The celebration is opposed by purists as magnifying the cult of Muhammad contrary to the true basis of Islam in which there are no intermediaries between man and God, with Muhammad regarded as nothing more than human. The feast is more popular in sentimental Pakistan, for example, than in the austere atmosphere of Saudi Arabia, where Mawlid is actively opposed.

The principal Shi'a feast of the Day of 'Āshurā on the tenth day of al-Muharram, originally a Jewish feast day also observed by the early Muslims, now commemorates the death of the Imam al-Husayn, the Prophet's grandson. The day has become a major festival in Shi'a countries and Karbalā, the site of the Imam's death, has become a place of annual pilgrimage that rivals Mecca for numbers of pilgrims. The central feature of the festival is a cathartic passion play depicting the event, together with a sombre street parade during which groups of young men cut their flesh and beat their bodies in mortification at the triumph of corruption over piety. Such display is regarded by Sunnis as contrary to Islam.

Lailat al-Qadr, or the Night of Power, is the anniversary of the first revelation of the Qur'ān to the Prophet through the agency of the angel Gabriel. Falling towards the end of the month of Ramadan, this is a night of intense devotion and prayer. 'Whosoever prays during this night,' Muhammad is reported to have said, 'in true faith and hope, will be pardoned his previous errors.'

II Understanding Shariah

Shariah, as we have seen, is the name given to a system of laws based on the Qur'ān and the Sunna, and constitutes the core of the 'social project' of Islam.

> We made for you a law
> So follow the Way
> And not the fancies of those
> Who have no knowledge.
>
> *Al-Jathiyah* (The Kneeling Down) Surah 45, verse 18

From the belief that the Qur'ān is the direct Word of God, the conclusion must follow that the laws to be found in the text are those prescribed by God for man. Similarly, since Muhammad is regarded as the Apostle of God, the guidance given to his followers through his Sunna must be divinely inspired. This in turn makes the concept of the Shariah spiritually irresistible for a Muslim as fulfilling the will of God, and simple believers often have difficulty understanding why political obstacles are so regularly placed in the way of achieving God's will on earth through the implementation of His laws.

In an ideal Muslim state the Shariah would govern all aspects of both personal religious practice and Muslim society at large by combining all the branches of law together. Thus under Shariah no distinction is made between the religious and the secular, between a sin against God, with which a Western legal system does not concern itself (blasphemy, for example) and a wrong done to society (theft, for example), nor between the regulation of a personal practice (saying prayers, for example) which falls far outside the scope of Western laws, and the terms of a civil obligation (paying taxes, for example). Under Shariah both blend into a single legal system of obligations, rules and punishments. Since all of creation, in Muslim belief, is an expression of the will of God, God cannot be excluded from any part of the life of the individual or the functioning of society.

Muslim law based on the Shariah has been compared in earlier chapters with the Common Law of England. The Common Law grew from a basic power (the once absolute and 'divinely ordained' power of the king) into a comprehensive civil and criminal system as well as a structure of constitutional practice around which the state was organized. Similarly the Shariah grew from a basic power (the Word of God in the Qur'ān and the 'divinely inspired' injunctions of the Prophet in the Sunna) into a detailed civil, criminal and constitutional system capable of governing all aspects of the state.

The Qur'ān contains almost eighty verses setting out pure law and approximately 500 verses of a general ethical and ritual nature, spread through almost all the Medinan Surahs. These general principles, as we have seen, are then elaborated and explained in a practical sense by the Prophet's Sunna. The Qur'ān and the Sunna, as the 'basic law' legislation of Islam, cover religious observance, inheritance, marriage, the condition of orphans, the emancipation of slaves, crime and punishment, property, international relations, and some economic and commercial matters. But this source of law ended, of course, with the final revelation of the Qur'ān and the death of Muhammad.

The development of both the Common Law and the Shariah after the original sources had disappeared (the 'divine rule' of kings, and the 'divinely inspired' Muhammad) was achieved by building on 'precedent', or the legal rulings and interpretations that had gone before. Precedent was then expanded and modified over time to meet evolving contemporary requirements, effectively building up new law on the foundations of the old, like the formation of a coral reef. This then led to the extraction of unifying legal principles from the body of accumulated precedent, a discipline known as *fiqh* to the Shariah, or jurisprudence in the case of the Common Law.

The bureaucracy of both legal systems also developed along parallel lines. As new law accumulated under the precedent system new institutions were required for implementation: courts, avenues of appeal, a system of suit and counter-suit, prosecution, defence and enforcement. Then these developing institutions, requiring rules with which to operate, themselves drove the further deepening and widening of the law, which in turn expanded the scope of the administration, and so on.

The need for a successor to Muhammad's temporal power created the caliphate. Once in existence, the caliphate expanded the laws originated by the agency of Muhammad, extending the precedents of his case by case decisions as recorded in the Sunna into new areas of law such as financial systems and criminal punishments (other than the fixed penalties already set by the Qur'ān). To administer and enforce the decisions of the caliphs as the Muslim empires expanded, a bureaucracy of experts was in turn required: judges, lawyers, legal consultants, scribes and secretaries. Then as the caliphate became absorbed in power and splendour under the ʿAbbāsids, the bureaucracy, together with the end of Muslim expansionism, slowly ate away at the role of the caliphs themselves until they became mere figureheads. Then, during the political fragmentation of the Muslim empires, the Shariah evolved into a separate institution, no longer dependent on the caliphate. Only 400 years later, under the Ottoman Empire, was partial unity of Islam restored, but by this time the Shariah had come to mean a legal system independent of and superior to any individual transient ruler.

As early as the tenth century CE, the jurisprudential concept of the Shariah had emerged from the three preceding centuries of Qur'ān and Sunna-based ad hoc decisions. The unfolding Qur'ān, the leadership of Muhammad and the Constitution of Medina may have provided for the relatively simple problems of a seventh-century society, but 300 years on the Shariah had developed into a form of comprehensive Muslim constitution, breaking away from the idiosyncrasies of individual rulers.

In the case of both the Common Law and the Shariah, however, the modern world has compromised the purity of the original legal organism. Legislation has overlaid the Common Law with multiple statutes, although the power of Parliament to create statute law is itself derived from the Common Law. Statutes now deal with the complexities of contemporary society which proved to be beyond the power of the courts to deal with through the precedent system (obvious examples are traffic regulations and the tax code). Similarly, conquest, colonialism and the process of gaining political independence in the twentieth century have overlaid the Shariah in Muslim countries with layers of legislation and codes, most imported from non-Muslim systems, making the practical difficulties of 'starting again' or 'returning to the purity of God's laws' insuperable in practice.

Fatwas in modern times

A fatwa, delivered by a qualified mufti, is an important source for a practitioner in Islamic law searching for a precedent, or a principle on which to build a judgement or an argument. But modern fatwas go further, intended to guide Muslims in matters of faith and law as encountered in their everyday lives. When faced with a family, business or personal problem, most Muslims do not have the knowledge or the resources to bring a court action or to engage the services of a lawyer (who would inevitably complicate the issue further still). Even for the wealthy, the prospect of litigation is daunting. In heavily bureaucratic Egypt, for example, and many Middle Eastern countries suffering from the same affliction, there are over 15 million outstanding cases bottled up in the courts involving, therefore, at least 30 million litigants, out of a total population of 70 million. Cases can take years, and are sometimes passed from generation to generation before final judgement is reached. An informal system of fatwas has, therefore, developed to bypass the sclerotic court system. For simple family matters, the sheikh of the local mosque can be consulted. But should the resulting fatwa be unsatisfactory, or for complicated issues, more sophisticated avenues are available. The party seeking redress can apply for a fatwa to a national newspaper (Al-Ahram, for example, the Middle East equivalent of the London Times) which usually has a panel of experts available to consider issues presented, and may reply to, or print, the result. Many broadcasting stations operate a similar service. In many large cities, religious universities operate a branch of Dar al-Ifta, the equivalent of a legal aid clinic, which originated with Al-Azhar University in Cairo, to which the problem can be taken, leading to the issue of a fatwa on the spot. Once an authoritative fatwa has been secured, in most cases the matter will be settled by direct negotiation between the parties following the ruling, helped along, no doubt, by the inaccessibility of the courts, and the religious overtones of the fatwa.

Here are two examples to illustrate the way the fatwa works.

Mustafa works in a bank, in a lowly position for which he is over qualified, but unemployment in his town is more than 30 per cent and nothing better is remotely available. His wife Zainab has no job and stays at home. They live frugally on his very meagre salary. Mustafa is deeply frustrated by his life, and tends to be short with his wife. He returns home one evening from work, even more stressed than usual, to find Zainab, with her friends, in a neighbouring flat and no dinner ready. He loses his temper with Zainab, and in front of her friends screams at her, 'I divorce you, I divorce you, I divorce you.' Zainab, with the help of her friends, packs her suitcase and moves back to her parents' house in the suburbs that same night. Mustafa is soon very regretful of his actions and pleads with Zainab to return. He is lonely and he misses her, and if the divorce really is to proceed, his nuptial agreement requires that he must pay to Zainab the deferred part of her dowry, which he cannot do. Zainab however, refuses, partly because she feels publicly insulted, but more importantly because she is concerned that if Mustafa's public acts of divorce mean that she is in fact divorced, she would now be committing fornication should she return to the flat. This in turn would lead to scandal and social ostracism. Mustafa seeks help from the sheikh of his mosque, but the sheikh feels unqualified to make a ruling. Mustafa then applies to a committee of local experts in the Shariah attached to a well-known *madrasah*, who consider the problem and issue a fatwa in Mustafa's favour. They conclude that since the Qurʾān in *Al-Baqarah* (The Heifer) at Surah 2, verse 230, requires that divorce must be irrevocable, and since Mustafa spoke his words in anger, and the purported acts of divorce were committed together and not at separate times, only a single act of divorce has been performed, and no divorce, therefore, has taken place. Zainab, who by now is not happy living with her parents and does not want to be a 'divorced woman', agrees to reactivate the marriage, once she is convinced that she will not be committing a sin. Just as importantly, she has the fatwa to show to any doubting members of her community.

Farouk is a wealthy old man, a widower, and the owner of a large agricultural property managed by his only son Muhammad. Farouk also has a daughter, Ramlah, who has made a bad marriage to a man with few prospects and poor health. Farouk dislikes his son-in-law and has refused over the years to offer any support to the couple, even though his daughter lives in reduced circumstances. Farouk dies, and under the Shariah, Ramlah is entitled to one half of the amount due to Muhammad, or one third of the whole estate. But Muhammad, already in possession of the farm as the manager, takes over all the assets of the estate, refusing to make any provision for Ramlah. Ramlah, who lacks the means to go to court, and aware how long a suit will take, applies to the Dar al-Ifta by letter for a fatwa. The fatwa received in reply is stern, quoting *Al-Nisā* (The Women) Surah 4 at verse 10:

> Those who unjustly
> Eat up the property
> Of orphans, eat up
> A fire into their own
> Bodies; they will soon
> Be enduring a blazing Fire.

But even though Ramlah is now an orphan, and the words of the Qur'ān appear to fit the facts precisely, Muhammad is unmoved. He still refuses to make allowance for Ramlah, challenging her to tell her story in court, which, as he well knows, she cannot afford to do, either in terms of time or money.

Fiqh

The comparison between the Shariah and the Common Law begins to break down, however, over the issue of jurisprudence or *fiqh*. In England the Common Law has built up a refined hierarchy of decision-making, stretching from the lowly Magistrates Court to the House of Lords. Decisions and their reasons are recorded at each level and over a period of time inconsistencies are eliminated by a system of appeals based on jurisprudential analysis, or in some cases legislation intervenes. But England is a small country with a unified legal administration. Islam, on the other hand, after receiving the basis of the Shariah through the revelation of the Qur'ān and the development of the Sunna, immediately spread out across Arabia and into Syria, Palestine and Persia. For the first 200 years after the death of the Prophet, therefore, a unified legal system was impossible. Judges from Mecca to Damascus to Kufa and beyond inevitably laid down a widely diverging range of decisions based on conflicting interpretations of the basic Shariah laws. The Caliph 'Umār, anticipating the growing problem, wrote to one of his senior judges in the early years of Muslim expansion, attempting to establish a basis for uniformity.

The letter is a remarkable statement of emerging Islamic jurisprudence and is worth reproducing here, both for the value of what is said, and as a window on the struggle for justice faced by early Islam, almost overwhelmed by the startling territorial progress the faith had made.

In the name of Allāh, Most Gracious, Most Merciful
From, the Slave of Allah, 'Umār ibn Al-Khattab, the Prince of the Faithful,

To, Abdullāh ibn Quays,

Salaam Aleka.

By these present know that judgeship is the burdensome duty placed upon you, but one which you have accepted. You are charged to analyse whatsoever matter comes before you, and once you have reached a clear decision, your judgement is to be executed. There can be no rights before the law without implementation by the law. Judge evenly between those who plead before you, and let not your face betray any preference, so that the nobleman seeking redress before you receives no favours over the poor man, and the weak will not therefore despair of justice. Make evidence the burden of the party which alleges, and place under oath he who denies the claim. Settlement of disputes between the parties, before judgement is rendered, shall be permitted between Muslims, except where matters contrary to the public good are concerned. Whosoever relies on evidence that is not present before the court, grant him a fixed period of grace in which to make good his claim, and if produced, consider such evidence on the merits, but if not produced within the allowed time, dismiss the claim. Thus will you establish the true facts of every case to come before you.

Where a previous judgement is subsequently found to be insecure, be not under obligation to follow your error. Justice is eternal and cannot be erased by contradictory precedent. Better to return to the right path, than to perpetuate injustice.

Evidence given by Muslims shall be presumed to be reliable, except in the case of those known to have given false testimony in the past, or those who have been subject to fixed punishments, or those deemed to be of untruthful character. For Allah alone knows the intentions of men, and on His guidance we rely to avoid the punishment of the innocent.

Exercise your discretion where a matter before you finds no guidance in the Book of Allah, or in the traditions of His Prophet. Employ analogy and deduction to extend the Shariah in the way of justice and the love of Allah.

Avoid sitting in judgement when angered, or lacking in resolution, and let not your ire rise against those appearing before you. For a judge must be just and so magnify the Word of Allah. There will surely be a great reward reserved for he who is sincere in the love of justice, even as against himself. Allah will assist him and vouchsafe him against harm from those whom he judges. But Allah does not countenance he who dissembles, and such a man's defects will be exposed, for Allah accepts only acts that are sincere.

If you pursue such justice, with what grace may Allah bless you, both in this world and the next.

Way Salaam.

(Translated by Paul Grieve and Dr Muhammad Serag)

During this early period, emphasis was on the personal merits of the individual coming before the court, on finding the appropriate just solution, despite the possibility of differing results in different geographical jurisdictions. Individual justice based on his personal knowledge of the parties and their circumstances was how Muhammad himself had approached his decisions, except for the cases where a clear and specific law from the Qur'ān applied.

In addition to the problem of fragmentation, in the first two Islamic centuries, *fiqh* was hampered by the sheer quantity of unorganized sources. We have seen how the Hadith, encompassing the Sunna, became a vast rising sea of reports of the Prophet's words and actions, few of which were reliable. To this the law was rapidly adding another substantial archive of decisions.

A legal practitioner in the Shariah during the early years of Islam, seeking to argue on behalf of a client, or to adjudicate the case before him, would pick and choose from the wide variety of sources in his search, since no consistent hierarchical system of reported cases was available. First the Qur'ān would be consulted as the Word of God, and if nothing was found relevant to a particular case, the Sunna of the Prophet would be examined. If no answer was to be found there either, general precedent from Medina would be sifted, and if there was no suitable comparison to be found from that source, lesser levels of local case precedent could be used, leading finally to the personal decision of the judge when all else failed.

During the high 'Abbāsid period of the eighth and ninth centuries CE (the third and fourth centuries AH) numerous schools of interpretation, or *madhabs*, appeared, attempting to rationalize this diversity. Four definitive schools of Islamic law finally formed, each offering a rationalized version of the sources, and differing only in emphasis and detail. These four schools still have relevance and are applicable today, even though their methodology is based on the teaching of eighth or ninth century scholars. And some of the original scholars themselves have come to be regarded over the centuries as 'Muslim saints', elaborately sanctified by hagiographies and legends, and usually referred to as 'imam', giving the word a further shade of meaning.

The Hanafi or Kufan School (from Kufa, a great literary centre in Iraq) was founded by Abu Hanifa (d. 767), but the school's principal theorist, Muhammad ibn al-Hassan ash-Shaybani (d. 804), is equally well known. Hanifi advocates an equitable and flexible approach to interpretation using 'legal discretion' or *istihsān*, to permit, where appropriate, a sense of abstract fairness to prevail over legal rigidity. Similarly, Hanafi emphasizes interior faith over outward acts of devotion. Since such teaching might appear to involve a choice being made between the original sources, the school emphasized a general Qur'ānic basis for their method.

> Those who listen
> To the word
> And follow
> The best meaning in it,

Those are the ones
Whom Allah has guided, and those
Are the ones imbued
With understanding.

Al Zumar (Crowds) Surah 39, verse 18

Hanafi also argues, based on the general provisions in the Qur'ān, that law could be created by an *ijmā* or a consensus of qualified legal authorities in successive generations, thus shaping the Shariah to suit changing circumstances.

Hanafi became the official school of the ʿAbbāsid era and of the Ottoman Empire and is thus the most widespread in the Muslim world. The system is used today in the legal systems of Syria, Jordan, Egypt and Pakistan, encompassing more than one third of the Islamic world. Hanafi also worked towards the codification of commercial laws relating to the traditional long-distance movement of goods and trade.

The Maliki or Medinan School is named after Malik b. Anas (716–95 CE) who lived his life in Medina. Malik was appointed as a judge and collected his decisions into a corpus on which the school is grounded, the *Muwatta'*, the first written compendium of laws in Islam. Malik's interpretation of *fiqh* was based on adherence to the literal word of the Qur'ān, the Sunna and legal precedents, drawn from decisions in Medina only, with emphasis on the decisions of the Companions of the Prophet. Malik's method was therefore based on *ijmā* as the source of law, like Hanafi. But Malik restricted the scope of consensus only to those practising law in Medina, past and present.

Istihsān was not permitted. The only departure from tradition contemplated by Malik was *istislah*, the accommodation of the public interest, provided that such new laws were strictly consistent with the core sources and were intended to protect the essential values of religion, life, intellect, lineage and property.

The Maliki School is dominant in Upper (or southern) Egypt and North Africa, but no longer in Medina (now within the Kingdom of Saudi Arabia).

The Shafi'i School is based on the writings of the Muslim thinker Muhammad b. Idris al-Shafi'i (d. 820 CE), whose principal work was

Al-Risala (*The Treatise*). Al-Shafi'i was a resident of Cairo, but was born in Palestine. He studied in Mecca, in Medina under Malik, in Iraq and Syria, and he was an expert in all the contemporary schools of *fiqh*. Al-Shafi'i was the most important jurist of Islam as well as a poet and a revered holy man. His memory remains forever popular with the poor of Cairo, among whom he is buried. Letters of supplication asking for relief from injustices suffered are still addressed to him and his tomb is considered to have the power to cure sickness, although this is contrary to strict Islam. Al-Shafi'i established the importance of the Sunna to the Shariah as complementary to the Qur'ān, and the mature concept of Sunni Islam can be said to originate with his work and that of his immediate followers. By restating and clarifying the 'divinely ordained' laws of the Qur'ān and the Sunna, al-Shafi'i sought to unify legal interpretation (although this was ultimately impossible across such a culturally and geographically diverse empire) and to resolve the growing conflict between *fiqh* based on the Qur'ān alone and tradition based on the reported practice of the Prophet. Further, the spread of forged Hadiths to justify unsound individual teachings threatened the unity and coherence of Islam. For this reason Al-Shafi'i sought to reduce the Sunna to only those sayings of the Prophet with a provable origin. He also attempted to limit the scope of scholars to impose their views through *ijmā*, by requiring that the necessary consensus should cover the entire community of legal scholars, which was patently impractical, rendering *ijmā* unworkable in practice.

Al-Shafi'i's greatest contribution to *fiqh* was in the development of *qiyas* as a rational basis for legal analogy. He did not approve of the narrow public interest requirement of the Malik school for the creation of new law, but he did not endorse the liberal *istihsān* of the Hanafi school. Al-Shafi'i's influence as a unifier was such that his legacy prevented the legal systems based on Medina or Kufa from breaking away completely from the mainstream. Nevertheless, in requiring that a judgement must conform to a secure Hadith to be valid, the Shafi'ite school imposed severe limitations on the adaptation of the Shariah to new situations. And indirectly, with the enhancement of the prestige of the Hadith, Shafi'ite rigidity contributed to the continuing 'manufacture' of Hadith to support unorthodox views, the very abuse that al-Shafi'i sought to curb.

Shafi'i's modern influence is strong in Syria, Malaysia and Indonesia.

The Hanbali School was established by the followers of Ahmad ibn Hanbal (d. 855) whose career was devoted to compiling traditional Hadiths. He travelled extensively in what is now the Middle East, verifying or rejecting a wide variety of traditions to produce his authoritative collection. Ibn Hanbal was a pupil of al-Shafi'i, but placed even more reliance on the traditional texts than his master. (Ibn Hanbal's extreme reverence for Muhammad led him, for example, to dye his hair dark red in reputed emulation of the Prophet.) In ibn Hanbal's view, the literal meaning of the core texts could not be departed from even by *ijmā*, and only in the rarest cases by *qiyas*. Hanbali was opposed to all forms of speculative theology and esoteric Sufism that could show no direct authority in the Qur'ān and the Sunna. This narrow and rigid reading of the Shariah is known as *taqlid*, or imitation, which can be translated as unswerving faith in the 'rightly guided' precedents, or as closed-mindedness, depending on your point of view. Hanbali is the opposing position to Hanafi, emphasizing good works and exterior acts over interior conviction as the true manifestation of faith.

After centuries of neglect, ibn Hanbal's extreme conservatism was adopted by ibn 'Abd al-Wahhab (d. 1792) via the writings of the Hanbali jurist ibn Taymiya (d. 1327). The followers of ibn 'Abd al-Wahhab, the ultra-puritan Wahhabi sect, became the ferocious power on which ibn Saud built his kingdom, and thus the Hanbali School came to be recognized as the official source of *fiqh* for Saudi Arabia. The Hanbali school has found modern relevance beyond Arabia, by advocating complete freedom in commercial matters, unrestricted by the contractual norms of precedent and the original sources.

Within Sunni Islam all four schools are generally tolerated in all jurisdictions. Where Shariah is practised, a combination of the social interpretation of Hanafi and the commercial *laisser-faire* of Hanbali prevails.

There is no disagreement between the *madhabs* as to fundamentals, although courts in different jurisdictions can produce widely differing results. Pluralism is reinforced by a well-established Hadith of the Prophet: 'The differences of opinion among the learned within my community are a sign of God's Grace.' This independence and flexibility prevented the schools from being subverted to suit the ambitions of transient temporal rulers. During the wars of religion that started in Europe in the sixteenth century, differing interpretations of the Christian scriptures were employed to justify competing acts of violence. In the Muslim world, however, this did not occur. Battles for temporal power within the fragmenting empire took place mostly outside the sphere of enduring faith.

Shi'a *fiqh*, like the Shi'a branch of Islam, took a different course from mainstream Sunni. The central difference between Shi'a and Sunni began, as we have seen, with the schism over the succession to Muhammad, with Shi'a belief recognizing only 'Ali and his successors as inheritors from the Prophet. From 'Ali, regarded by Shi'a as the First Imam, then through his sons al-Hasan and al-Husayn, the Second and Third Shi'a Imams, a line of twelve imams led the emerging community, the last from a continuing hidden state or 'occultation', to be discussed in more detail in the following chapter. Abu Hanifa studied under the sixth Shi'a Imam, Ja'far al Sādiq, the founder of Shi'a *fiqh*. But Shi'a rejects all four Sunni schools because, in the Shi'a view, only Shi'ite Imams can make fundamental decisions regarding the law.

Shi'a *fiqh* has considered and rejected both consensus and analogy in favour of the strict interpretation of the original sources, but subject to the elaborations of the first twelve Shi'a Imams. Traditionally the Shi'a idea of God's justice was rational, with God himself subject to natural law, obliged to punish evil and reward good. In modern times, however, Shi'a *fiqh* as a scholarly discipline has been overtaken by the theory of the *vilayat-e faqih*, by which ultimate interpretation of the Shi'a Shariah is in the hands of a supreme religious authority or *Faqih*, who alone is considered capable of producing the right solutions for the time. Although this is represented as *ijtihād*, allowing the sources to be reinterpreted, in practice the result is that the Shi'a clergy have given themselves wide scope to alter almost any law or opinion to suit the prevailing need.

Before the arrival of European colonialism during the nineteenth century, there was no universal 'rule of law' in Muslim societies, in the modern sense of those in power being themselves subject to the law, although, as will be discussed below, no ruler could rule successfully without the acquiescence of those who occupied positions in the institutions of society. But for the individual, the fortunes of war and the capriciousness of rulers were the overwhelming realities of the age. In practice this meant that the private law of the Shariah system (marriage, contract, inheritance, etc.) was constant, while public law (criminal, fiscal, international, etc.) was usually subject to change with each regime. Nevertheless, beneath the ups and downs of history, at an administrative level, the theory of *fiqh* developed the following legal framework for the Shariah, common to all the main schools of interpretation.

Furu al-fiqh, the 'branches of jurisprudence', codified the texts of the laws, the original sources of the Qur'ān and the Sunna, together with subsequent precedents, into *qanun*, classified under seven headings:

- *'ibādāt* – personal acts of worship and the laws governing the performance of the Five Pillars
- *mu'āmalāt* – relations and transactions between individuals
- *munākahāt* – family law from marriage to inheritance
- *jarā'im* – criminal law and fixed punishments
- *siyar* – international relations, the rules of war and peace, international treaties and the treatment of captives
- *qadā'* – defined the rules of evidence and the burden of proof, a subject with which the Islamic legal system was deeply concerned, as well as procedures for the appointment and dismissal of judges
- *māliyyāt* – determined the sources of fiscal law, including rules for payment of the *jizyah* tax for non-Muslims and the *zakāt* for Muslims, as well as the *kharaj*, or land tax, the principal source of revenues for the Muslim empires

Usul al-fiqh, the 'principles of jurisprudence', defined the underlying principles by which *furu al-fiqh* was formulated, by employing the following disciplines:

- *'Ahkām* categorized the law, which was principally divided between forbidden (*harām*), obligatory (*fard* and *wājib*), recommended (*mandub* and *mustahabb*),

permitted (*mubāh* and *jā'iz*) and disliked or frowned
upon (*makruh*). 'Ahkam also covers analysis of
causation, guilty intent, impediments to guilt such as
insanity, sanctions and punishments, and compensation.

● *'Adillāh* defined the sources of the law and the methods
by which the law is to be determined from the texts:

qiyas – the principle of interpretation of the sources
(the Qur'ān, the Sunna and precedents) by analogy,
consensus, or by reference to public policy. By using
qiyas a judge might exercise his discretion to extend
the ruling of one case to the facts of another by virtue
of a common element linking the two situations. Or,
when confronted by a situation not covered directly
by the sources, departures into new practice might be
justified by *ijmā*, the consent of the community,
generally meaning the 'ulamā', or recognized religious
scholars. Alternately, *ijtihād* offered a more liberal
solution to the same situation, contemplating, under
certain circumstances, the exercise of independent
judgement outside the scope of the original sources,
to deal with a new situation. This method was widely
used in the early days of Islam to incorporate into the
Shariah the laws and customs of subjugated peoples.

turuq al-tafsir – covered the rules for the
construction of documents, such matters as the
consistent interpretation of words, the rules governing
legalese, the significance of headings, appendices and
notes, and similar technical issues.

al-mujtahid – dealt with the qualifications required
of a practitioner in the law, from senior judges who
were authorized to make decisions based on *ijtihād*, to
the more junior levels, restricted to *taqlid*, or
following established authority.

The institutions of the Shariah

Islam expects every believer to take part in collective responsibility
for security and public order.

Ye are the best
Of peoples, evolved

For mankind.
Enjoining what is right
Forbidding what is wrong,
And believing in Allah.

Al 'Imrān (The Family of Imrān) Surah 3, verse 110

In an ideal god-fearing Muslim society, therefore, the function of the institutions of the Shariah related more to guidance and community improvement in the sight of Allah than to enforcement. The principal institutions of the Shariah in a typical pre-colonial Muslim society were as follows:

The family was (and still is) the principal building block of Islam. The traditional family structure was uncompromisingly patriarchal, but widely inclusive, so that generally every citizen of a traditional society would have been a member of an active family providing at least minimum nourishment, care and support. Much of the direct law of the Qur'ān and the Sunna is devoted to the improvement of family life. Inheritance laws for example, ensured that assets were distributed upon the death of the patriarch rather than passed to one individual, so that the whole family was protected.

Behind family life, centred on the mosque, stood the *waqf*, or religious charity, as the ultimate source of support. Property donated to the *waqf* 'belonged to God', and could not subsequently be sold or transferred. The income was for the benefit of the poor and needy, or for the common good in the form of the construction of a school, or drinking fountain, for example.

Civil order at the local level was in the hands of the *muhtasib*, somewhere between a market inspector and an ombudsman. With his assistants he was responsible for public order, for weights and measures, public health and moral standards.

Qadis, or judges, filled a wider role than a modern judge, presiding in a courtroom as well as overseeing the administration of the *waqfs*, and the welfare of orphans. As has been seen, the *qadi*'s function became more than the just disposition of the cases before him. As the Shariah developed, the *qadi* became the administrator of a settled and detailed legal system with an established body of law.

Where a *qadi*, or a ruler, or an individual, required a legal opinion, in much the same circumstances as a specialist barrister might be consulted in the UK today, a mufti would be retained to give a fatwa. Fatwas were unenforceable unless adopted by a *qadi* as a judgement, and rival fatwas obtained by contending litigants were common, often from rival schools of *fiqh*. Only under the Ottoman Empire were muftis given official status and rank. The position of Grand Mufti was often created by a Muslim ruler, giving the holder the authority to issue fatwas on wider national issues. Nevertheless, the position was often compromised by the political manipulation of the appointee's decisions.

The bureaucrats of the Shariah system (the clerks, assistants, sheikhs and teachers) received their education at a *madrasah* or Qur'ānic college, usually attached to a mosque and often physically divided into four parts, one for each of the main schools of *fiqh*. Below them the working population received a minimal education through the mosques, while above, merchant families employed tutors for their young. Practitioners in the law received an *ijāza*, or licence to practice after higher education at a Shariah college.

The elite of the systems became members of the *ʿulamā* (*ālim*, singular), the body of traditionally trained scholars who became jurists, judges, muftis or the administrators of *waqfs*. The *ʿulamā*, who acted as the guardians of the Islamic heritage, had no forum for the delivery of a unified opinion, but the tendency of individuals was strongly toward conservatism. Conservative elements of the *ʿulamā* resisted the introduction of printing, for example, the foundation on which the Western Reformation and Enlightenment were built. Indirectly, reaction to this conservative attitude led to the establishment of modern secular education, starting in Turkey and Egypt.

In most Muslim cities, trades and crafts – both manufacturers and sellers – were strictly ranked and separated topographically, with the nobler, such as the candle, incense and perfume merchants, closer to the mosque and the blacksmiths and potters set further away. A common interest built these sectors into guilds and professions, forming over the years a solid layer of society centred on the souk or bazaar. In practice, a ruler of traditional Muslim society would require the support of the bazaaris in order to achieve stability and exercise effective power, as the bazaar also operated as a bank, or even as a primitive form of central bank. At the end of the twentieth century, the influence of the bazaar could still be felt. The withdrawal of support by the merchants of Tehran from the Shah during the 1970s, and the financial support given to Khomeini in the early days of his exile, and later to his government-in-waiting in France, was ultimately crucial to the success of the Iranian Revolution.

At the core of the Shariah system was the *shurā*, or consultation process. In an earlier chapter, one of the reasons put forward for Muhammad's death without appointing a successor was that the Qur'ān in Surah 42, *Al-Shurā*, provided a framework by which the community itself could decide how to be governed. Muslims are enjoined at verse 38, to conduct their affairs by mutual consultation. The form that this consultation is to follow is not specified, however, and has been variously interpreted as meaning consultation between chiefs or family patriarchs, or between the *'ulamā*, the scholarly community, and so on. Had European colonialism not intervened, there is no reason why the *shurā* system could not have developed into a wider form of franchise, similar to a Western democracy, as the general level of education and sophistication of the population increased.

At the apex of the system, a ruler presided over his people as sultan, or, in the early days before the position became that of a figurehead only, as caliph. Ideally such a ruler would have seen himself as nothing more than a trustee, whose duty was to uphold the Shariah, not to rule as an autocrat. The words of Abu Bakr on taking power as the first caliph on the death of Muhammad come close to expressing the Muslim ideal: 'You made me your leader although in no way am I superior to you. Cooperate with me when I am right but correct me when I commit error; obey me so long as I follow the commandments of Allah and His Prophet, turn away from me when I deviate.'

But despite the injunction of the Qur'ān that a ruler should 'enjoin the good and forbid the evil', many were cruel, arbitrary and corrupt, although the fusion of law and morals in Islam, of religion and civil society, meant that a ruler could not rule without some level of consent from the ruled, and at least appear to be obeying the laws of God in the Shariah. Even when a tyrant ruled without such a consensus (a phenomenon that is hardly unknown even in the present day) the Qur'ān promotes obedience over revolution. Those in power must be endured, and ultimately they will be punished by God.

And thou wilt see them
Brought forward to the Penalty
In a humble frame of mind
Because of their disgrace.
Al-Shurā (The Consultation) Surah 42, verse 45

In practice, the administration of the Shariah continued undisturbed in the hands of the *'ulamā* at the level of religious practice, family law, commerce and inheritance. In the areas of criminal law, property and taxation a ruler may have been in a position to impose his own will within a certain geographical area, although the possibility exists in *fiqh* for the establishment of a *mazālim*, or complaints court. This tribunal operated in much the same way as the original Chancery Courts of England, applying the rules of equity where the common law courts had become deficient and rigid.

The familiar Western element that was missing from the institutions of the Shariah was the concept of the legal corporation: the trading company, the city, the state, the body that would transcend any one life, no matter how important that life might be in the present. Traditional Muslim tribal organization centred on the person of the chief and Islam was founded on the personality of one man of immense leadership capabilities. In the early years, the caliphate system followed the same pattern, with the fortunes of Muslim society closely tied to the fortunes of the leader.

There may be some substance to the theory that the 'corporate body' so common in every aspect of society in the West, from monarchy or presidency, to parliament and municipality, through social and charitable bodies, down to the humblest incorporated enterprise, derived from the Christian idea of a 'church', with a continuity separate from the personality of those temporarily in charge. Sunni Islam, in contrast, developed no tradition of corporate continuity, no 'church' or 'legal personality', being the religion of the individual standing in the local mosque who confronts his God directly, without the benefit or distraction of an ecclesiastical structure. The closest parallel to the continuum of the European 'corporate body' is the *waqf*, but the objective of the *waqf* was charitable not commercial and the concept never escaped into the mainstream of the Shariah.

A practical result of this cultural difference can be seen in the layout of a traditional Muslim city. Without a municipal corporation there was no forward planning, no dedicated public open spaces, for example, no grand boulevards. Rather, those individuals or families with the power to do so built where they pleased, principally houses and mosques, without being answerable to a higher guardian of the wider community interest.

The Shariah and Muslim nation-states

In the centuries after the establishment of the four principal Sunni schools of *fiqh* (and four further minor schools) no new school came into existence. Rather the four main methods of interpretation drew closer to each other to form the classical *fiqh* of the Shariah. This period is often portrayed as a time of stagnation, leading to the common belief, even among Muslims, that the Islamic legal system made no advance in over a thousand years from the tenth century CE to the present, and the period is sometimes referred to as the 'closing of the gates of *ijtihād*' or initiative.

The move toward conformity was in part a reaction to the devastating force of the Mongol invasion in the thirteenth century CE, when Muslim scholars sought to protect the core of Islam from destructive outside influences by adhering rigidly to precedent. But during the 400 years before the arrival of European colonization in Dar al-Islam in the nineteenth century, new law was indeed created by the exercise of *ijmā*, *istihsān*, *qiyas*, and even *ijtihād*. For almost half a millennium, Ottoman law, following the Hanafi school, improved and systematized commercial and criminal law to produce a consistent application throughout the empire. The Mughal Empire in India also made advances with the rationalization and codification of the law.

But the underlying conservatism of the Shariah also made a contribution to the success of the system, regulating lives, societies and commerce for 1,200 years, with such effect that Muslim culture became synonymous with legal order. Only in the nineteenth century was the conservative strength of the Shariah to become a weakness, making speedy adaptation to the arrival of the Western world almost impossible. Then, whatever response the Islamic legal system could have made to changing world circumstances, was frustrated by the rapid imposition of colonization and foreign legal systems on top of the historic layers of *fiqh*. This produced a confusion which many Muslim countries have yet to resolve over 100 years later.

The move away from pure Islamic law began with a round of legal reforms by the Ottoman Empire at the end of the nineteenth century, replacing most of the criminal laws of the Shariah with the French penal code, and attempting to rationalize Hanafi private law in the Turkish *Mejelle* code. This was soon followed by the imposition of British, French and Dutch law in the newly colonized Muslim territories, as well as the simplification and restriction of Islamic laws in order to make *fiqh* more easily administrable by European bureaucracies. As these new conditions appeared, Muslim modernists advocated the expanded use of *ijtihād* to replace the influence of the four traditional schools in order to meet the challenge of the times, but the move came too late.

The following potted histories give a brief overview of the present confused and fragmented position of the Shariah in four of the Muslim national states that emerged during the twentieth century.

From the conquest of **Egypt** by the Muslims in 640, until the arrival of the British in 1882, the country was ruled by the Shariah (principally the Hanafi school) which developed into a fully functioning system under the Ottoman Empire, although the *Mejelle* code was resisted by the Egyptian Khedives as part of their efforts towards independence from Turkey. But rather than gaining independence from Turkish rule, Egypt was occupied by the French, then the British, and the jurisprudence of the Islamic system was replaced with the Code Napoléon, together with some parts of the Italian legal code, translated into English and Arabic. Egypt became self-governing in the 1920s and by 1949 had put into effect the Egyptian Civil Law, which became a standard for the twentieth-century Arab world. This new code (dealing with civil matters other than family law, which remained under the Shariah) was prepared by the famous jurist Abdur al-Razzāq al-Sanhuri (the principal exponent of reconciliation between Muslim tradition and colonial reality). The code revised the inherited European system as well as reintroducing the principles of the Shariah, combined with the possibility of invoking precedents from as far back as the twelfth century CE. A further revision process based on the *fiqh* of the Shariah has continued over the years and is now formally recognized by the Constitutional Amendment of 1980, which requires that all enactments subsequent to that date conform to the Shariah. One anomalous result is that dancing girls are permitted on the television under the old laws, while at the same time the Qur'ān is the basic source of Egyptian law for the new. Another is that the Supreme Constitutional Court, responsible for hearing appeals based on the Shariah has come to be regarded as the guardian of personal liberties against the increasingly repressive legislation of the Egyptian government. The viability of this system of compromise owes much to the tolerant Egyptian character, but whether the resulting amalgam represents solid gradualism, or in fact satisfies no one, has yet to be determined.

After the creation of Transjordan by the British following the Cairo Conference of 1921, the old Ottoman legal system, based on the *Mejelle*, was continued. A process of revision of the Ottoman laws led to the adoption in 1976 of a new legal code for **Jordan**. Based loosely on the Egyptian Civil Code, the Jordanian Code extends much further, encompassing all branches of law, including the constitution. The principles of Shariah are specifically linked to the provisions of the code, and supported by administrative memoranda explaining the connection and giving the Shariah jurisprudence to which the new laws are related. Nevertheless, much of the criminal law section of the Code is based on European practice, and administrative regulations from the Highway Code to tax laws have also been imported wholesale from abroad. A hierarchical court system, based on the British model, was introduced at the same time, but here the connection between theory and practice has broken down. Although the Jordanian constitution provides for an independent judiciary, the government openly influences the courts, and permanent 'state of emergency' legislation, similar to that in Egypt and much of the Middle East, ensures that the entire system produces a result satisfactory to those in power. Of note is the adoption by the United Arab Emirates of the entire Jordanian Code, with only the names and the headings changed.

What is now **Pakistan** formed part of the Indian Raj, administered by the British separately from what is now India, using a codified version of Hanafi Shariah up to the middle of the nineteenth century, when a version of the English Common Law 'codified for export' was introduced. After the creation of Pakistan in 1948 as an independent country partitioned from India, the Common Law system was continued, despite the fact that the original ideal behind the establishment of Pakistan as a separate state was the utopian ideal of implementing the Shariah, which would allow Muslims to live 'under God's law'. Subsequent governments nevertheless continued the move away from Islamic law and towards a European form of legal code. During the 1980s an attempt to reverse this trend was made by General Zia al-Haq, who came to power by military coup. When his generals turned out to be as inept as their civilian predecessors, al-Haq announced the 'return to the Shariah' in an attempt to regain popularity and 'bring blessings' to Pakistan. In practice this meant little more than an amendment to the criminal code to provide for Islamic fixed punishments, and the imposition of mandatory *zakāt*, to be collected by the state for charitable purposes. But no fixed punishment has ever been administered in Pakistan, and while some proceeds of the *zakāt* are distributed to the poor, much of the money collected disappears into the state's murky accounts. Al-Haq's 'reforms' also included the establishment of a Federal Shariah Court as well as a Shariah bench in the Supreme Court, charged with bringing the old code into conformity with the Shariah, as well as hearing appeals based on Islamic law. Under al-Haq's civilian and military successors, the legal system in Pakistan has become increasingly complicated and sclerotic. This has been further aggravated by the introduction of mandatory Islamic banking regulations on comparatively short notice, to be discussed below.

The Ottoman Empire rejuvenated the Shariah after a long period of decline during the rule of the later ʿAbbāsid caliphs. Anatolia, or **Turkey**, benefited the most from Ottoman attention to legal codification and improvements which were based on the Hanafi school. The Ottoman legal system reached maturity in the sixteenth century CE under Süleyman the Magnificent, known in the Muslim world as Süleyman the Lawyer. Changes and improvements to the law were issued during the nineteenth century as a series of firmans, or jurisprudential decrees, with effect throughout the empire, achieving in this way partial codification and the start of the *Mejelle* system, promoted by the famous Muslim jurist Abu Saʾud al-ʿImady. Toward the end of the nineteenth century European law was progressively adopted parallel to the *Mejelle*, as areas of the law were withdrawn from the Shariah. After the defeat of Turkey in 1918 and the loss of empire, Atatürk initiated comprehensive reforms, attempting to create a modern state closely aligned with Europe, leaving the old Muslim world behind. As part of the reforms, the Shariah was entirely abolished in 1928, and the Swiss Civil Code was adopted, together with the Italian Criminal Code. This was an almost random arrangement, with Swiss law chosen merely because the Minister of Justice at the time had been educated in Switzerland. The code has nevertheless continued in use ever since, and comprehensive revisions came into effect on 1 January 2002 to conform with the standards of the European Community, although popular acceptance has been slow. The traditional Shariah system is still used in rural areas, three or four generations since abolition, as the basis of marriage law, women's rights, inheritance and property rights. The Turkish legal system does not recognize Shariah customs, however, and there is no provision in the code for a parallel system, or for appeals based on Shariah principles.

The Shariah today

In Western consciousness Shariah means something quite different from a comprehensive legal system thirteen centuries old. The Western press focuses instead on the well-known fixed corporal punishments prescribed in the Qur'ān. The Qur'ān does indeed set harsh penalties for certain crimes, which are, therefore, accepted as 'divinely specified'.

> As to the thief,
> Male or female,
> Cut off his or her hands:
> A punishment by way
> Of example, from Allah
> For their crime:
> And Allah is Exalted in Power,
> Full of Wisdom.
>
> *Al-Māidah* (The Repast) Surah 5, verse 38

In the era of the *Jāhiliyyah*, before Muhammad's ministry, Arabia was ruled by *lex talionis*, the law of the lawless desert, with no civil power such as a police force to restrain crime, so that only the certainty of all-out retribution from the victim's tribe or family maintained order. As we have seen, the Qur'ān reformed the Arab instinct to vendetta and intertribal warfare, diverting the desertman's energies from self-destruction to self-improvement. Savage fixed punishments derived from *lex talionis* were the means by which traditional tribal vengeance was controlled by the Qur'ān and channelled into a legal system acceptable to all. The victim's family could have their customary blood, but following a predetermined scale rather than through wholesale slaughter. The presumption of scholars is that the concept was taken from Judaism and the Torah, which contains the original statements of codified retribution.

> And if any mischief follow, then thou shalt give life for life,
> Eye for eye, tooth for tooth, hand for hand, foot for foot,
> Burning for burning, wound for wound, stripe for stripe.
>
> Exodus 21: 23–5

But the Shariah has moved on since the death of the Prophet in 632 CE, as has the Common Law. During the sixteenth century in England, a political opponent of the Crown could be tortured to death in public, or in the eighteenth century the penalty for mocking a Chelsea Pensioner could be death by hanging, or the punishment for a minor crime could be transportation to Australia. Though the legal provisions of the Qur'ān, unlike the Common Law, are considered to be divinely inspired and, therefore, cannot be 'repealed', in practice, repeal has been achieved by the progressive recognition over the centuries that the extreme penalties specified in the Qur'ān merely serve as symbols to emphasize the seriousness of certain crimes before God. Attempts by bloodthirsty Muslim literalists to implement such punishments, much to the delight of the Western press, are as abhorrent to Islam (the population of Saudi Arabia and Yemen excepted) as the spectacle would be in the West of a fringe community, the Isle of Man for example, under some 'law and order' government reverting to the old Common Law punishments of hanging and flogging in an attempt to recreate a mythical lost age of civil obedience and harmony.

Muhammad himself asserted that corporal punishments should be imposed only in the most blatant cases and preconditions were developed by precedent even in the early years of Islam that prevented implementation. In the case of adultery, for example, for which the Qur'ānic penalty is 100 lashes, the sentence could be imposed only if the accused confessed, or if four witnesses gave direct evidence of penetration. Since adultery is preferably a private act, such a requirement was unlikely ever to be met, and in addition a witness ran the risk of receiving 80 lashes himself if the accusation was found to be false and the accused acquitted. In the present day, in contemporary Pakistan for example, where amputation for theft is theoretically provided for by law, the preconditions required for implementation are such that the penalty has never been imposed. The thief must believe the victim to be unaware of the theft taking place; the stolen property must be of substantial value in a very poor country; the theft must have been from a place of safe-keeping; two witnesses are required to the act itself, and the punishment must not endanger the life of the criminal. Mitigation and mercy are urged repeatedly by both the Qur'ān and the Sunna and, in another interpretation, amputation as punishment for theft should not be implemented until 'all are well fed in a land of plenty'. A well-known Hadith says that rather a hundred guilty men should go free than one innocent be punished.

While the traditional Shariah punishments are thus unenforceable in a developed Muslim society, the United States, in the Muslim view, perpetrates much more shocking injustices in the present day. The American legal system is seen as favouring the rich and imposing capital punishment (which is supported by approximately 70 per cent of American voters) on the less fortunate almost exclusively, often after an extended wait on death row.

Over the centuries Muhammad's Commonwealth of Medina has come to be seen as utopian state in which the hand of God was present, directing a social system that realized God's plan for man on earth, leading to the promise of eternal paradise in the life hereafter. Since the death of the Prophet, Islam has endured a history of despotism and oppression in the name of God, similar to the uneven record of Christian rulers claiming divine authority to justify tyranny. But unlike the West, where the secular rule of law is now established and church and state firmly separated, in many Muslim countries the spirit of Shariah lives on. A few examples of the attempts in modern times to implement the Shariah as 'social reform' (in contrast to the purely legal implementation in the examples given above) will illustrate the difficulties.

In **Iran**, the regime of the Shah collapsed in 1978. He was a 'friend of America' and supported by the West, but by the mid-1970s his regime was a hollow façade that had lost all moral strength, for reasons that will be discussed in the next chapter. In the years following the revolution, the Islamic Republic was established to implement the Shariah, but almost twenty-five years later, the attempt has produced mismanagement on a huge scale, brutal repression and an administrative inflexibility that has brought most productive contacts with the outside world to a halt, while the country's misery index has risen to levels well in excess of anything experienced under the Shah. However, this failure, which is indisputable on a material level, is more attributable to the dark character of Shi'ism than to the inadequacy of the Shariah itself. In 1978 Khomeini was installed as Wali Faqih, 'chief jurisconsult', or the inheritor in some respects of the 'divinely-guided' Shi'ite Imams who began with 'Ali, Muhammad's son-in-law. Khomeini was even popularly seen as the representative on earth of the twelfth or Hidden Imam (although Khomeini never quite articulated a claim to infallibility). Who better, therefore, to lead the state in a hijrah to a new social order under God's law? In practice, however, pure Shariah was not implemented by the new state. Much of the civil code from the Shah's regime was retained and three conflicting court systems were allowed to develop: the old civil courts; Shariah courts intended to bring the law in line with the principles of the Shariah; and 'revolutionary courts' where no jurisprudence was followed and death sentences were swiftly passed on those considered inconvenient to the new regime. Moreover, during the two and a half decades of the Islamic Republic, the question of the implementation of the Shariah has been overshadowed by a struggle to resolve the riddle that lies at the core of the Iranian Revolution. How can the claim by the *'ulamā* and the Wali Faqih to absolute religious power cohabit with the will of the people, in whose name the revolution was nominally made? So long as Khomeini was alive, commanding obedience through the power of history and the force of his personality (similar to the position of Muhammad himself in Medina) the conflict was not visible. After Khomeini's death in 1989, however, an undisguised contest for power developed, having little to do with the ideals of the Shariah. On one side the conservative and theocratic *'ulamā* wield the weapon of the 'Word of God', and on the other, the almost democratically elected representatives of the people seek material improvement in what should be a rich country. To the credit of the people of Iran, this contest has taken place mostly within the framework of the revolutionary constitution, rather than through the use of armed force, as in many Arab countries. But the result has been to bring disgrace to the Shi'a clerical hierarchy, who were so ascetic in opposition, but who have demonstrated inevitable human weakness once in power, maintaining their position through abduction, murder and intimidation by show trial, while accumulating wealth and luxury for their membership through their control of state assets.

Afghanistan has a long history of devout Muslim observance, with 90 per cent of the population traditionally following the Hanafi school of Islam, which favours *ijtihād* and tolerance. An almost pure form of the Shariah was the law of the land until 1925 when a form of European civil code was introduced under British influence. A faculty was established at Kabul University to lead the integration of the traditional with the modern and to provide training for *qadis*. Sufism, the mystic side of Islam, was also very popular in Afghanistan.

Islam was also the motivating and unifying force through which British domination was finally broken. But with a similar though more urgent call to jihad to resist the Russian invasion of 1979, the old Muslim consensus was shattered. The arms and money pipeline from the American Central Intelligence Agency and Saudi Arabia via Pakistan promoted the idea of Islamic revolution rather than nationalist or tribal resistance to occupation, merely accompanied by belief. The influences were the violent Jamaat-e-Islamia Party of Pakistan, and the Sunni purists of Saudi Arabia, fanatically opposed to both Sufism and Shi'ism. Religious indoctrination combined with military training followed, creating the mujahidin, the ferocious fighting force that defeated Soviet Russia.

But the mujahidin were only successful on the battlefield. Their programme for the Islamicization of Afghanistan that was to follow the expulsion of the Russians was a complete failure. The attempt to impose a single interpretation of Islam on a diverse people was defeated by the strength of tribalism, while the traditional weakness of the Saudis, dependent on a single charismatic leader, was exposed when no such Afghani saviour appeared. Pure Sunni, Sufism and traditionally tolerant Hanafi all collapsed and the mujahidin became nothing more than corrupt and cruel warlords in a fragmented country.

The Taliban moved into this vacuum as a new force for Islamic reform, drawing on the stark teaching learned in the refugee *madrasahs* in Pakistan (of which at one time there were over 30,000). A comparison could be made with certain Christian sects, whose reading of the Bible concentrates on Creationism, accompanied by fire and brimstone, and who can always produce an obscure quote from the depths of the Old Testament to justify an extreme right-wing view. But the Taliban had nothing in common with Afghanistan's liberal Muslim roots. The essential driving force behind the movement was their interpretation of the life of Muhammad, who had himself taken up arms against an oppressive and corrupt oligarchy. And from within this new power the necessary charismatic leader appeared, the element that the former mujahidin had lacked. Mullah Omar, the Taliban leader, demanded total personal allegiance, effectively replacing the *shurā* consultation system with which the movement had started with his own decisions. Omar presumed to have himself named Amir-ul-Momineen, the Commander of the Faithful, or the 'head of Islam', the title taken by the early caliphs. On one occasion Omar even appeared before his followers from a rooftop wrapped in the cloak of the Prophet, a famous Afghani relic plundered from a sanctuary for the purpose.

The Taliban version of the Shariah concentrated on the literal text of the famously bellicose verses of the Qur'ān that date from Mecca's military threat to Medina, while ignoring fourteen centuries of development of Shariah *fiqh*. Rigidity and uncompromising extremism are contrary to the ideals of Islam, as we have seen, not to mention civil repression and the murder of Muslim by Muslim. No justification whatsoever for the Taliban is to be found in the text of the Qur'ān, or in the Shariah, other than the fixed criminal punishments discussed above and long out of use.

The reasons for this state of affairs can be explained, at least, by the initial desire of the *talib* body to cleanse Afghanistan of the ungodly destruction and corruption, fuelled by the West, that had gripped the country for the previous twenty-five years, from an era before most of the Taliban rank and file were born. And no matter how ardently the West may have wished to link the Taliban mentality with mainstream Islam, dwelling so often on the smashing of TV sets, public executions, the mandatory growing of beards and the reclothing of women, the image was no more valid than blaming the Vatican Curia (or the Archbishop of Canterbury) for the gunmen of Belfast.

Saudi Arabia is the most famous example in modern times of a state run under Islamic law. Ibn Sa'ud forged Saudi Arabia by alliances with, or victories over, most of the tribes of the Arabian peninsula, rather than by inheriting a post-colonial state within borders set by a European power, following the usual post-colonial experience. The Shariah in Saudi Arabia has thus been untouched by external influence and held in isolation by geography and history. The only non-indigenous laws are the traffic code and certain commercial regulations imported from Jordan and Egypt.

Ibn Sa'ud's all-conquering army consisted principally of warriors from the violent and puritanical Wahhabi sect, whose objective was the elimination of all 'innovation' in Islam and a return to the purity of the laws of the Qur'ān, as in the much idealized days of the Prophet's Commonwealth. As the price of battlefield victory therefore, the new state followed the ideology of the Hanbali school of Shariah, known as the most rigid form of Qur'ānic law and the interpretation on which Wahhabism is based. (Tradition says that Ahmed ibn Hanbal, the scholar who founded the movement, of whom ibn 'Abd al-Wahhab was a zealous disciple, refused to eat watermelon, that most innocent of fruit, since there was no exact precedent for such consumption to be found in the Sunna.) The result is a living example of *taqlid*, the rule of inflexibility and silence at the ultra conservative end of the possible interpretations of the Shariah. The social forces of the modern world beyond the boundaries of the state are physically excluded and simply not recognized. The Saudi royal family rules absolutely and publishes no accounts. The only consultative body, the *majlis-al-shurā*, is appointed by the king, and the 700 Saudi religious judges are a rigid self-protecting priesthood, mostly drawn from Qaseem, a region deep in the central desert and the stronghold of Wahhabism. Legal procedures are shab-bily opaque and punishments brutal, women have few rights (are not permitted driving licences, for example), reform is heavily resis-ted and the police are barely controlled. Precedent is not standard-ized so that decisions are inconsistent, and the cosy state monopolies are invariably protected. Under these circumstances, and in order to keep the country functioning, special tribunals have been estab-lished to deal with commercial matters, insurance claims, labour laws and patents, so bypassing the Shariah courts.

The Saudi reaction to the iconoclastic internet summarizes per-fectly the dilemma. Even Hanbalis cannot reject new technology out of hand while claiming that Islam is a religion for all ages, yet at the same time freedom of information cannot be tolerated. The response from the government has been to block access from Saudi servers to hundreds of thousands of sites worldwide, a form of censorship that is surely unsustainable.

When the borders of **Sudan** were drawn by the European powers in the nineteenth century, the animist Nilotic tribes in the pastoral south were arbitrarily combined with the ethnic Arab Muslim popu-lation of the north to create a new British colony, resisting the French to the west and the Ethiopian Amhars to the east. The north of the country had converted to Sunni Islam in the fifteenth century, and British occupation 350 years later was initially resisted with a religious fervour inspired by a self-styled Mahdi, or Messiah, Muhammad Ahmed. Once subjugated, British administrators kept the peoples of the north and the south separate, treating the south (by then partly Christian) in the same manner as the neighbouring 'black' colonies of Kenya and Uganda, while administering a codified form of the Shariah in the 'Arab' north under the Mohammaden Law Courts Ordinance.

Even before independence from Britain in 1956, however, the dangerously artificial nature of the country was exposed when the south began a revolt against the domination of the north. Fifty years later a devastating civil war continues, resulting in a huge popula-tion of internal refugees (second in the world only to Afghanistan). This racial and religious division of the country was exacerbated by the announcement of the introduction of the Shariah by the Khartoum government during the 1980s. Although the Shariah is supported by the northern tribes, among whom Sufism (known in Sudan as Ansar) is a long tradition, the reality has been something less than utopian. The announcement was nothing but opportunistic political cover for a mismanaged and failing economy, similar to the case of Pakistan, and resulted in little more than the pouring of alcohol stocks into the Nile and the inevitable reclothing of women, accompanied by the establishment of a committee to examine the existing patchwork of inherited colonial laws in the light of the principles of the Shariah. The country's constitution was in any event suspended and a state of emergency declared shortly after another in the series of coups that have followed one another since independence. But to the outside world the 'implementation of the Shariah' in Sudan quickly became synonymous with the terrible record of the military-backed government for genocidal civil war, the wholesale abuse of human rights (including murder, torture, mass abductions and slavery), the persecution of Christianity, and the reduction of much of the country to an aid-dependent dust-bowl.

Yet the problems encountered in these experiments do nothing to blunt the appeal of the Shariah to the majority of Muslims. The dream of a just and equitable theocratic society lives on, undimmed even by the record of the harsh dictatorships and narrow theocracies that have resulted. The alternative, the despotic suppression of such aspirations for the Shariah by force if necessary, may result in a temporary appearance of calm and order in the streets, but leaves the core issue dangerously unresolved.

The Shariah and human rights

The Universal Declaration of Human Rights adopted by the United Nations on 10 December 1948 was the product of centuries of struggle by subjects against their rulers. States based on physical coercion or a claimed 'divine right' to rule have largely been replaced in the West by societies theoretically organized on the basis of 'natural law', by which rulers only rule with the consent of the ruled, and even then subject to definite limits, principally the concept of human rights. The contrasting position of Islam is that the basis of a ruler's power is his trusteeship of the Shariah, by the will of God rather than by the consent of the ruled. Thus in theory, if not in practice, the treatment a subject may expect at the hands of the Muslim state should be a matter of divine law, not of human social contract.

The Qur'ān and the Sunna bear no apparent resemblance to a conventional legal code, or to a declaration of rights. But many of the core concepts of Islam, expressed almost 1,400 years ago, nevertheless match the high ideals of the UN Declaration.

● Slavery is not categorically prohibited by the Qur'ān, for seventh-century economic reasons, but slavery is judged to be against God's will and freeing a slave is extolled as a charity and a virtue. Small-scale domestic slavery nevertheless endured in the Arab heartland, and Prince Feisal, subsequently King of Iraq, famously appeared at the Versailles Treaty negotiations in 1919 accompanied by his slave. In the West, in contrast, active commercial slavery involving great numbers of captives, and sanctioned by law, continued through to the middle of the nineteenth century.

● The right to life and property was summarized in Muhammad's farewell address in the following words: 'Your blood and your property are sacrosanct until you meet your Lord.'

● The right to take part in government is covered by the Shariah institution of the *shurā*, discussed above.

● The *shurā* principle is only meaningful, however, if consultation takes place with freedom of expression. The Prophet himself allowed full discussion between his followers of the issues facing the Commonwealth of Medina. On subjects where a divine revelation in the Qur'ān had provided guidance, however, the will of God was not open to debate.

● The right to freedom of religion and conscience is specifically set out in the Qur'ān:

> Let there be no compulsion
> In religion: Truth stands out
> Clear from error.
>
> *Al-Baqarah* (The Heifer) Surah 2, verse 256

● The concept of fundamental human equality is repeated many times in both the Qur'ān and the Sunna, specifically summarized, once again, in the Prophet's farewell address. 'No Arab has superiority over a non-Arab as no non-Arab has superiority over an Arab, neither does a man of brown colour enjoy superiority over a man of black colour, nor does a black man enjoy superiority over a man of white colour except by piety.' The last three words of the quote raise an inevitable Muslim reservation to the concept of total human equality:

> Verily the most honoured of you
> In the sight of Allah
> Is he who is the most
> Righteous of you.
>
> *Al-Hujurāt* (The Chambers) Surah 49, verse 13

All men are equal before the law, therefore, but personal superiority can be earned through righteousness.

By the standards of today, however, there are serious omissions in the Muslim version of human rights such as the treatment of non-Muslim minorities, or the specific discrimination against women in inheritance and legal testimony. The blurring of the line between crime and sin is also problematic, as in the case of blasphemy, where freedom of expression under conformist Shariah soon comes up against limits far short of those regarded as inalienable by the West.

The advance made by the Qur'ān in creating personal rights under the conditions of the seventh century can be readily appreciated, coming long before similar measures were even considered in Europe. Ironically, the call for the implementation of strict Shariah in modern Muslim societies is often in response to the abuse of those same basic rights by nominally Muslim governments more than thirteen centuries later.

III Social Prohibitions

The well-known social prohibitions of Islam can now be seen in context as part of the Shariah, believed by Muslims to have a divine origin based on the words of the Qur'ān. Most of the prohibitions cut directly across Western practice, which regards the right of the individual to the 'life, liberty and the pursuit of happiness' as a self-evident truth having moral force, provided, of course, that no harm is done to others. For a Muslim the compulsion is reversed. Certain rules have been ordained by God and man, therefore, cannot criticize based on human logic or morality. A devout Muslim will explain that neither health nor social improvement is the reason for his or her obedience, nor is fear of punishment. God's commands are to be followed *bi la kayf*, 'without questioning how', leaving God to 'understand His own mystery'.

The more familiar prohibitions of Islam are as follows:

● Various meats are proscribed.

> He hath only forbidden to you
> Dead meat, and blood
> And the flesh of swine
> And that on which
> Another name hath been invoked
> Besides that of Allah.
>
> *Al-Baqarah* (The Heifer) Surah 2, verse 173

The flesh of donkeys and horses is prohibited, but camels are permitted. Birds with talons are not permitted, nor are animals with incisor teeth. The slaughtering of animals must be performed to certain standards, known as halal, covering cleanliness, the training of the slaughterman, the avoidance of suffering, and with the words *Bi-simi llāhi ar-rahmāni ar-rāhim*, repeated as the animal is despatched. Sunni Islam allows the consumption of all forms of seafood, but Shiʿa practice follows Judaism and prohibits the consumption of bottom feeders without fins or scales.

● The prohibition of alcohol was introduced progressively during Muhammad's ministry. By tradition, the reason for this was to allow the new community to renounce alcohol over a period of time. At first wine was permitted.

> And from the fruit
> Of the date palm and the vine
> Ye get out a wholesome drink.
>
> *Al-Nahl* (The Bees) Surah 16, verse 67

Indeed, wine was foreseen as one of the pleasures of paradise.

> Here is a parable
> Of the Garden which
> The righteous are promised:
> In it are rivers
> Of wine, a joy
> To those who drink.
>
> *Muhammad,* Surah 47, verse 15

Drunkenness was then prohibited at prayers.

> O ye who believe!
> Approach not prayers
> With a mind befogged
> Until ye can understand
> All that they say –
>
> *Al-Nisa* (The Women) Surah 4, verse 43

Then finally alcohol was prohibited absolutely.

> O ye who believe!
> Intoxicants and gambling
> Dedication of stones
> And divination by arrows
> Are an abomination
> Of Satan's handiwork;
> Eschew such abomination
> That ye may prosper.
>
> *Al-Ma'idah* (The Repast) Surah 5, verse 90

The traditional punishment for wine drinkers is flogging. This is not specified in the Qur'ān, however, or in the Sunna, but was introduced by 'Umar, the second caliph.

● Neither drugs nor tobacco were known in Medina, and no prohibition, therefore, appears in the Qur'ān or the Sunna. Drugs have, however, been considered as *harām* by Islam for centuries using *qiyas*, or the rules of interpretation, to equate hallucinogens with alcohol. Cigarettes are also theoretically prohibited as inflicting harm on the body, and thus contrary to Islam. The ruling is widely ignored, however, especially in the Middle East where, apparently, lung cancer has yet to be discovered.

● Homosexuality both between men and between women is specifically prohibited by both the Qur'ān and the Sunna, as is pederasty and anal penetration of a woman by a man. The Qur'ānic punishment was house arrest until the perpetrator repented and, as with adultery, four witnesses were required to the act itself. Homosexuality is now prohibited by the criminal codes of most Muslim states.

● Sex outside marriage is strictly forbidden, including between unmarried partners. The offence is widely defined, beginning with penetration:

> There is no sin after the association of other gods with Allah greater in the eyes of God than a drop of semen which a man places in the womb which is not lawfully for him.
> (Al-Bukhāri, *Kitab al Hudud*, The Book of Punishments)

and extending to lustful thoughts:

> Even to look at a woman with a passionate look is a sin.
> (Al-Bukhāri, *Kitab al Hudud*)

The prohibition can be circumvented by the *urfi* or informal (and usually temporary) marriage, in which there is no public declaration or registration. Although the arrangement is permitted by the Shariah and is the ambition of many university students in Cairo, for example, the families of the couple are usually hostile once they find out, and the long-term prospect of the bride in an extremely conservative Muslim society can be severely harmed if the relationship does not survive. Cairo newspapers frequently carry stories about *urfi* relationships ending in tears, and the bride seeking a backstreet hymen-repair operation.

An equivalent to *urfi* marriage is permitted by Shi'a *fiqh*, the *mut'a* or temporary marriage, expressly entered into for a fixed term. The custom is said to have existed during the time of the Prophet, but was banned by the second Sunni caliph 'Umar, which is probably why the exception was adopted by Twelver Shi'ism, who reject the authority of the first proto-Sunni caliphs. The practice is justified on the grounds that in this way human urges are recognized, while the children of such a union are legitimized and protected to the full extent of the law.

● Contraception is permitted by Islam, as sex is regarded as a gift from God, not merely for procreation. Abortion, however, is considered to be *harām* for destroying a life. Fatwas have suggested that no life can be considered to be present during the first forty days of pregnancy, and so early abortions should be allowed. But the current trend in Islam is to say that life begins with conception and that abortion is, therefore, not permitted under any circumstances, except where the health of the mother is endangered, certified by a doctor. Abortion is generally against the law in Muslim countries.

● Gambling is prohibited, defined as payment for an unknown return, which can vary from a large reward to nothing. Investing in stocks and shares, on the other hand, although risky, is permitted, since the investor at least receives a share certificate, whatever the final value of the paper may turn out to be.

The Queen Boat

Cairo is a dirty, dusty, crumbling metropolis of over 16 million people, so overcrowded that more than two million live in the cemeteries known as the City of the Dead. The city is also deeply conservative and very straight. There is little privacy at almost any level, especially for young people. Under such close living conditions, with cheap housing away from parents in short supply, everyone in each neighbourhood usually knows everybody else's business. There is very little nightife, therefore, outside the heavily guarded and very expensive American hotels, and there are few bars or clubs in the Western sense. The Nile, however, is wide where the dirty brown river passes through the heart of the city: three times as wide as the Thames, more than five times as wide as the Seine. So a river boat offers the seclusion not available on shore.

In the early hours of 11 May 2001, Egyptian security forces from the Interior Ministry stormed the *Queen Boat*, a floating bar and restaurant, arresting fifty-four male patrons. Many were beaten on the spot and others jumped overboard into the filthy water. While the men were held incommunicado by the police, the Cairo press (heavily scrutinized as well as prompted by the government) presumed their guilt with an immediate and popular campaign. The prisoners were 'devil worshippers' who practised 'debauched rituals' and 'gay weddings'. Homosexuals, a columnist urged, should 'face the death penalty'. Many of those arrested were allegedly from the 'privileged upper class' and had 'visited Israel'. Their names and photographs were published, with some pictures manipulated to show the subject wearing an Israeli uniform. All confessed 'within 12 hours', but during the subsequent trial evidence was produced showing that many had been whipped and subjected to electrical shocks or threatened with dogs, and 'medical examinations' had been carried out to prove that the men had performed 'immoral anal acts'.

In July the prisoners were put on trial, handcuffed and dressed all in white. The two main defendants were charged with 'exploiting the Islamic religion to spread extremist ideas', and practising homosexual sex 'as part of the group's rituals in front of the remaining defendants with the aim of insulting the heavenly religions and sparking civil strife'. The rest were accused of 'practising debauchery with men', as Egyptian law does not expressly prohibit homosexual acts. After a short hearing during which the defence accused the state of fabricating evidence, thirty-four men were convicted and received sentences from one to five years. Some of the defendants, the trial revealed, had not even been on the boat on the night in question, but were merely 'known homosexuals'.

But in the opinion of many observers, the use of the State Security Courts for the trial, from which there is no right of appeal, disclosed the Egyptian government's real motivation for the arrests. The State Security Courts were established twenty years ago to deal swiftly with terrorism, and the system has been used principally against the Muslim Brotherhood, Jama'ah Islamiyyah and Egyptian Islamic Jihad. After a long and brutal campaign against Islamism in Egypt, the government in 2001 declared victory. But still, under the repressive conditions within the country, the Brotherhood especially represents a continuing threat to security and attracts popular support in times of economic difficulty. By moving against homosexuals the government intended to undermine fundamentalist agitation based on the deterioration of public morals, demonstrating that the continuing state of emergency is not aimed only at fundamentalists, but protects society as a whole from undesirables of all kinds.

Human rights organizations with international connections were reluctant to become involved for fear of being accused of 'introducing homosexuality into Egypt'. Nor was the international community of much help to those convicted. Thirty US congressmen signed a letter in July 2001 protesting the arrests. But after the events of September 11th, no further complaints were heard.

IV   Women in Islam

As part of the recent swing in Europe and America towards total equality between the sexes, the status of women in Islam is frequently scrutinized by the Western press and consistently found to be deficient. Certainly by ideal Western standards of equality and freedom, women in Muslim countries live their lives as second-class citizens.

Muslim commentators make two useful preliminary points relevant to an examination of this issue from the outside. First, that marriage under Islam is not made in heaven, but is contractual. The arrangement should be viewed as similar to the 'partner' relationship in the modern Western sense, a couple living together only for as long as the relationship is worthwhile. In the poorer sectors of Muslim society (that is, among over 90 per cent of the population) the relationship is more a practical matter, with both parties working together in agriculture, for example, or small-scale commerce. Women under these conditions traditionally had recourse to the courts to end the relationship simply and speedily if the arrangement ceased to be satisfactory. In modern times, with the court system less accessible, the same end can be achieved with a suitable fatwa. Therefore, to regard married Muslim women in general as locked into tyrannical marriages as virtual servants is not a correct perception. Second, there is a direct link between wealth and the status of married women. An explanation for the limited freedom of women in some Muslim societies is that there are no jobs available for women in either a very wealthy society or in a very poor and backward society. Male-run governments, by keeping women at home, limit the workforce and mask economic failure. In Saudi Arabia, for example, women make up 50 per cent of university graduates, but only 4 per cent of the workforce, while unemployment among young Saudi males is unofficially over 30 per cent. In an open market, therefore, with no discrimination by sex, the unemployment figure would become unmanageable.

For all the contemporary criticism of the sexually unequal provisions of the Qur'ān, Islam greatly improved the position of women over the conditions prevailing in the *Jāhiliyyah* of the sixth century CE. Through Islam, women gained economic rights as individuals (to own their own property, for example, free of interference from their husbands) even if women were not fully equal to men, who were regarded as being in greater need as warriors and providers. Although traditionally women did not take part in *shurā* consultations, they enjoyed the right of *bay'a*: the opportunity to endorse, or otherwise, the result of the male *shurā* by shaking the hand of the leader, or abstaining in the event of disagreement. In theory, should enough women withhold *bay'a*, the authority of the *shurā* decision would be effectively compromised.

Under Islam women could give evidence in court, possibly for the first time in Arab society, but in some cases the word of two women was required to match the gravitas of a single male witness. The wholesale sexual exploitation of women, especially of captives, was replaced by a strict system limiting sex to the confines of marriage, although still favouring the male who is famously allowed four wives under the Shariah, and an easier divorce procedure. The Qur'ān addressed men and women equally, and sexual relations were to be conducted on the basis of equality and mutual fulfilment. Most importantly, the family and protection by the family, was made the centre of religious and social life: 'marriage is the half of religion', a popular Hadith confirms.

In the sixth-century Commonwealth of Medina, therefore, the Qur'ān represented substantial progress for women and enhanced status in a deeply patriarchal society. The perception of discrimination has only arisen subsequently as the world has changed, but the text of the Qur'ān as the 'word of God', has not. Thus in the twenty-first century, a narrow reading of the seventh-century text, as well as the many Hadiths on the subject of women, can easily become a rationale for misogyny, and 'proof' that men are spiritually and intellectually superior to women. Examples of such prejudice are many:

until recently women were confined to the home in Afghanistan, consistently refused the vote in Oman, barred from owning land in Bangladesh, prevented from travelling without the permission of a male relative in Saudi Arabia, or unable in almost all Muslim societies to enter into a formal marriage without the permission of a male guardian.

But even the limited improvements in the status of women made by the Qur'ān were soon eroded by conservative male society. The schools of legal interpretation that grew up in the centuries after Muhammad generally narrowed women's economic rights on marriage and upon divorce, for example. Strict rules were developed for the exclusion of women from prayer, from fasting or even touching the Qur'ān during menstruation, that were not to be found in the original authorities. Restrictive customs practised in the newly absorbed territories of the expanding Muslim empire were allowed to remain, all harking back towards the conditions of the *Jāhiliyyah*, when a woman was more a chattel than a person.

Judaism, Christianity and Islam are male-dominated religions rooted in ancient patriarchal traditions from a more primitive age. God is male (although theoretically neither male nor female in Islam) as are His various guises (Son and Holy Ghost), as are His disciples, prophets, priests, messengers, evangelists, caliphs and so on, possibly excepting some angels. Even at the beginning of the twenty-first century, more than half of Christendom (and 100 per cent of Jewry) matches Islam in excluding women from ecclesiastical authority, even though there is no direct rationale for such a policy to be found in the Gospels. In fact, the Qur'ān makes a consistent effort at gender equality, and the ironic verse 35 of Surah 33, *Al-Ahzāb* (The Confederates) was reputedly revealed in response to criticism from Muhammad's wife Umm Salama, who complained of gender bias in the revelations to date:

> For Muslim men and women
> For believing men and women
> For devout men and women
> For true men and women
> For men and women who are
> Patient and constant, for men

And women who humble themselves
For men and women who give
In charity; for men and women
Who fast, and deny themselves
For men and women who
Guard their chastity, and
For men and women who
Engage much in Allah's praise
For them has Allah prepared
Forgiveness and a great reward.

Women and the veil

An apposite instance of the patriarchal manipulation of history, religion and culture is the veil, which has become emblematic of the entire question of women's dress in Muslim society, and thus female status. The veil (or some other form of head covering) is one of the first issues to be taken up by male pressure groups demanding the implementation of the Shariah, since women in conservative Muslim societies have had the misfortune to become an icon of cultural identity and of family 'honour'. How women behave and appear in the street is often the emotive focus of the Shariah debate, with the much more significant question about how an alternative legal system would function in practice in a twenty-first-century state taking second place.

The word *hijāb* (meaning veil or screen) occurs seven times in the text of the Qur'ān, but on only one occasion does the context refer to women, and then specifically to the Prophet's wives.

And when ye
Ask his ladies
For anything ye want
Ask them from before
A screen: that makes
For greater purity for
Your hearts and for theirs.
                    Al-Ahzāb (The Confederates) Surah 33, verse 53

The injunction of this verse is exceptional, not universal, consistent with the Muhammad's struggle to have the privacy of his household respected even though he was a very public figure and lived in rooms behind the mosque, yet at the same time he wished to remain accessible.

The Qur'ān does enjoin modesty, however, instructing women (as well as men) in Surah 24, *Al-Nur* (The Light) at verses 30–1, to 'lower their gazes and be mindful of their chastity'. Women should not 'display their beauty and ornaments', but should 'draw their head-covering over their bosoms', except in the presence of their immediate family. A similar injunction occurs in Surah 33 *Al-Ahzāb* (The Confederates) at verse 59.

> O Prophet! Tell
> Thy wives and daughters
> And the believing women
> That they should cast
> Their outer garments over
> Their persons when abroad:
> That is most convenient,
> That they should be known
> As such, and not molested
> And Allah is Oft-forgiving
> And Most Merciful.

There is simply no Qur'ānic justification, then, for the veiling and segregation of women practised by many Muslims for centuries and still continued in some contemporary societies. In fact, there is evidence in the original Muslim sources that in Medina during Muhammad's lifetime women mixed freely and unveiled with men.

Nevertheless, the West should not assume that all women in Muslim societies wish to behave in the same way as women in London or Paris, for example. In traditional Muslim societies the veil is often welcome as distinguishing a woman as a member of the wealthy and privileged elite, a concept that reaches back to the historical distinction in dress between wives and slaves.

Voluntary female modesty as a form of self-protection is not unknown even among the liberated women of the West. There is, after all, an atavistic truth in Charlie Chaplin's observation that every man, on meeting an eligible female, calculates at some level and even if for no more than a fleeting moment, what his chances might be. This permanent biological readiness on the part of men is surely the real core of the problem. And the imposition of a conservative dress code on women is the matching admission by the men of such a society that they, rather than the women, cannot be trusted to control themselves and preserve order.

Female circumcision

The Qur'ān makes no mention whatsoever of female circumcision (or of the male version either) and no support is to be found for the practice in any secure Hadith. The point of connection is merely that the primitive practice of female circumcision is continued in some societies that also claim to follow Islam, almost exclusively in Africa. The practice expresses deep male fear of female sexuality, which is thereby acknowledged to be a force so strong that, should male control be lost, and women gain freedom of choice in their sexual expression, the prevailing patriarchal social structure would be overturned. Thus with the removal of the clitoris and often part of the labia minor as well, the demon is exorcized and the victim prevented for life from experiencing, and therefore seeking, orgasm. Such a result runs directly against the strong Muslim concept of mutuality in sexual fulfilment, for which there is definite and unequivocal authority to be found in the Qur'ān.

V   Islamic Banking

The commercial provisions of the Qur'ān reflect Muhammad's years as a trader. Contractual obligations are extensively covered in the jurisprudential interpretation of the Qur'ān and the Sunna, together with surety guarantees, promissory notes, bills of exchange and contracts of deposit. From these outline concepts, the Shariah jurists, notably the Hanafi school, developed the details of commercial instruments that facilitated the movement of goods over long distances, as well as warehousing, manufacturing and distribution. With these provisions Islam was hundreds of years ahead of Europe.

The best known of the commercial laws in the Qur'ān is the prohibition against *riba*, or usury, by which is meant collecting interest on money loaned.

O ye who believe!
Devour not usury,
Doubled and multiplied;
But fear Allah; that
Ye may really prosper.

> *Âl 'Imrān* (The Family of 'Imrān) Surah 3, verse 130

The conditions that produced this prohibition may be explained in modern terms. *Lex talionis*, the pre-Islamic law of the lawless desert, already discussed, recognized no bankruptcy procedure by which a debtor's indebtedness could be ended. Rather, a bankrupt could be imprisoned or enslaved, with the unpaid debt carried forward into the succeeding generation or generations. If, for example, a merchant were to incur a loss in an unsuccessful trading expedition, even through no fault of his own, such as in the case of robbery or a natural disaster, should any of his capital have been borrowed, the debt would nevertheless still have been owed, and traditionally doubled as the penalty for failure to pay on time. Compounding interest, which could not be ended by declaring bankruptcy, as would be the case today, would then have had the potential for destroying the man and his family in times when there was no state support, no insurance, or even *zakāt* to fall back on. Maybe Muhammad had seen such tragedies for himself.

The Qur'ān sought to prevent such commercial ruin by requiring first, that the collection of debts be limited to the physical assets of the debtor, with imprisonment or slavery for debt abolished, and second, that the investor could only be recompensed through a share of the profits, while taking an equal share of the risks. Thus in the example of misfortune given above, had all or part of the capital for the trader's expedition been supplied by an investor under the rules of the Shariah, the investor would have lost along with the borrower, rather than being able to recover his loan from the merchant's other assets, which, if insufficient, would have led to bankruptcy. Had the expedition been successful, however, the investor could have claimed his share of the profits rather than merely his interest. The arrangement was not limited to any fixed ratio between entrepreneur and investor, but could be made in any proportion agreed between the parties.

This may not have been an investor's preferred method of investing, since such an investment would require substantially more diligence than a loan secured against readily available and valuable assets. But if all were bound by the same rules, there would have been no alternative source of investment for those with capital and the system would have to work. Sharing risk and profit required honesty and trust, characteristics for which Muslim traders became famous throughout the world from the earliest days of Islam, setting an example wherever they went and as a result making converts the length and breath of their trade routes.

The ban on usury also touches on the question of the will of God. To charge a fixed rate of interest is to attempt to predetermine the future. But the future is known only to God, so how can rates be set in advance? The commercial practices established by the Qur'ān also had a moral dimension: profit is justified only when based on risk.

The modern application of this aspect of the Shariah is not so simple, of course, since the rule against usury has been strengthened by interpretation over the years to prohibit all risk-free non-participatory lending. The economic justification for this is that capital that participates in commerce contributes to the generation of community wealth, whereas money deposited in a bank at interest is out of circulation. In fact, the function of a modern bank is to recycle deposits as personal and corporate loans, and the depositor participates by running the theoretical risk that the bank will fail (although in practice this risk is often covered by government guarantees). But such conventional arrangements do not satisfy advocates of Islamic banking. All financial contracts must, on their face, share the risk between the parties. Equipment leasing or hire-purchase, for example, are recognized as within the Shariah, but an interest-bearing savings account is not.

In the wealthier Muslim countries, such as Saudi Arabia, Malaysia and the Gulf States, Islamic banking is available as an alternative to Western banking, but not forced upon the population, as is the case in Iran and the Sudan, and recently in Pakistan. Many international Islamic banking investment funds have developed over the past twenty-five years, including some run by Western banks, and managing billions of dollars, although the sector is still infinitesimally small compared with total worldwide investment. Even the size of the largest fund (Al-Ahli Global Trading of Saudi Arabia) has only recently passed the $1.0 billion mark. The fund as the investor, and the entrepreneur as the initiator and manager of the enterprise, share the risk, and the depositors behind the fund, who provide the capital, are paid a portion of the profit rather than a fixed rate of interest. Islamic funds are well suited to conventional trade in goods, for example, and have also extended their activities to include real estate and equity financing.

Shariah-approved transactions for the small consumer typically take the form of the purchase by the Islamic bank of an asset required by the consumer (who would in the West be the borrower with the funds borrowed secured against the asset). The customer then buys the article back from the bank at a 'mark-up' price, with payment of principal and 'mark-up' spread over a period of time. This double contract arrangement is very common in most Muslim countries, whether or nor the Shariah is mandatory, and is much the same as an interest-bearing loan in everything but name.

For the equivalent of business operating loans, however, Islamic banking provisions require a much closer relationship between the parties than between conventional lenders and borrowers. This has the perverse effect of making Shariah funds available to fewer clients than before, only to those who are able to persuade the lender that there will be sufficient profits (together with the original investment) from which to repay the stake, rather than sufficient assets outside the transaction with which to secure and repay the loan regardless of success or failure, as in the conventional banking system. The value of an asset as security is, of course, much easier for a bank to establish than future profits, and thus the shared risk relationship under the Shariah requires a longer view of the customer's business. The Islamic bank, being compensated only from profit which usually comes in last, is thus committed for the cycle of the transaction and cannot call in the loan unexpectedly, as is the case with the promissory note system in conventional Western banking. (The famous 'banker's umbrella': loaned on a sunny day, but immediately withdrawn when the rain begins.) The investor in a Shariah transaction is, however, a full partner with the entrepreneur and can influence the course of the venture commensurate with the investment.

The principal difficulty with Shariah banking is in relations with the outside world. Iran's poor management of the country's economy, for example, has led to the need for loans from western governments as well as private bond issues at interest in order to finance imports. More interest-bearing debt will follow as the country privatizes loss-making state enterprises. The government of the Islamic Republic has, therefore, been obliged to enter into contracts contrary to the Shariah or see their economy collapse. This dilemma has been rationalized by the ruling mullahs as acceptable since the lender is not Muslim, a reasoning that follows in the long Muslim tradition of leaving the financial details of business to Jews, Christians or Hindus.

Shariah banking in Pakistan

In 1999 Pakistan's Supreme Court ordered that only Shariah banking methods were to be used, starting in July 2001. Citizens assumed that little would change, as Pakistan had made failed attempts to convert to interest-free banking on previous occasions. But this time the military regime of General Pervez Musharraf backed Islamicization to increase political support, and the change is being actively perused, even though the transfer to the new system will inevitably drag on indefinitely. Even before implementation began, however, the government was obliged to head off wholesale bank withdrawals by confirming that the country's (interest-bearing) external and internal public debts would not be affected. But commercial loans to Pakistan have dried up nevertheless, leaving the country heavily dependent on funds from the West as soft loans or aid (a factor in Pakistan's rapid decision to join America's War on Terror).

A further problem has been the largely nationalized banking system, already weighed down by a high level of unpaid loans as a result of wholesale corruption. A process of privatization has begun, nominally to facilitate Shariah banking, with non-performing loans being transferred to the state to the tune of over $4 billion. (The preferred method of looting the state in the developing world is for those in power to grant their friends and relatives loans from a state-owned bank. The debts are never repaid, but the bank is then bailed out by the country's central bankers and by international institutions behind them, 'to protect the stability of the country's economy'. The individuals debts are then written off the accounts of the bank.) Islamic purists in Pakistan look forward to the day when every bank is a *paak*, or pure bank operated by Muslims for Muslims. But with the banks' profitability based on the success or failure of customers rather than on secured assets accompanied by the regular payment of interest, few may wish to invest in such institutions.

The changes to be made to the legal system in order to implement Shariah financing also raise practical difficulties. Under the Shariah the investor, or 'co-venturer', cannot secure and recover his investment against the assets of the borrower beyond the assets in the venture in question, since the source of repayment is to be by division of the proceeds and profit (or loss) only. If other assets could be seized in the event of failure then the risk would not be shared, and the very situation that the Qur'ān sought to avoid would have been recreated. Nor does Islamic law provide for the investor to be given security against the other assets of the entrepreneur even to ensure that the terms of the contract are met (rather than as security for the principal), with the inevitable result that Shariah funding is often difficult to raise.

But one beneficial result of the tightening of credit since the introduction of Shariah is to make businessmen more self-reliant, a very Muslim characteristic. Informal 'committees' of Muslim traders are now common in Pakistan, raising capital between themselves, which is then invested with members in rotation, to be repaid with a portion of the user's profits.

Problems also confront a Shariah compliant Pakistan on a macroeconomic level. By declaring the economy to be 'interest-free', the government has at one stroke emasculated control over monetary policy through the manipulation of interest rates (the most powerful weapon in the central banker's armoury). Further, if Pakistan wishes in the future to join the World Trade Organization in order to boost exports, the government will be obliged to allow foreign banks access to the domestic market, offering fixed interest returns.

Nevertheless, the move towards Islamic banking remains very popular in Pakistan. When the first 'riba-free' bank, the single-branch Meezen Bank, was launched in February 2002 after approval from the State Bank of Pakistan, expectations were high. 'This Bank,' said Naib Amir of the influential Jamaat-e-Islamia party, 'will get rid of the interest-based system, which is the root cause of the financial crisis the world over.'

Insurance has also come up against Islamic law, as providing against unforeseen events, which is to take a bet against the will of God. Insurance contains an element of gambling, since the policy-holder has no idea in advance what he or she will receive in return for payment of the premium. In practice these doubts have traditionally been answered by groups joining together to share the risk, through a primitive form of mutual self-insurance. In recent times more sophisticated Islamic insurance companies have been established, setting premiums for risk that vary with the profits earned by the insurer, so coming within the Shariah.

Islam is not opposed to worldly wealth, and the prohibition against *riba* has no socialist overtones. The Qur'ān praises the man who takes responsibility for himself and his family. *Zakāt* and voluntary donations purify the accumulation of wealth and the sanctity of private property is expressly assured. Affluence, like sexual fulfilment, is a God-given pleasure to be enjoyed. The constipated pace of development in the Muslim economies is caused by nothing more mysterious than the man-made impediments discussed earlier: the historic absence of the concept of the legal personality (principally the commercial corporation), the need to transcend the 'big basha' cult of the leader, and the failure of the big bashas in power to adhere to the core principles of the faith by eliminating tyranny and corruption.

VI   Jihad

Like 'fatwa' and 'Shariah', the word 'jihad', popularly believed to mean 'holy war', has passed into the English language. And like the others two examples, jihad, in the Westernized interpretation of the word, carries overtones of violence and extremism. In this view, jihad is a form of reverse Crusade by Muslims against the unbelievers. There is certainly an element of military language in the Qur'ān, since Muhammad's Commonwealth was only preserved through armed self-defence.

> To those against whom
> War is made, permission

Is given to fight, because
They are wronged – and verily
Allah is Most Powerful
For their aid.

Al-Hajj (The Pilgrimage) Surah 22, verse 39

Fighting maintained the unity of the early community, provided booty to cover the operating costs of the new state, and offered the reward of paradise eternal for those killed in 'God's service', although suicide operations were unknown in Muhammad's Commonwealth. With the jihad, the energies used for intertribal raiding were converted in the name of religion to the preservation and the expansion of Islam. Later, jihad was brought into service to intensify the wars against external competitors, from Abu Bakr's first conflicts with Byzantium, to the defence of the Ottoman Empire against the British in the nineteenth century, to the expulsion of Soviet Russia from Afghanistan by the mujahidin during the 1980s, and to the recent desperate attempts to drive the British and Americans from Iraq.

Such injunctions as the quotation given above can of course be interpreted in the present day as divine authority for heinous acts of violence. But the words themselves, which were revealed to Muhammad in the specific context of the attacks by pagan Mecca against Muslim Medina, do not make Islam as a faith responsible for the actions of a few. In fact, the Qur'ān intends that violence should be used only for defence, not for aggression.

Fight in the cause of Allah
Those who fight you
But do not transgress limits:
For, verily, Allah loveth not aggressors.

Al-Baqarah (The Heifer) Surah 2, verse 190

In contrast, Judeo-Christian mythology is rooted in the rewards promised by God to the Hebrews for their entirely unprovoked attacks against the Canaanites and the Philistines. Nothing in the Qur'ān can match Yahweh's bloodthirsty authorization to the Jews in the Book of Deuteronomy for the violent occupation of Palestine, to be discussed in the following chapter.

But the core concept of jihad is neither physical nor violent. Rather the word refers to the inner exertion of the individual to improve both himself and his community through moral discipline and commitment to Islam. The literal meaning of the word *jihad* is simply 'struggle', conveying the idea of a drawn-out contest with an intimate enemy who might at any time prevail. But that intimate enemy is the self, constantly subjected to the whispered temptations of *Shaytān*. Muhammad referred to this internal struggle as the 'major jihad', and regarded the physical defence of the Muslim community as the 'minor jihad' in comparison.

As we have seen, there is no church organization in Sunni Islam, no priests controlling the sacerdotal meditation by which salvation may be attained. Rather, Islam is achieved by attempting to live the pure Muslim life in the exterior material world. This requires a constant 'struggle in the way of Allah', involving all the believer's assets. His body is to be well maintained, his physical energies are to be directed toward the external obligations of the faith, from daily prayers to the haj, to the support of his family and the poor. His goods are to be used for the same purposes, while his spirit is to fight against temptation and strive for the ideals of Islam that have already been enumerated, from compassion to moderation. This incessant personal struggle for goodness is the true meaning of the word jihad.

> That ye believe in Allah
> And His Messenger, and that
> Ye strive your utmost
> In the Cause of Allah,
> With your property
> And your persons:
> That will be best for you
> If ye but knew.
>
> *Al-Saff* (The Battle Array) Surah 61, verse 11

Jihad also has a communal meaning, often associated with reformist movements that seek to purify Islamic society, usually by the imposition of stricter Shariah. Here the word takes on a political character, supported by a Hadith of the Prophet: 'The highest kind of jihad is to speak up for truth in the face of an unjust Sultan.'

6
THE DEVELOPMENT OF ISLAM

I Movements within Islam

The Shiʿa: the way of the Imams

We have seen in an earlier chapter how ʿAli, cousin of Muhammad and married to his youngest daughter (and only surviving child) Fatima, was passed over by the Companions during the *shurā* consultations that led to the appointment of Abu Bakr as the first caliph, following the death of the Prophet. And how, twenty-four years later, after the successive assassination of the second and third caliphs, ʿUmar and ʿUthman, ʿAli was finally elected as the fourth caliph or successor to Muhammad, only to have his rule contested by Muʾāwiyah, the man who was to become the fifth. We have also touched on ʿAli's subsequent murder by one of his own disaffected supporters, and on the later and even more significant incident when ʿAli's son, al-Husayn, the grandson of the Prophet, and many other members of his family were killed under dramatically tragic circumstances by the Umayyad usurpers of the caliphate.

At the heart of Shiʿa, or the Party of ʿAli, therefore, is a tradition of tragic and irreparable wrong. From the Shiʿa point of view, these black events represent God's testing of the faithful in anticipation of a great salvation to come.

On the death of ʿUthman, the third caliph, two groups had claimed the caliphate. On the one hand, the Emigrants and the Helpers (collectively known as the Companions), by then old men, asserted the right to make the appointment by traditional *shurā* consultation in favour of ʿAli. On the other hand, the Umayyad clan of the Meccan Quraysh tribe claimed to inherit power through their clansman ʿUthman. ʿUthman himself was a devout man and was married to Muhammad's daughter Raqaiyya. He had been one of the first to join Muhammad in the early days, breaking away from his Umayyad clansmen, the traditional holders of wealth and power in *Jāhiliyyah* Mecca. Later ʿUthman was forced into exile in Ethiopia to avoid persecution. But he was old and weak by the time of his appointment as caliph and his rule was compromised by the corruption of some of his Umayyad relatives, especially Marwan ibn al-Hakam, who was to be the seventh caliph. The resulting unpopularity of 'Uthman's caliphate among the Muslims produced the uprising that led to his murder. For the Umayyads to claim that the caliphate was now theirs, through a fraudulent *shurā* held among a few close supporters only, was an affront to Islam. This was especially so since Mu'āwiyah, the Umayyad claimant, who was 'Uthman's cousin and governor of Syria, was the son of the deeply mistrusted Abu-Sufyān, the latecomer to Islam who had opposed Muhammad right up to the day of the opening of Mecca.

The initial outcome of the *shurā* process favoured the Companions and 'Ali became caliph, but soon after his appointment the Umayyads began their opposition. They claimed that 'Ali, who was present in Medina at the time, was morally responsible for 'Uthman's murder and that as caliph he had done nothing to bring the culprit to trial and avenge the death of their clansman. (Although the Umayyads, once in power, did nothing to solve the murder either.)

As the dispute grew, 'Ali moved his headquarters into the former Sassanid Persian territories, while Mu'āwiyah assembled his forces in Damascus. Battle was joined at Siffin in 657 CE where, legend has it, the Umayyad forces rode into battle with manuscripts of the Qur'ān wrapped around the points of their lances to show their frustration with civil war between Muslims. In fact, this manoeuvre was only conceived by the unscrupulous Mu'āwiyah halfway through the battle, when he saw that he was losing to 'Ali's superior forces. Hostilities were nevertheless broken off inconclusively when the scrolls of the holy text appeared. The succession, as we have also seen, was then referred to arbitration, with the outcome confounded by the conflict between religion and politics, and by the irreconcilable concepts of free will, predestination and the will of God. After the collapse of the negotiations, without any resolution having been accepted by the negotiating parties, Mu'āwiyah rearmed and was soon in a strong enough position to advance against 'Ali once again. But before the fighting could resume 'Ali was assassinated by dissenters among his own supporters who had opposed the arbitration, and Mu'āwiyah thereupon proclaimed himself caliph.

The civil war did not stop with the death of ʿAli, but continued under his eldest son al-Hasan, and then under the younger son al-Husayn, who took the title of Imam. Al-Hasan's opposition lasted only a short time before he retired to Medina, bought off by Muʾāwiyah with a substantial pension and a succession of women (al-Hasan reputedly married and divorced a hundred times). Al-Husayn also withdrew from politics during Muʾāwiyah's lifetime and lived quietly in the Hijaz. But during his later years Muʾāwiyah had appointed his son Yazid as the next caliph, supported by another manipulated and fraudulent *shurā*, so when Yazid took power on his father's death al-Husayn renewed the family opposition to Umayyad rule, with the fatal results described below. When Muʾāwiyah had proclaimed Yazid as his heir, claiming that the decision was in the best interests of the ʿ*ummah*, he had been opposed by Abdul Rahman ibn Abu Bakr, son of the first caliph. 'By Allah,' Abdul Rahmān is reported to have cried, 'you are not concerned with any interest of the ʿ*ummah*, you plan to convert our system to the Heraclian. When one Heraclius died, another replaced him.' Muslims date the change in the system of caliphate succession from *shurā* to inheritance from this well-known jibe.

The Death of the Imam al-Husayn, Prince of Martyrs

In Shiʿa Iran the death of al-Husayn at the hands of the Umayyads is 'celebrated' annually by passion plays and narrations, in which every painful detail of the story is drawn out in an agony of vicarious suffering, with the audience sobbing and slapping their foreheads at each poignant pause. Often a criminal is released from jail on the day of the observance, on the condition that he plays the part of the arch-fiend (and Sunni) Yazid.

The incident took place at Karbalāʾ, Iraq, on the tenth day (ʿĀshurā) of the lunar month of Muharram in 61 AH (10 October, 680 CE). The Umayyad Yazid had been declared caliph as the son of Muʾāwiyah, an even more tyrannical, corrupt (and wine-drinking) individual in Shiʿa legend than his father. After al-Hasan's abdication as Imam in favour of his worldly pursuits, the position of leader of the House of 'Ali had passed to al-Husayn, 'Ali's second son, al-Husayn now raised the standard of revolt against the Umayyads, even though his promised support from the Muslim army in Iraq had failed to materialize. He claimed the right to the caliphate as the Prophet's grandson and preached 'death as martyrdom, and life with these oppressors as tribulation'. After a short campaign, Yazid's army commander, the ruthless ibn Ziyad, cut off the remains of al-Husayn's family and his few supporters in the desert, and the drama began.

Al-Husayn, understanding his hopeless situation, washed and perfumed himself with musk and ambergris, then donned Muhammad's sacred shawl, which had come to him through 'Ali, his father. Claiming to be under instructions from the Prophet, received in a vision, al-Husayn rode out on his great white horse towards the Umayyad army, with his baby son, 'Ali bin as-Husayn, Muhammad's great-grandson, on the saddle in front of him. The Imam called to ibn Ziyad that the baby was innocent and should be given water and preserved from harm, having regard to his great heritage. The response was an arrow which wounded the child and then al-Husayn himself. The Imam returned to his wife and handed her the baby, whereupon, by tradition, she sang a mournful song of womanly lament for the unfolding tragedy, although the baby was to survive as Ali Zayn al-Abidin Ali Asghar, the third Shi'ite Imam (and the only Shi'ite Imam to die in his bed).

The Imam then rode out again, together with his small band, to face his enemies. A storm of arrows rained down, so thick that when al-Husayn fell from his horse he was held clear of the ground by the multiple shafts protruding from his body. His head was cut off and presented to his young daughter, Ruqayyah, who was waiting behind the battlefield. She fell upon her father's remains, moaning and sobbing with such force that she too expired, still clutching the severed head. Every one of al-Husayn's companions was also put to death.

The brooding character of Shi'ism which flows from this dark history is poignantly expressed in the lines,

> Every day is 'Āshurā and
> Every place is Karbalā.

During Khomeini's campaign to topple the Shah of Iran during the 1970s, he made compelling use of the imagery of Karbalā. He cast himself as al-Husayn, the Shah as Yazid, and those being killed in the streets of Tehran by the Shah's troops as the martyrs at al-Husayn's side. The response was dramatic, and the heavily armed (and Israeli trained) forces at the Shah's disposal were overwhelmed, although at the cost of many civilian lives.

After the death of al-Husayn, a subsequent revolt under al-Zubayr by supporters of the 'old religion' (by which was meant the Prophet's Commonwealth) and the 'legitimate succession' (by which was meant the *shurā*) led to a brief period when there were two rival caliphates, but the dissenters were finally suppressed by Umayyad forces with great ferocity, which included the partial demolition of the Ka'bah in Mecca where the last of the proto-Shi'a forces had taken refuge. The Ka'bah was rebuilt, but the schism between Sunni and Shi'a would never be repaired.

The powerful tradition of Shi'ism had begun: a disciplined and ascetic inner life combined with stubborn political opposition against apparently overwhelming external odds, sustained by belief in the ultimate justice of God. For how could a state that had murdered the descendants of the Prophet in order to usurp power, and whose leaders were living in corruption and luxury while excluding the faithful from participation in the new 'divinely ordered' state, represent the will of God?

The key historical question that lies at the root of these events is why Muhammad died intestate.

During the weeks of his last illness Muhammad had ample opportunity to address the situation, and although he is known to have favoured Abu Bakr, Muhammad must have been aware that without specifically endorsing an heir, he would leave Islam in a state of crisis. Possibly Muhammad considered that the principles he had laid down during his ministry were strong enough to guide Muslims to the right choice: *shurā* specifically was by then a deeply rooted Islamic observance explicitly advocated by the Qur'ān. Or possibly Muhammad recognized that should he appoint a successor who then failed, Islam would be in even greater danger. But whatever the reason, Muhammad cannot have anticipated the depth of the schism that was to follow.

Muhammad is reputed to have recognized 'Ali as his successor in front of his followers at a place called Ghadir Khumm, during the return to Medina from the Farewell Pilgrimage to Mecca, and there were other possible indications of the Prophet's preference. But the words used on each occasion were tragically ambiguous, and had Muhammad's intention been clear, the Companions would not have hesitated to carry out his instructions. Yet from these obscure and undocumented incidents, the Shi'a came to believe that Muhammad had designated 'Ali as his successor, and that this was a 'divinely ordered act' and not merely a personal choice. And while 'Ali was certainly a blood relative of the Prophet and the first or second Qurayshite male to accept his ministry, he was Muhammad's cousin not his son. Further, 'Ali was only a young man in his early thirties at the time of the first *shurā*, an untested idealist and an inappropriate ruler for the experienced Companions who were in their forties and fifties.

The later armed opposition to 'Ali as the appointed caliph, by Mu'āwiyah, when both right and might were on 'Ali's side, was an entirely different circumstance. But again the House of 'Ali lost, this time through the cynical manipulations of the Umayyads. Here the Shi'a claim to have been wronged has substance. But the essence of Shi'a tradition and literature is that the injustice started with the appointment of Abu Bakr, and for this reason Shi'a do not recognize the first three caliphs who preceded 'Ali as 'rightly guided' by God, or even as legitimately appointed in a constitutional sense.

There was also a nationalist or racial element to the usurpation of 'Ali's title. Two decades previously the Sassanid Persian Empire had collapsed very suddenly when first penetrated by the forces of Abu Bakr, with complete control of the territory subsequently consolidated quite easily under 'Umar. The political and economic reasons behind the tremendous Arab conquests after the death of Muhammad have been explored in an earlier chapter. But there was a further religious reason for the quick Arab conquest of racially different Persia: the Zoroastrian faith was deeply unsatisfactory, based on a form of fire worship and a mythical future and final battle between good and evil, but offering little in the way of scripture or inspiration in the present. When, therefore, the all-conquering Muslim Arabs arrived with the strong and simple faith of Islam and the Qur'ān, with which they were overwhelming the Levantine world, almost the entire Persian population were converted. Yet the Persians were not Arabs, and with their long history of civilization they still regarded the invaders as a lesser, primitive people.

It was against this background that 'Ali moved to Kufah, in what is now Iraq, (formerly within the Sassanid Empire) to gather his forces against Mu'āwiyah, drawing key warriors principally from among the Arabs, but largely supported by the Persians of the old Sassanid lands. This gave the ensuing civil war and the period of Umayyad rule that

Worldwide Shi'a Populations

Country	Population	Muslims	% Muslim	Shi'a	% Shi'a
Afghanistan	29,928,987	29,629,697	99	5,926,697	20
Bahrain	688,345	688,345	100	481,842	70
Brazil	186,112,794	29,778	0.02	11,912	40
Ghana	21,029,853	3,364,776	16	1,000,000	30
India	1,080,264,388	129,631,727	12	19,444,727	15
Indonesia	241,973,879	212,937,014	88	1,000,000	0.5
Iran	68,017,860	66,657,000	98	60,535,590	91
Iraq	26,074,906	25,292,659	97	16,296,816	65
Jordan	5,759,732	5,414,148	94	115,195	2
Kuwait	2,335,648	1,985,301	85	595,590	40
Oman	3,001,583	2,851,504	95	43,741	1.5
Pakistan	162,419,946	157,543,348	97	32,484,348	20
Syria	18,448,752	16,603,877	90	2,951,801	18
Tajikistan	7,163,506	6,805,331	95	716,351	10
UAE	2,563,212	2,460,684	96	410,114	17
Yemen	20,727,063	20,623,428	99	6,888,228	33

These figures (for 2005) have been researched from public sources and are subject to dispute by both Sunni and Shi'a organizations. The worldwide division within Islam is estimated as 89% Sunni and 11% Shi'a of all denominations.

followed the flavour of Persian against Arab that remains today in the general division between Shi'a and Sunni. (Over time Shi'a was to divide internally but for the present purposes Shi'a means the majority *Ithnā'ashriyyah*, or Twelvers, the national religion of modern Iran.)

This latent racial aspect to the conflict between 'Ali and Mu'āwiyah goes some way to explain how Mu'āwiyah was able to recast 'Ali so cleverly to his Arab followers, from blood relative and son-in-law of the Prophet as well as duly appointed caliph into a 'pretender' and the leader of a 'rebellion'. This also accounts for the speed with which the Arab Umayyads were able to consolidate power behind them so successfully after Mu'āwiyah became caliph following 'Ali's murder (although not by the hand of an Umayyad) when their moral claim to rule was so patently thin.

Shi'a and Catholics

This early history of Shi'a has moulded the character and faith of the sect into a form substantially different from Sunni Islam, even though the two branches both practise the Five Pillars and share a common belief in the divine nature of the Qur'ān. In order to penetrate the differences between the two, there is a rough parallel to be explored between Shi'a and Catholicism on the one hand and Sunni and Protestantism on the other. The comparison may be superficial and not always a perfect fit, but for an observer from a post-Christian culture, the analysis is revealing nevertheless.

● Central to Shi'ism are a series of tragically wrongful deaths, starting with 'Ali and al-Husayn. The murders of the Prophet's direct descendants, truly shocking when measured against Muslim veneration of Muhammad as God's Apostle, have produced in the Shi'a a morbidity of character comparable to the Catholic obsession with suffering and death. Primitive Mediterranean Catholicism is usually replete with gory carvings of the Crucifixion, or darkly coloured pictures of Christ in his agony, or elaborate models of pierced and bleeding hearts. The Shi'a equivalent to this Catholic symbolism of suffering is copious quantities of blood: the blood of the martyr al-Husayn, to which is attributed the power of healing, or the red-dyed fountains in the martyrs' cemeteries for the war dead of Iran, for example, or the raising of blood through self-flagellation of the chests

and backs of young Shiʿa men during street parades on the Day of
ʿĀshurā, usually accompanied by a saddled and decorated white horse
representing the Imam's vacant stallion, also drenched in blood. Such
dramatic devices are entirely alien to both Sunnis and Protestants.

● The tragedy of Karbalā has became the 'original sin' of Shiʿism
matching the Catholic concept which, as we have seen, is entirely alien
to Sunni Muslims who, like Low Church Protestants, petition God
directly for their forgiveness as sin arises. Karbalā, in contrast, was a
sin, in the Shiʿa view, that will remain unforgivable and unredeemable
until the day of salvation at the end of the world. And like the Catholic
belief of Original Sin which sets the tone of the faith and creates the
need for salvation and thus for the Crucifixion of Christ, from the
tragedy of Karbalā flows the entire structure and character of Shiʿism.

● In Shiʿa belief, and directly contrary to the essence of Sunni
Islam, God continued to convey His divine will to man even after the
last words of the Qurʾān had been received by Muhammad. In place
of the 'corrupt' Sunni caliphate line, Shiʿa regard ʿAli as the first of
a line of Twelve Imams, sent by God to interpret and direct, following the death of the Prophet. Thus the Shiʿite Imams, like the
Catholic Popes making their 'infallible' pronouncements *ex cathedra*
as the inheritors of St Peter, built up a body of 'unerring' Shiʿa law
and textual elucidation over the first centuries of the Muslim era,
that diverges from the Sunna-based interpretation of mainstream
Sunni Islam. This Shiʿa claim to a divinely inspired succession to
Muhammad contrasts with the more limited political powers of the
Sunni caliphs, who are acknowledged to have been of this world
only. And since the Sunni Hadith was initially collected under
caliphs not recognized by Shiʿa, the Hadith that Sunnis narrate is
also rejected. Rather, the Shiʿa follow the teachings of their Twelve
Imams, from which the name for the main branch of Shiʿa has developed: *Ithnā ʿashriyyah*, or Twelvers. The Shiʿa leaders who came after
the Twelve Imams, stretching up to the modern day, are considered
to have inherited at least part of the mantle of the Twelve, leading to
the compelling conclusion that a man with such 'rightly-guided'
qualities should also be the temporal ruler of the Shiʿa state. Sunnis,
in contrast, believe that Muhammad was the Last of the Prophets
and that the Qurʾān is the Final Word of God, just as Protestants do

not recognize the appointment of St Peter by Jesus as the first Pope, or the subsequent ability of the popes as St Peter's successors, to receive continuing direction from above in the form of infallible dogma.

● The veneration by Shi'a of Fatima, daughter of Muhammad and wife of 'Ali, is readily comparable to the Catholic cult of the Virgin Mary. Fatima, according to legend, led a pure and blameless life and her son was cruelly put to death because of his inheritance. Even the term 'the Virgin Fatima' is used by Shi'a writers (although possibly meant in the sense of 'chaste' within her marriage, since Fatima had three children) as is the expression 'Holy Family', meaning Muhammad, his daughter Fatima, 'Ali his son-in-law, and the Imam al-Husayn, their son, together with his son 'Ali al-Asghar. This concept reaches into the heart of Shi'a practice and belief. The Shi'a version of the Shahādah, for example, is: 'I bear witness that there is no god but God, that Muhammad is the messenger of God, *and that 'Ali is beloved of God.*' The adoration of the 'pure woman' in the person of Mary or Fatima is also subtly connected in both Catholicism and Shi'ism with the tradition of cultural discrimination against women as protected objects performing limited roles.

● We have seen how a Sunni, like a Low Church Protestant, faces his God one to one, and is able to live his religious life quite satisfactorily without the assistance of sheikh or mullah. Shi'a, on the other hand, have developed an all-powerful ecclesiastical hierarchy based on the claimed inheritance of the divine power of the Twelve Imams. Shi'a are dependent on their mullahs for access to truth and salvation in almost the same way that access to the sacraments is in the exclusive hands of the Catholic priesthood. The *Faqih* or *Marji'* is the ultimate authority on *fiqh* and Qur'ānic interpretation, but the names also apply to any experienced Shi'a jurist qualified to issue a fatwa. Six ranks of clerics make up the formidable priesthood below, down to *talib alim*, or religious student. The effect of this hierarchy or *hawza*, on believers is that obedience to guidance given from above, in both religious matters and politics, provides a pure and certain course of action, almost absolving the faithful from personal responsibility. The resulting political power in the hands of a senior grand ayatollah who is also a *Marji'*, (Ayatollah Ali as-Sistani in occupied Iraq, for example) parallels the crucial intervention by Pope John Paul II to bring about the relatively peaceful liberation of Poland from Soviet control during the end of the Cold War. (John Paul is reputed to have threatened the Russians with personal jihad from the barricades, should Moscow have attempted the violent suppression of Solidarity.)

● The principal festival of Shiʿism, the Day of ʿĀshurā, marking the death of al-Husayn, is remarkably similar to the self-inculpating and cathartic tradition of a high Catholic Good Friday. In both rites the living take on guilt for causing the death of God's representatives on earth, abandoned to their respective betrayals at their moment of need by inadequate humans. Catholics suffer vicariously for the death of Christ, with crepe-draped statues, sombre music and even self-inflicted punishments, while Shiʿa parade through the streets whipping themselves until their backs run with blood. Defeat in both Shiʿism and Catholicism is celebrated in a way that presents the deaths of Christ and of al-Husayn as redemptive acts ordained by God, so that through their suffering good will finally prevail over evil and justice over oppression. In this way martyrdom turns a death that may appear historically to be a terminal loss, into a living victory, inspiring adherents through the generations with the promise of everlasting life, so that the cause of the slain lives on forever.

● Just as the Catholic Church for centuries regarded the priesthood as the sole custodian and interpreter of the Bible, similarly authorized Shiʿa versions of the Qurʾān depart from the plain and apparent meaning of the Arabic text so revered by Sunnis. For Shiʿa the text has a deeper meaning than the visible words, a hidden and esoteric truth only discernible by the initiated ʿulamā, who are free of the dross of human imperfections. Thus a modern Shiʿa interpretation of *Al-Isrā* (The Night Journey) Surah 17, verse 8, has no difficulty in extending the references to Jewish history to be found in this and the preceding surah, to cover the injustices of modern-day politics. The Shiʿa version is given on the left and the conventional Sunni version on the right.

After this ignominious defeat, it may be that God will turn to you once more in His Mercy and deliver you. But if you Jews	**It may be that your Lord May yet show Mercy Unto you; but if ye Revert to your sins**

continue with your designs on that 'promised land', spreading corruption and spilling blood in the process, We shall hammer you with the same power that We had granted you before, obliterating your race from the face of the earth. We have made the burning fires of Hell a prison for the unbelievers – a prison from which they will never be able to escape. (Exegesis by Muhammad Bāqir Behbudi)

**We shall revert
To Our punishments;
And We have made
Hell
A prison for those who
Reject all Faith.**

● Saints, relics and miracles are very much a part of Catholic practice, providing a means of intercession with God and a connection back to a simpler and more pious age. Protestants are more sceptical, generally regarding all such veneration as mumbo-jumbo that obscures rather than clarifies. In Islam the same divergence is readily apparent. The Twelve Shiʿa Imams occupy, like Christian saints, a midway point between the human and the divine, and powers are attributed to them which are not accepted by Sunnis. The great Umayyad mosque in Damascus, for example, contains a shrine said to contain the severed head of the Imam al-Husayn (although the head is also claimed to be in the al-Husayn mosque in Cairo) and is therefore a place of pilgrimage for many Shiʿa, with the result that the mosque is frequented by both sects. In the rooms surrounding the claimed relic, Shiʿa men with their dark beards and dark clothes, their attendant women in black from head to toe, beat their breasts as they recite their dirges calling for the Imam's miraculous intercession, tears rolling down their cheeks. The Sunni faithful remain unmoved, however, saying their individual prayers quietly in the adjacent main prayer room, but just as able to perform their devotions here as in the barest hall of the least inspiring corner mosque in the city.

Despite these similarities, there is at least one central flaw in these comparisons. Shiʿa are the minority in Islam, whereas in Christianity Catholics are the majority, and the exploitation of the moral superiority of permanent minority status as a form of victimhood is very much a part of the Shiʿa outlook.

Further, the character of Shi'ism is more overtly political than Catholicism, claiming to stand for absolute justice over all forms of worldly accommodation. Shi'a account for approximately 10 per cent of Muslims, but produce proportionately a great deal more heat. This is borne out in the present day with the refusal of the Shi'a Hizbullah forces in Lebanon to agree to any compromise with the State of Israel; by the 25 year economic and political stand-off between Iran and the USA, the Great Shayt'ān; and by continuous Shi'a opposition to the claim by the House of Sa'ud to be the legitimate Keepers of the Holy Places of Mecca and Medina despite 85 years of Saudi occupation.

The Imamite inheritance

Shi'a belief maintains that God has always provided His faithful with a Prophet, ever since Adam and the beginning of the world, and that He has promised that at no time will mankind be deprived of *hujjat*, or 'proof'. After Muhammad, the Shi'a also maintain, all subsequent guidance from God will be sent only through Muhammad's blood descendants, based on the Shi'a interpretation of verse 23 of Surah 42, *Al-Shurā* (The Consultation), which is not, of course, accepted by Sunnis:

> Say: 'No reward do I
> Ask of you for this
> Except the love
> Of those near of kin.'

The Prophet's 'family', in the Shi'a view, includes 'Ali, al-Husayn, and the following ten Imams descended through al-Husayn for a total of twelve. Through their heritage the Twelve Imams are considered to be infallible mediators between Allah and His creation and to have possessed the only true understanding of the hidden meanings of the Qur'ān.

When, therefore, the line of Imams appeared to come to an end at the close of the ninth century CE on the death of al-Hassan al-'Askari, the eleventh Imam, who had no apparent heir, the Shi'a community fell into profound disagreement about how to respond. Over time the answer evolved from a confusion of completing cults as the doctrine of the Twelfth or Hidden Imam, which remains the belief of the majority of Shiʿa today. According to this doctrine, al-Askari did not in fact die without an heir, rather he had a son and designated successor, but the child's birth was concealed because of the troubled times and fear of Sunni persecution. The son, however, named Muhammad, and known as the Imam Mahdi or Divinely Guided One, decided that he would have no successors and would not reveal himself to his followers, but would remain hidden, or in 'occultation'. In Shiʿa belief the Imam Mahdi has remained alive since the ninth century CE, but in hiding, from where he retains control over the affairs of the world. He will reappear one day in Mecca, when absolute justice will be established, marking the end of terrestrial time and 'all religion in the world will belong to Allah'.

This may be a difficult belief to credit from the outside. But the doctrine has a messianic quality which thus resonates with Judaism and with Christianity, which also claims that Christ (after rising from the dead) was taken from earth alive and will appear again at the end of the world. As an allegory, however, the construct reflects Shiʿa history and character most poignantly. Ten of the eleven Shiʿa Imams before the Imam Mahdi were martyred (the later ones following ʿAli and al-Husayn were reputedly stabbed or poisoned by the Umayyads or the ʿAbbāsids) and Shiʿa consider that their community has suffered centuries of usurpation and persecution at the hands of the 'illegitimate' regimes of the Sunni majority. Is not occultation until the coming of paradise an understandable response, therefore, to the tribulations of such an unjust world?

In practice, and in the absence of the hidden Imam Mahdi, the task of guiding the Shiʿa community falls upon the ʿulamā, consisting of the hierarchy of pious Shiʿa scholars and jurists mentioned above. And although an obvious difference in status is drawn by Shiʿa doctrine between the Imam Mahdi and his temporary 'vice-regents' on earth, the mystical presence of the 'divinely guided' Imams stands behind and reinforces the present-day rulings of the ʿulamā. Similarly, and to make a final comparison between Shiʿism and Catholicism, the papal claim to authority through St Peter, based on the claim that St Peter's ordination was by Christ (and therefore by God himself), forms the core validity of the Catholic Church, as well as the central dispute with Protestants.

Shiʿa has not always been in the minority in Islam. The fourth century AH (falling across the tenth and eleventh centuries CE) was the 'Shiʿa century', when for short periods dissident regimes claiming legitimacy through the family of ʿAli controlled large parts of the Muslim Empire, principally the Fatimids in Egypt and North Africa from 907 to 1171 CE, and the Buayhids in Persia, from 932 to 1062 CE. These regimes diverged from Sunni Islam over the legitimacy of the crumbling ʿAbbāsid caliphate, and combined both religious and political dissent in typical Shiʿa fashion.

Fully developed Twelvers Shiʿa did not combine with the power of the Persian state until the beginning of the sixteenth century CE, with the rise of the powerful Safavid dynasty. During the next two centuries Shiʿism was placed on a firm footing within the Persian-speaking territories (roughly equivalent to modern Iran), and the ʿulamā consolidated their role in religion, law and education as the inheritors of the Imams. The Safavids were in this way successful in turning the Shiʿa longing for salvation and freedom from tyranny into a force against the outside world. The Safavid Shahs achieved internal stability partly by force and partly by representing themselves as descendants of the seventh Imam. Later the divergent character of Shiʿism, and the separate religious identity of the Persian territories that resulted, would motivate the Shiʿa to resist for 500 years incorporation into the Sunni Ottoman Empire, leading to the modern state of Iran and the country's distinct character.

Over the course of Shiʿa history the ʿulamā have alternated between complete indifference to temporal power, regarding the state as unauthorized by the Imam Mahdi and therefore illegitimate, and seizing political control in order to establish the rule of God. The most recent swing from passive to active came in 1979 with the Iranian Revolution.

Schism and division

Today Islam is popularly seen as divided into Sunni and Shiʿa (the latter usually referring to the Iranian Twelver version of Shiʿism, the largest modern-day sect of dissenters from the Sunni mainstream). But Twelver or Imamite Shiʿism is only one of the divisions of the modern Shiʿa of ʿAli, and only one of many schismatic groups to be found in the history of Islam, or in the present-day Muslim landscape.

شيعي

MUHAMMAD

Fatima ═══ 'Ali (d.661)

AL-Hasan (d.669)   AL-Husain (d.680)

'Ali Zain al-'Abid (d.714)

Muhammad al-Baqir (d.731)

Ja'far al-Sadiq (d.765)

Isma'il (d.760)   Musa al-Kazim (d.799)

Muhammad al-Mahdi   'Ali al-Rida (d.818)

Muhammad al-Jawad (d.835)

'Ali al-Hadi (d.868)

Hasan al-Askari (d.874)

Muhammad al-Muntazar

Chart of the Shi'a Imams

The **Kharijites** ('secessionists') were the first to reject the com-
promises made by Islam after the death of Muhammad, demanding
that a successor be elected by all the Muslims, rather than by the
established Companions through the *shurā* process based on only a
limited franchise. A Kharijite, was responsible for the murder of
'Ali in retaliation for his negotiation with Mu'āwiyah, both of
whom the Kharijites rejected. Like the Wahhabis of Saudi Arabia in
a later century, the Kharijites counted many poor but fiercely pious
Qur'ān reciters among their number, and combined extreme desert
Puritanism with suicidal bravery during their repeated and ill-fated
rebellions against superior caliphate forces. Acts of piety were
stressed over inner faith, and sinners (by which Kharijites meant
most Muslims) were considered to have forfeited their membership
of Islam and thus become *kuffar*, or 'those who rejects the faith'.

Kharijite's influence is most strongly felt today through the 'Islamist' or 'fundamentalist' movements to be discussed below.

The **Murj'ites** ('suspenders of judgement') took the opposite point of view from the Kharijites in the debate about who was to be considered a Muslim. Murj'ites accepted anyone as a Muslim who had a 'knowledge of Allah in his heart', loved Him and submitted to Him, and who acknowledged this state orally. Acts of faith and good works could be 'postponed'. This view, later discredited as too permissive by Sunni Islam, served to facilitate conversions in the vast new lands being absorbed by the Muslim Empire.

Two other groups of early Muslims argued about another fundamental question: the nature of God and the degree to which man exercises free will. The rationalist **Mu'tazilites** attempted to resolve the ambiguity between God's unknowable essence and the references in the Qur'ān to God's body, His hands and face, and His throne (upon which He presumably sits like a human) by interpreting such sections of the text as metaphoric rather than literal. Even on the Last Day, following Mu'tazalite interpretation, man will see God only in his heart. Similarly Mu'tazalites refused to accept that the Qur'ān was eternal, for this would be to set a second eternal entity beside God Himself, a form of polytheism which is the worst sin of all. Rather, the book was believed to have been created by God, although at some point in time before the text was revealed to Muhammad, a conclusion based on Surah 85, *Al-Buruj* (The Constellations), verses 21 and 22.

> Nay, this is
> A Glorious Qur'ān
> Inscribed in
> A Tablet Preserved

Mu'tazalites also argued that man must be able to exercise free will, otherwise the exhortations to do good in the Qur'ān, and the threatened punishments for transgression, would be unjust. Of course, this problem cannot be reconciled in any faith that believes in the concept of an absolute deity.

Such rationalism was rejected by the **'Ash'arites**, based on the writings of Abu'l-Hasan al-Ash'arì (d. 935), who supported the literal meaning of the Qur'ān, bypassing the resulting difficulties by asserting that only God can know how the apparent conflicts are resolved. The references to God's appearance on the Last Day and His physical attributes are to be taken at face value. Similarly, the Qur'ān was considered by the ʿAshʿarites to be eternal rather than created, a seemingly arcane issue that nevertheless came to have wide political consequences. Al-Ashʿarī attempted to resolve the issue of free will by maintaining that there is no contradiction between God's omnipotence and man's freedom to act. The soul 'gets every good that it earns and it suffers every ill that it earns' (*Al-Baqarah* (The Heifer) Surah 2, verse 286). God has given man the perception of good and evil, and man is, therefore, free to choose within his own soul, even though God, in His omnipotence, must know what the predestined outcome will be. This ʿAshʿarite view prevailed over the rationalist Muʿtazilite arguments and is unfortunately the form of unsatisfactory belief followed by most Sunni Muslims in modern times.

After the murders of ʿAli and al-Husayn, the Party of ʿAli became the focus of political opposition to the de facto holders of power down the centuries, supported by an activist version of the Qur'ānic message. A revolutionary seeking to overthrow the existing order could always be sure of enthusiastic support if claiming to be descended from a usurped line in the Prophet's family (the nominal basis on which the ʿAbbāsids overthrew the Umayyads), or, even more effectively, if claiming to be the awaited Mahdi himself. Manipulated in this way, Shiʿism gradually divided into separate sects centred on claimed inheritance from different members of the Prophet's family and various different forms of messianic mahdism. The **Ismāʿilis** were the earliest recognizable Shiʿa schismatics, also known as Seveners for their belief that Ismāʿil, the son of the fifth Imam, Jaʿfar al-Sādiq, should have been the next in line, rather than his younger brother Musa. But Ismāʿil died during the life of his father Jaʿfar, so that Musa is regarded by the Twelvers as the legitimate line. But Ismāʾil, as the eldest son, is believed by the Ismāʿilis to be the Seventh Imam as a matter of divine revelation, which is where the Sevener line ends (for now) with Ismāʿil's occultation. Ismāʿilis themselves break up into differing sub-sects over this complex issue. For the Nizari Ismā ʿilis, or Khojas, the Aga Khan represents the living successor to their claimed line of Imams. The present Aga Khan is the forty-ninth successor, a very modern religious leader who is also head of a vast business and philanthropic conglomerate (incorporated under Swiss law) that sustains the sect as well as performing good works all over the world.

More extreme versions of imamism which are really beyond the pale of Islam, the **'Alawis** and the **Druzes**, for example, raised 'Ali and various combinations of imams to levels approaching deity. Similarly, Bahā'i, originating in nineteenth-century Iran, is based on claims by Sayyid Ali Muhammad Shirazi (executed 1850) and Mirza al-Husayn Ali (1817–92) to be the Bab and Bahā'u'llāh, or versions of the Hidden Imam. Bahā'i, a form of pantheism and therefore ferociously persecuted in Shi'a Iran, is now to be found in pockets around the world from New Delhi to Vancouver.

During the tenth and eleventh centuries CE, the Fatimid Shi'a ruled Egypt and most of North Africa, and for a short time even Mecca, Medina and Baghdad. The Fatimids claimed their religious legitimacy and imamhood through Fatima, daughter of Muhammad and wife of 'Ali. For most of this short period of Shi'ite ascendancy, Iraq and Persia were ruled by the Shi'ite Buyids, a dynasty whose power was more military than religious. Both sects dissolved into disputes over succession, and Sunni influence resumed in most of the Arab territories.

The case of Iran

Once something of the character and history of Shi'ism is understood, the modern history of Iran falls more easily into place. Shi'ism is messianic and thus above politics, yet at the same time Shi'ism can be turned into a strong political force in the hands of the *'ulamā*, who claim to exercise power in the name of the Imam in occultation. Further, the use of Twelver Shi'ism by the Safavid Shahs to underpin their political control handed substantial practical power to the *'ulamā* as the legal experts and judges of the regime, in return for their support. The *'ulamā* gained the right to collect certain taxes and administer the wealth of the *waqfs*, as well as the right to give *bast*, or sanctuary in holy places.

Safavid rule (1501–1666) enjoyed a period of glory and unity under Shah 'Abbās I (1588–1629) when Isfahan was one of the most extravagant capitals in the world, with 160 mosques, 50 colleges and 1,800 caravanserais. After the death of 'Abbās II in 1666, however, the Peacock throne was occupied by a series of debauched drunkards and military opportunists. Persia fell into a period of instability, fragmenting along tribal lines, with economic decline lasting until 1794 when order and unity were reimposed by the Qajar Shahs. During this period a number of centres of Shi'a learning and shrine cities of pilgrimage fell under Ottoman rule, Najaf and Karbalā, for example, beyond the western border of modern Iran. These cities subsequently passed from the Turkish to the British sphere of influence at the beginning of the twentieth century, and following the Cairo Conference of 1921 are today in Iraq, accounting for that country's mixture of Sunni minority and 60 per cent Shi'a majority (although no recent or reliable census is available to confirm this commonly accepted figure).

During the decline of the Safavids and the political chaos that followed, Shi'a *fiqh* began to question the legitimacy of any temporal rule other than that of the divinely guided Twelve Imams. This in turn led to the theory that in the absence of the Twelfth Imam in protective concealment, only the *'ulamā* could rule in his place, ultimately preparing the way for the Iranian Revolution of 1979 and the theory of theocratic dictatorship underlying the rule of Ayatollah Khomeini.

This doctrinal undermining of temporal power by the Shi'a clergy began in earnest under the Qajar Shahs (1794–1906), who, unlike the Safavids, did not even pretend to derive legitimacy through descent from the line of Imams. The power of the mullahs increased, supported by the wealth of the *waqfs*, and control over the collection of *zakāt*. The office of supreme authority in the Shi'a hierarchy was developed, the Wali Faqih or 'Vice-regent of the Hidden Imam', creating a potential rival to the Shah. The final decline of Qajar rule into corruption and chaos precipitated the first popular uprising in Persian history and an experiment with constitutional rule, though still subject to the power of the mullahs to oversee all new laws to ensure conformity with the Shariah. This attempt at an alternative system of government was short-lived, however, overthrown in 1925 by a coup supported by the Cossack Brigades and backed by the political power of Russia and Britain, who then divided the country between them into eastern and western spheres of influence.

An obscure cavalry colonel, Reza Khan Pahlavi, became Shah. Reza Khan made no dynastic claim of any kind, but he was a successful military man and for a while he was popular as the 'strong man' the country appeared to need. He set out to create a central-ized secular state and a powerful army following the example of Atatürk in Turkey, ruling in the absolute manner of the Safavids, while at the same time accumulating great personal wealth. The ear-lier constitutional advances were ignored and the influence of Islam and the power of the mullahs was suppressed. But in 1941 Britain and Russia replaced Shah Reza, whose pro-German leanings threat-ened the Allies' control of the Iranian oil fields. In the absence of any alternative, Reza Khan's young and pliable son, Muhammad Reza, became Shah. Now the final contest for power began between mosque and palace, that would lead to a revolution thirty-eight years later, an event comparable in significance in twentieth-century Muslim history with the fall of the Berlin Wall in Europe.

That Turbulent Priest

Sayyed Ruhollah Musavi Khomeini was born in 1902 in the small town of Khomein in arid central Iran. The family were local landowning notables, claiming as *sayyed* to be descended from the Prophet. Ruhollah's father was murdered by bandits during the lawless and semi-feudal era of the Qajar Shahs, when the boy was six months old. He was raised by his strong-willed mother, who took him, some years later, to witness the public hanging of his father's murderer. Khomeini's early schooling con-sisted of learning by heart large sections of the Qur'ān in Arabic and the sayings of the Shi'a Imams in Persian, backed by a regime of harsh phys-ical punishments that would today be considered abuse. But as a result, his memory for the standard texts was so complete that he could liter-ally recite backwards.

At seventeen, Khomeini entered the seminary in Qom as an orphan, both his mother and aunt having died of cholera. Within three years, in 1922, he had been permitted to wear the long clerical coat of the initi-ated *talabeh*, or seekers, and the black turban of the *sayyed*. By 1936 Khomeini had completed an arduous cycle of formal studies which had earned him the middle-ranking title of *hojjat-al-Islam*, or Proof of Islam. He had also married Qodsi, the fifteen-year-old daughter of a wealthy

Tehran cleric who was persuaded to end her opposition to the proposed relationship through a dream in which Fatima, the Prophet's daughter, urged her to marry. Qodsi was to be Khomeini's only wife and the marriage lasted sixty years.

Khomeini was also a poet and a student of mysticism. While never openly claiming to have completed the fourth of the Four Sufi Journeys (see below), Khomeini, according to his son, believed himself to enjoy a special relationship or union with God. As a consequence, Khomeini suffered isolation in the Qom seminary for many years, considered unfit by his peers to become a senior theologian. He developed an austere dissident voice, attracting a growing following of young radical clerics. He preached in favour of the Shariah and against the materialism and corruption of Shah Reza's rule, which he referred to ironically as the 'golden age'.

As an orphan Khomeini had already emulated the Prophet, and his ministry followed the same pattern as that of Muhammad, who made little progress as a prophet until he became a politician, while his eventual political success turned on his acceptance by his followers as a holy man and a prophet. Similarly, in 1962, after decades of preparatory preaching, Khomeini's political activism began.

After a weak start as an eighteen-year-old, Shah Muhammad Reza set out to implement Western-inspired reforms, known as the White Revolution. Women were to be given the vote, literacy encouraged in the countryside, state enterprises privatized and large land holdings redistributed. Military cooperation with the United States was increased and oil supplies to the West guaranteed, providing the Shah's regime, and the Shah personally, with enormous wealth. As popular protest grew against the reforms, Khomeini emerged as the leader of the anti-government movement. His sermons combined religion with attacks on the opulent, corrupt, wine-drinking, womanizing, dog-owning Shah who had styled himself 'His Majesty the Shadow of God'.

As Khomeini's stature and popularity eclipsed the other senior clerics of Qom, he moved up the ranks, to Ayatollah and to Grand Ayatollah, virtually, but not explicitly, claiming to speak on behalf of the Hidden Imam Mahdi. After two years of demonstrations and riots, Khomeini was exiled, briefly in Turkey and then to the Shi'a shrine city of Najaf in Iraq, where the Imam 'Ali is buried. He kept in close touch with the opposition within Iran, while at the same time amassing a substantial cash reserve through donations that flowed into his bank accounts from all over the Muslim world. Khomeini became the focus for dissent within Iran, openly preaching the theory of *velayat-e faqih*, 'government by the vice-regency of the qualified jurisconsult' during the continuing absence of the Imam Mahdi. Only after the impetus of revolution had brought Khomeini to absolute power would the Shah's opponents on the secular left discover that there was no room in this narrow vision of Iranian society for anything other than Shi'ite theocracy.

In the following years political oppression increased within Iran. The SAVAK, the Shah's security service, was pervasive, and opponents of the regime were imprisoned, tortured or executed without trial, including Khomeini's son, Mustafa, who died of a 'heart attack' during a visit from the Shah's agents. But Khomeini described the loss as 'God's hidden providence', and he may have exploited his son's natural death for political advantage.

The oil boom, starting in 1973, increased the Shah's expenditure on public infrastructure, but in practice the rich became richer and the poor suffered from high inflation. Small shopkeepers were imprisoned in a futile attempt to curb rising prices, and overnight a secular non-Islamic calendar was imposed, replacing the year AH with the date of the establishment of the Persian Empire by Cyrus the Great in 550 BCE, from whom the Shah now claimed descent.

Guerrilla activity began against the regime, and in response, in 1975, the Shah imposed a fascist form of political control through the abolition of all political parties, replaced by a single state organization, the Resurgence Party. All citizens were obliged to join and to subscribe, effectively alienating the entire population.

Khomeini began to issue fatwas from Najaf on smuggled tapes, contradicting government edicts. Iran pressured Iraq into curbing Khomeini's activities, leading to his move to France where he enjoyed full political freedom. A form of government in waiting, soon to be known as the Islamic Revolutionary Council, was set up in Paris, and an Islamic Republic was promised for Iran that would bring 'freedom, independence and social justice'.

By January 1979 the Shah was a broken man, hated by elements from every level of society. He was also suffering from cancer, and under President Carter he no longer enjoyed American support. The Shah left Iran for treatment in America, never to return. He died in Egypt the following year and is buried in a Cairo mosque. Within two weeks Khomeini had landed in Tehran, after his hijrah from Paris, welcomed by a crowd of two million.

To the masses, Khomeini was 'the Imam', with all the messianic meaning that word carries in Twelver Shi'ism. But what the Imam really stood for was widely misunderstood.

Within months the answer became clear, under a new regime of Hizbullah thugs and the Revolutionary Guard administering public floggings and amputations. Wholesale summary trials of political opponents were followed by immediate executions. And rather than democracy, Khomeini rigged public approval for a theocratic constitution that opened the way for dictatorship. He was installed as the Wali Faqih, or 'vice-regent on behalf of the Hidden Imam', following the theories he preached during his days in Qom. An appointed Council of Guardians was created, consisting of reactionary mullahs, to ensure that the decisions of the elected representatives of the people conformed to their idea of the Shariah. This was 'God's government', so that resistance became blasphemy, punishable by death. And instead of the promised rule of law, the white male staff members of the American embassy were taken hostage (with the women and blacks released), creating a national emergency and an international sensation that Khomeini manipulated in order to silence, in the name of national unity, all internal opposition to his sacred revolution.

Following on from the hostage crisis, an historic border dispute with Iraq escalated into an eight-year war. The initial attack by Iraq was taken by Khomeini to be 'God's hidden gift', allowing him to extend the national emergency and continue intense political repression indefinitely. Enormous physical damage was inflicted on western Iran during the war and almost one million young soldiers were killed or maimed.

At the same time, violent opposition to the Islamic Republic began. The assassination of mullahs by the People's Mujahidin was answered by the mass execution of political prisoners already in the hands of the government, and by the establishment of neighbourhood committees to control the population to a degree never approached by the Shah. By 1988, in response to the complexities and frustrations of government, Khomeini finally went so far as to claim outright that he ruled as the absolute 'vice-regent' of Muhammad, with the power, on behalf of the Islamic state, to overrule or modify any previous laws, including those based on interpretations of the Qur'ānic text. Religion was now at the service of state rather than the state serving religion, which had been the proclaimed basis of the Revolution.

Iran's war against Iraq (with Saddam Hussein, the Iraqi leader, supplied by the West and actively supported by the US Navy from the Persian Gulf) ended in stalemate. 'I drink this chalice of poison,' Khomeini told the Iranian people, referring to the ceasefire that halted the fighting without any territorial advantage gained, 'for the Almighty and for His satisfaction.' Shortly thereafter Khomeini fell ill with cancer and heart problems. He never spoke in public again.

As the end approached, Iran was falling into confusion. A new episode of terror began following an unsuccessful attempt by the People's Mujahidin to march on Tehran from the Iraq border as the war ended. Tens of thousands of young men already in jail for previous political transgressions were accused of counter-revolutionary sympathies and summarily shot or hanged.

Khomeini began to retreat into his Sufist mysticism and his cosmic vision, leading to his open criticism of 'stupid reactionary mullahs' who were failing to implement his will. These were, of course, the very words used by the Shah to describe the clergy before the Revolution, and exactly how the Western press viewed the Ayatollah himself.

On the day of Khomeini's death, 3 June 1989, there were scenes of orgiastic Shi'a grief across the country, repeated day after day, during which hundreds were killed and many injured. After a final frenzy at the Martyr's Cemetery in Tehran, when the Imam's body was almost lost to the insatiable crowds, Khomeini was finally laid sideways into his grave, facing Mecca to await the Last Day. Like the Commonwealth of Medina on the death of Muhammad, the Revolution was left to confront the future without the 'great architect'.

Iran's tumultuous example, the fusion of black Shi'a fatalism with violent world-challenging revolution, all sanctified by the 'will of God', has yet to be digested by Islam, more than twenty-six years after the overthrow of the Shah. However, the appointment of 'Ali Khamene'i as the Wali Faqih has in effect signalled the beginning of a separation of mosque and state, or the severing of the two different models of Shi'a Islam, active and passive, that had temporarily fused to provide the basis for the Revolution. Since 'Ali Khamene'i was only an undistinguished Hojjat-al-Islam, a middle-ranking cleric, at the time of his appointment, and not a Grand Ayatollah or a *sayyed* claiming descent from the Prophet's 'family' (both of which formed part of Khomeini's theoretical rationale for taking power) the concept that the supreme political ruler should also be the supreme spiritual authority had been breached. Khamene'i, still in office at the time of writing, makes none of Khomeini's veiled claims to rule on behalf of the Hidden Imam, or to be infallible. Rather, he merely fills an office under the constitution, and the perceived 'guiding hand of God' is no longer present.

Nevertheless, this has not prevented a determined clerical element, centred in Qom and on the mullahs of the Council of Guardians, from attempting to continue the exercise of Khomeini's absolute power in the implied name of the Hidden Imam. Opposing the theocrats are the 'liberals', who advocate a democratic working out of the religious and political legacy of the Revolution while taking into account the real-world secular problems of a mismanaged economy, lack of oil-production technology, international isolation, hidden unemployment well over 20 per cent, an accelerating brain-drain, a rapidly rising birth rate and 40 per cent of the population living in poverty.

The liberals have at times been able to command the support of the majority of the people. In 2001 for example, 77 per cent of voters supported the re-election of the reformist President Mohammad Khatami, himself a cleric. The West immediately regarded his successor, the austere Mahmoud Ahmadinejad, elected in 2005, as a setback for liberal reform. But the reformists had only themselves to blame. In the Khatami years the poor and unemployed were largely ignored in favour of elite 'liberal' politics, with the superficial seduction of Western culture appearing in the streets of Tehran, widely reported and photographed. But the 'new young Iran' obscured the continuing evil threat that America represents to most poor Iranians, which translated into a strong conservative vote.

But while the democratic institutions of the constitution may function more effectively in Iran than in almost any other Muslim country, real power is not in the hands of those elected. The unelected

Wali Faqih controls the army, the judiciary (which has jailed members of parliament for criticizing the administration), the security forces, and the country's contentious nuclear programme. The Wali Faqih also makes the final decisions on all economic and international affairs, and most importantly, he appoints the members of the Council of Guardians who can overturn any decision by any elected body, depose the president, or disqualify without cause any candidate from running for election. The basis for such rulings is that the action in question does not conform with the Shariah.

The Oppressed and the Martyrs

But there is an entirely different analysis possible of the politics of post-revolutionary Iran. In this version, the power struggle in Tehran has nothing to do with religion, with 'liberals' or 'conservatives', but has everything to do with power and money.

The wealth of Iran under the Safavid and Qajar shahs was divided between the shah's court and the well-endowed *waqfs*, administered by the mullahs, forming separate 'estates' of the political system. But when Reza Shah, the first Pahlavi, came to power by a coup, he was popular with the masses, supported by armed force, and he owed nothing to either the *waqfs* or the court. He could merely take possession, therefore, of whatever lands he coveted in the name of civil reform, with no distinction made between Reza's new personal assets and those of the government. In this way Reza became immensely rich, although claiming, of course, that he acted only as a kind of trustee on behalf of the common good. Part of his wealth was indeed used to stimulate industrial development in Iran, and to build the Trans-Iranian Railway (1927–38) for example. But in the process the Shah retained significant interests for himself in the projects he approved and financed. After Muhammad Reza Shah came to power in 1941, the accumulation of royal wealth continued, formalized in 1964 with the establishment of the Pahlavi Foundation. The Foundation, or *Bonyad* in Farsi, assumed ownership of the Shah's assets, amounting to more than 10 per cent of the entire value of the country. The Pahlavi Foundation built housing for the poor, promoted education and incubated industries, but at the same time diverted oil revenues, Western aid, defence contracts and a vast range of domestic business interests to create an even greater fund of wealth, much of which was moved out of the country into bank accounts controlled directly by the Shah and his family. And a new class of well-connected Iranians also grew wealthy in the process, controlling a high percentage of the companies listed on the Tehran Stock Exchange, and, like the Shah, secreting large sums abroad. The activities of this inside group effectively ended the previous monopoly of the bazaaris, the currency traders and import–export businessmen who had generously supported the religious establishment, and supported politically the pre-Pahlavi regimes. The result was strong backing for Khomeini from the Tehran bazaar, so crucial to his eventual success.

Almost immediately upon Khomeini's return to Iran in 1979 he created by special decree the *Bonyad-e Mostazafan va Janbazan*, or the Foundation, for the Oppressed and the Martyrs, known as the MJF. Within months the MJF had taken over the billions in assets of the Pahlavi Foundation together with much of the cash found in the Central Bank, and the further billions in businesses, cars, jewellery and private villas belonging the businessmen connected to the Shah, who had fled or been caught and executed. The MJF suddenly employed over 400,000 workers and reached into almost every Iranian household. At the same time the overseas assets of the Pahlavi Foundation (including the Shah's magnificent office tower at 650 5th Avenue, New York) were taken over by a subsidiary of the MJF, mostly with the acquiescence of foreign governments, anxious at the time not to offend the new Iranian government.

By 2002 the MJF had grown to employ 700,000 workers in 800 subsidiaries (including fourteen prisons), controlling industry, mines, transportation, general commerce, agriculture, tourism, construction, black-market contraband and further favourable state privatizations. Yet the MJF publishes no accounts and pays no taxes, has no public shareholders and operates outside all government regulations. The MJF also operates large enterprises outside Iran, principally in Germany and the US, which are convenient tools for avoiding international sanctions and prohibitions, or for channelling funds to support revolutionary causes such as the Hizbullah of Lebanon, or the Shiʿa tribes of Afghanistan.

Control over the membership of the board of the MJF lies with the 'conservative' mullahs and the state security apparatus, who together hold ultimate political power under the Revolutionary constitution.

(But not forgetting the bazaaris who now have the same relationship with those in power as the formerly favoured courtiers of the Shah, even, in the ultimate revenge, taking control of the Tehran Stock Exchange.) In the cynical view, their own survival is now more important to this nomenclature than any remaining Islamic ideals, and certainly more important than the case of the oppressed and the war wounded (most of whom, far from being helped, work in MJF manufacturing plants at slave wages outside the law). In this interpretation, the much-lionized crusading 'liberals' in Iran, previously led by President Khatami, are as much a part of (or are attempting to join) the ruling elite as the 'conservatives', since no one can participate in Iranian politics who does not accept the absolute power of the Wali Faqih in the first place, and is thus in fact 'conservative'. In this alternate version the arguments about 'reform' are seen as mere cover for both sides in the maintenance of lavish lifestyles and wide powers: a precise re-creation of the conditions which precipitated the 1979 Revolution.

The way of the Sufi

Sufism is 'Islam of the heart', the hidden counterpart to Muslim orthodoxy and the Shariah. This is the reverse side of the formality of the prayer routine and the other minutely choreographed external practices of the believer. Sufism is the desire to disconnect with the outside world and to connect directly and personally with the experience of God, independent of dogma. According to ibn Battuta, the fourteenth-century travel writer, 'the fundamental aim of the Sufi life is to pierce the veils of human sense which shut man off from the Divine and so to obtain communion and absorption into God'.

Sufism goes some way to bridge the divide between the unseeable and unknowable but 'just' and 'merciful' God of Islam, and the personal 'loving' God of Christianity, by making the religious experience essentially individual, centred on the love of God for the world of His creation. There are traces of Christian monasticism in Sufism and Muhammad himself is known to have had great respect for the Christian ascetics, such as the legendary monk Bahira. Hindu and Buddhist rituals also played a part in the development of Sufism.

The name comes from the Arabic word *sūf*, meaning wool, referring to the patched garments of coarse wool worn by the ascetic who has turned his back on the silken comforts of the world. Hence Sufism is 'to possess nothing and to be possessed by nothing', or the 'turning away of the heart from things to the Lord of all things'.

The substance of Sufism, therefore, beyond such inevitably unsatisfactory attempts to define the subject, is the journey of the spiritual traveller seeking God. If the Shariah is the main spiritual highway, leading the believer through the practice of the Five Pillars, through obedience to the divine laws, and through pious works, to achieve a state of blessedness in the world to come, then Sufism is the path that branches off, leading the seeker on an internal course towards personal knowledge of the eternal, while still in the present world. Mystic writing offers many variations on the theme of the path and the 'stages' or 'states' through which the journey passes, but for the purposes of this book four main 'stations' are identified.

The **First Station** on the seeker's path consists of repentance, not only for his or her sins, but also for the penitent's general 'heedlessness of Allah'. This state of fundamental repentance is accompanied by a complete re-submission to the will of God, and a corresponding reduction in the consciousness of self, or the ego, evidenced by immersion in piety and asceticism. The Prophet seeking illumination in his bare cave, was instructed in Surah 73, *Al Muzzammil* (The Enfolded One) at verses 1 and 2 to 'stand to prayer by night . . . and chant the Qur'ān in measured tones, and to remember the name of your Lord and devote yourself with complete devotion'. From this and many similar injunctions in the Qur'ān, the Sufi practice of *dhikr* developed, meaning 'the remembrance of God', a popular method by which the first Sufi station may be approached. From simple continuous chanting, alone or in groups, *dhikr* has become almost liturgical in form, while other varieties of ecstatic ritual extend to instrumental music and poetry recital, as well as to the famous trance-inducing dance, performed by Mevlevi Sufis and referred to in the West by the corrupted name 'whirling dervishes' (from the Persian word *darvish*, or beggar). Modern-day practice usually involves the constant repetition of the names of God, to be found as Appendix 4 to Chapter 3, or the chanting of the *tahlil*, from the first Pillar of Islam, *lā ilāha illā' Llāh*, accompanied by controlled breathing which, as in yoga, limits the supply of oxygen to the brain and induces a form of ecstatic trance.

The following verse from the Qur'ān is widely quoted as the beginning of the path of Sufism.

> Allah is the Light
> Of the heavens and the earth.
> The parable of His Light
> Is as if there were a Niche
> And within a Lamp
> The Lamp enclosed in Glass;
> The glass as it were
> A brilliant star
> Lit from a blessed Tree
> An Olive, neither of the East
> Nor of the West
> Whose oil is well-nigh
> Luminous
> Though fire scarce touched it.
> Light upon Light
> Allah doth guide whom He will
> To His light.

Al-Nur (The Light) Surah 24, verse 35

There is also a Hadith of the Prophet relevant to *dhikr*: 'There is a way of polishing everything and removing rust, and that which polishes the heart is the invocation of Allah.'

The **Second Station** of the sufi's journey is complete trust in God, which is described as 'abandoning every refuge except Allah', from obsession with the minutiae of dogma to all forms of personal wealth and comfort. The traveller attempts to leave the physical world and to cross into the metaphysical, challenging the spiritual barriers that separate man from God. To achieve this state of grace man must make *du'ā'*, or supplicate God, so defining the status of servanthood. Here God may reveal the true nature of the world through a way of understanding that is beyond the intellect. The seeker may be shown love, anger, frustration, fear and hope, which may then become visible to him in those around him, corresponding with the distance from, or proximity to God, of the soul in question.

In the **Third Station** the traveller returns from the state of worldly renunciation to fulfil God's will. He or she is once more a part of the world, but no longer separated from God, who is now omnipresent to the traveller. Here the seeker's ambition is to become to God as the 'corpse in the hands of the washer'.

The **Fourth or Final Station** of the Sufi journey is *fanā*, or passing into God, the ultimate aim of the successful mystic. God is loved for His own sake, not through fear of hell or hope of heaven, as in conventional subject–object worship. Here all impediments fall away and the traveller ceases to be aware of his or her own physical existence.

> *I am he whom I love, and He whom I love is I*
> *We are two spirits dwelling in one body.*
> *When thou seest me, thou seest Him,*
> *And when thou seest Him, thou seest us both.*
>
> Louis Massignon, 1983 *La Passion de l'al-Hallāj*
> *Martyr et Mystique de l'Islam*

This is the station at which the traveller becomes the teacher, able to guide and help others to reach God, just as Muhammad returned to preach to the men of Mecca after his experiences in the desert cave. This is the point at which the Ayatollah Khomeini considered himself to be ready to assume the *velayat-e faqih* or 'vice-regency on behalf of the Hidden Imam'.

When all the stages of the journey are complete the initial asceticism may be relaxed, and many well-known Sufi teachers have married, so founding saintly lineages.

In modern times Sufism might be considered to be 'low church' Islam, almost a form of folk religion, where devotion is more important than procedure, where religious ecstasy is sought and the niceties of doctrine are irrelevant. This contrasts with the purists typified by the Hanbali school and the puritanical Wahhabi sect of Saudi Arabia, for whom any deviation from the Shariah highway is apostasy, a crime which, until well into the twentieth century in Saudi Arabia, was punishable by death. This division of high and low church tends to follow racial lines, with African, Indian and Persian Muslims more attracted to Sufi practice, and the austere minimalist form of conventional Islam being almost exclusively Arab. For the same reason, few differences exist between Shi'a and Sunni Sufi practice.

A Sufi is taught by a sheikh, with the pupil–teacher relationship often lasting for years. Personal loyalty to a sheikh endures for life. Famous sheikhs have enjoyed wide reputations, passing their teachings down through the generations by way of their students and their students' students. Some have attained the status of saints, complete with elaborate tombs and a tradition of miracles, attracting a flow of pilgrims and regular supplicants.

In a modern context a Sufi practitioner might invite a friend to a *khalwah*, or Sufi meeting, of his *tariqah* (meaning 'path') or brotherhood, where the rites would be performed beginning with *dhikr*. The friend might then decide to join, in which case he would receive instruction from the sheikh of the brotherhood who would become his mentor. The new member would receive a 'covenant' from the sheikh, and in return the initiate would agree to obey the sheikh unconditionally. In this way some *tariqahs* maintain the pure origins of Sufism, linking members through their loyalty back to the founding sheikh, who is usually regarded by the membership as a saint. The Mevlevi, for example, or 'whirling dervishes', take Rumi himself (see below) as their founder and saint, and his ecstatic energy as their *baraka*, or blessing. Other modern brotherhoods are corrupt, however, both financially and spiritually, with the sheikh contributing little to the lives of the members, while living well on donations. Members of *tariqahs* will help each other in the outside society if possible, in very much the same way that members of European and American religious societies such as the Freemasons or Opus Dei come to each other's assistance.

From this short description it should be clear why Sufism has been so ardently persecuted in the past by Sunni Muslim orthodoxy. The gruesome execution of the Sufi master Mansur al-Hallāj, quoted above, in 922 CE (his hands and feet were cut off before he was hanged) is a well-known example. He was condemned for uttering the words *ana al-Haqq*, or 'I am the Truth', which he also chanted as the execution proceeded, as if he felt no pain. The words were taken to be extreme heresy against the guiding Muslim principle of the One God who 'hath not partners'. Sufi practices were also seen by Muslim orthodoxy as undermining the central importance of the mosque, creating a religion within a religion, and the cult of Sufi saints, who were (and still are) almost worshipped at their tombs, seemed to be reviving the old intercessionary religion of the clay idols of al-Lāt, al-Uzzā and Manāt.

In response to persecution, Sufism retreated into poetic allegory, using wine, song and human love as a code for religious ecstasy, which in many cases only added to the hostility of the strongly moralistic mainstream. To the conservative Shiʿa clergy, Sufism was especially alarming, potentially bypassing the entire hierarchical apparatus of the chain of Shiʿa Imams and their present-day dogmatic spokesmen, through direct fusion with the godhead.

The philosopher Abu-Hāmid al-Ghazāli (1058–1111 CE) was the master exponent of Sufism. His writing attempts to bridge the divide between the mystic and the orthodox, and between 'sober' and 'drunken' Sufis. In much the same way that St Augustine (354–430 CE) and the Augustinian monk Martin Luther (1483–1546 CE) re-evaluated Christian doctrines, al-Ghazāli re-examined the conventional Shariah highway, in which he found little religious truth, seeking a more satisfying path to direct knowledge of the divine. Al-Ghazāli abandoned the wealth and prestige of his professional life to wander from place to place, preaching closer communion with God by the suppression of the self. His reinterpretation of the Qur'ān and the Sunna in the light of Sufism was initially seen as an outright heresy by the orthodox mainstream. Later his work was to be more widely appreciated as giving a hidden mystic dimension to the standard outward acts of worship. Al-Ghazāli also strove to define the Sufi vocabulary of *dhikr* : *duʿāʾ* (supplication to Allah), *qirāʾah* (Qur'ān recitation), *fikr* (meditation), *rajāʾ* (real hope) and *ʿubudiyyah* (servanthood).

Jalal al-Din Rumi (1207–73 CE) is generally considered to be the greatest of the Sufi poets. His large volume of work, especially the *Masnavi-I Maʿnavi* (Rhyming Couplets of Spiritual Meaning) excerpted below, as translated from Persian by Reynold Nicholson, expresses the ecstasy of the 'drunken' Sufi seeking reunification with God, reaching beyond the bounds of Islam for a universal truth. The sea is a frequently used metaphor for the eternal in Rumi's poetry, giving form to the concept of human consciousness as an extension of the divine.

> *The grief of the dead is not on account of death; it is because*
> *they dwelt upon the phenomenal forms of existence*
> *And never perceived that all this foam is moved and fed by*
> *the sea.*

> *When the sea has cast these foam-flakes on the shore, go to the*
> *graveyard and behold them!*
> *Say to them: 'Where is your swirling onrush now?' and then hear*
> *them answer mutely: 'Ask this question of the sea, not of us.'*
> *For how should the foam fly without the wave? How should the*
> *dust rise to the zenith without the wind?*
> *Now, since you have seen the dust, perceive the wind; since you*
> *have seen the foam, perceive the ocean.*

Sufism in Africa

Sufism is also the principal medium for the spread of Islam in the present day, principally in Africa, but increasingly around the world.

By the end of the colonial era in the middle of the twentieth century, imperial history had divided Africa into the Sunni Muslim and Arabic-speaking north, and the largely Christian south, the latter split between a large range of denominations from Catholic to Seventh Day Adventist. FOCUS, a branch of the Islamic Foundation of Leicester, England, estimated that in 2000 there were 347 million Muslims in Africa (more than in the Middle East) and 359 million Christians. Islam is thought to have increased its membership ahead of Christianity since that date.

The frontier between Islam and Christianity, which generally coincides with the racial boundary between Africans of Arab blood and pure black, turns violent as the line passes through Sudan, as discussed in an earlier chapter. Nigeria also suffers from permanent tension between the Hausa-speaking Muslims in the north and the Christian Ibo and Yoruba tribes of the south, although jealousy over access to the privileges of the state is as much a factor in both conflicts as religion. Even though Islam is very much in the minority in sub-Sahel black Africa, competition with Christianity for converts is fierce. For both faiths this is now the principal missionary 'growth area' remaining in the world.

Christian communities in black Africa tend to be folksy versions of European churches, led by white or white-trained priests or ministers, who are part of an international church hierarchy. In addition, Christian missions often run clinics or schools. Converts are taught the elements of the faith before being formally received by baptism, and communal services are held on Sundays, punctuated by rhythmic hymn-singing and hand-clapping. Bells toll across the African landscape in imitation of Europe, and an adapted version of a European or American script is usually followed for services.

Missionary Islam, in contrast, relies on local African marabouts in the Sufist tradition, equipped with nothing more than a prayer rug, making simple *da'wah*, the call to worship Allah by following His Messenger. Conversion is a gradual process as local customs blend with the new religion, and there are many examples of whole tribes slowly converting together over one or two generations. Under Sufi influence, primitive belief in a primal animist force becomes the One God, with lesser pagan gods becoming Allah's attributes. Local spirits and ancestor-worship merge with the jinns, devils and angels of the Qur'ān, while witch-doctors and practitioners of healing cults turn into Sufi saints whose tombs become places of pilgrimage and *baraka*. Tribal incantations become Sufi *dhikr*, and polygamy can be retained. This is the same process, after all, by which many of the (non-idolatrous) customs of pre-Islamic Arabia were incorporated into the Shariah. And rather than the confusing array of Christian denominations, each with a different and more complicated dogma, but all requiring an immediate change in customary behaviour, Islam offers simplicity and gradualism, as well as a connection to the great traditions and mysteries of the anti-American and pre-colonial Muslim world. Entry is easy and instant, with the mere recital from the heart of the few words of the *Shahādah*. 'God is One' carries a simple compulsion for the nomadic illiterate and the short ritual of Muslim prayer can be performed anywhere, regulated by the passage of the sun. Most importantly, there is no imposition from above by a foreign white missionary superstructure, or even by a priest. Islam thus becomes a purely African religion, spread by Africans to Africans, free of any taint of colonialism or racism.

In the context of missionary Islam, the Tablighi Jamaat (or 'proselytizing party') should be mentioned, described darkly by *The Economist* as 'one of the most important and obscure of the world's Islamic movements'. In fact, the Tablighi is a non-organization, with no command, no publications, no officers and no funds. Rather the name refers to the practice by young Muslims of travelling for a year or more after school with the intention of strengthening the faith in other countries. The young preachers pay their own expenses, stay in mosques or the homes of imams in the host countries and organize their own programmes. While Muslim solidarity and unity is the objective, there is usually little of practical value in this world to show for the effort expended. The Tablighi does not operate as a volunteer workforce undertaking social improvement projects or teaching like the Peace Corp, and usually a severe language barrier exists between the mostly Arab-speaking travellers and local believers. Despite Western suspicions, Tablighi Jamaat is entirely non-political, and tolerated by all Muslim regimes, even the most repressive.

Black Muslims

The Lost-Found Nation of Islam, known as Black Muslims, is a response to the deeply felt need in the African-American community for pride based on identity, and for a black interpretation of the long and tragic history of slavery.

The Middle Passage, by which slaves were transported across the Atlantic under the harshest of conditions, was arguably the greatest wrong ever perpetrated on one ethnic group by another, yet the enormity of this chapter of Western history is dramatically obscure. Eight to ten million died in the transfer of slaves from West Africa to the Americas, but no dedicated memorial to the event has been erected in the United States (compared with over 250 to the Holocaust). Similarly, the issue of reparations for slavery (or even an apology), based on the precedent of the billions paid to the victims of Nazi brutality, never reaches the public agenda. The question, says the White House, is 'hopelessly mired in the past'.

There is little evidence, however, to support the assertion that Africans transported from West Africa brought Islam to America with them, or spoke Arabic. Islam was present in West Africa during the slaving centuries only along the borders of the Sahel desert, far from the coast. Slaves from East Africa, where the traders were mostly Arabs, were sent east and north, and not to the Americas.

The twentieth-century origin of the Black Muslim movement was an impression of Islam was taken up by black community leaders in America during the 1930s and 1940s. Although they had little detailed knowledge of the faith, they considered Islam to be the 'natural religion for the black man', since Christianity, in sharp contrast, had betrayed the universal ideals of Christ by becoming the 'white man's religion'. The 'racial pride' doctrines of the Nation of Islam, combined with rigid rules of self-discipline based on Islam, would, it was believed, combat the poverty and denigration to which blacks had long been subject, conditions which were worsening during the Great Depression of the 1930s, more than seventy years after emancipation.

The Nation of Islam was established in 1930 by Wallace D. Fard, an enigmatic black preacher from Detroit. He styled himself Farad Muhammad and claimed to have come to America from Mecca to save the black race by giving them an Islamic identity. Fard's doctrines, however, were entirely contrary to the all-inclusive and 'racially blind' basis of true Islam. He claimed that a Black God who had created the black race was the source of all light and power, while the white race was the creation of the devil in the form of a malign black scientist named Yacub, in rebellion against the will of the Black God. Farad acknowledged the Prophet Muhammad and the status of the Qur'ān as the Word of God, but claimed for himself the sole right to interpret the text. The solution to the black man's condition was seen as the complete separation of the races, either within North America or by the migration of African blacks back to the original paradise of Africa. Farad disappeared in 1934, reputedly returning to Mecca, after passing his ministry to his successor, Elijah Poole, a former Baptist minister and son of an itinerant Baptist minister, who renamed himself Elijah Muhammad and claimed to be the last of the prophets.

During the 1950s the organization turned militant, becoming openly black supremacist, anti-white and especially anti-Jewish, under the movement's most dynamic personality, Malcolm X. The movement began to split following the assassination of Malcolm X in 1965 and the death of Elijah Muhammad in 1975. In 1977 Minister Louis Farrakhan broke away, but the name 'the Nation of Islam' was maintained by the schismatics, as well as the aggressive racial rhetoric of Malcolm X. Thereafter, the leadership of the majority mainstream Black Muslims passed to Elijah Muhammad's son, Wallace Muhammad, who has since renamed himself Warith Deen Muhammad. Under Warith, some one million Black Muslims (including the boxer Muhammad Ali, formerly named

Cassius Clay and formerly the Nation of Islam spokesman) have renounced racism, renamed their organization the American Muslim Society and moved closer to the four or five million Sunni orthodox Muslims of America. But however bizarre the message of the Nation of Islam may appear, this fiercely conservative and disciplined faith has in many cases offered the hope of human dignity to the ghetto dweller, the drug addict, the prisoner, to all blacks battered and suffocated by the overwhelming dominance of the white man.

The Life and Times of Brother X

Malcolm Little was born in Michigan in 1925, the seventh child of the Reverend Earl Little, a one-eyed Baptist minister who preached black-race purity and a return to Africa on the 'Black Train Homeward'. Malcolm's father and five of his six uncles were murdered, or lynched by the Klan, and his mother was the product of a violent sexual assault by a white man, which accounted for Malcolm's reddy-brown complexion, and he came to hate 'every drop of that white rapist's blood that is in me'. The Reverend beat his wife and children savagely and regularly, and Malcolm also grew up hating Christianity.

After his father's death Malcolm's family fell into complete poverty, often eating nothing more than boiled dandelion greens. His mother went insane and the children were placed in foster homes. Malcolm left school at fifteen and moved to Boston where he began as a shoe-shine boy, moving up to a life of hustling and petty crime in New York. He grew tall and handsome, he wore a zoot suit and conked his hair to look like a white man. He became a well-known lindy-hopping hipster on booze and reefers, and he found himself a white girl with shiny red lips and a Cadillac convertible. When America went to war, Malcolm persuaded an army psychiatrist that he was insane like his mother, and his climb up the Harlem crime hierarchy continued unbroken, graduating to bank hold-ups, running liquor, the white-on-black sex trade and hard drugs.

While Malcolm was serving ten years in jail on fourteen counts, from armed robbery to possession of firearms, his brothers and sisters joined the Nation of Islam. During visits to the jail they converted Malcolm to the creed of Wallace D. Fard. A correspondence subsequently began with Elijah Muhammad, and Malcolm was persuaded to see himself as the personification of evil, and Elijah Muhammad as divine. He started to pray facing the east, gave up cigarettes and ate no more pork. He taught himself to read and write by copying out the dictionary in the prison library and he developed a revisionist explanation of world history that expanded on the black eugenics theory originated by Farad (who often appeared to Malcolm in his cell in a vision). In the prison debating society Malcolm learned how to speak in public.

Released on parole in 1953, Malcolm joined Detroit Temple Number One of the Nation of Islam. He renounced the name of Little, the name presumed to have been given by slave owners to his slave ancestors, and was given his 'X', representing his lost African name. Two years later, Malcolm became Minister X, sent by Elijah Muhammad back to New York to open Temple Number Seven, where Malcolm turned his 'jungle mind' and his talents as a street hustler to proselytizing and organizing. He was an emotionally charged speaker, inventing catchphrases such as 'Black is beautiful', 'respect', 'tell it like it is' and 'the power within', that were to come into general use by young whites in the 1960s.

In 1959 the reverse-racist 'white devil' message of the Nation of Islam (named 'Black Muslims' by the press) exploded in the American media, and Malcolm X became both a black star for his combative speeches, and an object of white fear and hate, as well as a target for FBI and Internal Revenue Service surveillance. By the early 1960s there were over one hundred Nation Mosques (as the Temples were renamed) and Minister X, now a national figure, was seen as the power behind the ailing Elijah Muhammad. Jealousy began inside the organization, followed by death threats from both within and without, and when Malcolm X uncovered Elijah Muhammad's secret life of debauchery in his mansion in Phoenix (justified by quotations from the scriptures), he was ejected.

Before launching his own organization, the Muslim Mosque Inc., Malcolm performed the haj in Mecca (where he was popularly taken to be Cassius Clay), where he found the 'true religion' of the Oneness of man under God in the multiracial, multicultural brotherhood of the pilgrimage. From Mecca, Malcolm wrote to the Nation of Islam repudiating the race-based doctrines of Elijah Muhammad. He changed his name to El-Hajj Malik El-Shabazz and he dropped the word 'negro' from his vocabulary in favour of 'Afro-American'. He returned to America after a tour of emerging African states, to the 'long hot summer' of 1964, with racial tension coming up to the boil. He was repeatedly accused of 'stirring up the Negroes' and called 'the angriest Negro in America', while his arguments in favour of Muslim orthodoxy based on his personal experiences were breaking the power of the Nation of Islam within the African-American community.

By early 1965 Shabazz was preaching that Mississippi was 'anywhere south of the Canadian border', while attacking Elijah Muhammad for 'religious fakery', and he knew that his life was in danger from all sides. Armed clashes began in Harlem between supporters of the Nation of Islam and the Muslim Mosque Inc., and Shabazz's house was fire-bombed. But the New York Police Department refused to respond to the repeated death-threats and offered no protection. That same year Shabazz was gunned down as he began a speech to an all-black audience at the Audubon Ballroom. 'Alaykum Salaam' he shouted immediately before the shots were fired, as if he knew what was about to happen: 'Peace be with you'. The assassins escaped and were never apprehended, but that night the Nation of Islam Mosque Number Seven was burned to the ground.

In 1999 the US Postal Service issued a commemorative stamp in honour of Malcolm X. The radical had become respectable.

II What is a Fundamentalist?

Discussion of this difficult topic should begin with definitions. The very nature of Islam, the direct relationship of Man to God, is 'fundamentalist' in that all Muslims believe in the 'fundamentals' of the Qur'ān as the Word of God, which they can read and obey for themselves. But in arriving at a personal and often militant meaning of the Qur'ān, without reference to the methods of interpretation described earlier, the reader is disregarding the centuries of accumulated wisdom of Islam. Such a reader should more correctly be referred to as a 'literalist', believing in the superficial meaning of the words. Well-known examples of literalist interpretation among the monotheistic religions are belief in the Seven Day Creation, or the Judgement on the Last Day. But 'fundamentalist' is the popular tag, and cannot be avoided.

Accusations of naivety and narrow-mindedness are often aimed at fundamentalism, but interpretation is also at the heart of conflict in the religious mainstream, both in Islam and in Christianity. St Matthew's Gospel 16:18, reports that Christ said to Simon Barjona, his principal disciple, 'Thou art Peter, and upon this rock I will build my church'. Then in Matthew 26:26, Christ takes bread, which he blesses and breaks, saying, 'Take, eat; this is my body'. These words are accepted by all Christians as part of the Gospel, yet a literalist interpretation has led to the Catholic doctrines of papal authority and transubstantiation, both of which are rejected by Protestants. Opposing meanings given to the words were then used as the religious gloss to centuries of political and economic wars between rival Christian kingdoms, and remain at the core of the issues that still separate Catholics and Protestants today.

Similarly, the Qur'ān in Surah 33, *Al-Ahzāb* (The Confederates), verse 33 describes God's intentions for Muhammad's family as follows:

> And Allah only wishes
> To remove all abomination
> From you, ye Members
> Of the Family, and to make
> You pure and spotless

From these innocent-seeming words endless dissent and bloodshed was to flow as the Party of 'Ali broke from the proto-Sunni majority to become the predominantly Persian proto-Shi'a minority, claiming that only the descendants of 'Ali and the 'family' of Muhammad could interpret the ultimate truth of the Qur'ān. Then the original conflict would lead to centuries of further conflict on various pretexts, down to the meaningless massacres of Iranian teenage troops during the Iran–Iraq war of 1980 to 1988, urged forward by their religious leaders' promises of 'martyrdom' and a 'place next to 'Ali in paradise'.

In modern-day Islam, fundamentalism is the reaction against compromise with modern secular society as well as the expression of a desire to maintain or rediscover the core values of the faith. From the early schism over the succession to Muhammad, to the overwhelming of Dar al-Islam by the materialist West in the twentieth century, Muslims have been subjected to division, discredit, imperialism, colonialism, tyranny, corruption, and more recently to reoccupation, both economic and military. Islamic fundamentalism seeks to sweep away this flawed history and re-establish *al-Islām*, submission to the will of God, following the pure principles embedded in the Qur'ān and (for Sunnis) in the Sunna. This is a force within Islam that goes back to the first days of the Party of 'Ali and the Kharijites, or usually back further again to the 'rightly guided' Commonwealth of Medina. But how the rule of God on earth is to be accomplished, and whose interpretation of the will of God is be followed are, of course, the reefs upon which such voyages have repeatedly foundered.

Current fundamentalism comes from disillusion and despair, therefore. Faced with the continuing victory of ungodliness and injustice, a fanatical minority feels driven to undertake acts of violent defiance. Nor is this radicalizing process unique to Islam, but is to be found at the fringes of many other religions where politics and ideology cross over: the Real IRA, for example, the breakaway group from the Irish Republican Army; the Bajrang Dal, associated through the Rashtriya Swayamsevak Sangh with the Hindu Bharatiya Janata Party, once the leading party in the political coalition in power in India; the Branch Davidians of the Seventh-Day Adventist Church; or the Jewish 'settlers' of Gush Emunim (The Block of the Faithful), murderously inserting themselves into occupied Palestine in the name of God, to name but a few.

And for the fanatical literalist, Islam offers ready comforts. Surah 42 *Al-Shurā* (The Consultation) relates at verse 13 that Islam was 'enjoined on Abraham, Moses and Jesus'. Even before the Qur'ān, therefore, man was Muslim, and, as to the future, 'to Allah we belong and to Him is our return' (*Al-Baqarah* (The Heifer) Surah 2, verse 155). Thus no absolute dividing line is recognized between the time before an individual life, the time of present life, and the time of the afterlife. The will of God stretches back to creation and forward into infinity. If, therefore, religious duty is believed to embrace an act that will result in the perpetrator's suicide (or is so manipulated by others), the result is not the finality of death, but martyrdom, rewarded by instant and everlasting reunification with God at the push of a button, confirmed by His own words:

> Think not of those
> Who are slain in Allah's way
> As dead. Nay they live,
> Finding their sustenance
> In the presence of their Lord.
>
> *Al-Baqarah* (The Heifer) Surah 2, verse 154

But the significance of this verse and others similar, depends once again on interpretation. A Muslim scholar could argue from history that nothing in Muhammad's life justifies extending the meaning of the word 'slain' in the text, to the carrying out of a deliberate act of suicide. Certainly Muhammad never ordered or manipulated a Companion into committing intentional suicide for the Muslim cause (to be distinguished from personal bravery on the battlefield).

The first Islamist organizations of the twentieth century were the Society of Muslim Brothers in Egypt, founded by Hasan al-Banna (assassinated by the Egyptian state in 1949), and the Jammat-e-Islamia in Pakistan led by Sayyid Abu'l-A'la al-Maududi (d. 1979). Both men came from religious families with strong ties to Sufism, and both began by interpreting British imperialism as a new crusade against Muslim values. Both organizations opposed the imposition of the Western-style nation-state on to the emerging independent Muslim entities of Egypt and Pakistan. They also opposed the moral decay of the nationalist leaders of Egypt and Pakistan who cooperated with the departing British, then took power themselves, only to produce, in so many Muslim countries, the gross mismanagement and corruption that has been discussed earlier.

Not surprisingly, therefore, both the Muslim Brothers and the Jammat-i-Islāmi have been suppressed on various occasions, first by the British and then by the subsequent nationalist rulers. The Muslim Brothers, although in permanent and sometimes violent opposition to the nation-state, have attempted to offer a practical and moral alternative to the governments in power by establishing a network of small cooperative industrial enterprises throughout Egypt, as well as schools, athletic programmes, public health initiatives and social services for the poor. These charitable, almost secular activities, and many like them run by fundamentalists across the Middle East, represent a move to soften the extremism of the last twenty years. Many Islamist groups are similarly seeking to put into action the often repeated maxim of Muslim reformers, who wish not to modernize Islam, but to 'Islamicize modernity'. The programmes are also intended to show that Islam works and corrupt secular governments do not.

The Islamist organizations with the highest international profile have emerged not as might be expected, from the slums of Cairo or Casablanca, but from the conflict between the State of Israel and the Palestinians, discussed below in more detail. Beyond the specific injustices perpetrated on the Palestinian people by the British and subsequently by the establishment of the State of Israel, the mere presence of Israel in what was once Arab territory, stretching pristine and Muslim from Syria to the Yemen, has come to stand for all the humiliations that Arabs believe they have suffered during the past century at the hands of the West. Here politics, religion and utopian ideals, together with guerrilla action, all combine to produce the unstable conditions that began with the frustrated Arab Revolt against Turkish rule in 1917, and still make up our newspaper headlines day after day.

Fatah (the Palestine National Liberation Movement) began at Cairo University in the early 1950s with the assistance of the Muslim Brothers. Fatah, however, has always seen itself as a classic liberation movement fighting a colonial power (the State of Israel) with the religious dimension present but playing a secondary role. The organization under the late Yassir Arafāt exercised complete control over the umbrella resistance group, the Palestine Liberation Organization (PLO) from the late 1960s, but under what is now the 'old guard' of Arafāt men, Fatah lacks effective power over most of the armed splinters nominally within the organization and run by the next generations. Until the first mass uprising, or intifada of 2001, Fatah defined the nature of Palestinian opposition to Israel, which has moved through three stages. Fatah first began with direct commando raids against Israel, but was soon diverted by a second stage of armed action against other more reluctant Arab countries, notably Jordan, which expelled the Palestinian militias in 1970 in order to avoid domestic chaos and another war with Israel (which came anyway). After a second expulsion of Fatah, from Tripoli to Tunis following the Israeli invasion of Lebanon, the third stage began in the mid 1980s when political negotiations with Israel opened, based on Fatah's renunciation of violence and recognition of the Jewish State. The resulting Oslo peace process led to the establishment of the Palestinian Authority, an embryonic independent state, dominated by the old Fatah. But Oslo put off the difficult issues of the 'final status' of Jerusalem, Israel's permanent borders, and the question of Jewish settlements within Palestinian territory (which Israel permitted to double in number during the ten years of Oslo, and to accelerate further since), and the right of refugee return. So when negotiations with Israel broke down, wide Palestinian discontent at the entire process surfaced in the form of the second intifada, precipitated by the armed entry of General Ariel Sharon (who subsequently became the Israeli prime minister) into the Muslim Haram al-Sharif, also claimed by Judaism as the Temple Mount, the duality of which is discussed below. Armed organizations within Fatah (the Tanzim, Force 17, the Hawari Special Operations Group, etc.) once again came into direct confrontation with the Israeli Defence Forces. The massive destruction of Palestinian towns in response to the resistance led to loss of both control and respect by the Palestinian Authority, which is prevented by Israel from carrying weapons, deprived of transportation and communications, and used by Fatah bosses as a job patronage scheme in a ruined and impoverished society.

Hizbullah (the Party of God) is a Lebanese Shi'ite organization, inspired and financed by Iran's Revolutionary Government. The organization began in 1983 with devastating attacks on American, French and Israeli forces in occupation of Lebanon, and Hizbullah was principally responsible for Israel's withdrawal from South Lebanon in 2000. This quasi-victory over the all-powerful Israeli Defence Forces showed resistance groups in Palestine that the military defeat of Israel might be possible, and contributed to the eruption of the second intifada of 2001, even though the direct influence of Shi'a Hizbullah in Sunni and Christian Palestine was limited. Here was another example of how a popular movement supported by religious conviction could overcome a superior and better equipped force, just as the Iranian Revolution had defeated the Shah (and by association the US), just as the Mujahidin of Afghanistan had defeated the Russians, and just as Israel itself had defeated the combined Arab forces in 1948, 1967 and 1973 (although the word 'defeat' is disputed by Arabs in relation to the 1973 war).

The civil war in Lebanon (1975–90), followed by the Israeli occupation, produced devastation and poverty in the Shiʿa communities of South Lebanon. The non-military part of Hizbullah attempted to ameliorate the situation with ambitious programmes for housing, schools, help for small farmers and the reconstruction of mosques, extending down to the distribution of food, water and care for the families of 'martyrs against Israel'. However, with Israel departed, and Iran's vital financial contributions limited by permanent domestic political and financial crisis and confrontation with the America, Hizbullah's support among Lebanese Shiʿa has dropped well below 40 per cent, and the entire Shiʿa community is probably less than half of the population of Lebanon (no reliable census is available). The nominal objective of Hizbullah remains to establish an Islamic revolutionary government in Lebanon, but this has been further frustrated by the start of reasonably successful country-wide and multicultural elections.

Hamas is the informal name of the Islamic Resistance Movement. The word is an acronym of the official name, spelling 'zeal' in Arabic, which is popularly interpreted to mean 'exaltation' or 'enthusiasm'. The Movement was established in 1988 by the Gaza branch of the Muslim Brothers, left over from the earlier Egyptian occupation of Gaza. The spiritual head of the movement was Sheikh Ahmad Yassin, a partially blind, quadriplegic imam, who was murdered in his wheelchair by Israel in 2003. Hamas runs educational, social and religious programmes in occupied Palestine as well as vocational training, job creation schemes and small businesses. In Gaza, in the absence of formal government, Hamas is one of the main providers of social services, from schools to clinics. But the organization is best known for uncompromising opposition to the Oslo peace process and to the PLO recognition of Israel, backed by frequent attacks on both Israel and the PLO, intended to expose the weakness of the PLO and to stop any further compromise with Israel. Hamas was first active during the later stages of the first intifada that began in 1987, and played a large part in the second intifada of 2001. The Battalions of ʿIzz al-Din al-Qassām is the branch of Hamas that specializes in training suicide bombers (named after a Palestinian guerrilla leader, killed by the British in 1935). Despite the overwhelming Israeli reprisals against Palestinian civilians in response to suicide attacks, Hamas is extremely popular in the West Bank and Gaza and represents the only serious (and incorruptible) threat to the (corrupt) power of the PLO and the Palestinian Authority. The Palestinian Authority alternates between trying to co-opt and corrupt Hamas, and doing Israel's bidding by imprisoning members. But on another level Hamas is useful to Israel as the new demon of the peace, now that the PLO no longer operates as a resistance organization, allowing Israel to continue to equate opposition to occupation with 'international terrorism'. The strong social arm of Hamas has given the organization the opportunity to begin a successful campaign to gain political control through elections. This, and other examples to be discussed later, will soon test the honesty of American preaching of 'democracy' in the Middle East, when Hamas becomes the dominant political force in the Palestinian territories through democratic elections.

Palestine Islamic Jihad (PIJ) began in the 1970s among the disaffected youth of Gaza, fenced in by the Israeli Defence Forces under atrocious prison gulag conditions (the fourth most densely populated urban area in the world). The movement is related to Islamic Jihad, a militant anti-Western protest group present in various independent incarnations in a number of Muslim countries from Egypt to Indonesia. Considered the most complex, secret and dangerous of the Palestinian activists, the PIJ stands for uncompromising armed opposition to the very existence of the State of Israel, expressed by Sheikh Tamimi, one of the founders of the movement, as a refusal to 'accede to a Jewish state on our land, even if it is only one village'. The PIJ is reputed to be funded by Iran, even though the movement is predominantly Sunni and based in Damascus. The movement's first operations were conducted in Lebanon during the 1980s, in conjunction with Hizbullah. Recent PIJ operations include burning Israeli crops, the murder of Palestinian collaborators, attacks on Israeli buses and suicide missions against Israeli targets. The PIJ's objective is a united Islamic state covering all the Arab territory previously ruled by the Ottoman Empire. The spiritual leader of the PIJ, Fathi Shaqaqi, was murdered by the Israeli secret service in Malta in 1995.

Al-Qaeda (the Base) is now an all-consuming idea, a *salafi* rallying cry across the Muslim world that will never be suppressed. Al-Qaeda is a franchise, and not the worldwide organization sought by the American government as an ideological opponent to replace communism, and so continue the domestic crowd control justified by perpetual war under a 'war President' (the ultimate Orwellian achievement).

The original radical Muslim complaint was against the presence of US forces in Arabia, the Muslim Holy Land, but opposition to the State of Israel, and to America as Israel's backer, became the principal expressed grievance from 2000 on. Then the American occupation of Iraq, causing at least 25,000 civilian deaths so far, together with vast civil destruction, has provided the hot opportunity for the idealistic call to arms to be implemented.

The precise stimulus for such acts as those of September 11th, 2001 in New York, and July 7th 2005 in London, and the daily suicide operations in Iraq, may still be beyond comprehension in the west. Certainly 'criminal' or 'terrorist' are patently unsatisfactory and simplistic labels, as well as historically self-serving. But the murkiest outlines of the motivation of the perpetrators may be perceived by considering the cumulative impact of a number of events in Muslim history discussed earlier: the status of the Qur'ān as the undiluted Word of God, yet open to gross misinterpretation; Muhammad's absolute victory over the power and corruption of the Meccan *Jāhiliyyah* from an initial position of almost complete isolation and weakness; and the reverence of Muslims for the Holy Land of the Hijaz, therefore of Arabia, and by extension, of all Muslim lands. To this the tragic history of Afghanistan acted as a catalyst for the formation of al-Qaeda, creating the 'Arab Afghans' already referred to, young men trained, hardened and financed, whose deep beliefs, together with their frustrations at the new *Jāhiliyyah* of Western influence, saw no other means of expression. They became the '50 cells around the world' of al-Qaeda, allegedly consisting of 'over 70,000 members', that US Defence Secretary Donald Rumsfeld attempted to identify in October 2001. But subsequent events, especially the new running sore of Iraq, have demonstrated that this phantom will never be destroyed, even if the personal inspiration of Osama ibn Laden were to be eliminated.

Marxist-Leninist liberation movements such as the **PFLP** (Popular Front for the Liberation of Palestine) are not, of course, Islamist. Despite such high-profile actions as the assassination of a right-wing minister in the Israeli government in October 2001, a combination of the shock of the capitulation at Oslo together with the demise of the Soviet Union has led to the effective collapse of the nationalist groups, leaving the field to the religious organizations.

Whatever the specific short-term operational objectives of an armed Islamist organization may be, the ultimate ideal always remains: to correct what Muslims see as the injustice of Western impositions on Muslim societies and to reverse what the West sees as the irreversible process of Westernization of the worldwide nation-state based on the separation of politics and religion. This raises, once again, the unanswerable question about what would replace the nation-state in the Islamist vision, and the adequacy of the Shariah to operate a modern society. As a broad generalization, the Palestinian resistance movements described above express to various degrees an intention to reinterpret the Shariah to produce some as yet undefined system of government relevant to modern conditions, rather than proposing to reconstruct an archaic vision of the Prophet's seventh-century Commonwealth in the style of the former Taliban.

III The Future

Clearly Islam faces the general challenge of withstanding the counter-spiritual effect of rising materialism and increasing personal freedom that has reduced Christianity in Europe to little more than cultural and historical texture. But even if Islam can stand up to the seductive power of Western culture, there are three principal areas of tension in the Muslim world where the outcome could have a decisive effect on the character of Islam in the twenty-first century: Muslims in Europe; Palestine and the State of Israel, and Islam and Democracy.

The 'clash of civilizations', so famously predicted by the American political scientist Samuel P. Huntington during the 1990s, has not come to pass. No revitalized and unified Islam has emerged as a threat to the liberal materialist values of the West, equal to the former pressure from communism, despite the repeated use of the words 'war' and 'crusade' by President Bush following September 11th, 2001, and matching apocalyptic language from Osama ibn Laden and the former Taliban government of Afghanistan, calling on every Muslim to 'rise up to defend his religion'. There is little danger of a new Warsaw Pact of cohering Islamist governments joining together effectively against the West. But progress (by the West as well as by Muslims) on the vital issues to be discussed below may influence whether Islam is to maintain the fever pitch of turmoil that started in the 1980s and still boils on. Will this unjust world, in the view of many Muslims, continue to be divided between the 'us and them' of Dar al-Islam (the abode of Islam) and Dar al-Harb (the abode of unbelievers), or move toward a workable balance between faith and realpolitik?

Muslims in Europe

A recurring joke in France is that the *énarques* (graduates of the École Nationale d'Administration), the country's famously highly trained corp of senior civil servants, are so clever that they have calculated the precise date on which the French social system will go bust (popularly believed to be Bastille Day 2025). The birthrate in France, like all European countries, has fallen to a level that will no longer sustain current population figures, which are projected to start falling by the year 2010. By 2030, if the projections are accurate, 30 per cent of French men and women will be over sixty as against 18 per cent in 2000, and there will be under three workers to support each retiree, rather than the present four. There are three possible alternatives for Europe in response to these figures. First, the economies of Europe could shrink, leading to a commensurate reduction in living standards, accompanied by the abandonment of entire towns and villages; secondly, government social services including healthcare could reduce by 50 per cent or more, combined with a rise in the pensionable age to seventy or seventy-five; thirdly immigration could be substantially increased.

None of these solutions will be welcomed by European voters and no forthright policy proposals are therefore likely to be put forward by any politician who wishes to be re-elected. In practice, however, the shrinking economy will no doubt be avoided at all costs. At the same time, government pensions will be reformed and privatized, but only reluctantly and only slightly ahead of the demographic curve and the growing crisis. And through all this, immigration will be permitted to rise, in addition to increasing illegally.

According to a recent UN study, Germany, for example, requires over three million immigrants per year in order to maintain the present ratio of workers to pensioners (although the calculation was made without counting on the politically difficult possibility of extending working lives and reforming services, which is now the central issue in German politics). However, the consequence of even one million immigrants per year into Germany, the rate forecast by the respected DIW think tank of Berlin as required by 2020 merely to maintain the present workforce, would bring about a significant change in the character of German society, further accentuated over the following generations if immigrant birthrates were to prove higher than those of the ethnic population, as has been the case during the last decades. The present immigrant (and mostly Muslim) population of Germany already makes up 8 per cent of the total, and even that proportion has resulted in an extremely high level of racial tension, as discussed earlier.

If, or when, such increases in (mostly Muslim) immigration into Europe occur, the present cycle of alienation among new arrivals will become much more serious unless there is a far-reaching modification in the attitude of host countries. Typically, the first adult members of an immigrating family consider themselves lucky to have escaped the violence and poverty of their homeland and they work hard in their new country, generally living quietly in a depressed urban area close to others from the same country of origin. Their children, however, who in many cases are not automatically citizens under present laws, find themselves in a concrete ghetto, isolated between two cultures. They cannot adopt their parents' experiences and values, acquired under quite different circumstances, yet are unable to succeed in a Western culture, a problem often made worse by viciously competitive school systems that stream the less articulate away from access to better jobs at an early age.

The result is chronic disaffection and unemployment, often expressed in wholesale community violence, which is usually hidden from view as fast as possible. On Bastille Day in France in 2001, for example, 130 cars were burned in Paris alone, by rioters of overwhelmingly North African Muslim origin. But little was reported in the press, and beyond the standard call for more police, no public discussion about the reasons for the riot took place. The shocked 'law and order' response by the French government to the much more serious riots of 2005, which were too big to hide (10,000 cars were torched) may develop into a further method by which French leader can avoid facing this core problem of twenty-first century European society.

In Oldham and Bradford in the British Midlands, millions of pounds of damage was done by white versus Pakistani versus police riots in 2001. All sides acknowledged in the press over the following days that nothing had changed since the last round of riots five years previously, and that the ghettoization of the Pakistani and Bangladeshi communities was deteriorating not improving. This cycle is then completed by young second and third generation immigrants, who feel themselves permanently excluded by society and turn to Islam, making the religion into a badge of protest, misinterpreted to justify aggression, but at the same time confirming the faith as the culture of the segregated underclass.

A further difficulty is that Islam itself has little precedent for participating in society as a minority religion. The life of a good Muslim is ideally lived under the Shariah, where all aspects of life, internal and external, from religious observance to family and criminal law, are defined by a single system. Without the acceptance of a boundary between civil law and religious obligations, combined with the core belief that the unerring Word of God is expressed in the Qur'ān, Islam is difficult to accommodate in a determinedly secular Western society where almost all views are equally respected and none is seen as either right or wrong.

Nevertheless, the further Islamicization of Europe appears to be demographically inevitable, with Muslims rapidly becoming the largest practising religious community in most European countries. This will obviously bring dramatic change, from an increase in the number of minarets competing with church spires on the skyline of European cities (or in the suburbs anyway) to streets filled with a much more hybrid and multiracial population. Failure to meet this challenge and to make the accommodations necessary could sour relations between Islam and the post-Christian world even further, and undermine the very social viability and continuity that immigration is intended to promote.

Palestine and the State of Israel

The Pentateuch tells the story of the Hebrews, one of the many Semitic tribes that established themselves four to seven thousand years ago in the Fertile Crescent that is now Lebanon, Syria, Iraq, Jordan, Israel, Gaza and the Occupied West Bank. The books relate how the Hebrews become a captive slave-race in Egypt, then after their escape they are promised the land of Canaan for their own in perpetuity, the legendary land of milk and honey.

But Canaan, Philistia or Palestine, was already occupied by the indigenous Canaanites, Jebusites and Philistines (among others) and a protracted and bloody battle for possession followed, fuelled, on the Jewish side, by the purported instructions of the Hebrew God as related in the Book of Deuteronomy.

> When the Lord thy God shall bring thee into the land
> whither thou goest to possess it, and hath cast out many
> nations before thee, the Hittites, and the Girgashites, and
> the Amorites, and the Canaanites and the Perizzites, and the
> Hivites, and the Jebusites, seven nations greater and mightier
> than thou;
> And when the Lord thy God shall deliver them before
> thee, thou shalt smite them and utterly destroy them;
> thou shalt make no covenant with them, nor shew mercy
> unto them.
>
> (Deuteronomy 7: 1–2)

A succession of Jewish prophets and rulers follows the invasion, and the name of the land in the Jewish text is changed from Canaan to Israel and Judah, with Samaria added later.

The Palestinian side to this saga is much less well known, since the non-Jewish written record is almost non-existent, a defect that has weakened the Palestinian cause right down to modern times, in which the Palestinians consistently lose the propaganda (as well as the physical) war. So that the Pentateuch, whether fiction, fraud or historical fact, has become the framework within which all other theories and sources are placed. Nevertheless, the Palestinians, even in the Torah, are the proto-inhabitants of Canaan, supported by the archaeological record of Jericho, for example, which takes Canaanite and Jebusite occupation back 7,000 years.

But during the last three centuries BCE, as Palestine became a part of the Persian Empire, then fell into the empire of Alexander the Great, then came under the Egyptian Ptolemies, followed by the advance of the Roman Empire into the Eastern Mediterranean, the history of Palestine moves out from under the shadow of the Torah. Myth gives way to historical fact. The Romans took possession of Jerusalem in 63 BCE and were to rule Palestine for the next 700 years, until the defeat of Byzantium by the advancing Muslims in 636 CE, with the surrender of Jerusalem accepted by the Caliph 'Umar two years later.

In 39 BCE the Emperor Augustus appointed Herod as King of Judea (the southern part of Palestine) on behalf of Rome. Herod ruled for thirty-five years until 4 BCE, during which time he built Jerusalem into a substantial city. The centrepiece of Herod's work was a large stone platform extending high above the city, on the site of the present-day structure of the Muslim Haram al-Sharif, the Dome of the Rock and al-Aqsa mosque. Herod's project included a forum and a market up on the platform as well as a form of Jewish temple.

After Herod's death, Rome took back direct control of the whole of Palestine. The Jews resisted imperial rule and major rebellions were put down with great force by the Roman army in 70 and 135 CE. On the first occasion Jerusalem, which the Jews had used as a fortress, was largely destroyed. Herod's temple was burned and the remains pulled down, although the structure of the platform still stood. On the second occasion the Hebrew element of the population was expelled from Jerusalem by the Romans with the edict: 'It is forbidden for all circumcised persons to enter the city and to stay within the city.' Jerusalem was then rebuilt as a Roman city and renamed Aelia Capitolina, dedicated to the pagan god Jupiter Capitolinus. Jews were permitted to enter the new city only once each year to lament the destruction.

So began the Jewish worldwide diaspora, but semi-voluntarily, since Jews were not expelled by the Romans from greater Palestine, only from the City of Jerusalem. The State of Israel claimed to end the Jewish diaspora condition by the Proclamation of Independence of 1948, referring to the Jews as 'exiled from the Land of Israel', but this was not quite truthful. Pagan Rome continued to rule Palestine until 324 CE, after which the Empire became Christian and Christianity then claimed Jerusalem until the arrival of Islam a further 300 years later.

There was no trace of Herod's temple or even the temple to Jupiter remaining by the time the Caliph 'Umar entered the city to take possession half a millennium after the Roman destruction and rebuilding. Merely the outline of Herod's platform had survived, on which, after reconstruction, the Umayyads built the Haram still standing today.

In the diaspora, Jews maintained their traditions of 'divinely' ordained superiority, keeping themselves to themselves and rarely integrating with their hosts, while succeeding in a range of intellectual and business endeavours, being barred from most others. In Europe the Christian response was resentment, persecution, expulsion and murder, of which some of the more infamous examples are the Spanish Inquisition, the massacres of Jews in England during the Crusades, the Jewish pogroms in Eastern Europe and Russia in the nineteenth century, culminating in the Holocaust of 1933 to 1945.

Meanwhile, in Palestine, over the centuries following the Roman destruction of Jerusalem, the non-Jewish population of Palestinians continued to live on their land as landlords and peasants, just as they had done for the preceding millennia, and converting from paganism or Christianity to Islam with the arrival of the Muslims. Some Jews moved back to Jerusalem during later Roman Christian rule, and subsequent Muslim rule, but Jews made up no more than 15 per cent of the city's population under the Turks, and were not present in any significant numbers in the surrounding countryside.

At the end of the First World War in 1918, with the defeat of the Ottoman Empire, Palestine was divided from the previous Turkish ruled Arab territories and became a separate British colony, although technically a League of Nations Mandate. Zionism, the movement by Jews to colonize Palestine as a solution to persecutions in Russia and Poland, had begun on a small scale at the end of the nineteenth century, and Jewish immigration was encouraged by Britain starting in 1921. Jews began to arrive in Palestine in what were then large numbers, despite opposition from the native Palestinian population. Britain's policy was devised almost single-handedly by Churchill, whose personal support for Zionism served to reward the political and financial assistance which both he and his father had received from the Jewish community in Britain. Jewish enterprise, Churchill

predicted, would soon improve the lot of the backward Arab peasants. Meanwhile Prime Minister Lloyd George's endorsement of
Churchill's initiative was based on his low church (and Welsh) belief
in the Old Testament as the Word of God. Biblical mysticism linking the return of the Jews to the Promised Land with the Second
Coming had been popular in Victorian England, and the influential
cult of Freemasonry was based on a detailed elaboration of the myth
of Solomon's Temple, which a number of British expeditions had
attempted unsuccessfully to find. Lloyd George had also represented
the Zionist movement as the society's solicitor in Britain in the years
before he joined the government.

During the 1930s Britain progressively lost control of Palestine,
and following the end of the Second World War and the revelation
of the horrors of the Holocaust, Britain was unable to resist wholesale Jewish immigration into Palestine. The resulting proposal by the
UN to divide Palestine between Jews and Arabs was opposed by the
Arab nations on the basis that partition would reward progressive
Jewish usurpation. War followed in 1948 between the armed Jewish
settlers and the Arab armies. Chronic political disunity and lack of
military organization among the Arabs, together with Western political and material support for the Jews (the British left them arms and
equipment, for example) led to the defeat of the Arab armies and the
declaration of the State of Israel. Further defeats were inflicted on
the Arabs by the smaller but better equipped Israeli Defence Forces
in 1967 and 1973. During the course of these wars a majority of
Palestinians were expelled from their lands and villages by the victorious Jews, to become permanent refugees on the West Bank, in
Gaza, Jordan, Syria and Lebanon.

The wars of 1948 and 1967 have become the core of the dispute
between Israel and the Palestinians. Jewish historians claim, and
Israeli children are taught, that the Palestinians ran away before the
arrival of the advancing victorious Israeli army, voluntarily vacating
their properties which were then expropriated by the new Jewish
state. The Palestinians, on the other hand, claim that a free people
was forcibly evicted by Jewish wars of conquest motivated by the
desire to take over Palestinian lands and possessions right down to
the household furniture. Palestinians also suspect that under the
right international circumstances, such as another major Islamist

attack on America, Israel could launch a further war of conquest and push the remaining Arab population of the West Bank out into Egypt and Jordan, to create Eretz Yisrael, or Greater Israel. (This proposal for 'population transfer' is referred to by the Israeli right-wing as 'the Jordanian solution').

These events resonate precisely with the words of Deuteronomy quoted earlier and the Torah is unashamedly used, even in modern times, as the justification for Israel's actions. 'This country exists as the accomplishment of a promise made by God Himself,' Golda Meir claimed when prime minister of Israel. 'It would be absurd therefore to call its legitimacy into account.'

In 1948 the State of Israel was immediately recognized by America and the European nations. The horrors of the Holocaust were seen as giving the Jews a moral force, with the Palestinians left to their fate, and the new State of Israel expressly linked the creation of the new state to the recent genocide in Germany and Poland. The huge museum in Jerusalem to the Holocaust, for example, ends the story with the declaration of the State of Israel and the defeat of the Arabs, two years after the liberaton of the camps. 'People pursued by a monster,' the Jewish writer Isaac Deutscher explained, 'cannot help trampling on those who are in the way.'

But in the Palestinian view, starting in 1948 Israel became an imperial military power and a settler-racist state, with no more moral, historical or hereditary right to exist than any other armed aggressor of history. In this interpretation, Israel's appetite for territory and the harsh treatment and expulsion of the indigenous occupants of the conquered lands match the years of white rule in South Africa, the Chinese occupation of Tibet, or the ethnic cleansing of Kosovo by the Serbs. Only world reaction, led by America, is different.

Palestinians claim that the true nature of the State of Israel, from violent origins through occupation and repression, is obscured from the world by the influence of the Jewish community on American domestic politics, especially through the well-funded activities of I-APAC (the Israel America Political Action Committee) and the political and financial support of millions of evangelical Christian Zionists in America whose belief, once again, is that the Second Coming is linked to Jewish possession of the Christian Holy Land. Press reports regularly portray Israel as 'under attack', 'moderate',

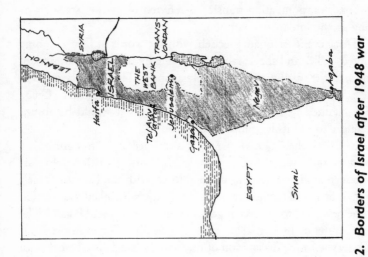

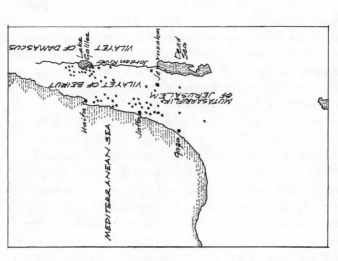

1. Jewish settlements at the time of the Balfour Declaration, 1917

2. Borders of Israel after 1948 war

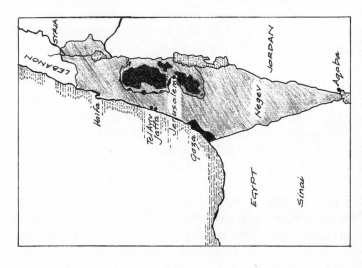

4. Remaining Palestinian controlled areas 2005

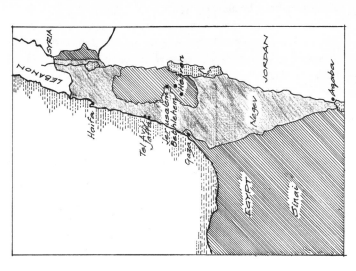

3. Borders of Israel after 1967 war

'democratic' and 'Western', while the Palestinians are denigrated as 'terrorists' and 'fundamentalists'.

The confrontation between Israel and the Palestinians attracts disproportionate interest in the West because of a unique blend of characteristics. Palestine is the cradle of Judaism and Christianity, and to a lesser extent of Islam, while Jerusalem is claimed as requisite to all three faiths. The territory occupied by Israel thus commands the attention of 1.0 billion Muslims, 1.7 billion Christians and 13 million Jews. Palestine is also the flashpoint between two historically cantankerous cultures, and where an apparently Western, First World and heavily armed nuclear power faces the Muslim threat. Palestine is also the physical centre of the old world, as well as calling up the economic issue of the West's security of oil supply. The Palestinian cause, along with the liberation of Tibet, is the last of the great anti-colonial movements of nineteenth and twentieth century history, stirring the idealism of many on the left in the West, as well as connecting to a legacy of freedom-fighting by which many Arab states gained independence. While the State of Israel itself, in the words of the London *Guardian*, is 'an American colony', supported by billions of American dollars and endless American arms, and therefore cannot be allowed to fail.

Even more mortifying for Arabs, the continuing crisis with Israel demonstrates the internal weakness of Arab society itself and exposes the impotence of the sound and fury with which the nattily suited Arab leaders and their 'semi-official' presses respond. The Palestinians have been dispossessed for fifty-seven years, and under military occupation for thirty-eight of those years, yet in all that time the combined forces of the oversized Arab armies, the economic power of oil, and Arab diplomatic efforts, have produced no relief whatsoever. Ironically, the State of Israel, riven by deep internal dissension over religion and politics, holds together in large part only because of the external threat from the surrounding Arab countries.

But should a genuine peace (resolving the 'final status' issues of a viable Palestinian state: the Jewish settlements in the West Bank, the status of Jerusalem, and the right of refugee return) ever be agreed between Israel and the Palestinians, the core of the tension between Islam and the West would be removed at a stroke. All the other conflicts in which the name of Islam is invoked would be reduced to the status of mere regional questions. Arab governments would no longer be able to exploit the issue of Israel in order to divert attention from their own internal failures and the appalling conditions under which most Arabs live. Then the core values of Islam, which this book has attempted to explain, would have to prove themselves out in the open.

Powerless in Gaza

Slums of the poor world have filled this observer with overwhelming but almost inadmissible emotions: pity, disgust, frustration, human shame, and most strongly of all, the desire to run and to forget. The same feelings that might grip a meat-eater on visiting an abattoir. And deeper still there is racism. Britain too once had terrible slums, but through enlightened (white Anglo) self-interest, all have gone. 'They' (post-colonial black Africans of the Kibera slum in Nairobi, for example) are to blame therefore, not 'us': in the end, we say, only they can help themselves.

Beyond the personal confusion brought on by the experience, the slum is where the harsh grip of the world status quo on the individual is most vividly demonstrated. So that walking through a slum trivializes all other forms of political observation. Because the slum illuminates from the bottom the true nature of the society above: the history, the injustice, the greed, the callousness, the ignorance and the self-delusion.

But the slum that is Gaza is different. This is a form of open prison for an entire inconvenient people that no secret theory of racial superiority can explain away. Here 1.4 million indigenous Palestinians are squeezed into a barren sandy strip between row upon row of electrified wire on the land side, and the sea on the other, patrolled by the Israeli navy equipped with the latest and fastest American vessels. Here the former owners of the whole land of Palestine live in cinder block hovels, blown with garbage, and sewage running down the streets under the donkey carts. Latticed by wires, decorated with 3D graffiti and punctuated by carbonized car wrecks from Israeli helicopter assassinations. Populated by extended families whose escaped relatives on the outside have proven themselves worldwide as doctors, teachers, professionals and businessmen. Then every few streets a low building behind a high wall is decorated with verses from the Qur'ān on green and yellow banners. Hamas (and a locked United

Nations food distribution centre) is the only organizing presence to be seen, the only sign of hope or help in this dreadful claustrophobic place.

And once again the light of perception shines from below, out from the windows of these jailhouses, to illuminate the truth. Here in Gaza, out at the unseen edge of the repression of the Palestinians, the secular majority of metropolitan Israelis could no longer support the religious crazies of the Gush minority, who have so successfully hijacked the levers of the Israeli state in recent years. Three soldiers were required to protect every one of the 8,000 Jewish former 'settlers' in Gaza against the surrounding Palestinian population who outnumbered them 200 times. This was a situation that could no longer be sustained, making disengagement inevitable. Even the Israeli god of the Torah did not promise Gaza to the invading Jews (Joshua 10:41, etc.), only Judea and Samaria, now central Israel and the occupied West Bank. But the Gush and their captive government in Jerusalem were never going to give up territory for nothing, even if the land in question was illegally occupied, of no value and unprotectable. So in return for the withdrawal that was inevitable anyway, but widely praised around the world as 'opening the way for peace', and 'courageous' or 'historic', what payment did the Gush extract in return?

● In the short term, an opportunity was provided for worldwide publicity, and for the power of victimhood to be enhanced. Hour after hour on American television Jewish settlers, clutching at their prayer books and screaming their lines, were carefully carried away one by one by five or six Israeli Defence Force soldiers. But no Jew died in the protest, or was even hurt, and all have been compensated, so the lie-ins meant nothing compared with the hugely destructive treatment visited on the Palestinians for over fifty years at the hands of the same army, but hidden from view. Attempt to equate, for example, the vacating of the Gaza Jewish settlements with the regular demolition of Palestinian houses. The residents of the former left in moving trucks, together with all their possessions, for a new home provided by the state, and up to $300,000 per family in compensation financed by America. The latter are given no more than five minutes to remove a few clothes, a few pots and pans before an American Caterpillar tractor tears into the house, leaving the destitute residents weeping in the muddy street. In any event, Israel hardly 'withdrew'. Israeli forces still seal the land borders of Gaza, and the coast, with the self-reserved 'right' to reoccupy should the Gaza Palestinians protest their fate with any form of counter-attack. No airport is permitted, and the small sea ports are blockaded, with even deep-sea fishing prohibited.

● No Jewish-built house was to be occupied by Palestinians, so that no moving-in scenes with overtones of victory could follow the 'tragedy' of the moving out. Despite the hundreds of Palestinian homes occupied by Jews since 1948, most without any compensation whatsoever, and despite the desperate housing shortage in impoverished Gaza, all the Jewish houses in Gaza were wantonly destroyed and left as rubble.

● The withdrawal liberated 8,000 militant Jewish settlers with cash in their pockets and religiously sanctioned vengeance on their minds to reinforce the settlers of East Jerusalem and the West Bank. And the huge but harmless drama of Gaza will ensure that no further 'retreat' is ever again politically possible.

● As has been discussed, the Palestinian Authority has been prevented from maintaining order in Palestinian-controlled areas. The force has been emasculated by Israel, and corrupted and factionalized from within. The PA will fail therefore to police the expanded Gaza society and the incorruptible Hamas programmes will prosper both on the ground and politically. But then Israel and America, who have made every attempt to blacken Hamas to the world, will be able to say, 'You see what happens when we try to trust the Palestinians? The terrorists take over.'

● Most significantly of all, during the month of August 2005, as the world watched the charade in Gaza, the Jerusalem Envelope was completed in record time, Israeli crews working on the 25-foot high concrete barrier day and night. As Gaza was left behind by Israel, Jerusalem was entirely surrounded. More Palestinian familes were split or isolated by the route of the 'apartheid wall', and another 150,000 Jews were added from illegal West Bank settlements to Greater Jerusalem (including Ma'ale Adomim, the largest settlement in the West Bank with a population of 30,000). So that a core condition to Middle East peace was physically violated, the heart of any future Palestinian state cut out before birth.

Prime Minister Sharon of Israel described the events in Gaza as 'heartbreaking'. Palestinians have shed few tears.

Islam and Democracy

In a previous chapter the extravagant claim was made that if free democratic elections were ever to be held in the Muslim world, some version of an Islamist party, proposing to implement the Shariah, would come to power in almost every Muslim country. But what would happen then? How would such governments bring the Shariah into the twenty-first century? And, more importantly, would a government that considered its programmes to be 'implementing God's law', be prepared to leave office peacefully after a subsequent democratic defeat?

This is unlikely to be tested, however, since democracy and Islam are kept firmly apart by history, culture, the corruption of the current crew of Muslim rulers, and ironically, the intervention of America forcing a democratic charade at the end of a gun. The twenty-two Arab Muslim states are the least democratic ethnic group in the world. At the end of the twentieth century the average tenure of their rulers was a feudal twenty years, with Syria becoming the first 'hereditary Muslim republic' with the accession to power of Bashshār al-Assad. While in 2001, six of the eight most repressive countries in the world, according to World Audit, were under Muslim regimes: Afghanistan (under the former Taliban), Iraq (under the former Ba'thist regime), Libya, Saudi Arabia, Somalia and Sudan.

The building block of traditional Arab society was the desert tribe with the sheikh at the head, achieving his position partly through inheritance and partly through strength of character. Ibn Saud, the most powerful Arab ruler of modern times, died intestate like Muhammad. 'After my death,' he told his family, 'let the best man win.' The contest would, however, have been limited to a small group of direct male heirs, and the winner would have to gain support from key members of the tribe based on his physical and mental qualities, his leadership abilities, and above all on the perception of his *baraka*, or luck and charisma. Once in power the sheikh's supporters would become his 'clients' and to a large extent he could only rule effectively with their continuing consent. A network of benefits would therefore develop, through which the sheikh would maintain loyalty. Such benefits would range from delegated power to regular gifts, to privileged personal access, while down at the level of the ordinary tribesman, the sheikh would have to prove himself the 'father of his people'. A successful sheikh would know the history and troubles of each family, regular feasts would be held, and the sheikh's wives would ensure the loyalty of the women of the tribe with visits and gifts. A sheikh's prestige and authority would never recover from the reputation of *bakhil*, or 'stingy one'.

Once the sheikh was in power, however, there was no easy way to be rid of him. There is authority for the entire 'ummah to decide that their ruler should be replaced for not following the laws of God. But in a contemporary political context even the preliminary meetings necessary to establish such a consensus would be broken up by the existing government and the participants imprisoned. And the Qur'ān offers little encouragement for violent revolution or coup d'état.

> Oh ye who believe!
> Obey Allah, and obey the Messenger,
> And those charged
> With authority among you.
>
> *Al-Nisā'* (The Women) Surah 4, verse 59

In modern times, this traditional power hierarchy can be readily perverted to the creation of a dictatorship based on a quasi-fascist system of channelled support. The extraordinary resilience of the regime of Saddam Hussein in Iraq, for example, only brought down by the external might of the US, was based on a network of clients spread throughout the country following the tribal pattern. Clients were rewarded for loyalty and tied into the fortunes of their leader through the award of key government posts, or state contracts, or import licences and control over foreign exchange, among other benefits. Hussein's clients among the rural sheikhs were similarly implicated, with grants of land and recognition of authority. Then each senior client developed lesser clients down the line. At the same time, ultimate security for the regime was the responsibility of members of Hussein's Tikrit clan, whose fortunes were directly merged with those of their leader. It is estimated that Iraq's population of 20 million was in this way controlled by a cadre of no more than

500,000 people, despite a Sunni–Shiʿa divide and sustaining dreadful damage during a number of wars, as well as the economic devastation (and corruption) of UN sanctions.

Iraq, of course, was an extreme example, but a version of the leader–client system is at the root of the corrupt tyrannies that control many Muslim countries, often reinforced by exaggerating the absolute rule of the Prophet, misquoting the Hadith, and misinterpreting the words of the Qurʾān. 'Sixty years with an unjust Imam,' Muhammad is reported as saying, 'is better than a single night of anarchy.' But this is not a secure Hadith.

Yet Islam appears to accommodate the concept of democracy. The Qurʾān provides at least a starting point for democratic development, although the limited passages relating to the *shurā*, or process of consultation, are imprecise.

> So pass over
> Their faults, and ask
> For Allah's forgiveness
> For them; and consult
> Them in affairs of moment.
> Then, when thou hast
> Taken a decision
> Put thy trust in Allah.
> For Allah loves those
> Who put their trust in Him.
>
> *Al ʿImrān* (The Family of ʿImrān) Surah 3, verse 159

Wide claims are made based on such verses: that Islam invented democracy, or that *shurā* is the foundation of the Shariah, and therefore comparable with any Western system. In fact there are only two references in the text of the Qurʾān to *shurā*. Both are of a general nature and in the case of Surah 3, above, apparently addressed to a figure of traditional authority already in power rather than to any upwardly hopeful member of the rank and file.

But even if the Shariah, through a liberal *ijtihād* based on the *shurā* principle, had developed a Muslim tradition of democracy, before colonialism and subsequent post-colonial liberation imposed a perverted veneer of the Western version, the concept would have been severely limited. Because the core difficulty with 'democratic Islam' is that the will of the people can never be supreme, but must always be subject to the will of God, from whom flows all power.

> Allah has promised, to those
> Among you who believe
> And work righteous deeds, that He
> Will, of a surety, grant them
> In the land, inheritance
> Of power.
>
> *Al-Nur* (The Light) Surah 24, verse 55

Similarly, a secure Hadith declares unequivocally that 'no one is entitled to obedience if he disobeys his Creator'.

But who is to judge who 'among you believe', and who is qualified to exercise power as God's vice-regent on earth? Who is to interpret what God meant in the inexplicit words of the Qur'ān? Who is to judge whether a ruler is obeying or disobeying his Creator? This is the precise point where liberal and conservative, democracy and theocracy, collide in Iran, the leading example of an attempt in the Muslim world at a functioning Islamic state.

The British Parliament, as the supreme power in the land, could legalize any innovative social activity desired or tolerated by the voters who are the ultimate source of that body's power: gay marriage, for example (which has already been achieved) the unrestricted sale and consumption of drugs, the legalization of prostitution and so on. But in a Shariah state even the unanimous vote of an elected parliament could not pass such laws because such activities are contrary to the Qur'ān. This, therefore, is where the chasm opens, for if the power of the democratically elected representatives of the people is to be limited, who is to define those limits? Who is to interpret what is and is not the will of God?

In the Iranian example, as we have seen, the answer to these questions is that the ultimate power to interpret falls into the hands of a few mullahs and jurists, the Council of Guardians, and finally to one man, the Wali Faqih, a cleric in power for life and responsible to no one other than God. Elected governments may come and go, but final authority does not pass, and the will of the people cannot dislodge those who have appointed themselves to act in the name of God.

The ideal ruler in Islamic tradition, as envisaged by the Qur'ān, under whom *shurā* would function as a form of democracy within the bounds of the Shariah, would be a man (although the Qur'ān does not prevent a woman from ruling) knowledgeable in the law and possessed of the qualities of justice, virtue and piety. But this is merely to restate the threadbare concept of utopia, while in practice in the real modern examples, the consequences have been dire: a dictatorship of clerics, extravagant abuse of human rights, diplomatic isolation, gross economic mismanagement and increasing poverty, all accompanied by the perversion of everything egalitarian that Islam ideally stands for.

In the Western view there is only one solution to this dilemma: the separation of church and state, with the will of the people supreme. The secular state becomes a purely political creation, mercifully free of divine help, with personal salvation by whatever means left to the discretion of the individual. But, as we have seen, this is a concept that contradicts the very basis of Qur'ānic law and the very text of the Qur'ān. In the Islamic ideal, not only is there no distinction between 'the things which are Caesar's' and 'the things that are God's' (Matthew 22:21) but rather the laws of God in Islam are to *replace* the purely man-made state. 'Say', Muhammad is instructed in Surah 6, *Al An'ām* (The Cattle) at verse 71: 'Allah's guidance is the only guidance and we have been directed to submit ourselves to the Lord of the worlds.'

The virtuous upward circle of peace, prosperity, accountable secular democracy, tolerance, and the rule of law, leading to more peace, more prosperity and so on, has been vindicated by many examples over the last century, and not only in the West. But in many Muslim countries, the apparently irresolvable conflict between Islam and democracy has developed into a diabolic downward circle of violence, intolerance and dictatorship while we the West, who could easily exert influence on our Muslim client-states to reform, in fact fear the outcome of the very democratic measures which we so regularly preach. For if a truly free election imposed from the outside will inevitably transform a passive but corrupt virtual dictatorship into an unstable and probably undemocratic Islamist state, is it not better to ensure that democracy and the rule of law remain nothing more than rhetoric? Or, as internal pressure mounts in a corrupt Muslim state for reform, which might in turn lead to elections and so to reactive Islamism, is it not better for the West to continue support for an existing compliant and familiar regime regardless of a few excesses and inconveniences?

This is how hypocrisy is justified, how corrupt ruling elites are propped up in many Muslim countries, and 'extremists' suppressed, with the financial markets reassured and the somnambulist citizens of the West promised that all will soon be right with the world. But this is also how Muslim anger rises under the lid. These were the conditions that led to the Iranian Revolution, for example, with the disastrous results already described.

Under the Lid

Stand of the edge of Thahrir Square in Cairo, at the centre of a city of 17 million, at the cultural heart of 1,400 years of Islam, but among the ordinary men and women of Egypt for whom life never seems to improve. How does the Muslim world look from here? How could the daily routine of violence and corruption be made to disappear? And if the will of the people, expressed freely and democratically, really were to be implemented in Muslim countries, as America purports to wish, how *could* the Muslim world look?

- In place of a repressed minority divided between Turkey, Iraq and Iran, the Kurds would be a new nation with a seat at the UN. Kurdistan would thrive in peace, with human rights and religious freedom restored.

- In place of absolute nomadic poverty and constant hostility from Algeria, Morocco, Mali and Niger, the Tuaregs would be another new nation, able to relate the plight of their people to the outside world. The Polisario of the former Spanish Sahara would also be free of Moroccan repression and possibly joined with the Tuareg in a free southern Saharan nation.

- In place of the National Democratic Party, which would vanish instantly, Egypt would be free of neo-pharaonic rulers and governed by a coalition of able professionals led by the Muslim Brotherhood. The new government would struggle with Egypt's bureaucracy, with the armed forces, with poverty and unemployment, and with much reduced American help.

- In place of the State of Israel, a new multicultural state would border Egypt, Jordan and Lebanon, in which Jews would be a minority (after the exercise of the Palestinian right of return) but accepted as full citizens in a tolerant society inspired by the many precedents in Islamic history in which Jews have participated in Muslim administrations (although the reverse has never once been the case).

- In place of the bloodstained *pouvoir*, Algeria would be governed by the FIS, and no doubt many in the secular middle class would leave for France. But Europe needs suitable migrants much more urgently than the obsolete concept of racial purity.

- In place of the unsustainable expense of the House of Saud, Arabia would be ruled by conservative Bedouin methods based on *shurā*. Women would not be liberated in the Western sense, full elections would never be held, nor accounts published, but the instability of the country, so feared by the West, would be gone.

- In place of Iraq, the eighty-year-old hangover from the Churchill's Cairo Conference would finally be cured. The Kurds would leave for independence, the Shiʿa would ally with or join Iran, and the Sunnis would join with an expanded Syria in a quasi-Shariah state free of Alawite rule.

- In place of the state-wide repression of the al-Sabbāh family, Kuwaitis would complete the transition to a form of Shariah democracy, now impeded by their rulers.

- In place of a constant state of emergency, the Jordanian constitution would be upheld, the king would play a constitutional role only, and middle-class technocrats allied to the Muslim Brotherhood would take power.

- In place of military rule, Pakistan would muddle along as an ineffi-
  cient democracy, with power alternating between the People's
  Party and the Muslim League. The threat from India that justifies
  Pakistani military and nuclear power would be eliminated because
  Kashmir would have voted to leave Indian control and join Pakistan.

- In place of American hegemony, Afghanistan would be independent,
  but still not a democracy, ruled by warlords and an overlord in
  Kabul. Poppy production and internal strife would dominate the
  state, which would be Islam's basketcase for the foreseeable future,
  overwhelmed by history, race, climate and decades of destruction.

Small wonder, therefore, that few Arabs believe American rhetoric as
meaning anything more than sham elections in which US interests are
given the veneer of local approval. The most recent example of US
democracy in the Middle East was the re-election of the client regime of
Hosni Mubarak in Egypt in 2005, when the hugely popular opposition,
the Muslim Brotherhood, was banned, with the leader of the party,
Hassan el-Brince, imprisoned for the duration together with fifty-seven
other senior members of the party.

7

TRAVELLING IN DAR AL-ISLAM

I Culture, Religion and Social Progress

Although relegated to the last chapter of this book, the culture of twenty-first century Dar al-Islam, or the Muslim world, is important. Culture in the wider sense of 'way of life' can either facilitate or hinder social progress, and the culture of a country is what the traveller sees on the streets, meeting the people and visiting the sites.

A comparison was made in Chapter 1 between the economies of South Korea and Egypt, which in 1950 shared the same level of GDP, as well as similar levels of foreign aid. But now, more than half a century later, the two countries return figures of $9,400 GDP per head and $1,290 respectively, according to *The Economist, World in Figures*.

Despite Egypt's superior location, self-sufficiency in oil, and the 'unearned' benefits from the Suez Canal, South Korea has moved ahead to become the twelfth largest economy in the world, through the development of a sophisticated manufacturing sector producing everything from vehicles to electronics. Egypt, in contrast, now languishes in forty-first position, and with an ominous fertility rate almost double that of North Korea. There are, no doubt, many secondary reasons for this startling discrepancy, but surely the primary explanation must be South Korea's culture of thrift, hard work, lack of tolerance for corruption, education and discipline, increasingly consolidated by democracy, and the fact that most of these characteristics are largely missing in Egypt.

The European culture of learning and improving is the bedrock of the industrial and knowledge revolutions that have come to dominate the world. Similarly the disciplined self-reliant desert culture of Arabia, released by Islam from the self-defeating bondage of inter-tribal warfare, carried the seventh century Muslim horsemen into the heart of the Byzantine and Sassanid empires to create the caliphate as a new world power. How wrong, therefore, the Nazi writer Hans Johst was, when in 1934 he had one of his characters say, 'whenever I hear the word *culture* . . . I release the safety-catch on my pistol'. In retrospect the words could be seen as carrying a prediction of the great wreckage that was to follow on from the National Socialist hijacking of centuries of German culture.

The core of the complicated and controversial link between culture and social progress has rarely been better expressed than in the words of Daniel Patrick Moynihan, twenty-four years an American senator, and that extinct beast among politicians, an intellectual free of preconceptions: 'The central conservative truth is that culture not politics determines the success of a society. The central liberal truth is that politics can change a culture and save it from itself.' Moynihan's conservative truth is certainly self-evident in most Muslim societies. The question facing Islam is whether the inherited culture of the Qur'ān is capable of incubating the liberal changes necessary for social success in the twenty-first century, as was the case in the seventh century example given above, when Islam adapted fast to new circumstances.

As we have seen throughout this book, many of the right ingredients are theoretically present in Islam to support progress, from honesty and hard work to group social responsibility, but these possibilities are all too frequently frustrated by human agency. The general failure of Muslim society to educate women, for example, and give access to the workforce (not to mention political power), when there is no Qur'ānic justification for such practices, is a clear example of culture, rather than Islam, impeding economic progress. Another illustration, the 'Big Basha', or 'Saladin Syndrome' in Muslim society, which has also been considered, visibly undermines individuality and initiative, while tacitly condoning all manner of abuses, none of which is justified by pure Islam.

To explain the diverging paths of progress in South Korea and Egypt as the social result of *inshah' allāh*, or 'if Allah wishes' would be tempting. For if God, following His own inscrutable reasoning, has willed a man to be poor, ignorant and malnourished, that is how he will be and nothing can be done. Protestantism in general and Calvinism in particular were also once based on belief in the predestination of the 'pre-damned' and the 'pre-saved'. Yet the values of Northern Europe, subsequently spread to North America, have gone on to create the greatest bastions of wealth and progress the world has ever known, by inverting the culture to define the 'pre-saved' as men and women demonstrating such qualities as self-motivation, honesty, patience, tenacity, hard work, competitiveness and so on. But Sunni Islam, as we have seen, has no cultural hierarchy from which such practical leadership could flow, with the result that even the most prominent Muslim scholars are mere individuals, deploying deep spiritual training and human compassion, but with little knowledge of, or influence over the outside world.

Possibly the question is so complex, a combination of religion, history, politics, psychology, anthropology, geography and probably a lot more, that no clear explanation can be given for the difference between the present conditions of North Korea and Egypt. But progress does not have to be measured solely in terms of Gross Domestic Product. A Muslim would point to the many aspects of his or her culture that are considered to be more important than worldly wealth. A Westerner would certainly answer that this is merely to restate the problem, because productivity in the Western view is the ultimate source of civilization, in the form of good healthcare, a liveable urban environment, education, arts, civil rights, recreation, and all the other existential benefits that make up the backbone of an improved 'way of life'. (Although, to take a different viewpoint, stressed South Korea has more than ten times the Western average of alcohol-related vehicle accidents, and Egypt has none.)

America has also flirted with cultural importance. Less than a month after the attacks on Washington and New York on September 11th, 2001, as their massive military response was in preparation, the civil response was announced: the US was to be rebranded. A Madison Avenue sage (Charlotte Beers, former head of both J. Walter Thompson and Ogilvy and Mather, whose career was established by her successful brand marketing of Uncle Ben's Rice) was installed as the Under Secretary of State for Public Diplomacy, to pull off the biggest assignment in advertising history. Rather than Barbie, *Baywatch* and Chicken McNuggets, America was to be known henceforth for tolerance, democracy and freedom: the qualities which for the American people, whatever the rest of the world may think, define their society. Possibly, however, the nature of the mandate said more about the true nature of American culture than the ensuing publicity campaign ever could. Charlotte Beers and her successor left after only months in office, to be succeeded in 2005 by Karen Hughes from the senior management of the Bush re-election campaign. At her nomination hearing only two senators were present, confirming that the office has lost its effectiveness (and budgetary priority). To the Muslim world, what the US does is more important than what the government says.

Muslims, on the other hand, look to their faith and their history for the exact mirror image of America's ambitions as a defence against the strength of the 'universal culture' of the liberal West. Probably at no other time in the history of Islam, which for centuries was a dominant force and rarely a defensive one, has culture been so important to the Muslim world. 'We will be modern,' this observer is told by Muslims time and time again, 'but we will not be *you.*' But how social and economic progress will be speeded up in Muslim countries in the 'knowledge era' without deep penetration by the West is never convincingly explained.

II   God Without an Image

Even though America is probably the most religious country in the Western world, with 85 per cent of the population professing belief in a god, religion was not considered in Ms Beers' mandate as forming part of American culture. Religion in America is considered to be entirely contained within the word 'freedom', the basis of the United States Constitution (which does not once mention the word 'god'). Faith for Americans is a free personal choice and therefore, in theory, has no place in the group activities of national politics and culture. Even school prayer is banned by a long-standing Supreme Court interpretation of the Constitution. In practice, of course, US elections are won and lost through religious support, as if the President's job description included 'Chaplain-in-Chief'. And a low-level battle rages constantly in US courts and legislatures between secularists attempting to uphold the strict separation of church and state, and religious groups intent on government funding for religious schools and 'faith-based' initiatives.

But in Islam culture *is* religion and the two cannot be separated. Just as mosque and state fuse in the ideal Shariah society to become a complete 'way of life', so all cultural expression in Islam should similarly centre on *tawhid*, the very core of belief, the affirmation of the Oneness of God, the Unknowable, the Unseeable, the transcendent Creator, encapsulated by the words of the First Pillar of Islam: 'I bear witness that there is no god but God and that Muhammad is the messenger of God.'

When a Muslim artist views his art through this inescapable prism of belief, therefore, his task is to portray *tawhid*. But exactly contrary to Christian practice, the Oneness of God is not to be found reflected in the human form, as in the Christian tradition of man created in the 'image of God', or God 'made flesh' in the form of Christ, a universal subject of Western art. Animal form is also beyond the reach of Muslim art as part of God's animate creation, and the stricter interpretations of Islam even regard the reproduction of trees, flowers and landscape as offensive. Rather, the entity of the Muslim God is by definition beyond definition, and simply inexpressible, so the *inexpressible* is what the Muslim artist must find a way to express. (This should not be confused, however, with the *attributes* of God, many of which are detailed in the Qur'ān.)

The traditional solution to this conundrum is to stylize the impalpable Godhead with the 'arabesque' geometric design (see p. 406) that extends away in all directions *ad infinitum*, giving the impression that there is no boundary between this world and the next. The object decorated in this way, textile for example, wood, ceramic tiling, pillars, domes, pottery, or the page of a book, becomes a weightless transparent statement of *tawhid*, with no distinction between the physical and the spiritual, and thus exudes a sense of profound tranquillity. The pattern has no static focal point, but moves seamlessly from one module to the next, providing an artistic rendering of the frequently repeated Qur'ānic concept, that wherever one turns, there is the presence of Allah.

In Islam, therefore, portraying the physical world through examples from nature or the human form is at best a mere secular effort, at worst a vain and self-centred pursuit. There is no Muslim equivalent of Picasso, or el Greco or Fra Angelico (and certainly no Rodin or Toulouse-Lautrec) because what is seen as the slavish representation of extant creation by Western artists is of no value in a religious culture that seeks to reach for the divine and bypass everything that is not God. Victorious Muslims first entering the churches and palaces of the Byzantines, and coming face to face with the intricacies of Christian religious representational art, must have thought themselves to be in the very shrines of idolatry. But, nevertheless, the works of art of Christendom were left unmolested, since between the peoples who share Allah's book, His angels and His Messengers, 'We make no distinction between one and the other' (*Al-Baqarah* (The Heifer) Surah 2, verse 285).

Modern Western scholars have attempted to link the arabesque to molecular patterns seen under a microscope, or natural crystalline formations, concluding that Islamic art 'unknowingly imitated the work of God'. But this line of analysis is in itself contrary to the true motivation of Muslim art. Rather, a parallel could be drawn with the work of Paul Klee, Rothko or Joan Miró, whose patterned art and reductionist ambitions resonate more closely with Muslim objectives.

This sensitive Islamic theory of inexpressibility developed over time into a body of rules that specifically prohibited the depiction of animal and human life-forms in mosques. Both al-Bokhari and Muslim report that the Prophet said: 'Those who make pictures will be chastised on the Day of Judgement and it will be said to them, "Now put life into that which you have made".'

Over the Muslim centuries the status of representational art depicting animals or human portraiture has deteriorated from being merely extra-religious to become 'against Islam'. So, by extension, any creativity not harnessed to a communal religious objective has come to be discouraged by Muslim culture as a deviation from the true path of submission. Representational art is not specifically prohibited by the Qur'ān, but once this 'God-centred' attitude had developed, well-known passages like the lines below were used to support the idea that the descriptive artist blasphemes with his art, by coming close to competing with God.

> To Him is due
> The primal origin
> Of the heavens and the earth.
> When He decreeth a matter
> He saith to it: 'Be,'
> And it is.

> *Al-Baqarah* (The Heifer) Surah 2, verse 117

This interpretation explains the skill and the inspiration lavished by Muslim craftsmen on the ornamentation of such non-contentious and faceless objects as weapons, furniture, metal work, stone and ceramics.

Representational art, sculpture, and carving in particular, is also uncomfortably close to the creation of idols. The overthrow of idolatry in favour of the One God is the central message of Islam, and was the apogee of Muhammad's career. Ibn Saʿd (d. 844 CE), an early biographer of the Prophet, describes the scene:

> The Prophet, may the prayer and peace of Allah be with
> him, entered Mecca as the conqueror; the people converted
> to Islam, some willingly and some reluctantly. The Prophet,
> may the prayer and peace of Allah be with him, still on
> his mount, made the ritual circuits around the Ka'bah,
> where 360 idols were displayed. And every time he passed
> by an idol, pointing his cane be declaimed, 'Truth has come
> and falsehood has vanished, for falsehood by its nature is
> bound to vanish.' And as this sentence was pronounced,
> each idol slid from its pedestal and smashed to the
> ground.

This event was the symbolic implementation of monotheism in Arabia, but a more sinister interpretation of these events can also be made. In the chaotic pagan world of the *Jāhiliyyah*, every household and every man and woman had their individual god, to be touched or spoken to at every turn: when travelling, when entering or leaving the home, and especially in times of stress. These idols in their thousands and their hundreds of thousands were personal and each one was different, so that idolatry thus represented a form of freedom of thought, or *shirk*. But the word *shirk*, which appears 160 times in the Qurʾān, was reconstructed by Islam to mean something completely different: the eternally unforgivable wrong of worshipping something or someone other than, or as a partner with, Allah. Believers, like the men of Mecca themselves after the opening of their city, are offered peace and security by Islam, as well as the promise of paradise eternal. But the penalty is obedience to God and His Prophet in the present, and the relinquishing of freedom of thought on an artistic level. More dangerously, as we have seen, this can be developed into the concept of religious conformity to be manipulated by tyrants into acceptance by their subjects of limits to economic enterprise, civil rights and democracy.

Exceptions to the prohibition against animal and human figurative art do exist, however, particularly among the first and second generations of Muslims following the death of the Prophet, and later quite widely among non-Arab Muslims. Most famously, the Umayyads from primitive Mecca, unsophisticated by the standards of their recently acquired Byzantine subjects, hired Christian artists to embellish their new monuments. The floor and walls of the court-yard of the Great Mosque in Damascus (completed in 714 CE) were originally covered with a green and gold mosaic depicting a popu-lated Qur'ānic paradise against a background of fantastic succulent trees and multi-hued flowers. At the end of the nineteenth century, however, fire destroyed this great work except for a few perimeter wall sections. 'It was surely the hand of God,' this observer's official guide concluded as we stood together on the edge of the renovated courtyard, now relaid in stark marble, desert bare and blindingly white in the summer heat. In Umayyad Spain, in another example, great lions were carved to support the basin in the Court of Lions in the Alhambra palace in Granada.

After the European Renaissance of the sixteenth century CE, some forms of representational art spread to the Muslim world, but neither character nor emotion were ever fully expressed. The Hadith that became a tradition, or a rule, had effectively removed interpre-tive art from the Muslim repertoire, even when some representation was tolerated. Even today no Muslim text attempts to illuminate religion with pictures. No pictures of the Prophet hang on the walls of mosques or in the homes of any Muslim. Photography is now widely accepted, however, and even the most conservative of Muslim newspapers includes photographs of the men and women in the news. The absolute prohibition remaining in the modern day is against human statuary, although even this is occasionally breached by egomaniacal political bosses.

On the other hand, Muslim abstract art of all kinds, shows a pro-found appreciation of colour and light, with the most successful cre-ating the impression of an opening to the infinite. In the opinion of experts the brilliant hues of Persian and Turkish pottery have rarely been surpassed anywhere in the world, for example, and the use of colour by Muslim artists in the design of prayer rugs, carpets and illuminated books is without comparison.

III   Mosque Architecture

The highest form of Muslim art, however, is mosque architecture. With the design and construction of a mosque the artist magnifies God, the mosque provides the physical setting for the practice of Islam, and usually stands at the heart of a Muslim community. Further, those involved with such a project follow the example of the Prophet himself from the early days of the Medina Commonwealth, when Muhammad built the first mosque with his own hands.

For these reasons Muslim cities are everywhere dotted with informal mosques, in addition to the readily visible free-standing mosques. These little prayer rooms are situated in basements and alleyways, in office buildings and petrol filling-stations. As we have seen, no dedication of a mosque is needed beyond pious intention, making the process of establishing a corner mosque very simple. In fact the whole earth is considered to be a mosque and prayers can take place in any suitable location (except bathhouses, camel pens and any other unclean place). In addition, many Muslim regimes offer a tax concession for the building containing such a mosque, although this in turn brings both mosque and mullah to the notice of the authorities. Verse 18 of Surah 9 *Al-Tawbah* (The Repentance) is commonly found displayed in an informal mosque to show that the area is set aside for worship.

> The mosques of Allah
> Shall be visited and maintained
> By such as believe in Allah
> And the Last Day, establish
> Regular prayers and practice
> Regular charity, and fear
> None at all except Allah.

Formal mosque design, on the other hand, *al-masjid al-jāmi'*, intended for use by an entire community, falls into three categories.

● The courtyard mosque follows Muhammad's original layout and is common in hot climates. The building consists of a rectangular court of which one wall faces the *qibla*, or direction of prayer towards Mecca. The *qibla* end is roofed, or enclosed for some distance back, with aisles created by the supporting columns. In normal daily use, this part of the mosque, which is often carpeted, is of sufficient size for those wishing to pray. On Fridays or feast days the courtyard is used to accommodate extra rows of the faithful, lined up to match the covered aisles. In more sophisticated variations on the design, a cloister of columns rather than a bare wall encloses other three sides of the courtyard.

● The cruciform *madrasah* mosque, widely used in Persia and Egypt from the twelfth century, consists of a courtyard, usually open to the sky, enclosed by four large covered halls, each of equal size, opening on to the central courtyard. The halls are free of columns and usually raised by one step above the level of the courtyard. One of the four halls will contain the *qibla* wall and will be in constant use. The other halls are filled when necessary with rows matching those facing the *qibla*. The origin of the design was as a *madrasah* with one hall each for the four principal schools of *fiqh*, often with accommodation for the students on other floors behind or above. Lessons would be held in the halls by the mullah of each school.

● The third type, the domed mosque, favoured by the Ottoman sultans, is entirely enclosed, and is thus the design usually followed in temperate climates. The typical profile of a European mosque is a dome in copper or marble over a rectangle. The prayer hall is under the dome and consists of one large room with few columns, in which the faithful line up facing the *qibla* wall.

The elements of a mosque consist of the prayer hall facing Mecca, with the *qibla* wall designated by the *mihrab*, an empty niche, often made of intricately carved stone. A *minbar* or pulpit, usually made of wood and ornately decorated, faces the congregation, from which the Friday *khutba* is given. A few aisles back from the *qibla* wall a *maqsura*, or raised platform, accommodates Qur'ān reciters, local chieftains, or a speaker who will repeat the words of the *khutba*, or the invocations during prayers, as they are spoken to those further away (but made redundant in modern times by the dubious advance of electronic amplification). Women, who are always segregated at prayer, are usually provided with a balcony above the prayer hall, or a screened area to one side. Modern mosques include extensive plumbed washing facilities for ablutions, separated from the main part of the mosque or hidden in the basement in the case of modern buildings. In early mosques an ablution fountain often stood at the entrance to the courtyard, or in the case of the cruciform *madrasah* design, in the middle of the courtyard. Ablution fountains were often free standing roofed structures of great artistic merit. The most easily distinguished feature of a mosque is the minaret, from which (before the advent of amplification) the muezzin called the *azān* five times per day. Minarets provide a simple method by which the origin, influence and dating of a mosque can be readily established.

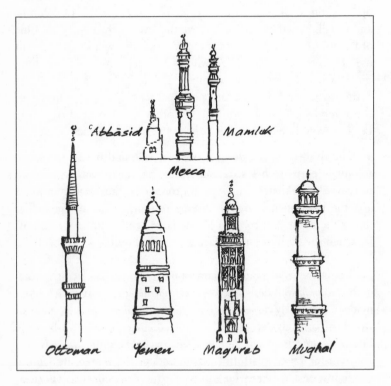

Minaret design

IV   The Harams

Mecca and Medina

Mecca (or more correctly, *Makkah al-Mukarramah*, Makkah the Blessed) and Madina (*Madinat al-Nabiyy*, the City of the Prophet, also known as *al-Madinat al-Munawwarah*, Medina the Radiant, or the Radiant City) stand apart from all other Muslim holy places. These are the cities where irrefutably Muhammad was born, undertook his ministry, created his ideal Commonwealth, died and is buried. For this reason Mecca and Medina, each centred on a much extended and now vast mosque, are *haram*, or sacred precincts. Non-Muslims may not enter, and for believers special rules of behaviour apply.

Standing before the Ka'bah in Mecca is an overwhelming experience: for a believer, the structure is the Primordial Temple, reflecting the presence of God, and lies on the cosmic axis connecting heaven and earth. The pilgrim is at the very centre of Islam, the *qibla* of prayer from all around the world, and at the final destination of his or her pilgrimage. History is all around, stretching back, in Muslim legend, to the very beginnings of human existence on earth. A few kilometres outside the city, on the plain of Arafāt, Adam and Eve found each other again after falling from the Garden of Paradise. The city is where, in fact as in legend, Adam built the first 'house of rest', the original Ka'bah, on the present site, and later again, this is where Noah's ark settled after the flood. Here also, Ibrahim, the father of monotheism, brought Hājar and her son Ismā'il at the direction of God, abandoning them in the desert to His mercy, which was fulfilled in the form of the well of Zamzam. Later, when the child had grown into a boy, Ibrahim prepared to offer Ismā'il in sacrifice, again on divine orders. Then, in thanks to God for His intervention, preventing the consummation of the sacrifice, Ibrahim rebuilt Adam's Ka'bah and initiated the haj. Finally Muhammad, born and raised in the city, returned victorious from Medina as the Messenger of Allah to cleanse the Ka'bah and reinstate the haj, together with the religion of the One God.

Since the death of Muhammad, through fourteen centuries of tumultuous Muslim history, the title of the 'Custodian of the Two Holy Mosques' of Mecca and Medina has ranked in importance second only to that of Caliph. And since the abolition of the caliphate in 1924 the office of Custodian may be said to be the most important in Islam. Although traditionally associated with Muhammad's Hashemite clan of the Meccan Quraysh tribe, the al-Saud family assumed the role when in 1926 the British permitted the expulsion by ibn Saud's forces of al-Hussein ibn Ali, the last Hashemite Amir of Mecca. The entire Ottoman vilayet of the Hijaz was then merged into what was shortly to become Saudi Arabia.

The site of the city of Mecca is described in the Qur'ān through the words of Ibrahim himself as 'an infertile vale'. The city sits in a hard rocky valley, and the surrounding area is incapable of any agricultural production, even with the modern provision of copious water. Rather it was the presence of the Ka'bah that determined the original position of the city, and trade and service industries connected to religion have sustained the population ever since, stretching back into the days of the *Jāhiliyyah*. Fear of the loss of revenues from religious tourism and associated trade fairs, should the religion of the One God prevail over the idolatry of the many, was at the heart of the Qurayshite opposition to monotheism and Muhammad's ministry.

The economic base of the city today is not significantly different, although tremendous physical changes have overtaken Mecca during the last fifty years. Pilgrims have increased from 100,000 during the haj season of 1950 to 3 million in 2004, of whom more than half come from countries other than Saudi Arabia, despite recently imposed country quotas. The lesser pilgrimage of the '*umra* attracts a further 3 million visitors each year, a figure which is growing at the rate of 25–30 per cent per annum. Prince Sultan ibn Salman, head of the Saudi tourist promotion agency, predicts a total of 34 million visitors to Mecca annually by the year 2020.

The al-Saud family has spent over $35 billion in recent years on pilgrimage facilities and on extensions to the mosques of both Mecca and Medina, but still more is required to accommodate the anticipated growth. The hospitality trade to pilgrims now employs four times as many workers as Saudi Arabia's oil industry, and new high-rise developments for tourism are sweeping away large parts of the traditional narrow streets and brick houses of old Mecca, creating yet more economic activity. In parts of the city, land is now priced at $60,000 per square metre, many times more than values in the centre of Hong Kong, London or New York.

The Holy Mosque, the largest in the world, is more a feat of accommodation than architecture. After the second Saudi extension was completed in 1995, the mosque has become a vast open-air amphitheatre accommodating more than 500,000 worshippers at once on multiple levels, facing the Ka'bah in the centre. The exterior walls of the building are topped by five pairs of huge minarets, and plazas around the exterior provide space to pray for further hundreds of thousands of pilgrims.

The materials and finishes of the entire structure are of the highest quality, set to last for centuries. Marble, granite and mosaic, brought from the best sources all over the world, often worked with the most intricate designs, cover every surface. The mosque is also supplied by services to a matching standard of excellence: air conditioning, toilets and ablutions (the latter fed by the water of the well of Zamzam), lighting systems, crowd control systems, sound systems, CCTV, emergency exits, a bus depot and multiple underground parking garages.

Medina, in contrast to Mecca, is surrounded by greenery. The Medinan oasis is fed by bountiful deep wells of fresh water and the sandy soil when irrigated produces famous pomegranates, dates and sugar-sweet grapes. Although here, too, real estate development has changed the face of the city and now covers many of the formerly productive orchards.

Medina is often referred to as soft, or 'feminine', to accentuate the contrast with the harshness of Mecca, 320 kilometres distant. Medina, for a believer, flows with the special *baraka* of Muhammad. His presence is felt everywhere, while the ground is sanctified by his remains. These sentiments explain the name 'Medina the Radiant'.

Although not forming part of the route of the haj, Medina is usually visited by pilgrims after the rituals at Mecca are complete. The central attraction of the city is the Prophet's Mosque, of which the core is the building constructed with Muhammad's own hands in the years after the hijrah, and which became the model for mosques the world over. The Prophet's Mosque has been hugely enlarged over the years (and the original construction by the Prophet is no longer visible), again using materials of the finest quality. But in all respects, size, elaboration, services and impact, the Prophet's Mosque ranks second to the Holy Mosque of Mecca. The Prophet's Mosque contains the Prophet's tomb, with Abu Bakr and ʿUmar, the first and second caliphs, lying beside him. Pilgrims cannot enter the tomb, and must offer their prayers from outside a series of elaborate golden gates.

The Prophet's Mosque is entirely enclosed and heavily air-conditioned, topped by a dome in a deep dusty green, the shade that has become the colour of Islam, representing precious desert fecundity and thus the Mercy of Allah (although the dome is now dwarfed by the ten enormous minarets of the later extensions). A large plaza behind the mosque, there being more space in Medina than in the flinty valley that limits Mecca, brings the total number of believers that can be accommodated simultaneously at the mosque for prayers to one million.

Jerusalem: *Isrā* and *Miʿrāj*

The two great Muslim buildings of Jerusalem, the Dome of the Rock and al-Aqsa Mosque, known together *al-Haram al-Sharif,* the Noble Sanctuary, constitute the third haram of Islam. The 'Rock' for which the Dome is named is a dark wedge of natural bedrock, rising almost two metres out of the ground directly under the Dome. Here the traveller encounters the very spot where Judaism (and therefore Christianity) and Islam intersect. This, in Muslim legend, was the destination of the Prophet's Night Journey, or *Isrā*, and the departure point for the Prophet's ascension to heaven, or *Miʿrāj*. But this is also the same rock that in Jewish belief Abraham used as the altar for the sacrifice of Isaac (which in Muslim belief took place outside Mecca). 'Al-Aqsa' Mosque, the second building, means 'the Farthest' Mosque, named by reference to the opening lines of Surah 17, *Al-Isrā* (The Night Journey):

> Glory to Allah who did take His Servant for a Journey by
> night from the Sacred Mosque (in Mecca) to the Farthest
> Mosque (in Jerusalem).

The Jerusalem site is considered by Muslims to be a haram because by tradition Muhammad was present in the city, as he was in Mecca and Medina. For this reason, informally among Muslims and often in the Western press, the Jerusalem Haram is referred to as the 'third holiest site in Islam'. But the presence of the Prophet in the city, whether mythical or existential, is unresolved, so that Jerusalem is of lesser importance, and unlike Mecca or Medina, has never been an exclusively Muslim city.

Although Islam is currently in possession of the Haram, underlying ownership is claimed by the State of Israel. Jews, together with many Christians, know the site as the 'Temple Mount', referring back to purported Jewish use of the site in pre-Islamic times. The place is also referred to by Torah and Old Testament enthusiasts as 'Mount Moriah' after Genesis 22:2, where the description of Abraham's sacrifice begins, even though only the 'land of Moriah' is referred to in the story, and not any 'mount'. But these apparently minor nuances conceal an explosive potency, even in the twenty-first century. The militaristic penetration of the Jerusalem Haram in 2000 by General Sharon (later Israeli prime minister, and frequently described by President George W. Bush as a 'man of peace') in order to assert Israel's 'eternal' ownership of the site 'up to the heavens', was the event that sparked what came to be known as the al-Aqsa intifada. The uprising resulted in the violent deaths of more than a thousand non-combatant civilians. (Sharon had also contributed to the start of the earlier intifada of 1987, by moving into a requisitioned house in the Arab quarter of the city.)

The competing claim to the Haram by Palestinians begins with the indigenous residence of their Jebusite ancestors. Excavation has uncovered the Jebusite acropolis of Sion, south of the present walls of the Old City of Jerusalem, linked to an established settlement named for the Jebusite pagan god Shalem (making the city Ur-Shalem, from which the name Jerusalem is derived) and constituting a recognizable pre-Jewish civilization dating from the fourteenth century BCE, or possibly earlier.

Jebusite civilization was followed by occupation of the same ground by successor tribes of proto-Palestinians, of which the best known are the Canaanites and the Philistines. The tribal name 'Philistine' is the origin of the word Palestine, from the 'land of Filistia' (and manipulated by Torah propagandists to mean, according to the *Oxford English Dictionary*, 'uncultured person, one whose *interests are material and commonplace*', a derogatory term that is surely well overdue for oblivion like 'nigger' or 'yid'). Then recognizable Palestinians appear after the conquest of Palestine by Alexander the Great in the fourth century BCE, followed by the Egyptian Ptolemies and the Greek Seleucids. Finally, Palestinians live in the full light of history from Roman times onward.

The period of more than 1,300 years stretching from the Jebusite settlement of Ur-Shalem to the arrival in Palestine of the Roman Empire in 63 BCE, is the period allegedly occupied by the Torah stories: the leadership of Moses, the Exile and the Wandering, David then Solomon's rule from Jerusalem, the establishment of the Twelve Tribes of Jacob, the construction of the First Jerusalem Temple, the construction, destruction and reconstruction of the Second Temple, and a few subsequent periods of Jewish political rule. But other than the text of the Torah, no support whatever exists for these events, either on the ground (one of the most ardently excavated areas in the world), or in the records of neighbours who are claimed to have been involved, principally Assyria, Egypt and Babylon.

In the Palestinian view, therefore, the Torah stories are entirely unsubstantiated. Rather, Judaism is considered to have emerged from a monotheistic tribal cult which slowly divided the Yahwist Hebrew tribe from the pre-existing pagan Jebusite and Canaanite tribes to become the Jewish faith. In the Palestinian view, Hebrew history was created retroactively, taken from various scraps, myths and the traditions of others, to form the books of the Torah, and only assembled in final form during the first century CE, with the presence of the discommodious Canaanites explained away as the progeny of the non-Hebrew concubines of the mythical Abraham.

By the time the first outside conquerors arrived in Palestine from the northern coast of the Mediterranean in the fourth century BCE, the Hebrews were an organized elite society, and various accommodations were made with the new powers, beginning with Alexander the Great in 332 BCE. But in 164 BCE, during the decline of the Greek Seleucid Empire that followed Alexander and his successors, the Egyptian Ptolemies, the Hebrews revolted against outside domination under the leadership of Judah Maccabee who established a short-lived Jewish state. The Maccabees then evolved into the aggressive House of Hasmon, which forced the population of much of Palestine to choose between conversion to Judaism and expulsion, in an attempt to create a permanent Jewish majority. With these events the 1,300 pages of the Old Testament and the Apocrypha come to an end and only then merge with archaeologically and independently supported history.

The defeat of the Jewish House of Hasmon by the Roman general Pompey in 63 BCE led indirectly to the appointment of Herod the Great as king of Judea by the Roman Senate in 40 BCE, a character well known to every Christian for the story of his legendary attempt to murder the baby Jesus. Seven hundred years of Roman rule in Palestine were now about to begin and the Christian era was dawning. Over the following two millennia after their defeat by Rome, Jews would be only a tiny minority in Palestine, and hardly present even in Jerusalem, with Palestinian possession, as the overwhelming majority, continuing as before, reaching back to the start of history.

From an outsider's point of view, however, this Muslim counter to the Torah tradition is clouded by the unambiguous reference in the Qur'ān ('the unerring Word of God') to the Promised Land, which is the principal founding myth of Israel (Surah 5, *Al-Mā'idah* (The Repast), verses 20–26, and Surah 17, *Al-Isrā* (The Night Journey), verses 2–8). Then the construction of the Dome of the Rock directly over the rocky outcrop claimed by Judaism as sacred was a clear statement of Muslim belief, at least at the time of the construction, that on this same site had once stood one or more Jewish temples (in the last of which Christ, in the Christian version, had preached and overturned the tables of the moneylenders). By choosing this particular place, therefore, Islam was giving physical substance to the claim of the new faith in the Qur'ān to be the inheritor and perfector of all that had gone before. The Palestinian explanation of the present state of affairs in Jerusalem, based on archaeology, may therefore appear to be inconsistent with the Qur'ānic version. But the Qur'ān expects all three 'Abrahamic' religions to be dealt with equally and to cooperate, rather than to allow differences to become a source of territorial contention.

The Christian claim to Jerusalem receives the same Muslim response, since Jesus in the Qur'ān was not the Son of God, but 'no more than a Messenger.' In this version Jesus was taken alive up to heaven and not crucified, thus eliminating at a stroke the sanctity of

such key Christian sites in Jerusalem as the Via Dolorosa of the
Stations of the Cross and the Church of the Holy Sepulchre. And in
any case, Muslims also emphasize, no evidence exists to support the
story of Christ in Jerusalem (or anywhere else). Here again the
Dome of the Rock gives physical substance to Islam's mission to
'correct' the misinterpretations of previous beliefs by emblazoning
the admonishing words of *Al-Nisā* (The Women), Surah 4, verse
171 (among others) around the inside of the Dome.

> So believe
> In Allah and His Messengers
> Say not 'Trinity': desist
> It will be better for you.
> For Allah is One God
> Glory be to Him:
> Far Exalted is He above
> Having a son.

Herod ruled the southern part of Judea from his capital of
Jerusalem on behalf of Rome until 4 BCE. He undertook the reconstruction of the city, including most importantly the great project
that today constitutes the 10-hectare platform on which the Haram
sits, originally the site of a form of Jewish temple. But Herod, whose
father was a non-Jewish Idumean and whose mother was a pagan
Arabian princess, corrupted pure Jewish values, and he also built
pagan temples, including one to the 'god' Augustus Caesar, Herod's
last patron. Only well after Herod's death was the temple project
completed and finally adopted as fully Jewish, a mere ten or so years
before the temple was then destroyed by the Romans. There is no
evidence of any kind to define what was on the site before Herod's
work began, certainly nothing has been found to substantiate the
Jewish claim that the rebuilt Second Temple preceded Herod's
temple in the same location. The Jewish Western Wall, or Wailing
Wall, is only from this period therefore, and no earlier.

After the two Jewish uprisings against Rome, and devastation of
70 and 135 CE that followed, no Jews were left in Jerusalem, and the
forced converts to Judaism from Hasmon rule soon resumed their
pagan ways. Rome then converted from paganism to Christianity
in 324, together with some Palestinian natives, and Jerusalem

quickly became a very Christian city, then a part of the Byzantine Empire, the inheritors of Rome in the eastern Mediterranean. Churches were built, most famously the Church of the Holy Sepulchre, and the city filled up with monks and nuns.

With the defeat of the Byzantines by the Muslims in 636, the Palestinians step forward from the shadows of history to become Arabized, mostly converted to Islam, and subjects of the caliphate. Muslim rule of Palestine was to last for the next thirteen centuries, significantly interrupted only by the bloody episode of the Crusades, and ending with the defeat of Turkey by the British in 1918, precipitating the end of the Ottoman Empire. During these Islamic centuries, while the practice of Judaism and Christianity continued, Jerusalem became an important centre for Sufi study, a seat of Shariah jurisprudence and was famous for specialized crafts such as bookbinding.

The most visible legacy of the Islamic centuries, after the glowing presence of the Haram, is the fortified wall that surrounds the Old City, built by the Ottoman Sultan, Süleyman the Magnificent between 1536 and 1540. A truly remarkable, although perilous, walk can be taken (when the Israeli Defence Forces permit) along the top of the ramparts around three sides of the city from the Stork Tower to the Dung Gate.

'Umar ibn al-Khattab, the second caliph of Islam, entered Jerusalem probably early in 638, five years after the death of Muhammad and two years after the battle of Yarmuk, with the proclamation: 'You are guaranteed your life, your goods and your churches, which will be neither occupied nor destroyed, as long as you do not do anything blameworthy.' Full freedom of worship was declared, there was no bloodshed, and even the monks and nuns could stay. According to Muslim tradition 'Umar was then taken to Herod's platform where he recognized the place as that described to him by Muhammad as the destination of the *Isrā*, and the site of the *Mi'rāj*. There was no building to be seen, neither pagan Roman, nor Herodian, and 'Umar and his men set about clearing dung and rubbish from the site. A rudimentary wooden mosque was built, incorporating the rock outcropping at one end.

Over fifty years later the Umayyad dynasty set out to give physical form to the Muslim attachment to Jerusalem with the

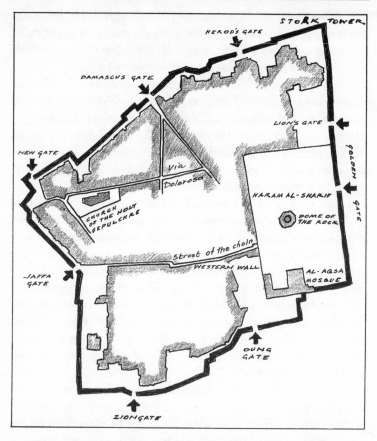

Map of the Old City of Jerusalem, The Haram, Western Wall and the Church of the Holy Sepulchre

construction of the Dome of the Rock and al-Aqsa Mosque. Although the true motivation for the extravagant attention given to Jerusalem by the Umayyads may have been to undermine the prominence of Mecca and Medina during the time of the schismatic caliphate based in the Hijaz, following the murder of the Imams 'Ali and al-Husayn. From a distance, the great golden cupola of the Dome, seen against the grey and white stone of the packed buildings and multiple steeples behind, gives the city an aura of transfigured sanctity, as if rising above the minutiae of dogma and politics. But this is a tragic illusion.

The Dome is the oldest example of Islamic architecture, and consists of a support cylinder, then the dome above, set on an octagonal ambulatory, the prototype of the Ottoman domed mosque. The external fabric has been extensively refurbished over the centuries with great dedication to craft, so that now the finishes on both interior and exterior are blindingly rich and complex. The golden cladding of the Dome, although the most famous element of the mosque, is only recent, dating from the 1920s and paid for by public subscription from Muslims all over the world.

Al-Aqsa Mosque is a lesser structure, although, unlike the Dome, it serves as a functioning mosque for the remains of the Palestinian community of the Old City. The mosque was built shortly after the Dome, but was twice destroyed by earthquakes within the first sixty years, as well as on a number of occasions subsequently, then the building was partly burned by a deranged Australian tourist in 1969. The present building is unremarkable, therefore, notable only for the marble columns donated by Benito Mussolini in the 1930s and for the elaborately painted ceiling commissioned by King Farouk of Egypt.

The Mysterious Ending of al-Hākim bi-amr Allāh

Muslim rule of Jerusalem was not without episodes of violence. The most turbulent period began with the coming to power in Egypt of the Fatimid caliph al-Hākim (996–1021 CE). At the age of fifteen al-Hākim had his regent assassinated and began his rule as an absolute despot, following only his mood of the moment. He embraced Shiʿa fanaticism and instigated severe repression of Christians and Jews, both wealthy minority communities. He ordered the destruction of churches, convents, monasteries and synagogues, wine and beer were prohibited to all, shoes for women were banned, jewellery was outlawed, as were singing girls, raisins, honey, rocket salad, lupines, barking dogs, chess and walking at

night. Government officials were frequently executed or publicly muti-
lated for no apparent reason, so that the entire population lived in uncertainty and fear.

Near the end of his reign al-Hākim allowed himself to be persuaded
by Shiʿa Ismāʿili extremists that he was the reincarnation of the Divinity.
He no longer washed or changed his clothes and wandered alone for
days in the hills outside the city. During one of these absences al-Hākim
simply disappeared. The popular explanation on the Cairo street was that
he had been assassinated by his libertine sister who feared for her life,
or according to another rumour, al-Hākim had entered a monastery
under an alias, where he ended his days.

But al-Hākim's extraordinary rule is more than a footnote to history.
A saintly or even divine interpretation of the life of al-Hākim led to the
formation of the Duruz or Druze sect within Shiʿa Islam. As part of his
final delusions, al-Hākim permitted a supporter, Hamza ibn ʿAli, to elevate
his status beyond that of imam to the level of the One, a higher degree
than even the Prophet. After al-Hākim's disappearance, the Druze
(named after Muhammad ibn Ismāʿil al-Darazi, the first Druze sheikh)
became a separate religion from both Shiʿism and Sunni, based on
the projected return of al-Hākim as the messiah. After Hamza himself
withdrew, in order he claimed, to return with al-Hākim, the preparation
for al-Hākim's return was adopted as the religious rationale for a
series of rebellions against the caliphate. Over many subsequent generations a Druze orthodoxy evolved, and the rebels of Syria became an
entrenched community in the mountainous back country of the
Lebanon. The Druze remain an aggressive force in modern Syrian and
Lebanese politics.

The Roman Emperor Constantine, in addition to his conversion of
the Empire to Christianity, also restored Christian unity with the Council
of Nicea (modern Nice) in 325, ending a series of schisms over the nature
of God and the Trinity. The most substantial of the works commissioned
by Constantine was a church to mark the reputed but disputed place of
Christ's burial. In 1009 the richness of the Church of the Holy Sepulchre,
by then almost 700 years old and the object of centuries of pilgrimage
and donation, came to the caliph's attention. Al-Hākim was infuriated by
reports that the Christian priests of the Holy Sepulchre were claiming
superiority for their religion by appearing to bring 'Holy Fire' down on to
the altar of the church during an annual rite named the Saturday of the

Light, commemorating the removal of Christ's body from the Cross. The trick, a blasphemous outrage in the Muslim view, was achieved by igniting balsam oil with oil of jasmine to produce an astonishingly bright combustion from a suspended lamp controlled by a pulley, giving the effect of a miraculous white presence descending from heaven. Orders were issued from Cairo for the demolition of the structure, which was quickly accomplished stone by stone. Centuries of Muslim tolerance in the city had been fatally undone in just a few months.

Under al-Hākim's successors, the Church of the Holy Sepulchre was rebuilt by the Jerusalem Christian community, a disappointing structure compared with the original church built by Constantine. But even though the new construction was complete more than forty years before Jerusalem fell to the Franks of the First Crusade, with such disastrous results for all sides, al-Hākim's actions had lit a fatal fuse. 'An accursed race', Pope Urban II declared in 1095 in his announcement of the First Crusade, 'has destroyed the Church of God'.

The tradition of the Prophet's *Isrā* and his *Mi'rāj*, that lies at the heart of Muslim Jerusalem, is little known or appreciated in the West. But the underlying message is undeniably pluralistic: during his mythical travels Muhammad meets and takes advice from a number of acknowledged Judeo-Christian prophets, and Muhammad clearly yearns to bring Muslims into the heart of mainstream monotheism from the isolation of pagan Arabia. The story already related on page 52, is a fixture in Muslim culture, resulting in a deeply felt connection to physical Jerusalem. The *Isrā* and the *Mi'rāj* were the proof given by Saladin, for example, in a letter to Richard Coeur de Lion of Muslim ownership of the city.

As an example of the extent to which Islamic tradition has embellished the story of the *Isrā* and the *Mi'rāj*, the Appendix to this chapter reproduces a version of the tale from *The Life of Muhammad* by Emile Dermenghem, which in turn draws on a number of original and little-known sources.

Jerusalem also remained in the forefront of the consciousness of diaspora Jews during their almost total absence from the city for two thousand years following the Roman destruction. And in the ultra-orthodox view, the coming of the Messiah and the end of the world will be hastened by the construction of a Third Temple on the site of the alleged previous temples, now occupied by the Haram. This literalist belief in the Second Coming, linked to the construction of the Third Temple, is also shared by many American fundamentalist Christian Zionists, located principally in the South and the Midwest of the US, and forming a substantial pro-Israel lobby exercising great influence in the Republican Party.

The Haram and the Western Wall were captured by Israel by armed force during the 1967 Arab–Israeli war, and added to the parts of the Old City already captured in 1948 (described by Israel as the 'unification' of Jerusalem). Ever since, every effort has been made by Israel to de-Arabize and Judaize Jerusalem, and to persuade the world to recognize the city as the capital of the Jewish state, rather than Tel Aviv, the first capital of Israel. A number of small Jerusalem mosques have been destroyed by Israel since 1967, without any serious local or international repercussions, but the connection of the Prophet himself to the Dome of the Rock has (so far) made the Haram untouchable by Israel, despite severe and unrelenting pressure on the Israeli government from the ultra-orthodox messianic right, intent on building the Third Temple. This observer has been warned many times, that should the Dome of the Rock be touched by Israel, global Muslim anger would rise to a level that would threaten world order. 'Every Arab would be ready for martyrdom.'

This contention over the title deeds to Jerusalem can be summarized as three sets of unanswerable questions:

1. The claim by each of the three religions to a divine connection with Jerusalem is based on belief only. There is nothing tangible in the city to authenticate the story of Abraham, the First or the Second Jewish Temple, the execution of Jesus Christ or the Night Journey and the Ascension of the Prophet. Thus the three sites, the Western Wall, the Church of the Holy Sepulchre and the Haram, which mark these alleged events, are physical incarnations of faith, not of provable fact. Can faith alone create title to territory? And if so, which one of the three contenders should prevail?

2. If the answer to the preceding questions is a logical 'no', then Israel's present occupation of Jerusalem is based on nothing more than conquest by force of arms in 1948 and again in 1967. But is not the Palestinian, or the Muslim, claim to possession of Jerusalem also based on armed force, in the form of the defeat by the Caliph 'Umar of the Byzantine Empire? Do not the Israeli victories of 1948 and 1967 (and the prior facilitating British victory of 1918) merely reverse the earlier Muslim military victory? Should not Muslims accept defeat, therefore, just as they previously accepted victory? The differences, however, between the events of 636 and 1948/1967, between 'Umar's possession of the city and the arrival of the Israeli Defence Forces at the gates of the Haram, are significant. First, the Muslims opened, or 'liberated', rather than conquered Jerusalem in 636, in that the native Palestinian population was thereafter no longer under the rule of European Byzantine Christians, but under the Arab Caliphs and the Shariah. No population transfers were precipitated, and all three faiths were still free to worship in their Jerusalem shrines, and live their lives as they pleased. The arrival of Israel in 1948 and 1967, on the other hand, represented occupation by force by an essentially Western power and by a religion with a long history of hostility and intolerance. Muslim property was confiscated wholesale by the State of Israel, Muslim houses were immediately demolished to make way for the plaza that now faces the Western Wall, and more than half of the Palestinian population of Jerusalem became permanent refugees. If, therefore, Israel's possession of Jerusalem is permitted to stand, how is this different from such recent precedents as Kuwait, the Falkland Islands, Kosovo and East Timor, where world opinion and righteous arms reversed unjust occupations?

3. This characterization of Israeli behaviour as 'occupation' might be seen in a different light, however, if Hebrew and Jewish history could be said to confer aboriginal title on Israel, as the country's constitution claims, by referring to 'ancestral lands', the right to 'reconstitute a National Home' and 'the redemption of Israel'. This would mean that the present spectacle is really nothing more than cousins fighting over a common heritage, rather than a colonial power occupying conquered lands after subjugating a native people. Even

the extremist revisions of Palestinian history recognize some common Semitic ancestry with Jews, and in modern terminology the Jews who resisted Rome were freedom fighters and the Romans were colonists. Certainly a classic historic injustice was done by the Romans to the Jews upon their defeat, with hundreds of settlements razed according to the historian Dio Cassius, and over half a million Jews killed. But like faith, does ancient history create title? Should the events from 1,900 years ago allow, in the present, a man from Russia, Ethiopia or the United States, who claims a Jewish mother and thus qualifies for immediate Israeli citizenship, to dispossess indigenous Palestinians from their houses and farms by force of arms, when those who in fact committed the original offence, the Romans, are long gone? And are those who resist such forcible displacement on this occasion freedom fighters or terrorists? Certainly the leaders of the revolt against Rome are celebrated as heroes in modern Israel. And even Israel does not claim that Jews were the sole indigenous inhabitants of Palestine, or that the Palestinians (as Canaanites and Philistines) were the ones who invaded from Sinai and appropriated their Jewish lands.

V Ten Treasures of Islam

Beyond the three harams, Islam has created a vast architectural heritage, to which this guide cannot begin to do justice. However, many great Muslim sites are effectively inaccessible to most tourists, being either too remote, as in the case of Samarkand or Bukhara, or behind a political barrier or in a war zone, as in the case of Herāt, Samarra or Baghdad. As a compromise, therefore, ten treasures of Islam have been selected, that encompass a substantial part of the geographical stretch of Islamic history, but are accessible at the present

1. **The Great Mosque of Damascus**, Syria. Built by the Umayyad Caliph al-Walid I from 706 to 715. On completion, this breathtaking structure was understandably regarded by Arabs as one of the wonders of the world. The transept, dome and aisles reflect church architecture of the late Byzantine period, and much of the workmanship was undertaken by craftsmen sent to work in Damascus by the Byzantine Roman Emperor. The mosque replaced the basilica of St John the

Baptist, shared for decades between Islam and Christianity, and the mosque still reputedly encompasses the tomb containing St John's head. The earlier Christian church incorporated walls from a Roman temple to Jupiter, which were then integrated into the mosque. The floor and walls of the courtyard were once decorated with over 44,000 square feet (4,000 square metres) of gold mosaic, depicting the entire Islamic world of the period set in a paradise of lush vegetation. Most of the mosaic was destroyed in the fire of 1893.

2. **The Mosque of ibn Tulun**, Cairo, Egypt. Built between 876 and 879 by the ʿAbbāsid governor of Egypt, Ahmad ibn Tulun (835–84) who began in the Caliph's service as a slave. The mosque reflects the design of the great courtyard mosque in Samarra (Iraq), the ʿAbbāsid capital during the period, and has, therefore, been interpreted as a deliberate symbol of ʿAbbāsid rule over Egypt. However, contemporary historians record that the concept of the mosque came to ibn Tulun in a dream, and that no political message was intended. There are, however, clear indications that Samarra influenced the design. Brick piers rendered with stucco in the Mesopotamian style support the roof of the prayer hall and the surrounding cloister, in place of the stone columns traditionally used by Egyptian builders, and many of the carvings follow earlier motifs from Samarra. But the Samarra mosque, now in ruins, is not only of substantially different proportions to the mosque of ibn Tulun, but also has a quite different atmosphere. Samarra is bare yet triumphal, the walls supported by a pattern of obese brick towers, with overtones of fortification. The mosque of ibn Tulun, on the other hand, is serene, a remarkable expression of the infinite in built form, making subtly powerful use of light and shadow, and contrasting with the chaos of the surrounding city. The building has recently been extensively renovated, without any reduction in architectural impact.

3. **The Great Mosque (La Mezquita)**, Cordoba, Spain. La Mezquita, on the other hand, was a definite political statement, the centre of Muslim Cordoba, which by the tenth century CE was the largest city in western Islam, and many times the size of the modern town. The mosque was built in 786 by Abd al-Rahmān I, founder of the Spanish Umayyad dynasty, in place of the church of San Vincente in the south of the city, which until then was shared by

both Muslims and Christians. The Alcázar, the centre of Umayyad government, was built alongside the new mosque, symbolically fusing mosque and state in the Shariah tradition. Every subsequent ruler of Muslim Spain claiming descent from Abd al-Rahman I added to the structure, showing special respect for his memory. The pernicious piercing of the mosque by a Christian cathedral, which took 300 years to complete, has already been discussed (page 149). But in an alternative interpretation of the effect of this addition, the presence of a Christian shrine may have saved the Muslim structure from neglect and decay after Cordoba reverted to Christianity, to be followed later by the expulsion of the Moors from Spain and then by the bigoted days of the Inquisition. The *qibla* end of the courtyard is covered with a series of saddle roofs creating rows of two-storey arcades, giving a luminous, weightless feel to the prayer hall, a physical opening on to the infinite. Of great interest are the support columns, recycled from Roman and Visigoth periods, mostly mismatched as to capitals and circumference, and buried at various depths into the floor to provide a uniform spring point for the rows of brick and stone arches that are the dominant feature of the interior design. Ironically, following the history of Muslim tolerance in Spain, and the sharing of churches and mosques, La Mezquita today is heavily patrolled by armed guards, not against 'terrorism', but to prevent any attempt at Muslim-style prayers, for which offence the perpetrator is immediately put back on his feet and arrested.

4. **Sultan Hasan Mosque**, Cairo. This great building is the classical example of a *madrasah* mosque, built to accommodate students from the four schools of *fiqh*. Each school was housed in a separate wing facing on to a large main courtyard dominated by an elaborate and still original ablution fountain. The instruction areas are vaulted enclosures 130 feet high (40 metres) open to the front, with living accommodation behind and above. A prayer hall of immense proportions completes the facility. Following the Mongol destruction of Baghdad in 1258, Cairo had become the world centre for Muslim studies, and from this *madrasah* students dispersed throughout Islam bearing their knowledge of the Qur'ān, the Hadith and the Shariah. Completed in 1363 CE by the Mameluk rulers of Egypt, keen to overcome their lowly slave origins, the structure is as

brilliant a feat of architecture as the European Gothic cathedrals from the same era, combining the built environment with the ever-blue open sky to create a glimpse of infinity. The mosque is almost deserted except on Fridays, so that the visitor can sit uninterrupted and sense the peaceful power of the place. Even the jostle of Cairo traffic fails to penetrate the tranquillity.

5. **The Dome of the Rock** and **al-Aqsa Mosque**, in Jerusalem have been described earlier in this chapter. Of great interest to the traveller in Dar al-Islam is that this site may be visited and the mosques entered, despite the status of haram, when the other two harams in Mecca and Medina are strictly forbidden to non-Muslims. The Jerusalem Haram is closely guarded by the Israeli Defence Forces, and subject to capricious decisions about who can and who cannot enter. Muslims, other than young men, are usually allowed access, so that wearing a Palestinian scarf and clutching a Qur'ān will usually result in permission at the door, even if accompanied, in the case of a white visitor, by a sceptical look and a body search.

6. **Kutubiya Mosque**, Marrakesh, Morocco. This is the outstanding work of the Almohad dynasty, rulers of Morocco together with parts of Islamic Spain and what is now Algeria and Tunisia from 1130 to 1269 CE. The administrative and spiritual capital of the empire was Marrakesh, and the Kutubiya Mosque, built in 1158, was the principal mosque of the city, replacing an earlier mosque built on the same site in 1147, but which was razed when the Sultan discovered that the orientation of the *qibla* towards Mecca was incorrect (by only 10 degrees or less). The Almohads were Berber Muslim purists, prohibiting all architectural decoration other than geometric. The stark arresting design that resulted, relieved only by rows of multifoil arches, makes sensational use of the bright light and open skies of the city. The 220 ft (67.5 metre) square minaret of the mosque, topped with intricately intersecting arches and a smaller 'lantern' tower, defines the skyline of Marrakesh. The Almohads were driven from Spain by the Christians in 1212, but left behind a second great mosque and minaret in Seville, known as the Giralda.

7. **The Alhambra**, Granada, Spain. This great fortified city up on the spine of a hill overlooking the city of Granada, backed by the

snow-covered Sierra Nevada beyond, is the culmination of Islamic architecture in Spain. The excitement of seeing the walls and towers from the highway, appearing above the deep green Mediterranean trees is more than fulfilled walking through the Puerta de la Justicia. The wonders of the interior demand at least two full days of appreciation: the Palacio de Comares and the Torre de la Cautiva built by Yusuf (1333–54 CE) from the Nasarid family responsible for the completion of the complex after more than 300 years of construction from the eleventh century on; the Palacio de los Leones, a masterpiece of Islamic decoration and culture; the military garrison, the Alcazaba, looking down on Granada from the battlements; the Palace of Charles V, from the height of the European Renaissance after Spain was lost to the Muslims during the fifteenth century. The Spanish government operates a *parador* in one of the buildings in the centre of the fortress, where even one summer night spent after the departure of the tourists, and one dawn, can give the traveller some dim idea of the achievement and splendour that was once Muslim Spain.

8. **Taj Mahal**, Agra, India. 'the honour of the terrestrial world . . . in a garden bearing the works of Paradise . . .' The story of this mausoleum is well known: the great love of the Mughal Shah Jahan for his wife Mumtaz Mahal, who died delivering her fourteenth child, and the Shah's overwhelming sorrow, so strong that his hair turned white in three days. Followed by the arrival of Mahal's body in Agra and the Shah's resolve to build a version of paradise on earth for his beloved. The result, eleven years later (built 1632–43 CE) was the Taj Mahal, drawing on the substantial wealth and sophistication of the Mughal Empire, which covered a larger area than modern India and ruled hundreds of millions of people. The complex originally consisted of tombs for Mahal and Jahan, a mosque, subsidiary tombs intended for the Shah's other wives, a guesthouse, the famous garden and pool, the four equally famous minarets. Then outside the walls a *waqf* estate consisted of bazaars and caravanserais as well as thirty villages to pay rents to cover the cost of the maintenance, services, charities and recitings of the Qur'ān ordered by the Shah in perpetuity in the mosque (but long since discontinued). The inlaid stone that covers the building is also familiar, but less well known are the

plant designs that decorate the interior walls, and the calligraphy of extensive excerpts from the Qur'ān woven everywhere into the decoration. The monument became a shrine to femininity over the following years and a Mughal dynastic sanctuary until the end of the Empire. The last Mughal emperor was captured by the British in the gardens in 1857 and taken to Rangoon where he died in captivity. Today the Taj Mahal is threatened by tourist exploitation, surrounding development and pollution, as well as a low level of interest from the Indian state against the background of continuing Hindu–Muslim tensions.

9. **Shah Mosque**, Isfahan, Iran (now renamed the Imam Mosque by the Iranian Revolutionary government). Isfahan under the sixteenth and seventeenth century Safavid Shahs was one of the largest cities in the world and the principal trading hub between the East and Europe. Shah Abbas I (1587–1620), in addition to consolidating Shi'a as the national religion of the Persian Empire, undertook vast urban renewal works in Isfahan, which included the construction of a maidan, or central city square larger than Tiananmen Square in Beijing. The largest building in the project, the mosque, is centred on the back line of the square, then turns internally by 45 degrees so that the *qibla* faces Mecca. This monumental mosque, built between 1611 and 1630, was intended as the centre of the city. A great *iwan*, or portico, leads in from the square flanked by two minarets, then to a second portico entrance with matching minarets behind, and on into the domed prayer hall, flanked by smaller chambers for winter prayer and *madrasahs*. The decoration of the building is transcendent, entirely executed in mosaic and tile using a full colour range, but with blue predominant. The designs include vases, vines, prayer mats and extensive stylized excerpts from the Qur'ān. The tiles at the back of the prayer hall appear to suffer in quality, possibly because the building was completed after the death of Abbas, and because many tiles were replaced during the 1930s. Isfahan declined after the siege and capture of the city by the Afghans in 1722, then trade collapsed with the introduction of ship transport between China and Europe. The city and the mosque were extensively renovated by Shah Pahlavi Reza in the twentieth century, and Isfahan was recently designated by the United Nations as a

World Heritage Site. The city is very cold in the winter (with little heating) and very hot in the summer, and visits require extensive planning and visa negotiations.

10. **Bad Shāhi Mosque**, Lahore, Pakistan. This huge building is regarded as the finest (and last) of the Mughal works. Constructed between 1672 and 1674, the completion coincided with the start of the decline of the Empire, marked by the abandonment of more distant provinces in a time of financial over-extension, leading a century later to the evolution of Lahore into the capital of Sikhism. The building is a courtyard mosque in red sandstone, entered through domed portals in contrasting marble and approached by three-sided monumental steps that seem to foreshadow the Victorian architecture of the British Raj. The interior decoration of the cusped arches at the entries display semi-abstract floral designs of a quality equal to the Taj Mahal. The mosque holds 5,000 of the faithful, and is the largest mosque on the Indian subcontinent.

VI Thirty-five Famous Muslims

Culture also finds a strong human dimension in the people who characterize an age, by weakness or strength, for good or for evil. Westerners are familiar with the men and women who make up a picture of their own times and history. Churchill, Hitler and Stalin, most famously, stand at the heart of twentieth-century history, then Ronald Reagan, the Hollywood actor who became one of the most popular presidents in American history and presided over the end of communism; de Gaulle remains a symbol of Gallic intransigence and European reconstruction; Mozart, the billiards player who could carry a complete opera in his head, or Beethoven or Picasso the eternal modernist; and Newton, Darwin and Einstein, whose scientific discoveries precipitated the long decline of Christianity. But who are the equivalent names in Muslim culture? The men and women Muslims would describe with little hesitation as rooted in their consciousness?

Few of the names that follow will be familiar to Westerners, and others may not seem to be suitable icons. Many others not included here have already been mentioned in earlier chapters, such as Abu Bakr, 'Ali, and Nasser. But these entries were chosen by the many Muslims who were consulted in the preparation of this book (all Sunni except one Shi'a who chose Fatima). Some Muslims replied, of course, that only God can judge who is admirable and who is not. As al-Ghazāli wrote, 'never despise any human creature, for Allah has hidden sainthood among His bondsmen, and it may be that the person your eye scorns is one of His saints'. This is how the devout cleaner and humble bringer of tea at the American University in Cairo comes to appear on the list. On a practical level, these are also some of the well-known personalities that a traveller in a Muslim country will encounter, as street names, for example, or in conversation as heros celebrated in Muslim history for bravery, piety, vision, or even those who stand for the way Islam should not be.

Muhammad (Muhammad ibn 'Abd Allah 571–632) Messenger of Allah and so named by God. The last in a line of prophets stretching back to Adam and the Creation. His character and his religious and political achievements are set out in this book as in so many others.

'**Umar** ('Umar ibn al-Khattāb, d. 644). Second caliph from 634, following Muhammad and Abu Bakr. Father of Muhammad's wife, Hafsa. In a parallel with St Paul and the early Christians, 'Umar was a persecutor of Muhammad on behalf of the pagan Meccan clans, who then converted to Islam with great conviction, in self-revulsion after wounding his sister and her husband, who were believers. He was inspired by verses 1–7 of Surah 20, then recently revealed, which the couple had been attempting to conceal in their clothing.

'Umar became one of Muhammad's strongest supporters and as caliph he was responsible for the spread of Islam into Syria, Persia and Egypt, taking possession of Jerusalem personally with his famous ecumenical entry into the city in 638. He was taller than his followers and powerfully built, he had a passionate and impetuous nature, but the example of his predecessor, the shrewd and patient Abu Bakr, gave 'Umar the example he needed to combine statesmanship with personal leadership to such effect. 'Umar established the *diwān*, or Register of Muslims, the basis for both the distribution of wealth captured during the conquests, and for a definitive tribal genealogy reaching down to the modern day. 'Umar continued Abu Bakr's efforts to collect the elements of the Qur'ān into a coherent whole. 'Umar as caliph became ascetic and disciplined, he scourged his own son (who subsequently died of his wounds) for drinking wine and he attempted to impose order on his conquering armies. He was murdered by a deranged Persian slave.

Fatima. Daughter of Muhammad and his first wife Khadijah, wife of 'Ali ibn Abi Tālib, mother of al-Hasan and al-Husayn. The only child of Muhammad to establish a line of descendants. All his other children either died in infancy, or their first generation of descendants suffered the same end. Fatima became the object of veneration throughout the Muslim community due to her closeness to the principals of the early community and the events that shaped the subsequent history of Islam. References to Fatima in Islam are punctuated with the appellation al-Zahrā', the Shining One. Parallels have also been drawn earlier between the traditional veneration of Fatima, especially by the Shi'a, and the Virgin Mary. Fatima, like Mary, is the eternally bereaved and sorrowing mother (specifically for the death of her mother and father and the murder of both her husband and her second son), personifying the secret and forever unfulfilled wishes of womanhood, in contrast to the unceasing aggression and destructive nature of man.

Fatima was probably born five years before the start of Muhammad's ministry, the fourth of Khadijah's four daughters. She is said to have cleaned off the refuse, excrement and sheep's entrails thrown over Muhammad during the period of his rejection by the men of Mecca, and to have moved to Medina after the hijrah, suffering humiliation in Mecca before her departure. In Medina, both Abu Bakr and 'Umar asked Muhammad for Fatima's hand in marriage, but 'Ali was chosen as learned and wise, and the first to embrace Islam (although according to other sources, this honour goes to Abu Bakr, with 'Ali as the second). 'Ali and Fatima, like most of the Emigrants, were initially very poor, living in primitive conditions, until the first military successes. The marriage produced the two famous sons, al-Hasan and al-Husayn, two daughters and a third son, still-born. The marriage was famously rocky and

'Ali sought permission to take a second wife, but was refused by Muhammad who is reported as saying 'what offends Fatima, offends me also'. 'Ali in his frustration would follow arguments with his wife by lying on the ground outside their house, his clothes covered with dust. On one such occasion Muhammad brought 'Ali to his feet, brushed the dust from him, and teased him as Abu Turab, or the Dusty One. Fatima tended Muhammad's wounds after the battle of Uhud, and took to sorrowing in the cemetery of Medina for the Muslim dead. According to Shi'a legend, Fatima took a divinely ordered part in the Prophet's ministry, first as one of the five People of the House, or the family of the Prophet (Muhammad, 'Ali, Fatima, al-Hasan and al-Husayn) and secondly as a witness at the Mubahala, a contest to be held between Muhammad and the Christians of Najran to determine the primacy of either the new religion or the old. The contest was to have been preceded with a curse, 'May God curse over the one that is wrong . . .', which it was believed would destroy one or other of the communities. In the event the Christians capitulated before the contest, and the event was subsequently mysticized by Shi'a interpretation to make the People of the House into God's witnesses, confirming that the line of succession was to be from the 'Holy Family' only, the basis of the schism between Sunni and Shi'a.

Fatima was dominated by love of her father, and has come to be known as Umm Abiha, Mother of her Father (unsatisfactorily compared in popular devotions with the role of Mary as Mother of Christ). Her sole political act was to refuse to acknowledge the *shura* of Abu Bakr as the first caliph, chosen rather than 'Ali for whom she had campaigned. When approached by Abu Bakr asking for her *bay'a*, she refused and 'Umar threatened to burn her house. These events were to deepen the hatred by the proto-Shi'a for the first three caliphs, which was aggravated further by a subsequent dispute between Fatima and Abu Bakr over land owned by Muhammad, which Fatima claimed as her inheritance, but which Abu Bakr retained for the benefit of the entire community. Fatima died shortly after the Prophet in 11 AH and was buried in Medina, but the location has been lost.

The legends surrounding the life of Fatima are many, especially among the Shi'a. Angels assisted at her birth because no Meccans would help the wife of the hated Muhammad, the choice of ʿAli as her husband was announced by the angel Gabriel, the wedding was attended by 70,000 angels, and food was provided from heaven, she did not menstruate, lost no blood during birthing and produced her children through the left thigh (Mary produced hers through her right). Miracles are attributed to Fatima, and she is said to be the first to enter paradise after the Resurrection. Fatima is associated with light: she is a lamp that illuminates the heavens, or the horizon, or the light of God's creation falls upon her as upon all members of the Prophet's family.

ʿĀʾisha (ʿĀʾisha bint Abu Bakr 614–78). The third, and popularly believed to be the 'favourite' of Muhammad's wives. ʿĀʾisha became Muhammad's principal or 'managing' wife, deriving this position from a combination of her father's prominence in the Muslim community, her personality and her beauty. ʿĀʾisha's relationship to the Prophet has been touched on elsewhere, including her alleged infidelity and Muhammad's ensuing revelation, but she also played an important role in Muslim history after Muhammad's death.

ʿĀʾisha was born in Mecca, the daughter of Abu Bakr, and was married to Muhammad at the age of six, although the relationship was not consummated until ʿĀʾisha was at least ten. By agreement among Muhammad's wives, ʿĀʾisha nursed the Prophet during his final illness and he was buried in the floor of her simple single chamber. Muhammad's wives achieved great status during his lifetime, coming to be known as 'mothers of the believers', a title still in use today. The penalty, however, was that none was permitted to remarry, and on Muhammad's death, ʿĀʾisha was left a childless widow of eighteen.

During the rule of the first two caliphs, her father Abu Bakr for two years, and then ʿUmar, with whom she was on good terms for ten, ʿĀʾisha played no part in community politics. During the rule of ʿUthman, however, ʿĀʾisha sided with the opposition to the increasing domination of the Umayyads, although she was not a supporter of ʿAli, and did not condone ʿUthman's assassination. In Mecca she organized a small army to avenge ʿUthman's death and marched to Basra in Iraq, where ʿAli had established his headquarters (in Kufa), for the coming battle with the Umayyads under

Mu'āwiyah. 'Ali's forces engaged 'Ā'isha's party in what was to be known as the Battle of the Camel as the fiercest fighting took place around 'Ā'isha's litter. 'Ali prevailed, but treated 'Ā'isha with respect, although her commanders were killed. Thereafter she lived quietly in Medina, reconciled first with 'Ali, and then with Mu'āwiyah, after 'Ali's assassination. In her later years 'Ā'isha became noted for her learning, her ability to recite the Qur'ān, as well as a large selection of Arab poetry. Twelve hundred Hadiths were ascribed to her, but only 300 were retained by al-Bukhari as authentic. 'Ā'isha died during Ramadan 678, and even up to the last, her approval or disapproval was important to community leaders.

Jābir ibn Hayyān (Abu Musa 721–815) was known among the Christians of the Middle Ages as Geber, as a famous alchemist and practitioner of medicine. He was a student of the Shi'ite Imam Ja'far al-Sādiq, of the Shi'a imamite inheritance, from whom he learned the way of the Sufi. He first practised his craft under the Umayyads, and is reported to have collaborated with Khalid ibn Yazid ibn Mu'āwiyah who shared the same interest. After the end of Umayyad rule, Jābir ibn Hayyān was patronised by the 'Abbāsids who showed great interest in science and culture, and in particular by the Baramkid family promoted by the 'Abbāsids. Jābir ibn Hayyān made great contributions to the emerging sciences of chemistry, astronomy and philosophy, as part of the Islamic centuries of progress influenced by Greek texts, with the result passed back to Europe at the start of the Renaissance.

Hārun al-Rashid (Hārun bin Muhammad bin 'Abd Allāh, 786–809). The 'good' Hārun al-Rashid of the *Arabian Nights*, and fifth 'Abbāsid caliph. Many pivotal events in the history of Islam took place during al-Rashid's reign, which also marked the acceleration of the corruption and decline of the 'Abbāsid dynasty, and the start of the disintegration of the united caliphate that had begun with Abu Bakr and the 'rightly guided' caliphs. Al-Rashid became caliph in his early twenties, and his rule is famous for ceremony and splendour, elaborated and exaggerated by the tales told by Muslim merchants who were by then travelling all over the Levant, and as far as China. But in fact his authority was consistently challenged by uprisings in both Syria in the east (where much of the population still held Umayyad sympathies) and in the west in Ifriqiya, with frequent Kharijite and Alid rising in response to poor government administration and high taxation. New dynasties broke away from the caliphate in the Maghreb and along the North African coast in what is now Tunisia. At the same time, the Yemen was in rebellion for a decade.

Al-Rashid's fame as a caliph lies in his campaigns against the Byzantines to the north, which he led personally, achieving many battlefield victories. He is reputed to have established diplomatic contact with Charlemagne, whose subjects were permitted to undertake the Christian pilgrimage to Jerusalem. The result at the end of his reign, however, was that Dar al-Islam had made no progress against Dar al-Harb, and the borders remained unchanged. The disintegration of the caliphate was accelerated on al-Rashid's death by his decision to divide the Muslim lands between his two sons.

Al-Kindi (Abu Yusuf Ya'qub ibn Ishāq, 801–73), prominent Arab philosopher of the 'Abbāsid Caliphate. Al-Kindi was born in Kufah in Iraq where his father was an 'Abbāsid governor and descendant of the royal Yamanite Kindah tribe from southern Arabia. He was sent to Baghdad as a young man to complete his training, where his scholarship brought him to the attention of the 'Abbāsid caliph al-Ma'mun. The caliph founded an observatory and an extensive library in Baghdad, the House of Wisdom, the only major library to be established since the great library of the Ptolemies in Alexandria, which was burned during the later Roman Empire. Al-Kindi was appointed to the library as a young man, with responsibility for curating and translating the caliphate's collection of Greek manuscripts. He never left Baghdad, continuing with his studies and his writing while in and out of favour under successive caliphs. Al-Kindi was the 'Arab Philosopher' and the only pure blood Arab to achieve such status in the field. He wrote commentaries to translations of Aristotle and Plato, and developed his own theories in arithmetic, astronomy, optics, space and time, medicine and music. His most important work is *A Book on First Philosophy*, defending the development of philosophy and answering those who denigrated the subject. Al-Kindi is honoured in Islam for his theories of convergence between Greek philosophy and Islamic teaching, and for his formulation of a technical and philosophical vocabulary in Arabic

Abu Jaʿfar al-Tabari (839–923), Muslim polymath and historian of Persian origin from Tabaristān (now in northern Iran), who devoted his life to writing on law, medicine, poetry, history, grammar, ethics and mathematics. He was persecuted in Baghdad for attempting to establish a school of jurisprudence to challenge the Hanbalis and Shafiʾites. Al-Tabari's most famous work is the *History of the World*, reputedly consisting of the lost text of over one hundred original volumes. The work begins with the early prophets, covers the pre-Islamic rulers of Persia, followed by the life of Muhammad (including extensive commentary on the Qurʾānic verses relating to the subject) and ending with the Muslim era to the year 915 CE. Al-Tabari combined oral sources gathered during this extensive travels with earlier written histories, including a Persian translation of the Book of Kings from the Torah. The *History of the World* makes no attempt to join the sources together into a coherent narrative, but the multiple and often contradictory versions of the same events offer a rich view of the depths of Arab tradition. Much of the reconstruction of the history of the early period of Islam is based on material collected by al-Tabari.

ʿAbd al-Rahmān III (Al-Nasir li-Din Allah ʿAbd al-Rahmān, 889–961), the most famous caliph of Muslim Spain and the first caliph of a united al-Andalus. ʿAbd al-Rahmān III came to power at the age of twenty-three, and ruled for more than half a century, 912–61. He completed the pacification and unification of southern Spain by defeating rival Arab aristocrats and occupying their centres of local power. He consolidated the borders of al-Andalus with the Christians to the north, and he fought the Egyptian Fatimid dynasty for influence over the Maghreb. ʿAbd al-Rahmān turned Cordoba into a sophisticated Muslim metropolis, rivalling the great cities of Islam in the east and certainly far grander than any contemporary European city. The culture of Umayyad Spain has been touched on earlier, made possible by the peace and political unity established by ʿAbd al-Rahmān.

Abu 'l-Kāsim al-Firdawsi (932–1021), Persian poet from Tus, who lived a modest life on an inherited estate. Firdawsi was commissioned to set the Book of Kings from the Torah into verse, which led to his composition of *Shāhnāmah* (the Book of Kings, but an original work not to be confused with the Torah), an epic poem of sixty thousand lines covering the entire history of pre-Islamic Persia, including myths and legends, ending with the Arab conquest in the seventh century CE.

Avicenna (Abu 'Ali al-Husayn ibn 'Abd Allah ibn Sinā, known as Avicenna from the Hebrew Aven Sinā, 980–1037), the most influential of all Muslim philosophers, both on Islamic thought and on medieval Christian philosophy. An Ismā'ili from Bukhara (now in Uzbekistan), Avicenna had mastered all the sciences of his time and memorized the Qur'ān by the age of sixteen or seventeen. He practised medicine as well as serving in various court capacities and he concurrently compiled a universal encyclopedia of philosophy. His works on medicine were influential down to the seventeenth century. Avicenna attempted to resolve the problem of how the imperfect existential world could have derived from the Unity of God. He wrote extensively on psychology, following Aristotle by dividing man's nature into vegetative, animal and rational, and he analysed the phenomenon of prophethood in Islam, attempting to define the components of prophetic character. Avicenna died in jail during a dispute with his patron, the ruler of Isfahān in Persia.

Al-Sharif al-Idrisi, geographer of the twelfth century CE, thought to have been born in 1100. He worked in the court of Roger II, Norman King of Sicily, who drove the Muslims off the island but retained the services of Muslim scholars. Al-Idrisi produced the first known comprehensive work of descriptive geography, the *Book of Roger*, after his protector. How far al-Idrisi travelled is not clear, but he wrote with admiration of Rome as a place of 1,200 churches and 10,000 baths, and 'the palace of a prince called pope'.

Al-Ghazali (Abu-Hamid Muhammad bin Muhammad al-Tusi al-Ghazali, 1058–1111). In his early twenties, al-Ghazāli rejected the Sufi tradition of his native Tus (now in modern Iran) and became an absolute sceptic. He moved to Baghdad where he was recognized as an intellectual and teacher of canon law. But by the age of forty, 'God had restored to him his belief' and he returned to the way of the Sufi. Al-Ghazāli took up the life of the wandering dervish, leaving the pleasures of the city and his brilliant career behind. He replaced philosophy, which he found to be flawed and inadequate, with 'experience' and direct perception of the love of God. From this base al-Ghazāli preached reform of the rising rigidity of Islamic thought, the restoration of simple faith and the inclusion within Islam of all those who embraced the broad principles, rather than the outward acts of practice. Religious certainty could only be found through ecstatic experience, rather than through obsession with form or reason. In this al-Ghazāli built on the teaching of al-Shafi'i, and his devotion to intellectual and emotional freedom informed indirectly the works of Thomas Aquinas and Pascal.

Avenpace (Abu Bakr Muhammad bin Yahiā bin al-Sā'igh al-Tujibi al-Andalusi al-Saraqusti ibn Bajah, d. 1139), ranked as a philosopher by ibn Khaldun equal to Averroes in the West and Avicenna in the East. Also known for his poetry and popular songs, as well as for his works on mathematics, astronomy and botany. The details of his life are obscure, but he served as vizier to a succession of Muslim rulers in the principal towns of Muslim southern Spain. Avenpace (his Latinized name) was born in Saragossa and died in Fez in the Maghreb. Many of his works survive, however, a few in the original Arabic, some in Hebrew and Latin. His most famous work is *Tadbir al-Mutawahhid* (Rule of the Solitary), which describes the path by which the soul may unite with the Divine. The route is described in Neoplatonic terms of increasing abstraction from the physical world, until finally the Active Intellect is reached.

Ibn Tufayl (*c.*1110–86), philosopher of the Maghreb, but born in Spain, of whose family and education nothing is known. He served as adviser to a number of North African rulers, and promoted the career of Averroes. Ibn Tufayl's fame rests on his authorship of *Hayy ibn Yaqzān* (meaning 'the living son of the wakeful one', or Allah), a work of philosophical romantic fiction and probably the first novel ever written in Arabic. The plot of the book is based on the discovery of Arab Neoplatonic philosophy through the device of an intelligent man placed alone on an island from childhood. Through reason alone the narrator constructs the whole of the Muslim system of Greek-influenced philosophy for himself. The child narrator is fed by a fawn, which then ages, dies and decays, a process for which the author searches for meaning.

Saladin (Al-Malik al-Nassir Yusuf bin Ayyub Salāh al-Din, 1138–93). Born in Kurdish Tikrit (now in modern Iraq), Saladin was the son of a senior functionary of the ʿAbbāsid dynasty, but little is known of his youth. During the decline of the ʿAbbāsids, Saladin, a Sunni, emerged to overthrow the Fatimids, the Shiʿite Ismāʿili dynasty that ruled Egypt from Cairo. Saladin's eventual Ayyubid empire covered much of the modern Middle East, although nominally still under the caliph of Baghdad. Saladin is most famous among Muslims for his jihad against the Crusader occupation of Palestine. The combined Crusader armies were defeated at the battle of Hittin (1187) and subsequently expelled from Jerusalem. This reversal was responsible for the failure of the Third Crusade. But there were eight Crusades in all, and the Franks were not driven from the Arab lands until over a century after Hittin. The final defeat of the Franks was accomplished by the Mameluks, who also overthrew Saladin's Ayyubid empire. Saladin was deeply religious, at once compassionate and ruthless, but his personality has been obscured by later romanticization, including Western writings such as *Ivanhoe* by Sir Walter Scott.

Averroes (Abu ʿl-Walid Muhammad ibn Ahmad ibn Muhammad ibn Rushd 1126–98). Born in Cordoba, Averroes was the intellectual star of Umayyad Spain. After studying law and medicine he turned to philosophy when asked by the caliph whether the universe was eternal, or had a beginning. 'I was so overcome with terror,' Averroes recounted later, 'that I could not answer.' He wrote commentaries on Aristotle, and on Plato's *Republic*, as well as on works of Greek science, the body of work for which he is most famous. Although his own philosophical ideas are not considered to be original, his attempts to show that the Creation was a continuing force rather than a single event in the past, earned him the compliment of condemnation by both Muslim and Christian orthodoxy. Averroes also wrote extensively on the nature of the human soul, but decided finally that the answers to his questions could only be provided by revelation. He died in Marrakesh in the service of the Almohad caliph, after a period of banishment and persecution for his views. Averroes' rationalism influenced the Jewish scholar Maimonides as well as Thomas Aquinas.

Ibn ʿArabi (Abu Bakr Muhammad ibn ʿAli, Muhyi ʿl-Din al-Hatimi al-Taʾi al-Andalusi, 1165–1240), celebrated Sufi pantheist and mystic. Born in Spain he lived for over thirty years in Seville, but then made a visit to the East from which he did not return. He professed Muslim belief and practised Islam, but believed that man's 'inner light', with which he considered himself to be illuminated in a special way, was the sole guide to faith. He regarded all being as One and all religions as equal and in this was associated with the Qādiriyya Sufi order. Ibn ʿArabi claimed to have seen the beatified Muhammad and to have learned the final (and the 100th) Greatest Name of Allah. His views inevitably offended many, he was often denounced as a heretic, and in Egypt groups formed to carry out his assassination. Ibn ʿArabi wrote extensively, his most famous works were a complete system of mystic knowledge in 560 chapters and a series of poems addressed to a Meccan lady scholar with whom he fell in love.

Jalal al-Din Rumi (1207–73), the third and best known of the trio of Sufi masters of the twelfth and thirteenth centuries whose influence has spread throughout Islam, of whom ibn ʿArabi was the first and ibn al-Fārid the second. As a boy, Rumi fled with his father, also a Sufi mystic, before the Mongol invasion, to settle in Konya, now in central Turkey. Whereas ibn ʿArabi wrote with the fixed purpose of discovering definitive philosophical and logical responses, Rumi's journey was mystical and experimental, intended to lead to gnosis, or the direct intuition of God. Rumi's poetry, reportedly composed under the influence of mystical rapture and written down by his students, throbs with passion and life, reaching, according to the late Professor R. A. Nicholson, 'the utmost heights of which a poetry inspired by vision and rapture is capable, which alone would have made him the unchallenged laureate of mysticism'. A long lyric on the theme of sacred love, for example, begins:

> *I was all tears, I became all laughter*
> *I was dead, I became alive;*
> *The grace of love came*
> *And I became perpetual happiness.*

Rumi remains extraordinary popular today. Translations of his poetry by the American Coleman Bark have made Rumi one of the bestselling poets in the US for several years.

Ibn Taymiya (Taqiyy al-Din Ahmad ibn Taymiya, 1268–1328), a prominent activist in the line of Muslim reformers that stretches from Ahmad bin Hanbal in the ninth century CE to Muhammad 'Abduh who died in the twentieth century, and forward again to those advocating the renewal of Islamic principles today, from the sophisticated militant to the humblest marabout. Some in the historical line, like ibn Taymiya, were regarded as mujahid during their lifetimes, others have been revered as mujahid only in later generations.

The objective of ibn Taymiya's reform, or *islāh*, is to return to the principles of the Qur'ān and the Sunna as the immutable word of God and His Prophet, based on the famous verses:

> Let there arise out of you
> A band of people
> Inviting to all that is good
> Enjoining what is right
> And forbidding what is wrong:
> They are the ones
> To attain felicity.
>
> Ye are the best
> Of Peoples evolved
> For mankind
> Enjoining what is right
> Forbidding what is wrong
> And believing in Allah.
> If only the People of the Book

Had faith, it were best
For them: among them
Are some who have faith
But most of them
Are perverted transgressors.
        Al-Imrān (The Family of Imrān) Surah 3, verses 104 and 110

Salafiyya, of which ibn Taymiya is widely regarded as the origi-
nator, is a movement within *Islāh* taken from the expression *al-salaf
al-salih*, the 'pious forefathers' (discussed in Chapter 2). By *Salafiyya*
ibn Taymiya meant those who transmitted the core of the faith in
any generation, together with the ideals for living the virtuous life.
Salafiyya is a particular interpretation of the general *islāh* concept of
a return to first principles of Islam, as well as representing an
attempt at the reconciliation and agreement within Islam advocated
frequently by the Qur'ān.

Ibn Taymiya was born in Damascus to a family of refugees from
the Mongol invasion. He attained the status of expert in the Qur'ān
and the Hanbali jurisprudence by the age of twenty-one, when he
began teaching at the Umayyad Great Mosque. He sought to eliminate from Islam all innovations since the times of the 'pious ancestors', including the system of Hanbali jurisprudence in which he
had been educated, as well as the *fiqh* of the other three schools. Ibn
Taymiya considered that truth was to be found only in the text of
the Qur'ān and the Sunna, which could be applied directly to contemporary conditions by *ijtihād*. This view was an effective repudiation of the prevailing orthodoxy, which preferred to view the
original sources through the lens of accumulated precedent and
practice, with the result that ibn Taymiya suffered numerous periods
of incarceration in the jails of the regional rulers of Egypt and Syria
who followed the disintegration of the 'Abbāsid caliphate. He died
a prisoner in the Citadel in Damascus.

Ibn Taymiya emphasized obedience to God and His prophet, and
to those in authority, following the words of the Qur'ān, but he
regarded the proper exercise of power as a religious duty, requiring
the ruler to follow the will of God, through the Shariah as the laws
of God. The ruler enjoys validity therefore, only for so long as he is
the instrument for the Muslim community to implement God's

commandments. This concept, in particular, has provided substantial support to those opposed to corrupt Muslim regimes in the modern day, and was a notable factor in the assassination of Anwar Sadat, President of Egypt. Although mystical revelation was accepted as a valid path to religious knowledge, ibn Taymiya ferociously opposed all Sufi innovations, such as saints, elaborate memorials and intercession, as contrary to the absolute Oneness of God. The Mu'tazilites, the Shi'a, the Kharijites and Muslims influenced by Greek philosophy were also vilified as deviationist. He was the author of numerous religious works, many written in prison, and even the few that have survived are still influential in the twenty-first century.

Ibn Battuta (Shams al-Din Abu Abdullah ibn Abdullah al-Tanji, 1304–77), born and educated in Tangier, from the Berber tribe of Lawāta. Ibn Battuta graduated from the Māliki school of *fiqh* and could have followed his father who was a judge. But ibn Battuta immediately left Morocco, apparently intending to perform the haj. In Alexandria he began to dream of flying on a big bird towards Yemen, then east and south. As an ambitious traveller he had the portable skill of a trained Islamic judge, while his journeys fell during the exhausted peace following the Mongol invasions and withdrawal. After a long stay in Mecca, where he fell in love and performed the haj five times, he began his first epic journey, to the Yemen and across the Indian Ocean to what is now Kenya, through the Persian Gulf to the Crimea, to Afghanistan and finally to Delhi. A later journey took ibn Battuta to the Maldives, India once again, Bengal, Indonesia and China, returning to Morocco by way of Europe during the Black Death. He completed a further journey across the Sahara and back before recording his adventures in a book famous throughout Islam, *The Travels*. Along the way he was tempted by numerous distractions, from the Sufi life, to women. But ibn Battuta retained his faith and his restless spirit, and he developed a wide tolerance which shines through the text. The book was translated by the British Orientalist H. A. R. Gibb in the nineteenth century, and recently reissued in a much more readable and abridged version by Tim Mackintosh-Smith.

Ibn Battuta died in Marrakesh, and nothing is known of his career after his return.

Ibn Khaldun ('Abd al-Rahmān ibn Khaldun Waliyy al-Din, 1332–1406), North African judge, administrator, historian and adventurer. Ibn Khaldun held a number of senior administrative posts in the fractured sultanates of the Maghreb and Spain. He earned a reputation for treachery and manipulation and spent periods in jail, but he ended his career as a civil servant and statesman as Grand Qadi of the Malikite school in Cairo. He lost his entire family in a shipwreck soon after his last appointment and devoted the rest of his life to pious works and his writing. Ibn Khaldun's most famous book, *Muqaddimah*, deals with all branches of Arab sciences and literature, treating sociology as a science, but religion as a spiritual mystery beyond reason. *Muqaddimah* was the book of the age, and ibn Khaldun's judgement and depth of thought have ensured that the work remains one of the foundations of Islamic philosophy, inspiring eminent modern historians and analysts of Islam including Marshall Hodgson, Albert Hourani and Malise Ruthven.

Muhammad ibn 'Abd al-Wahhāb (1703–92), born in what is now Saudi Arabia, but for many years an itinerant teacher in Iraq and Persia. Abd al-Wahhāb was strongly influenced by the writings of ibn Taymiya, and like his mentor sought to reform Islam through the elimination of all innovation since the days of *al-salaf al-salih*. But Abd al-Wahhāb narrowed the meaning of the term to the Prophet, his Companions and their immediate heirs, and took the Prophet's seventh-century CE Medina Commonwealth as the best possible model for society achievable on earth. Axiomatically, no subsequent variations could represent an improvement. Similarly, the Hadith carrying the Sunna was to be followed in every detail (even though, as we have seen, many of the Hadith were fabricated). In this way, ibn Taymiya's relatively open-minded search for truth behind the current orthodoxy, through the re-examination of the original texts, became in the hands of Abd al-Wahhāb a new rigidity of terrifying intensity. Claiming to be the instigator of new thinking based on a return to the holy texts, Abd al-Wahhāb became instead a blinkered follower of the minutiae of a byegone era.

As with ibn Taymiya, the main targets of Abd al-Wahhāb's call for a 'return to God's law', were Sufi saints, the construction of elaborate mosques and tombs, all practices and traditions not specifically authorized by the Qur'ān and the Hadith, as well as such practices as smoking and the use of prayer beads. Abd al-Wahhāb's extreme puritanical views led to his expulsion from his native 'Uyayna oasis, to which he had returned from his wanderings to preach. He left with his family and made an alliance with Muhammad ibn Saud, who soon became ruler of the central Arabian Nafud. Under their arrangement, Abd al-Wahhāb would provide the religious motivation for al-Saud's political ambitions, and in return Abd al-Wahhāb would set religious policy for the conquered territories, which would become a 'theocratic state'.

Abd al-Wahhāb's fortunes now rose along with the House of al-Saud, and after his death at the age of eighty-nine, *Wahhabiyya*, or Wahhabism, grew to be the dominant religious force in the entire Arabian peninsula, and was subsequently exported to Afghanistan under the Taliban regime. The religious zeal of Wahhabism was the principal inspiration of the Saudi forces that eventually reunited Arabia after centuries of fracture. No prisoners were taken as the ferocious Wahhabist Brotherhood (or *Ikhwan*) consolidated power, massacring all opponents as deviants and infidels. Abd al-Wahhāb also emphasized the commendable Islamic principles of equality and cooperation, but even this positive aspect of the movement was quickly eroded by the development of privilege in Saudi Arabia based on pedigree of birth.

Al-Afghani (Jamal al-Din al-Afghani, 1839–97), one of the most influential Muslim activists of the nineteenth century, devoting his life to the renewal of Islam, and the ideal of replacing colonialism with a reunited Muslim empire, including both Sunni and Shi'a. Al-Afghani was a Persian Shi'ite, despite his name, but he concealed his origins in order to be able to advocate Islamic unity. He was cultured but ascetic, and well read in Muslim medieval philosophy. He taught and lectured widely, and was at the same time involved in resistance against foreign domination and domestic oppression in Afghanistan, India, Persia and Egypt. He preached wherever he went in an inflammatory style for a return to first Islamic principles. Al-Afghani was the inspiration for the modern regeneration of the *salafiyya* movement and for the Muslim Brotherhood, as well as the personal mentor of Muhammad 'Abduh, in the Sufi tradition of *pir* and *murid* (master and disciple). He ended his wide travels as the guest, then the virtual prisoner, of the Ottoman sultanate. He was charged with directing the assassination of the Shah of Persia in 1896, but died of cancer while awaiting extradition from Turkey. Al-Afghani's great concern was with Islam as an entire way of life, rather than with the detailed formulation of dogma. He wished to close the gates on the West and rebuild the crumbling edifice of Islam in a new and different way. He died disappointed by the internal divisions of Islam that prevented the realization of his vision. He is claimed as the intellectual source for many of the advocates of *salafiyya* today, but cerebrally he belongs to none of them.

Muhammad 'Abduh (1849–1905). 'Abduh gained a place at al-Azhar University, Cairo, although he was from a poor country background. He was an Egyptian modernist and reformer who attempted to prepare Islam for the advent of the modern world. 'Abduh drew a distinction between the essential doctrines of Islam (belief in God, the revelation of the Qur'ān as completing the prophetic cycle, moral responsibility and final judgement) and the social teachings of the faith, including the laws of the Shariah. But in contrast to the core beliefs, passed down by a line beginning with the Companions of the Prophet and thus immutable, 'Abduh regarded social morality and the Shariah as relating to particular circumstances and so open to change as circumstances changed. 'Abduh's movement follows in the *salafiyya* tradition therefore, but in this case the objective of the call for a return to the original immutable texts is to move forward not backward.

The essence of 'Abduh's intention for contemporary Islam was to meet the scientific and political challenge from the advancing West by modernizing, while at the same time adhering to the famous maxim of Malik ibn Anas, 'the later success of this (Muslim) Community will only ensue through those elements which made for their initial success'. Thus the original sources of the Qur'ān and the Sunna are to be applied through piety and trust to modern questions through *ijtihād*, or innovation, replacing *taqlid*, or the slavish imitation of past tradition and practice (into which the Wahhabist version of *salafiyya* had fallen, although claiming the contrary). 'Abduh's version of *salafiyya* became the inspiration for nationalist anti-colonial move-ments in Tunisia, Morocco and especially Algeria, placing emphasis on political rights, political action and education. The Muslim Brotherhood, operating principally in Egypt through to the present day, was a direct outgrowth of 'Abduh's version of *salafiyya*, and is what is generally meant today by *salafi*.

But 'Abduh would not have been encouraged by the modern *salafi* movement, since he ultimately embraced Western rule by returning to British Egypt after extensive travels, entering the legal profession, rising to become a judge and finally the Mufti of Egypt, an imperial appointment. His famous rulings, based on the Maliki school, allowed public interest to overrule the constraints of prece-dent, and he attempted to separate social progress from the practice of religion, the formula, he believed, that had allowed the West to progress. Lord Cromer, the British Consul General in Cairo, and the virtual ruler of the country went so far as to describe 'Abduh, in his memoirs, as an agnostic.

Muhammad Iqbal (1873–1938). Born in the Indian province of Punjab, now in Pakistan, Iqbal grew up during the period when Islam in British India was in decline. His life was dedicated to the restoration of the faith as both a spiritual and a temporal order. He studied philosophy at Cambridge University, received a doctorate from Heidelberg University where he was a student of Nietzsche, and was called to the London bar in 1908. On his return to India he was the first advocate of a separate state for Muslims, but he was not considered a threat to imperial order by the British and he was knighted for services to education. Iqbal's main legacy is poetry, written in the mystical Persian style, offering an explanation of human destiny that made him a cultural hero. Religion is presented as the only source of salvation and emancipation. Iqbal idealized the early Muslim community, in which he saw the realization of man's spiritual and worldly potential, with the perfection of the soul reflected in the excellence of social relations. The inner truth of Islam had, in this view, been hidden from subsequent generations by obscurantist religious interpretation and wayward rulers. Only by reconnecting with the root values of Islam, could the perfect society be recreated. Iqbal was, therefore drawn into the argument, that history is not a product of divine will, the general Muslim view, but rather lives and destinies could be directed by the individual. Iqbal used the language of Sufism, but avoided the traditions with his message that improvement could only be achieved by embracing the problems of the existential world, not by their rejection.

Iqbal is regarded as the intellectual father of Pakistan, but he did not live to witness the terrible birth of his nation, which was left to 'Ali Jinna, leader of the Muslim League. Iqbal did not believe that Pakistan would prosper under upper-class Westernized Muslims as inheritors of the British Raj, but at the very least the creation of the state offered the opportunity for social improvement through a 'return to the original purity of Islam'.

Sayyid Qutb (1906–66), Egyptian exponent of the 'just Islamic society' and principal influence on the Muslim Brothers, following the assassination of the founder Hasan al-Banna (1906–49). He preached that man could only be free when released from all forms of oppression, from colonialism to corruption, from human desires to the 'priesthood' (by which Qutb meant the religious establishment centred on al-Azhar University in Cairo), and subjected only to the laws of God, as expressed in the Qur'ān and the Sunna. Qutb's famous treatise *Signposts on the Path* (written in prison and contributing to his execution) is seen as the beginning of revolutionary Islamism. 'The Western Age is finished,' he wrote, 'only Islam offers hope for the world.' Qutb based his political mission on his core concepts of *jāhiliyyah* and *hakimiyya*, both adapted from Maududi (see below)and strengthened.

By *jāhiliyyah* Qutb meant the corruption of all aspects of Muslim life by decadent Western culture, creating a society as rotten as that destroyed by Muhammad in Mecca. But he advocated more than 'defending Islam', to embrace aggressive action in order to eliminate the cancer, just as Medina overcame Mecca. Qutb went so far as purposely to misinterpret the Qur'ān to justify individual action against injustice. Surah 5 *Al-Mā'idah* (The Repast) at verse 45 reads:

> And if any fail to judge
> By the light of what Allah

Hath revealed, they are
No better than wrongdoers.

Qutb interpreted the word 'judge' to read 'rule', giving apparent authority to declare the ruler *kafir*, or an unbeliever, so justifying violent means. In any event, the passage in context clearly refers to the standard of behaviour required of Jews and Christians.

By *hakimiyya* Qutb meant divine 'sovereignty on earth', which he believed would be achieved through the force for good in the Qur'ān. From this has developed the rejuvenating Qur'ānic concept by which a true Islamic state will be worked out when the opportunity arises by the committed professional classes of the modern age (rather than through traditionalist mullahs and sheikhs), using the core concepts of Islam in ways that have never before been attempted. This experiment could possibly begin immediately upon the outcome of a free vote in most Muslim countries, if such a referendum were ever to take place. *Hakimiyya* has become a militant slogan throughtout Islam for the opposition to the status quo, but does not answer the practical questions.

Qutb was nothing if not committed, and since he gave his life for his beliefs he has achieved the status of *shaheed* or martyr (especially as he was imprisoned twice, horribly tortured and humiliated, tried by a politically rigged court, and underwent a barbaric execution). Qutb moved from being a supporter of the revolution of Nasser to an opponent, and during a period of civil unrest in the mid-1960s he was arrested. His followers prepared for violence and martyrdom to achieve their version of social justice, but were held in check by a ruthless state of emergency which is still in force today. Later members of the Brotherhood were accused of directing the assassination of Egyptian President Anwar Sadat in 1981, although the actual perpetrators were not members. The Muslim Brotherhood was also responsible for an attempt to overthrow the dictatorial regime of Syrian President Hafiz al-Assad in 1981, which was put down with great loss of life.

Qutb was also an influential literary critic, and was the first to promote the works of Neguib Mahfouz, initiating the Egyptian literary revival of the 1940s and 1950s. Later Qutb rejected his literary work and claimed to wish that he had never made the effort.

Umm Kulthum (Dakhliyya Tamayya z-Zahira, 1904–75), the most treasured Arab musician of the twentieth century. Umm Kulthum's genius for interpretation of classic songs occupies a place in the hearts of Arabic speakers comparable to Western appreciation of Ella Fitzgerald (for her impeccable scats) combined with Kathleen Ferrier (for her lyrical renditions of traditional songs). Daughter of a village imam and *mukri* in rural Egypt, she began performing as a young Qur'ān reciter, dressed as a boy. But the unusual timbre of her singing voice and the force of her interpretations freed her from traditional social restrictions, propelling her to national prominence shortly after moving to Cairo. Umm Kalthum usually sang with a large orchestra skilfully conducted to accompany her famously spontaneous improvisations on classic *qasā'id* literature that could extend a song for an hour or more before a rapt audience following every nuance. But she was also 'popular', able, like Sinatra or Pavarotti, to speak directly to the heart of the uninitiated listener through her monthly radio concerts and ultimately through motion picture musicals. Her career lasted over fifty years and her love songs and poetry recitals are still heard nightly on radio stations throughout the Arabic-speaking world. Umm Kulthum supported Nasser and the 1952 Egyptian coup, and she was largely responsible for maintaining Arab solidarity after the defeat of the Six Day War of 1967, with a tumultuous tour of the affected countries. The grief at her funeral in Cairo in 1975 exceeded the street emotion at Nasser's death five years earlier.

Sayyid Abu'l-Aʿla al-Maududi (1903–79), also known as Jamaat-e-Islamia, and founder of the Jamaat Islamia party in Pakistan which has been active since the inception of the state in 1947. The goal of the party is the conversion of Pakistan from a Muslim homeland to an Islamic state and the establishment of the Shariah as the sole law of the land. The Jamaat has an extensive network in Britain, based on the Islamic Mission and the Islamic Foundation in Leicester. The party is backed by Saudi Arabia and has links to Dawlatul-Islam, the Bangladeshi political party advocating the same policies.

Maududi's writings explain Islam as an entirely self-contained system of laws, beliefs and social practice requiring application rather than innovation or dilution by outside ideas, especially any influence from the corrupted West. For this reason Maududi is widely read by Sunni activists and he is one of the few non-Arab writers on Islam to be translated into Arabic.

Maududi's political career began with the ambition to convert the whole of India to Islam, and he only reluctantly accepted the establishment of Pakistan as a separate Muslim state. Like Iqbal he had little confidence in the rulers left behind by the Raj to advance the cause of Islam. Maududi was imprisoned for sectarian agitation (his death sentence was commuted) and the fortunes of the Jamaat only rose when harnessed by General Zia ul Haqq to gain support for his military rule. Since Maududi's death the Jamaat has become a minority party associated with factionalism and violence against the Shi'a minority.

Anwar Sadat (1918–81), President of Egypt from 1970. Born in a poor Delta village, Sadat became an army officer, commissioned at twenty. He opposed British rule and joined the Muslim Brotherhood, attempting various political assassinations and collaboration with the German forces in Africa under General Rommel. Sadat participated in Nasser's July Revolution of 1952 and was a member of the Revolutionary Command Council. On Nasser's death Sadat became President. He severed ties with Russia and moved the economy towards capitalism. Sadat was responsible for the attack on Israel in October 1973, which after initial Arab success ended with the Israeli forces only sixty miles from Cairo. Economic reforms after the war promoted by the West led to inflation, lowering of public morals and riots, with Egyptian troops firing on their own citizens. At the same time the cost of living rose sharply to the detriment of the poor and the advantage of the rich. After armed attacks on the government, Sadat attempted to appease the opposition by allowing Brotherhood exiles to return, and moderate Brotherhood programmes to develop.

By diplomacy Sadat reopened the Suez canal and recovered the Sinai peninsula captured by Israel, through an Egyptian–Israeli Peace Treaty and a spectacular but outrageous visit to Israel in 1977. The central Palestinian question was left unresolved, and Sadat was filmed praying in the al-Aqsa Mosque under Israeli guard, so implying Israeli sovereignty over the Haram. Sadat became increasingly dependent on America and out of touch with the worsening problems of ordinary Egyptians, surrounding himself with corrupt courtiers. He began to respond to political opposition by re-arresting Brotherhood members and by Nasserite torture, imprisonment and execution of dissidents, while at the same time attempting to present himself to the people as a village patriarch who understood the intricacies of crops and livestock. Sadat was assassinated while reviewing troops on the eighth anniversary of the 1973 'victory' over Israel. Sadat became a ridiculous figure, criticized for his meaningless titles, splendid uniforms and his attempts to bring quotes from the Qur'ān into his speeches, but in the decade after his death his reputation recovered and he is seen today as ending the oppressive Socialism of Nasserism.

Yassir Arafāt (Muhammad Abd al-Rauf Arafāt al-Qudwa), born to Palestinian parents in Egypt in 1929 and attended Cairo University after taking part in the 1948 Israel–Arab war. He was President of Palestinian Students' Union (1952–57), served in the Egyptian army and later founded Fatah in Kuwait and subsequently became Chairman of the Palestine Liberation Organization in 1969. He attempted to accommodate all points of view within the PLO, with the result that the PLO was unable to set a consistent policy and was constantly under attack from within by radical factions. Fatah was expelled from Jordan when operations against Israel began to destabilize the Jordanian state and Arafāt moved to Lebanon, taking over much of the south of the country, which he ran as a state within a state. When Israel invaded Lebanon, Arafāt and his supporters were cornered and evacuated to Tunis. From Tunisia Arafāt lost touch with ordinary Palestinians suffering under Israeli military occupation in the West Bank and Gaza. When he returned, as head of the Palestine Authority established by the Olso peace process as a stage towards Palestinian statehood, he was seen by his own people as largely irrelevant and corrupt, while the construction of Israeli settlements in occupied Palestine and the expropriation of Palestinian land continued.

The administration of the PA turned out to be as ineffective and as corrupt as the PLO, unable to bring the various elements in the Palestinian resistance together. The result has been the deterioration of relations with Israel, leading to the closure of Palestinian towns by the Israel Defence Forces, severe economic hardship, and frequent violent incursions by the IDF into Palestinian territory. At the beginning of 2002, with Arafāt virtually imprisoned in Ramallah and considered by Israel to be 'irrelevant', a 'terrorist' and a 'murderer', the solution to the impasse between Israel and the Palestinians seemed to be as far away as ever.

Arafāt died in Paris in 2004 and was buried in Ramallah with full honours. A moderate from the PLO, Mahmoud Abbas, was elected in his place. But within months the same canard reappeared. Abbas would only be a suitable 'partner for peace' with Israel and America if, under conditions of Israeli occupation, internal economic collapse, military balkanization and the continued expansion of Israeli settlements, Palestine first transformed itself into a functioning democratic state, disarmed and compliant.

Naguib Mahfouz (b. 1911), Cairo-based novelist and for many years employed by various Egyptian ministries. Author of over thirty novels and thirteen collections of short stories, the first published in 1939. His work is Arabic narrative of universal appeal, rich in nuance and flowing smoothly from realism to ambiguity and back. Many of the characters created by Mahfouz are expressions of the hopes and frustrations of Egyptians and Arabs generally, and appeal to a wide audience. The view of the world is generally gloomy, occasionally illuminated by minor advances towards the author's distant and probably unachievable utopia. The strongest characters have a sense of their own impalement by time and politics, while the villains are ambitious, shallow and usually successful.

Mahfouz is best known for *The Cairo Trilogy*, three novels almost filling the function of a social history of Egypt from the end of the First World War until the overthrow of King Farouk by Nasser in 1950. This achievement alone brings Mahfouz up to the stature of Dickens, Balzac or Tolstoy. Mahfouz was awarded the Nobel Prize for Literature in 1988, the first Arab to be honoured (although for a novel written thirty years earlier). In 1994 Mahfouz was stabbed in the neck by two Egyptian fanatics who accused him of blasphemy. Mahfouz survived, but his health has never fully recovered.

Mohammed ElBaradei (b. 1942), Director General of the International Atomic Energy Agency (the IAEA, a United Nations organization composed of 139 nations, reporting to the Security Council on nuclear arms proliferation and working to promote peaceful nuclear use). From a prominent Cairo family and son of a former president of the Egyptian Bar Association, ElBaradei rose from law school graduate of Cairo University to a specialist in international law with the United Nations. He began his third term as Director General in May 2005, despite US opposition due to Elbaradei's assertions early in the Iraq crisis of 2003, that, following IAEA inspections, no weapons of mass destruction were to be found in Iraq. ElBaradei has subsequently refused to condemn the alleged nuclear arms programme in Iran before proof of such activities has been found, and was thus able to maintain working relations with the Iranian government. Elbaradei is admired for his methodical and entirely fair 'non-aligned' approach to international difficulties, summarized by the following excerpt from his essay in the *New York Times* in February 2004: 'We must abandon the unworkable notion that it is morally reprehensible for some countries to pursue weapons of mass destruction, yet morally acceptable for others to rely on them for security.' For his fearless efforts Dr ElBaradei, together with the IAEA, was awarded the 2005 Nobel Peace Prize. Seen by many as a criticism of US policy, ElBaradei interpreted the rationale of the award as a message from the Nobel committee to 'keep doing what you are doing'.

Ahmad Zuweil (b. 1946), born and educated in Egypt, Zuweil earned his PhD at the University of Pennsylvania, and is at the time of writing Linus Pauling Chair Professor at the National Science Foundation Laboratory of Molecular Science at the California Institute of Technology, Pasadena, California, directing a team of 150 postgraduate researchers. Zuweil became known worldwide with his award of the Nobel Prize for Chemistry in 1999 for his work in the field of atomic research, 'making it possible to observe the movement of the individual atom in a femto-second (invented by Zuweil): a split second that is a millionth of a billionth of a second'. Zuweil lives in the US with his wife, a physician in public health, and his four children. He is the first scientist of Arab origin to win a Nobel Prize in the sciences. During the celebrations he said that he owed his determination to his mother, who placed a sign reading *Doctor Ahmad Zuweil* on his bedroom door when he was ten years old.

Shehta (Shehta Morsi Tolba, b. 1964), the eldest son of a farming family in the peasant village of Manzal Hayyān-Hihya in the Governate of Sharqiyya in northern Egypt, 100 km from Cairo. The family, consisting of his father and mother, brother, sister-in-law, Shehta and his wife, and a total of six children, live together in the family house on a farm of less than one acre. The farm has been in the family for generations and in the last decade has received electricity and improved irrigation, although the farm has never paid any taxes. Shehta's father works the farm which provides the family with food and some surplus to barter. Shehta received no education, helping his father from the age of eight until drafted into the army at the age of eighteen. Like his father, Shehta could neither read nor write until taught elementary Arabic by the army. On discharge, Shehta found a position at the University as a cleaner, and holds the same position twenty years later. He commutes to and from Cairo every week earning $100 per month, which, with his brother's small salary as a government worker, is the only income the family has.

Like his father, who attends the village mosque for every one of the five prayers every day, Shehta is innately devout. His first task in the University was to clean the ablutions in a dormitory for girls where he earned the girls' respect by his complete discretion and modesty. The future Queen Noor of Jordan attended the University and subsequently remembered Shehta on a visit to her old school by assisting his family with a small donation. Shehta is regarded by the Arabic Language Department where he now works as a paragon of honesty and trustworthiness.

Shehta chose his wife for himself, merely by sight, but sought the permission of her father before even talking to the young lady herself. They were married a year later and now have three small boys. Shehta and his brother work on the farm on Fridays and Saturdays so that the children are free to go to a new village school where they learn Arabic, English and Arithmetic. The eldest child has excelled by learning the first half of the Qur'ān by the age of eleven.

Two questions interested this observer after Shehta had related his life story.

'Have you consciously ever given in to Shayt'ān?'

'When I was engaged to my wife, I did not even sit next to her for one year.'

'What is your ambition for the future?'

'I would like my father to perform the haj, if God wills. And I would like my children to be taught at school.'

VII   Face to Face

Muslims are notoriously touchy about their faith, although a more sympathetic comment would be to say that Muslim beliefs are deeply held, and that this can have the effect of elevating some seemingly minor matters of protocol into important issues. The traveller in Muslim countries generally, and Arab countries in particular, needs to know how to avoid giving offence and how to establish a rapport based on respect for the religion and culture of Islam.

But behaviour varies widely between Muslim communities around the world, just as life in Marseille differs from life in Edinburgh even though both cities are European and nominally Christian. The factor common to all Muslim countries is that the religious dimension to everyday life is much stronger than the Christian equivalent. The key is to be aware of the difference between those observances derived from the Qur'ān and those that are little more than regional superstitions.

Dress code. Moderation is urged by the Qur'ān in all things. To regard Muslim attitudes to dress as 'sexist' or 'old-fashioned' is unproductive therefore, since the rationale for the code, if not for the minor details that vary from culture to culture, is ordained by God for the stability of the community. Sexual display and appetite are treated by Islam as similar to the appetite for food or drink: a basic instinct to be recognized frankly and enjoyed under the right circumstances. But sexuality is to be restrained in the interest of the higher attainments of which humans are capable: public order and personal dignity, for example. This contrasts sharply with Western values which usually put the freedom of the individual ahead of community standards, which are themselves often ill defined. But in all Muslim countries an unnecessary display of female flesh will be seen as offensive rather than liberated, while in some communities the reaction will be outright confrontation. What may be normal around a swimming pool at an American hotel in Beirut will rapidly become a provocation on the streets of Lahore. A suitable outfit for a woman for outings in an Islamic country would be a dress with a high neckline and a hem down to the calf with arms covered to the wrist. A head of exotic flowing hair is much more arousing in a Muslim country than in the West and coiffure should be at least restrained if not covered, in order to avoid disconcerting looks or even attempts to touch. Men should avoid wearing shorts in cities and certainly on Fridays. A Muslim cannot enter a mosque or pray with bare legs, or arms exposed up to the shoulder. This makes most leisurewear unworkable for a believer since prayers take place five times per day. The wearer of shorts in a Muslim country will therefore be an exception on the street and should not be surprised if he finds that he or she is attracting attention.

A strong sense of **personal privacy** goes with Qur'ānic modesty: knocking and awaiting permission to enter a room, for example, excusing oneself before leaving the presence of others; not standing in a doorway and blocking the passage of others. In the early days of the Prophet's ministry, his door was always open, which he found to be an increasing hardship especially since his household included a number of women who should not have been exposed to random visitors. Later, a verse of the Qur'ān was revealed giving Muhammad permission to require visitors to knock and await his invitation to enter.

A more cultural than religious custom governs the use of the **left and right hands**. Traditionally heaven is on the right hand and hell on the left, finding some common ground with the double meaning of the word 'right' in English and *droit* in French and the older association in both languages of left with 'sinister' or *sinistre*. Thus the left hand is reserved for unclean acts, wiping the anus, carrying shoes or anything soiled. Conversely the right hand is used for eating, for shaking hands and for passing items into the hand of another person. Less importantly, the right foot should pass over the threshold first on entering or leaving home, showing respect for one's dwelling and invoking protection from the dangers that lie beyond. A Muslim might accompany his arrival or departure, or any other activity of the day, with the words '*bismi'llāh*', 'in the name of God'. This right-biased instinct is also present on a crowded street in a Muslim city. Moving to your left to allow another pedestrian to pass on your right will generally result in the reciprocal reaction from those approaching. Moving to your right will often result in a collision because in popular Muslim mythology the devil's power is neutralized if he is passed by on the stronger right. Arabic writing begins on the right of the page and any serious composition will probably begin with an invocation to God, also starting from the right-hand side of the page. This practice has an eerie resonance in modern science, which has linked left-handedness with a propensity to schizophrenia, dyslexia and stuttering.

Elaborate greetings are part of Arabic legend and apply to Muslims in general. Behind the myth lies another Qur'ānic injunction: to have respect both for yourself and for others. This is reflected in a high standard of politeness at a personal level that can easily be construed by a Westerner as being phoney. Muslims usually take the time, for example, to wish you good-day or goodbye in a style that is communicated directly and with conviction. Shaking hands as a greeting is normal, while between Arabs especially kissing expresses close personal friendship. However, this would never apply between a man and woman who are not married, and even between men the kiss is usually placed on the shoulder or in the air and not on to the cheek.

On the other hand, frequent warnings in the Qur'ān against hypocrisy form another important aspect of Muslim personal protocol. 'God is closer to you than the vein in your neck,' the Qur'ān says and He alone knows your intentions, rendering the acting out of a falsehood purposeless. Compliments should, therefore, not be given if not meant but should never be omitted where due. A Muslim should accept without difficulty a politely expressed difference of opinion, or a frank expression of negative or upset feelings.

A common misunderstanding between Westerners and Arabs, but not all Muslims of course, centres on **communication**. Arabs will attempt to avoid a direct 'no' to a request, especially to a friend or colleague. The answer may in fact be 'no', but another way must be found to express the position. This may take the form of point-ing out difficulties, or adding conditions then doing nothing. In this way the willingness shown by the words is more important than the action, which may not take place anyway for many different reasons, and in the mean time the friendship has not been impaired by point-blank refusal. In the other direction, the same applies: if the requestee is unwilling to perform an act, and makes that clear indi-rectly, he or she will not be pressed, and a superficial excuse will be accepted. The universal expression *inshah' allāh* expresses exactly the uncertainty that covers over a refusal. A request may take on a deeper meaning, however, when asked 'for my sake' by the requestor, and such expressions reveal a certain urgency, as well as the acknow-ledgement of a reciprocal debt to the requestee. The frustration of a Westerner trying to 'get to the bottom line' or to 'cut to the chase' is therefore predestined, and to break the code is both unproductive and rude.

God is woven into every aspect of Muslim life. Almost every Muslim born becomes a believer, whether or not he or she is a devout practitioner. So there are many **everyday expressions** that carry religious significance. Examples of such phrases, that can be easily memorized and would earn the speaker instant appreciation, are given in Appendix 3 to Chapter 3.

There are no uniform or text-based rules for **visits to mosques** by non-Muslims. Practice differs from culture to culture but a wel-come is usual to other 'Peoples of the Book'. Visiting is specifically prohibited in Morocco and Tunisia, as well at most Shi'a shrines. Certain universal rules apply to the behaviour of the visitor, whether the mosque to be entered is in general use or a historical monument. Fridays must be avoided as well as times of daily prescribed prayers which are announced by the call of the muezzin. In a mosque the dress code mentioned above is obligatory, with the addition for women of a scarf tied close around the face. Men should not wear shorts and should cover their arms down to the elbow. Shoes must be removed even though some sites frequented by tourists may provide shoe covers or slippers. The question of foot infection from slippers is sometimes raised by Western visitors, but this is not valid from a religious point of view and the choice is between following the rules in your socks or bare feet, or not entering the mosque. In addition, the visitor should show respect for the mosque by behaving quietly and modestly and children should be controlled. No photographs should be taken of Muslims at prayer in a mosque.

Relationships. Here the wide difference between what is usual in the West and what is acceptable in a Muslim country is quickly apparent. Once again this is not a question of 'backwardness' or 'repression' but a sincerely and universally held belief based in faith as to the correct way in which relationships should be initiated and conducted. Men and women may hold hands in public without giving offence, but an embrace or kissing is completely unacceptable. Relations between husbands and wives are private and sacred and should never be displayed in a public place. Such relations between unmarried people are prohibited anyway, so that the issue of public display does not arise. Women holding hands or linking arms are unremarkable, even between two men this is taken as a sign of friendship because overt gay behaviour in public is almost unknown. Unmarried men and women can meet in formal situations, even through a casual acquaintance at work or in a shop, but any attempt to 'pick up' on the street will lead to nothing more rewarding than severe embarrassment for both sides, even in a large modern city like Cairo.

Travelling as an unmarried couple or gay couple. Homosexuality is not a personal matter of 'choice' in Islam as the Qur'ān prohibits such behaviour, which is viewed as a threat to the community. The difficulties encountered by a gay couple in a Muslim country will depend on both the country visited and the facilities used. International hotels will probably be accommodating in all except the countries following the Shariah. In a hotel with local management two men or two women sharing a room would probably be accepted without comment as no sexual relationship would be suspected unless deliberate evidence were given. However, a man and a woman with different names on their passports would usually be prohibited from taking a room together unless proven to be married or brother and sister.

A woman travelling on her own must first take all the personal safety precautions recommended for any journey, from New York to Paris, but in a Muslim country, in addition, the dress code should be followed closely at all times. In the vast majority of situations, a woman in the street wearing long clothes and a headscarf will receive full respect and encounter no difficulties. In most Muslim societies cafés are the customary preserve of men only, but in a restaurant women should be able to obtain service on their own with no awkwardness. However, street society is largely male and this may lead to discomfort for a single woman, especially in crowded places at night. In many Muslim countries trains and buses have separate compartments for women, with the balance of the coaches mixed rather than separated.

Visiting a Muslim home. The visitor can expect to be overwhelmed by food and drink, starting with the welcoming offering of fruit juice made from natural products: tamarisk, licorice or guava, rather than a bought bottled drink. In response the visitor should bring a small gift, candy, flowers in the more affluent societies, or fruit, but never alcohol. The nature of the invitation should also be considered carefully. If a man is invited without reference to his wife or partner, he should go alone and expect to find that the occasion is for men only with the women of the house elsewhere. If the invitation is expressly for a couple then the company will generally be mixed, but may separate later.

Bargaining in a Muslim country is another subject of legend when in fact the practice only applies to bazaars or sometimes taxis. The Qur'ān prescribes that fair measure be given, so although bargaining for price is acceptable, representations as to quality, weight or refinement should be accepted as offered. If there is any reason for doubt, it would be preferable not to buy the article than to question the definition that has been given. Some guidebooks recommend an elaborate bargaining procedure in which the tourist offers half the asking price then goes through the charade of walking away. None of this is necessary and bargaining should begin with the purchaser comparing prices in the market and developing a reasonable expectation of final price that does not insult the seller. Bargaining should be done on a friendly and straightforward basis and will be accepted in the same spirit.

Official and unofficial guides. At some tourist destinations the visitor is overwhelmed by souvenir sellers, touts and self-styled guides, at the Pyramids in Giza, for example, or approaching the souk at Marrakesh. The annoyance of saying 'no, thank you' every few seconds, or even having your path blocked by a donkey, a camel or a shop agent until you acquiesce, can be overcome by engaging the services of an official guide. In his or her company there is instant peace. Be sure, however, to choose a guide licensed by the government with a card, a badge and photograph ID.

Tipping. Here judgement should be based on Western practice, with one important distinction. Attempting to tip an inappropriate level of service can give deep offence. If in doubt, your appreciation should be expressed with nothing more than a sincere 'thank you'. Some examples of who should not be tipped are language teachers, private drivers, officials, police, office workers and hotel managers.

Style of address. The intimacy intended in the West by using a first name does not apply in Arabic, where a person's full name will consist of his or her personal name, the personal name of the father and the grandfather, followed by the family name for a very wide family. His or her first name, therefore, is the only personal name he or she has. This applies equally to both males and females, and a woman does not change the composition of her name on marriage. The names of earlier generations listed in the name can be preceded by *ibn* as 'son of' or *bint* as 'daughter of', which can lead to an impossibly long recitation, so that in practice earlier generations are dropped successively. First names are usually used with the prefix Mr or Mrs or Professor or Doctor where a level of formality exists. The family name, which in some cases may not exist, may reflect an origin or a *metier*, such as Hijazi (from the Hijaz) Halaby (from Aleppo) Najjar (carpenter) or Tawil (tall). The common prefix to the family name of *al-* is merely the definite article, and carries no connotation of past or present nobility or distinction. The names given above could equally be written as al-Hijazi, al-Halaby, al-Najjar, or al-Tawil.

Appendix

Excerpt from *The Life of Muhammad* by Emile Dermenghem

In the middle of a solemn quiet night when even the night-birds and the rambling beasts were quiet, when the streams had stopped murmuring and no breezes played, Mahomet was awakened by a voice crying, 'Sleeper awake'. And before him stood the Angel Gabriel, with radiant forehead, countenance white as snow, blond hair floating, in garments sewn with pearls and embroidered in gold. Manifold wings of every colour stood out quivering from his body.

Gabriel led a fantastical steed, Burāq (Lightning), with a human head and two eagles' wings; it approached Mahomet, allowed him to mount and was off like an arrow over the mountains of Mecca and the sands of the desert towards the North . . . the Angel accompanied them on this prodigious flight. On the summit of Mt Sinai, where God had spoken to Moses, Gabriel stopped Mahomet for prayer, and again at Bethlehem where Jesus was born, before resuming their course in the air. Mysterious voices attempted to detain the Prophet, who was so wrapped up in his mission that he felt that God alone had the right to stop his steed. When they reached Jerusalem Mahomet tethered Burāq and prayed on the ruins of the temple of Solomon, with Abraham, Moses and Jesus. Seeing an endless ladder appear upon Jacob's rock, the Prophet was enabled to mount rapidly to the heavens.

The first heaven was of pure silver and the stars suspended from its vault by chains of gold; in each one an angel lay awake to prevent the demons from climbing into the holy dwelling places and the spirits from listening indiscreetly to celestial secrets. There, Mahomet greeted Adam. And in the six other heavens the Prophet met Noah, Aaron, Moses, Abraham, David, Solomon, Idris, Yahyâ (John the Baptist) and Jesus. He saw the Angel of Death, Azrail, so huge that his eyes were separated by 70,000 marching days. He commanded 100,000 battalions and passed his time writing in an immense book the names of those dying or being born. He saw the Angel of Tears who wept for the sins of the world; the Angel of Vengeance with brazen face, covered with warts, who presides over the elements of fire and sits on a throne of flames; and another immense angel made up half of snow and half of fire, surrounded by a heavenly choir continually crying, 'O God, Thou hast united snow and fire, united all Thy servants in obedience to Thy

laws'. In the seventh heaven where the souls of the just resided was an
angel larger than the entire world, with 70,000 heads; each head had
70,000 mouths and each mouth had 70,000 tongues and each tongue
spoke in 70,000 different idioms singing endlessly the praises of the
Most High.

While contemplating this extraordinary being, Mahomet was carried
to the top of the Lote-Tree of Heaven flowering at the right side of
God's invisible throne and shading myriads of angelic spirits. Then after
having crossed in a twinkling of an eye the widest seas, regions of
dazzling light and deepest darkness, traversed millions of clouds of
hyacinths, of gauze, of shadows, of fire, of air, of water, of void, each
one separated by 500 marching years, he then passed more clouds – of
beauty, of perfection, of supremacy, of immensity, of unity, behind
which were 70,000 choirs of angels bowed down and motionless in
complete silence. The ground began to heave and he felt himself carried
into the light of his Lord, where he was transfixed, paralysed. From here
heaven and earth together appeared as if imperceptible to him, as if
melted into nothingness and reduced to the size of a grain of mustard
seed in the middle of a field. And this is how Mahomet admits having
been before the Throne of the Lord of the World.

He was in the presence of the Throne 'at a distance of two bows'
length or yet nearer', beholding God with his soul's eyes and seeing things
which the tongue cannot express, surpassing all human understanding.
The Almighty placed one hand on Mahomet's breast and the other on his
shoulder – to the very marrow of his bones he felt an icy chill, followed
by an inexpressible feeling of calm and ecstatic annihilation.

After a conversation whose ineffability is not honoured by too
precise tradition, the Prophet received the command from God that all
believers must say fifty prayers each day. Upon coming down from
heaven Mahomet met Moses, who spoke with him on the subject.

'How do you hope to make your followers say fifty prayers each
day? I have had experience with mankind before you. I tried everything
with the children of Israel that it was possible to try. Take my word,
return to our Lord and ask for a reduction.'

Mahomet returned and the number of prayers was reduced to forty.
But Moses thought that this was still too many and made his successor
go back to God a number of times. In the end, God exacted no more
than five prayers.

Gabriel then took the Prophet to Paradise where the faithful rejoice
after their resurrection – an immense garden with silver soil, gravel of

pearls, mountains of amber, filled with golden palaces and precious stones.

Finally, after returning by the luminous ladder to the earth, Mahomet untethered Burāq, mounted the saddle and rode into Jerusalem on the winged steed.

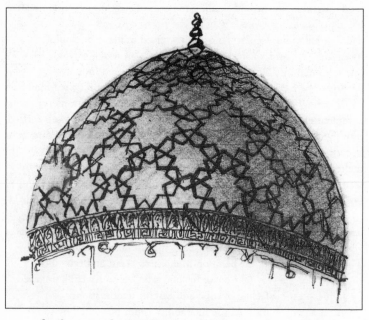

Arabesque decoration on the dome of a mosque

GLOSSARY

General note on use of accents
᾽ : sign of *hamza*, creating a stop between letters.
ʿ : sign of *ain*, creating a guttural edge to the following letter.

Abraham: (or Ibrahim in Arabic) patriarch of both Muslims and Jews, father of Ishmael born of his Canaanite wife Hajār, and of Isaac born of his Hebrew wife Sarah. Extolled in the Qurʾān as obedient to Allah, and his story is therefore a matter of faith.

AH: *Anno Hegirae*, in or since the year of the hijrah, the emigration of Muhammad from Mecca to Medina, and the start of the Muslim calendar.

ʿAlawi: schismatic Shiʿite sect of northern Syria, forming the power base for the Syrian Baʾth Party and the al-Assad family, past and present rulers of Syria. Not to be confused with the Sunni Alawite dynasty, present-day kings of Morocco.

ʿalim: (plural *ʿulamā*) a recognized man of knowledge in *fiqh*, in the interpretation of the Qurʾān, or in the history of Islam. A scholar.

ʿAshʿarite: schismatic Sunni sect following al-ʿAshʿarì, a literalist interpreter of the Qurʾān.

ʿĀshurā: the tenth day of the lunar month of Muharram. The day of the martyrdom of the Imam al-Husayn, and a day of Shiʿite mourning and fasting.

āya: (plural *ayat*) a verse in the Qurʾān, with the secondary meaning of 'sign' (from Allah).

azān: call by the muezzin of a mosque to prayer in congregation.

Ba'th: meaning 'renaissance'. The name of a political movement, principally in Iraq and Syria, the Ba'thist Party, taking power as nominally socialist, but ending in tyranny and corruption.

Bahā'i: a Shi'ite schism, following Sayyid Ali Muhammad Shirazi (executed 1850) who preached pantheism and world peace. Ferociously persecuted in Iran and now spread worldwide.

baraka: blessings or spiritual energy flowing from an event, person or a place, attributed to the Mercy of Allah.

basmala: contraction of the widely used expression 'In the name of Allah, the All-Merciful, the All-Compassionate'.

bay'a: a handshake to recognize a consensus or to acknowledge allegiance. The female version of *shurā*.

burāq: the miraculous beast which transported Muhammad during the *Isrā*. Mythically in the form of an ass with wings.

burqa: a loose outer garment for females covering the entire body, with a grill for the eyes. A version of which is worn by many Muslim women, most famously in Afghanistan.

CE: Common Era, meaning the Western method of calculation of years, but expressed without religious bias. Also BCE, Before the Common Era.

da'wa: a simple form of proselytization by the call to prayer, usually by a *marabout*, or penniless wandering missionary. The method by which Sufi Islam has spread in Africa.

Dar al-Harb: the 'House (or land) of Conflict' meaning the borders of Islam where the faith confronts non-Muslims.

Dar al-Islam: the 'House (or land) of Islam' where the faith and Shariah reign.

dhikr: the remembrance of Allah, by mental discipline, song, dance, spoken invocation, or rhythmic repetition, among other methods.

diwān: the collective memory of a tribe, a family, or of Islam, expressed as poetry. Also as Diwān, the muster-roll of soldiers during the early expansion of Islam, becoming a tribal genealogy still maintained in Mecca.

Eid al-Adha: the Festival of the Sacrifice, the celebration at the end of the haj, or pilgrimage, falling on the tenth of the lunar month of Dhù'l-Hijja, associated with the sacrifice of an animal to commemorate Abraham's aborted sacrifice of Ishmael.

Eid al-Fitr: festival ending the fast of Ramadan, falling on the first day of the next lunar month of Shawwāl.

fanā': Sufi self-obliteration in the love of Allah, based on the interpretation of a Qur'ānic verse.

Fātiha: the first surah of the Qur'ān, used as a general form of prayer, similar to the Lord's Prayer.

Fatimid: Ismāʿili dynasty claiming descent from Fatima, daughter of Muhammad. Rulers of parts of North Africa, including Egypt from the ninth to eleventh centuries CE.

fatwa: (plural, fatāwā) a legal ruling covering a current issue based on the *fiqh* rules of interpretation. Much mis-used for political purposes.

fiqh: jurisprudential core of the Shariah, based on the Qur'ān, the Sunna for Sunni *fiqh*, and on the writings of the Imams for Shiʿa *fiqh*.

firman: a form of fatwa issued by the Ottoman Empire, with the status of legislation.

Five Pillars: described by Muhammad as 'the Five'. The basis of

Muslim practice consisting of *shahādah* (profession of faith), *salāt* (daily prayers), *zakāt* (poor tax), *sawm* (fasting) and *haj* (pilgrimage).

hadith: the reported sayings of the Prophet. *Hadith Qudsi* (or Holy Sayings) are hadith that report the words of Allah as given by Muhammad.

haj see the Five Pillars.

hakimiyya: 'divine sovereignty on earth'. A twentieth-century political slogan supporting the movement toward the implementation of the Shariah.

halāl: consumption permitted by the Shariah, usually meaning the required method of butchering animals and preparing food. Similar to 'kosher'.

harām: forbidden by the Shariah.

Haram al-Sharif: the Holy Sanctuary (haram: sanctuary) by which is meant the Dome of the Rock and al-Aqsa mosque, both standing on the same enclosed platform above the Old City of Jerusalem.

Hijaz: the province of the Ottoman Empire on the Red Sea, formerly an independent part of *Arabia deserta*, containing the cities of Mecca and Medina, where Muhammad was born, assumed his prophethood, and died. Now part of Saudi Arabia.

hijrah: also hegira in Latin and used to describe Muhammad's departure from Mecca and his journey to settle in Medina.

hujjat: meaning the 'proof' by which Allah will always provide guidance to the world. Also used for a middle rank (*hujjat-al-Islam*) within the Shi'a hierarchy of mullahs.

ihrām: the rules of behaviour and the state of mind required for the observance of the rituals of the haj and the *'umrah.*

ihsān: the state of complete sincerity before Allah, as he sees the believer, and the believer sees Him.

ijāz: uniqueness, as applied to the Qur'ān and to mankind.

ijmāʿ: consensus among the 'ulamā' on areas of *fiqh*.

ijtihād: the process of innovation by which the Shariah can be extended to subjects not directly covered by Qur'ānic precedent, or by other clear authority.

imam: another word for sheikh or mullah, as religious and political leader. Also as Imam, meaning the successive leaders of the Shiʿa, all descended from ʿAli.

imān: acceptance of the faith of al-Islam.

inshah'allāh: 'If Allah wills.'

intifada: uprising, usually with reference to resistance by Palestinians against Zionist occupation.

Isā: Jesus Christ, a Jewish prophet of Islam.

Ismāʿilis: a schismatic sect from Shiʿa, following the seventh Imam, rather than the twelfth Imam of the Shiʿa majority.

Isrā: the Night Journey of the Prophet from Mecca to Jerusalem and back on the twenty-seventh of the lunar month of Rajab. The *Miʿrāj* of the Prophet, in which he was admitted to the outer levels of paradise, took place during the *Isrā*.

istihsān: legal discretion, to permit where appropriate, a sense of abstract fairness or equity, to prevail over legal rigidity.

istislah: the accommodation of the public interest in legal decisions, provided that the essential values of religion, life, intellect, lineage and property are protected.

Jāhiliyyah: the Time of Ignorance in Arabia, covering the one or two centuries before the ministry of the Prophet, during which the Arabs abandoned the monotheistic religion of Abraham and practised polytheism and idolatry.

jihad: struggle, both personal and military. Associated with resistance by the individual to temptation, and with the battles fought by the first Muslims to protect their religion.

jinn: residents of an invisible parallel world, referred to in the Qur'ān, and therefore a matter of faith.

jizyah: protection tax paid by non-Muslim residents to the Muslim empires. Generally equivalent in value to *zakāt*, from which non-Muslims were exempt (see the Five Pillars).

Ka'bah: the stone cube, now at the centre of the Great Mosque of Mecca, built by Adam to mark his forgiveness by Allah, later restored by Abraham. The holiest place in Islam.

kafir: (plural *kuffār*) more than a non-believer, a person who specifically rejects Allah and the Prophet.

khalwa: spiritual retreat from the world in order to remember Allah.

Kharijites: the first Muslim schismatics, advocating pure salafist Islam (see *salafi*) and rejecting as non-believers all who depart from the Shariah, even in minor matters.

khutba: a sermon delivered before noon prayers, especially on Fridays, following a set form and rendered in austere language.

lex talionis: the law of the lawless desert based on retribution and like for like.

madhab: school of jurisprudential interpretation of the Shariah based on the work of an original master. The four main Sunni schools are Hanafi, Maliki, Shafi'i and Hanbali.

madrasah: a traditional school for boys and girls based on study of the Qur'ān.

marabout: see *da'wa.*

masjid: place of prostternation, or mosque.

mihrāb: niche or other marking in the wall of a mosque showing the direction of prayer toward Mecca, or *qibla.*

minbar: raised chair, or steps from which the *khutba* is delivered, often a highly decorated structure in the Arabesque manner.

Mir'āj: see *Isrā.*

muezzin: faithful member of a mosque congregation trusted to make the call to prayer.

mujahid: a fighter in the name of Allah, who participates in a jihad, covering both personal and external struggles.

mujtahid: a scholar qualified in *fiqh* to undertake *ijtihād.* Many different levels of accomplishment are recognized, in all specialist areas of the Shariah.

mullah: see imam.

Murj'ites: liberal interpreters of the Qur'ān who 'suspend judgement' of individuals, and accept anyone as a Muslim who has a 'knowledge of Allah in his heart'.

Mu'tazilites: rationalist interpreters of the Qur'ān, believing for example that on the Last Day, man will see God only in his heart.

prostternation: a word coined in this book to describe the core act of prayer, with seven points of the body on the floor.

qasida: extended rhyming ode of pre-Islamic Arabia, recited from memory and generally praising a benefactor, desert life, or a particular tribe.

qibla: the direction of prayer, toward the Ka'bah in Mecca.

qiyas: logical deduction by analogy, a method by which *fiqh* may be extended to cover new situations not specifically dealt with by then existing legal texts and authorities.

Quraysh: one of the principal tribes of Arabia based in Mecca, of which Muhammad was a member. Holders of great power and wealth both before and after the advent of Islam.

rak'a: (plural *raka't*) the prayer routine consisting of thirteen different postures accompanied by recitals and whispered prayers.

Ramadan: the lunar month during which Muslims fast through the day. See the Five Pillars.

rasul: messenger, the title by which Muhammad referred to himself, rather than the more popular, but strictly incorrect, 'Prophet'.

rightly-guided: the term used for the first four caliphs (successors to Muhammad) who were appointed by *shurā*, and uniquely qualified through their personal association with Muhammad. Sunnis accept all four, Shi'a accept 'Ali only (the fourth caliph).

salafi: from the Arabic expression *al-salafi al-salih*, meaning 'the pious forefathers' and referring to the Companions of the Prophet and their way of life in Medina under the Muslim Commonwealth from the hijrah to the death of Muhammad. Adopted during the twentieth century as 'salafist' of 'salafiyya', to mean a movement that seeks a return to the (perceived) original values of Islam.

sa'y: a stage in the haj and the *'umrah* that involves walking seven times between two of the hills of Mecca to commemorate the search by Abraham's wife Hajār for water for the baby Ishmael.

sayyed: a Muslim able to trace his, or her family history back to the family of the Prophet. Secondary meaning of teacher.

Sha'ban: the eighth lunar month of the Muslim calendar.

Shahādah: the affirmation of Muslim belief, 'I bear witness that there is no god but God, and that Muhammad is the messenger of God'. See also the Five Pillars

shaheed: martyr who dies fighting a jihad. The term was never applied to suicide during the early days of Islam, when such 'operations' were unknown.

Shariah: system of Islamic law, comparable to the Common Law of England, based on the Qur'ān, the Sunna for Sunni, and the exegetics of the Imams for Shi'ites.

Shaytān: the devil, mythically Ibis, the fallen angel. Comparable with the story of Lucifer.

Sheikh: see imam, with a secondary meaning of leader or superior.

Shi'a: schism from mainstream (Sunni) Islam, following disagreement over the appointment of the first caliph after the death of Muhammad, and who was (or is) qualified to lead Muslims. Followers of 'Ali ibn Abu Tālib.

shirk: idolatry in the *Jāhiliyyah*, redefined by Islam to mean the eternally unforgivable wrong of worshipping something or someone other than, or as a partner with, Allah.

shurā: consultation process for making communal decisions established by the Shariah, similar to a limited form of democracy.

skullcap: *kippa* in Hebrew. The small round covering worn on the crown of the head by traditional Jewish males, especially on the Sabbath. The knitted version denotes membership in the Gush, the

Zionist settler movement advocating the violent creation of a Greater Israel, including Gaza and the West Bank.

souk: market place, also known as a *medina* in North African cities such as Marrakech.

Sufi: a follower of Sufism, the mystical aspect of Islam, practising internal rather than external religion. Liberal and individual, thus contrary to traditional Sunni or Shi'a practice.

Sunna: the example of the life of the Prophet, from his actions and his sayings, the latter gathered as the Hadith. The source of the division between Sunni and Shi'a Islam, the latter accepting only guidance from descendants of the Prophet (see also Shi'a).

surah: chapter of the Qur'ān, which consists of 114 surahs.

Tablighi Jamaat: non-political 'gap year' programme for young Muslims to visit other Muslim countries and explore differences and similarities. Also operates as a form of low-profile missionary movement.

tajwid: one school in the art of Qur'ān recital, giving each consonant full value.

Takbir: the name for the Arabic expression, *Allāhu Akbar*, 'Allah is the Greater'.

taqlid: imitation, or a narrow reading of the Shariah based on unswerving faith in the 'rightly-guided' precedents. Seen as closed-mindedness by advocates of *ijtihād*.

tariqah: as *Tariqah*, meaning the Way or the Path of Sufism, or as *tariqah* meaning a Sufi brotherhood following a particular sheikh.

tasmiyah: the invocation that opens all surahs of the Qur'ān (except one) 'In the name of God, the Merciful, the Compassionate'. Also see *basmala*, the shortened version.

tawāf: the first rite of the haj, seven passages around the Ka'bah (anti-clockwise).

tawhid: the core of Muslim belief, the affirmation of the Oneness of God, the Unknowable, the Unseeable, the transcendent Creator, encapsulated by the words of the First Pillar of Islam.

tilawa: a school in the art of Qur'ān recital with a varying pitch, similar to plainsong.

Touareg: nomadic Berber tribe of the Sahara and the Sahel. Famous for bravery and independence. A race deprived of a homeland by the legacy of colonialism.

Twelvers: *Ithnā'ashriyyah,* or the Shi'a majority following the teachings of twelve imams, descendents of 'Ali. The national religion of modern Iran.

Umayyad: the Umayyah clan of the Arabian Quraysh tribe. The wealthiest grouping within the tribe and traditional holders of power in Mecca. Opponents of Muhammad, but later forming the first dynastic (Sunni) caliphate after the murder of 'Ali.

'ummah: the body of Muslims worldwide as a distinct and cohesive community.

'umrah: the lesser pilgrimage to Mecca, similar to the haj, but can be performed at any time of year.

urfi: temporary marriage based on a contractual agreement. Often leading to the subsequent compromise of the female party as a divorced woman.

Vilayet: a large administrative district or province in the Ottoman Empire, usually headed by a Turkish governor, but generally administered by native functionaries.

Wahhbis: adherents to the Qur'ānic exegesis of ibn 'Abd al-

Wahhāb, a zealous literalist, and founder of the ideology on which the Kingdom of Saudi Arabia has been built, based on *taqlid.*

Wali Faqih: the Vice-Regent of the Hidden Imam, the ultimate authority in Twelver Shiʿism. Based on the Shiʿa belief in the occlusion of the Twelfth Imam. The power that overthrew the Pahlavi dynasty in Iran.

waqf: a religious trust supported by public subscription that stands behind every mosque, for the purpose of owning and maintaining the building and supporting charitable works.

wasat: the way between two extremes covering consensus in decisions, personal modesty, and peace between Muslims. Based on Surah 31, verse 19 of the Qurʾān, and many other examples.

zakāt: see the Five Pillars.

Zamzam: The well opened by Allah (and now under the Great Mosque in Mecca thus) saving the life of the baby Ishmael. Also see *saʾy.*

INDEX

To order further *Brief History* titles just fill in this form *(cont. over page)*

No. of copies	Title	Price	Total
	A Brief History of 1917: Russia's Year of Revolution Roy Bainton	£8.99	
	A Brief History of the Birth of the Nazis Nigel Jones	£7.99	
	A Brief History of the Boxer Rebellion Diana Preston	£7.99	
	A Brief History of British Kings & Queens Mike Ashley	£8.99	
	A Brief History of British Sea Power David Howarth	£9.99	
	A Brief History of the Celts Peter Berresford Ellis	£7.99	
	A Brief History of Christianity Bamber Gascoigne	£7.99	
	A Brief History of the Circumnavigators Derek Wilson	£7.99	
	A Brief History of the Crusades Geoffrey Hindley	£7.99	
	A Brief History of the Druids Peter Berresford Ellis	£7.99	
	A Brief History of the Dynasties of China Bamber Gascoigne	£7.99	
	A Brief History of Fighting Ships David Davies	£6.99	
	A Brief History of Globalization Alex MacGillivray	£8.99	
	A Brief History of the Great Moghuls Bamber Gascoigne	£7.99	
	A Brief History of the Hundred Years War Desmond Seward	£7.99	
	A Brief History of Infinity Brian Clegg	£8.99	
	A Brief History of Medicine Paul Strathern	£9.99	
	A Brief History of Mutiny Richard Woodman	£8.99	
	A Brief History of Napoleon in Russia Alan Palmer	£7.99	
	A Brief History of Painting Roy Bolton	£9.99	
	A Brief History of the Royal Flying Corps in World War I Ralph Barker	£9.99	
	A Brief History of Science Thomas Crump	£8.99	
	A Brief History of the Tudor Age Jasper Ridley	£7.99	
	A Brief History of Vikings Jonathan Clements	£7.99	
	P&P & Insurance		£2.50
	Grand Total		**£**

Name: _____

Address: _____

_____ Postcode: _____

Daytime Tel. No. / Email: _____
(in case of query)

Three ways to pay:

1. **For express service telephone the TBS order line on 01206 255 800 and quote 'BHI'. Order lines are open Monday – Friday 8:30a.m. – 5:30p.m.**

2. I enclose a cheque made payable to **TBS** Ltd for £ _____

3. Please charge my ☐ Visa ☐ Mastercard ☐ Amex
   ☐ Switch (switch issue no. ...) £ _____

   Card number: _____

   Expiry date: _____ Signature _____
          (your signature is essential when paying by credit card)

Please return forms (*no stamp required*) to, Constable & Robinson Ltd, FREEPOST NAT6619, 3 The Lanchesters, 162 Fulham Palace Road, London W6 9BR. All books subject to availability.

Enquiries to readers@constablerobinson.com.
www.constablerobinson.com

Constable & Robinson (directly or via its agents) may mail or phone you about promotions or products. Tick box if you do not want these from us ☐ or our subsidiaries ☐.